SHORT-TERM PLAY THERAPY FOR CHILDREN

Short-Term Play Therapy for Children

Edited by

Heidi Gerard Kaduson
Charles E. Schaefer

THE GUILFORD PRESS
New York   London

© 2000 The Guilford Press
A Division of Guilford Publications, Inc.
72 Spring Street, New York, NY 10012
www.guilford.com

Printed in the United States of America

This book is printed on acid-free paper.

Last digit is print number: 9 8 7 6 5 4 3

Library of Congress Cataloging-in-Publication Data

Short-term play therapy for children / [edited by] Heidi Gerard
Kaduson, Charles E. Schaefer.
     p. cm.
  Includes bibliographical references and index.
  ISBN 1-57230-520-7
  1. Play therapy. 2. Children—Counseling of. 3. Family
therapy. 4. Child psychotherapy. I. Kaduson, Heidi Gerard.
II. Schaefer, Charles E.
RJ505.P6S53 1999
618.92′891653—dc21   99-051928

We wish to thank our children—
Jay, Nicole, Kymberly, Karine, and Eric—
for teaching us the true meaning of play.

About the Editors

Heidi Gerard Kaduson, PhD, specializes in evaluation and intervention services for children with a variety of behavioral, emotional, and learning problems. She is past president of the International Association for Play Therapy and codirector of The Play Therapy Training Institute, Inc. She has lectured internationally on play therapy, attention-deficit/hyperactivity disorder, and learning disabilities. Dr. Kaduson's publications include *The Quotable Play Therapist, The Playing Cure, 101 Favorite Play Therapy Techniques,* and the forthcoming *101 Favorite Play Therapy Techniques* (Vol. II). She maintains a private practice in child psychotherapy in Hightstown, New Jersey.

Charles E. Schaefer, PhD, a nationally renowned child psychologist, is Professor of Psychology and director of the Center for Psychological Services at Fairleigh Dickinson University in Teaneck, New Jersey. He is director emeritus of the International Association for Play Therapy and has written or edited more than 40 books on parenting, child psychology, and play therapy, including *The Therapeutic Use of Child's Play, The Therapeutic Powers of Play,* and *Family Play Therapy.* Dr. Schaefer maintains a private practice in child psychotherapy in Hackensack, New Jersey.

Contributors

Sue A. Ammen, PhD, RPT-S, Ecosystemic Clinical Child Emphasis, Clinical Psychology Program, California School of Professional Psychology, Fresno, California

Alisa Bahl, MA, doctoral candidate, Department of Psychology, West Virginia University, Morgantown, West Virginia

Phyllis B. Booth, MA, The Theraplay Training Institute, Chicago, Illinois

Loretta Gallo-Lopez, MA, private practice, Tampa, Florida

Marjan Ghahramanlou, MA, doctoral candidate, Clinical Psychology Program, Fairleigh Dickinson University, Teaneck, New Jersey

Thomas G. Hardaway, II, MD, Department of Psychiatry, Texas A & M University Medical School, Temple, Texas

Amy D. Herschell, MA, doctoral candidate, Department of Psychology, West Virginia University, Morgantown, West Virginia

Heidi E. Jacobsen, MA, doctoral candidate, Clinical Psychology Program, Fairleigh Dickinson University, Teaneck, New Jersey

Heidi Gerard Kaduson, PhD, RPT-S, private practice, Hightstown, New Jersey

Susan M. Knell, PhD, Meridia Behavioral Medicine—Cleveland Clinic Health System, Cleveland, Ohio; Department of Psychology, Case Western Reserve University, Cleveland, Ohio

Sandra Lindaman, MSW, The Theraplay Training Institute, Chicago, Illinois

Carol Mader, MEd, Lancaster–Lebanon Non-Public School Services, Manheim, Pennsylvania

Cheryl B. McNeil, PhD, Department of Psychology, West Virginia University, Morgantown, West Virginia

Violet Oaklander, PhD, Violet Oaklander Institute, Santa Barbara, California; Adjunct Faculty, University of California Extension, Santa Cruz, Santa Barbara, and San Diego, California; Adjunct Faculty, Lewis and Clark College, Portland, Oregon

Charles E. Schaefer, PhD, RPT-S, Department of Psychology and Center for Psychological Services, Fairleigh Dickinson University, Teaneck, New Jersey; private practice, Hackensack, New Jersey

Janine S. Shelby, PhD, Santa Monica UCLA Medical Center, Rape Treatment Center, Santa Monica, California

Julia A. Trebing, PsyD, CPT-P, BCETS-D, Creative Therapies at the Playroom, Stamford, Connecticut

Risë VanFleet, PhD, RPT-S, Family Enhancement and Play Therapy Center, Boiling Springs, Pennsylvania

Preface

In the age of managed care, few mental health practitioners can dispute the need for becoming adept in providing short-term therapy. Professionals have a need to work quickly and efficiently in order to help children with psychological difficulties in short periods of time. While we may be able to choose from various techniques, we must further examine the theoretical orientation and procedures by which we can promote quicker change and long-lasting results.

Short-Term Play Therapy for Children brings together chapters that detail for clinicians proven methods by which to conduct play therapy in a short-term format. Many of the authors have been using a shorter approach to play therapy for many years. It is now more important than ever before to get this information out to clinicians. Managed care dictates many limitations on how we work as child psychotherapists. To facilitate work within these limitations, we have put together several types of play therapy that have been created with managed care in mind.

This book provides short-term approaches to individual play therapy for children, family play therapy, and group play therapy. As will be shown, short-term approaches can be used to address a wide variety of issues and problems, including fears and phobias, grief, trauma, classroom disturbance, and attention-deficit/hyperactivity disorder. Strategies include cognitive-behavioral play therapy, gestalt play therapy, client-centered play therapy, structured play therapy, filial play therapy, Theraplay, and parent–child interaction therapy.

Through these many approaches, clinicians will be able to see, in detail, how play can be used in a time-limited way. The chapters have treatments broken down into sessions to further facilitate the clinician's understanding of the process.

While it is clear to all of us that we can do a lot in a short-term format, it must also be noted that therapists have many limitations. Short-term play therapy is not effective for all children, but for those who can benefit from such therapy, this book provides step-by-step, state-of-the-art approaches. Whether one's orientation is psychodynamic, cognitive-behavioral, child-centered, or any other, this book can serve as a guide toward a better understanding of how to help certain children in specific ways.

Understanding the process is very important to each therapist's implementation of play therapy for children. Whether it is by the use of miniatures, relationships, or games, play therapy is becoming the best way to help children in our troubled times. With these chapters, we hope also to stimulate the reader's own creativity to devise even more innovative techniques that will facilitate the goal of helping children with psychological difficulties in short-term therapy.

HEIDI GERARD KADUSON, PHD
CHARLES E. SCHAEFER, PHD

Contents

PART II: FAMILY PLAY THERAPY

PART III: GROUP PLAY THERAPY

SHORT-TERM PLAY THERAPY FOR CHILDREN

PART I

INDIVIDUAL PLAY THERAPY

1

Cognitive-Behavioral Play Therapy for Childhood Fears and Phobias

Susan M. Knell

INTRODUCTION

Fears in Childhood

Fears are a normal part of childhood. For most children, fears are mild, age specific, and transient (King, Hamilton, & Ollendick, 1988), and most fears decrease with age. Although each child's fears will be determined by his or her individual learning history, particular fears seem to cluster at certain ages. Nonetheless, there are many common threads among children. The infant, whose fears seem to be concrete and centered around the immediate environment, may show behavior reflective of fear in response to loud noises or strangers. As the child grows, fears of imaginary figures (e.g., monsters) may evolve (Jersild, 1968). The older child and adolescent are more likely to be fearful of more anticipatory, abstract, global stimuli and events (Gullone, 1996). These older youths' fears also tend to be more cognitive. As the child's imagination grows, fears, too, become less concrete and more imaginative.

Age-related fears are often transitory and of short duration. Studies have suggested that children ages 2–6 years have an average of three fears, and that 40% of 6- to 12-year-olds have as many as seven fears (Miller, 1983). There is evidence that parents tend to underreport their children's fears; that is, when children are asked directly, they report more fears than indicated by studies relying on parent reports (Ollendick, King, & Frary,

3

1989; Ollendick, Matson, & Helsel, 1985). Findings also support the commonly held clinical belief that girls not only report more fears than boys, but they also report a higher intensity of fear (e.g., Ollendick et al., 1985; King et al., 1988).

Children often learn to be fearful of objects or situations after experiencing an unpleasant event associated with the stimuli. Such experiences might be severe, or the child might have received much attention during or after the event. The child's experiences, cognitive development, expanding resources, and reactions of parent and caretakers are often helpful in overcoming fears. As the child gets older, his or her increased cognitive abilities and experiences provide more resources, which allow the child to respond to fearful situations in increasingly adaptive ways (Campbell, 1986).

Many childhood fears will come and go without any intervention. Others, which continue beyond the expected age range, may grow in intensity if not challenged and may generalize to other situations. For example, the child who is fearful of being in a room with the door closed may soon be fearful of elevators, cars, and other places where doors must be closed. When anxiety is so intense or pervasive that it leads to unwanted psychological distress and/or maladjustment, there is cause for concern, for such fears can become phobias.

Phobias, intense fears that are not age related, are irrational because there is no real danger. It is estimated that only 3–8% of the population exhibit excessive fears (King et al., 1988). Simple phobias are evident in only a small sample of children and make up only a small number of cases referred for treatment (Silverman & Nelles, 1990). The number of children referred for fears is believed to be smaller than the number of adults referred, perhaps reflecting parents' relative lack of awareness of their children's fears, as well as a relative lack of trained professionals to deal with the problems of children.

Literature suggests that mild fears or simple phobias are transient, developmental phenomena that resolve over time (Silverman & Nelles, 1990). For more complex fears, studies suggest that treatment does shorten the recovery time, which has been estimated to be from 1 to 5 years if left untreated (Agras, Chapin, & Oliveau, 1972; Hampe, Noble, Miller, & Barrett, 1973). Given the distress caused by these extreme fears, it seems warranted to provide relief through psychotherapy rather than letting the fear run its natural course.

Children with extreme fears are often not brought to the attention of mental health practitioners in a timely fashion. In a study of children presenting with simple phobias, Strauss and Last (1993) found that these children, on average, were brought to treatment approximately 3 years following the onset of their phobias. Additionally, children with debilitating fears may be brought to therapy for another presenting problem, and the fear may be uncovered as part of a thorough assessment of their functioning. When the fear is the primary concern, treatment is usually sought because of the significant interference the fear is presenting either for the child or the family. Examples include children who cannot separate from their parents and therefore cannot benefit from school or other age-appropriate activities, children who are too fearful to ride elevators and, thus, must use stairs, or children who are fearful of school, peers, or other everyday experiences.

Assessment of Fears in Children

Assessment of childhood fears usually involves parent interview, child interview and/or play interview, observation, and, with older children, the use of clinical screening measures and fear survey instruments.

An understanding of the developmental appropriateness of the child's fears is critical. This developmental perspective sheds light on the appropriateness of treating the child's fears. However, even fears that are common and age appropriate may deserve intervention. If a child's fear is excessive, lasts a long time, and/or interferes with his or her functioning, it may be clinically significant and worth treating. For example, separation anxiety is normal in young children. However, if it interferes with the child's ability to go to school, interact with peers, or participate in day-to-day activities, it should not be ignored.

Part of the assessment should include an understanding of how the child and family typically deal with the fearful object/event, and what coping strategies (or lack thereof) have been developed. How does the fear impact on the child and family's day-to-day functioning? Have family members changed their routines to accommodate the child's fears? What efforts have the parents made to help the child, and how successful or unsuccessful have these efforts been? The extent and nature of the child's exposure to feared stimuli are also important. For example, a child who is afraid of roller coasters is not likely to need treatment. A child who is afraid of elevators, and who lives in a high-rise apartment in a large city, will probably require some kind of intervention unless the fear is short-lived.

Observation of the child's response to discussion of the feared object or situation can be important. The nature of the fear may become more obvious in watching the child's reactions to such a discussion. At times, in family discussions, factors that maintain the fear may become more evident. Some fears can be assessed in real life, so that the therapist can observe the child's actual response to feared stimuli. When possible, such observation can be an important part of the assessment. For example, observing a fearful child on or near an elevator or school can be easily arranged. Other feared stimuli may entail more "prearranging." Finding the circumstances through which to observe a child fearful of thunderstorms, or one who is afraid of hurricanes, may be challenging but not necessarily impossible.

Self-report surveys can be used with older children. Most commonly used are the State–Trait Anxiety Inventory for Children (STAIC; Spielberger, 1973), the Revised Children's Manifest Anxiety Scale (RCMAS: "What I think and feel"; Reynolds & Richmond, 1978), and the Fear Survey Schedule for Children—Revised (FSSC-R; Ollendick, 1983). These surveys are not geared for preschool and early school-age children. Other, nonstandardized tasks to help assess fears include use of a "fear thermometer," where 0 represents no fear and the top of the thermometer represents extreme fear (Introduced for use with adults by Walk, 1956). Such a task is not reliable, but it does help the younger child quantify his or her fears in a concrete, understandable format. It also can be adapted for use with very young children.

It is also important to assess and understand any changes in the family situation or environment that may have contributed to the child's fears. Lifestyle changes, such as moves, may prompt changes in the child's sense of safety or security, and thus may contribute to changes in levels of fear. Traumatic events, such as divorce, abuse, or family illness/death must also be understood in terms of the impact they may have had on the child's fears.

Treatment of Fears

A wide range of literature exists on treating children's fears and phobias, with most published work providing case studies of treatment of fearful children. Past work includes clinical material from a variety of theoretical positions, including psychoanalytic, Adlerian, Rogerian, and behavioral views (see Morris & Kratochwill, 1983, for a brief summary of these positions as they relate to fearful children).

Across orientations, most practitioners would agree that fearful children need to learn to cope with that which is feared, or learn not to be afraid (Miller, 1983). Recent case studies have suggested much support for cognitive-behavioral treatments. Even before short-term therapy was accepted, treatment for childhood fears was typically described as brief (four or five sessions) (Ollendick, 1979). Much recent literature describes behavioral interventions stressing fear reduction, and including the interventions of systematic desensitization, contingency management, modeling, and cognitive-behavioral techniques.

Indications for Cognitive-Behavioral Interventions

One of the primary goals of cognitive-behavioral therapy is to identify and modify maladaptive thoughts associated with the child's symptoms (Bedrosian & Beck, 1980). Maladaptive thoughts refer to ideations that interfere with the individual's ability to cope with experiences (Beck, 1976).

With fears, maladaptive thoughts may include self-statements such as "I am too fearful to do this" or "I cannot get over this fear."

A significant component of overcoming fear is gaining control over the fears. This may involve learning that one can deal with the feared stimuli, learning to manage feelings associated with the fear, and learning specific coping skills to deal with fear. Cognitive-behavioral interventions provide such learning opportunities as well as the specific skills necessary to overcome fear. In play therapy, children may master a feared object by taking on the role of one who does not fear it. They may act in ways that suggest they are not afraid. By "pretending" and practicing, the child may overcome the feared stimuli. Traditionally, more psychoanalytically oriented child therapy saw the function of this type of role playing as a basis for the beginnings of self-control (Loevinger, 1976).

Cognitive-behavioral play therapy (CBPT) is designed specifically for preschool and early elementary-school-age children. It emphasizes the child's involvement in therapy by addressing issues of control, mastery, and responsibility for changing one's own behavior. CBPT is designed to be developmentally appropriate and to help the child become an active participant in change (Knell, 1993a, 1994, 1997, 1998, 1999). In addition to phobias (Knell, 1993a), CBPT has been used for children presenting with a wide range of diagnoses, such as selective mutism (Knell, 1993a, 1993b) and encopresis (Knell & Moore, 1990; Knell, 1993a), as well as children who have experienced traumatic life events, such as divorce (Knell, 1993a) and sexual abuse (Knell & Ruma, 1996).

COGNITIVE-BEHAVIORAL PLAY THERAPY WITH FEARFUL CHILDREN

Setting/Materials

CBPT is usually conducted in a playroom with a wide array of play materials available. A typical play therapy room is well stocked with toys, art supplies, puppets, dolls, and other materials. The more directive and goal-oriented techniques of CBPT may require more materials to meet the needs of a child's specific presenting problems. Sometimes, it is not necessary to buy toys for specific situations because of the child's ability to be creative and flexible with existing toys. At other times, the therapist may need to buy specific materials that meet the needs of a specific child. For example, a child fearful of sitting on the toilet may be able to play with a doll on a plastic bowl that resembles a toilet. Or the child may not be able to "pretend" in this way, and may have an easier time using a specifically designed dolls' play toilet.

Although play therapy is usually conducted in a playroom, the fearful child may need to be treated *in vivo*; that is, the child may need to be seen in a setting that more closely resembles the fearful situation. Thus, the child fearful of elevators may be seen in and around an elevator; the school phobic child may need to be treated at or around the school; and a child afraid of dogs may need to be seen in a setting where dogs are allowed.

Treatment Stages

CBPT takes place as the child moves through several treatment stages, which have been described as the introductory/orientation, assessment, middle, and termination stages. After preparation for CBPT, the assessment begins. During the middle stage of CBPT, the therapist has developed a treatment plan, and the therapy is turning to a focus on increasing the child's self-control, sense of accomplishment, and learning more adaptive responses to deal with specific situations. For fearful children, this will incorporate a wide array of cognitive and behavioral interventions specifically geared toward helping the child with his or her fear. Generalization and relapse prevention will be incorporated into the middle stages of therapy so that the child can learn to utilize new skills across a broad range of settings, and to begin to develop skills that will enhance the chances of setbacks after therapy is completed. During the termination phase, the child and family are prepared for the end of therapy (see Knell, in press, for more description of these stages in CBPT).

Treatment Interventions

A variety of treatment techniques are utilized in cognitive-behavioral play therapy with fearful children. Given the limited cognitive abilities of young children and the anxiety that accompanies fears, play therapy offers fearful children the opportunity to express their feelings in a safe environment. Some of the most important interventions in cognitive-behavioral work with fearful children are behavioral interventions (e.g., systematic desensitization, contingency management, and modeling) and cognitive techniques.

BEHAVIORAL INTERVENTIONS

Systematic Desensitization. Systematic desensitization is the process of reducing anxiety or fear by replacing a maladaptive response with an adaptive one (Wolpe, 1958, 1982). This is accomplished by breaking the association between a particular stimulus and the anxiety or fear response that it usually elicits. The stimulus is presented, but the anxiety is prevented from occurring. For adults, this is usually done by teaching muscle relaxation, where a state of calm is incompatible with anxiety (Jacobson, 1938). Children over the age of 6 years can be taught modified relaxation techniques (e.g., Cautela & Groden, 1978), although some children may find other techniques more useful. With children, other methods to induce relaxation are often used, such as calming play activities or visualization of calming scenes. Schroeder and Gordon (1991) even suggest the use of laughter, giving the example of the child imagining a feared monster dressed in red flannel underwear!

Systematic desensitization involves the person imagining a hierarchy of anxiety-provoking scenes in combination with these incompatible responses. In addition to imaginal desensitization, *in vivo* desensitization, where the anxiety-provoking stimuli are confronted in real life, is also used. While some authors argue that *in vivo* desensitization is superior to imaginal exposure (Emmelkamp, 1982), others suggest a blend of both imaginal and *in vivo* exposure (James, 1985). With children, *in vivo* desensitization has become increasingly popular, largely because of the difficulties that children have both in imagining fearful stimuli and acquiring a state of relaxation (King & Ollendick, 1997). Ultee, Griffioen, and Schellekens (1982) found *in vivo* desensitization to be more effective than imaginal desensitization with 5- to 10-year-olds, whereas both were equally effective with older children.

In setting up *in vivo* desensitization paradigms, it is important that the therapist have control over the feared stimulus (e.g., a cooperative dentist, an elevator that is not in a busy building and can be held at a floor for brief periods of time). Systematic desensitization is a powerful intervention with fearful children. It is most useful when the child exhibits high levels of physiological reactivity (e.g., racing heart) and extreme avoidance (King et al., 1988). It also may be less effective than other interventions when the phobia is primarily due to a lack of skills, or for fears reinforced by significant others.

In addition to a number of single-case studies, a number of group studies evaluating systematic desensitization have been reported with children and adolescents (see review in King & Ollendick, 1997). In seven studies, with children ages 5–15 years, systematic desensitization was found to be more effective than either no treatment or wait-list control conditions.

An example of the use of systematic desensitization with a young child was provided by Knell (1993a). A 5-year-old boy, Jim, was fearful of closed spaces after having been accidentally locked in a bathroom by his younger sister. Several hours passed before he could be removed from the bathroom. Consequently, Jim refused to stay in any room unless the door remained open. This specific fear generalized, and soon Jim was fearful of any place where the door was closed behind him, including any room, elevators, or car doors. A fear hierarchy, which incorporated assessment data collected from Jim and his mother, was developed (see Table 1.1). Twenty-three items, ranging from Jim's least fearful (playing with toys in a large room, with the therapist in the room and the door open) to his most fearful (riding in the elevator between floors) situation, made up the hierarchy. Graduated stages in the hierarchy were presented to Jim *in vivo* as he was instructed to play and make simple, positive self-statements, largely consisting of affirmations of his ability to manage the tasks. Playing with certain toys appeared to be relaxing and incompatible with Jim's anxiety, and were used to help Jim manage increasingly anxiety-provoking items on the hierarchy. When he showed any sign of discomfort, the therapist returned with him to an easier, previous step. Jim seemed to derive satisfaction from his increasing ability to manage these previously difficult situations, and he liked the positive feedback regarding his progress that he

TABLE 1.1. Systematic Desensitization Hierarchy for a 5-Year-Old Afraid of Being in a Room with a Closed Door

Large room, therapist in room

  1. Playing with toys, door open
  2. Playing with toys, door half closed
  3. Playing with toys, door open 1 inch
  4. Playing with toys, door closed but not shut tight
  5. Playing with toys, door closed.

Small room, therapist in room

  6. Playing with toys, door open
  7. Playing with toys, door half closed
  8. Playing with toys, door open 1 inch
  9. Playing with toys, door closed but not shut tight
 10. Playing with toys, door closed

Small room, therapist not in room

 11. Playing with toys, door open
 12. Playing with toys, door half closed
 13. Playing with toys, door open 1 inch
 14. Playing with toys, door closed but not shut tight for 10 seconds
 15. Playing with toys, door closed but not shut tight for 30 seconds
 16. Playing with toys, door closed but not shut tight for 1 minute
 17. Playing with toys, door closed for 10 seconds
 18. Playing with toys, door closed for 30 seconds
 19. Playing with toys, door closed for 1 minute
 20. Playing with toys, door closed for 2 minutes

Elevator, with therapist

 21. Standing in elevator with doors held open
 22. Standing in elevator with doors closed, and exiting on same floor (reopening door immediately)
 23. Riding elevator to next floor

received from his therapist and mother. After Jim was able to successfully move through the hierarchy, he was able to overcome his fear of closed doors.

Emotive Imagery. Emotive imagery, a variation of systematic desensitization, was developed by Lazarus and Abramovitz (1962). The therapist evokes images of self-assertion, pride, affection, and other anxiety-inhibiting responses through the use of hero images (e.g., Superman, Winnie the Pooh) in a fantasy that includes the child. The therapist induces positive affect and then gradually introduces the feared stimuli into the story. A fear hierarchy is developed, but the hero figure, rather than for muscle relaxation, is used as the anxiety inhibitor. From a systematic desensitization paradigm, the emotive imagery is thus the incompatible response to the feared stimuli, and the therapist involves the feared stimuli into the story in a systematic, and graduated fashion.

A recent study (Cornwall, Spence, & Schotte, 1997) used emotive imagery as a treatment for clinically significant darkness phobia in a sample of 7- to 10-year-old children. After a period of six sessions (6 weeks) of emotive therapy, the children in this group were significantly less fearful of the dark based on child and parent reports, and a behavioral darkness probe task.

Contingency Management. "Contingency management" is a general term that refers to techniques that modify a behavior by controlling its consequences. Positive reinforcement, shaping, stimulus fading, extinction, and differential reinforcement of other behavior (DRO) are all forms of contingency management. Management programs can be set up within the play therapy sessions or in the natural environment.

Positive Reinforcement. Positive reinforcement is an important component of almost every treatment for childhood fears. It is used with fears by specifying a target behavior, determining a reinforcer, and making the reinforcement contingent on the occurrence of the targeted behavior. It often involves social reinforcers (e.g., praise) or material reinforcers (e.g., stickers), and can be direct (e.g., praising the child with separation anxiety for venturing off to school without his or her mom) or more subtle (e.g., reinforcing independent play, which ultimately would lead to more confidence in the ability to be away from a parent figure). Reinforcement can come from the therapist as well as the parents and significant others who have been trained by the therapist to use appropriate reinforcement as the child conquers his or her fears.

For many children, chart systems that specify the desired behavior and reward can be extremely useful. Chart systems can help operationalize the desired behavior and ensure that the reinforcements are given in a systematic way. For example, a child fearful of sleeping in her own room, can have a chart that specifies she will receive a sticker for going to bed within a certain time frame after being asked, will stay in her room without constantly complaining or leaving the room, and will stay in her bed all night. Such reinforcement also helps the child see that she can master the feared situation and provides fairly immediate feedback for her positive behaviors.

Shaping. Shaping is a way of helping a child get closer and closer to a targeted goal. The child is given positive reinforcement for closer and closer approximations to the desired response. Eventually, the child reaches the desired behavior. One does not expect a fearful child to overcome his or her fears at once. Thus, the child who sleeps with his parents, because he is fearful of sleeping in his own room, could be shaped by providing reinforcement of his efforts in small steps (e.g., sleeping on the floor next to his parents' bed, sleeping on the floor in the hall toward his own room, sleeping on the floor in his room, sleeping in his own bed).

Stimulus Fading. A child may have some of the skills for a behavior but only exhibit the behavior in certain circumstances or with certain people. In these situations, stimulus fading may be used. The therapist helps the child use positive skills in one setting, and then helps the child transfer the skills to other settings. This is often seen when a child's responses may be different with each parent.

Stimulus fading was used with a 4½-year-old who was fearful of sleeping in her own room (see "Case Illustrations" section later in this chapter for a more detailed description of the treatment in this case). At first, the parents reported that she had not slept in her own bed since they moved into their new home 1½ years previously. Upon gathering the history, the parents remembered that the child had stayed in her room approximately 1 year earlier, when her father had been responsible for putting the child to bed. At that time, he had decided that "Mom was not allowed" around at bedtime (other than to say good night to the child), and the child had had no difficulty going to sleep under these circumstances. Unfortunately, she had gotten sick and regressed to her previous behavior. In part, treatment consisted of using the father as the primary parent to get the child ready for bed. After a reasonable routine was established, and the child was sleeping through the night in her room, the mother was gradually faded back into the bedtime routine.

Extinction and DRO. Some children exhibit fears because they have been (or are being) reinforced for performing them. In such cases, the reinforcing behaviors will need to be removed in order for the child to stop being fearful. A common reinforcing behavior is parental attention. After evaluation, it may become clear that the parents' attention is a major contribution or causal factor in the child's fear. Behaviors can be extinguished by withholding reinforcement. Extinction does not teach new behaviors, so it is frequently used in conjunction with a reinforcement program. A child can be reinforced for learning a new behavior at the same time that another behavior is being extinguished. This can be done through DRO. Thus, behaviors that are different from or incompatible with the maladaptive behavior are reinforced.

Modeling. Modeling is well researched and used frequently with fearful and anxious children. Modeling allows the child to see nonfearful behavior in the anxiety-provoking situation and demonstrates for the child a more appropriate response for dealing with the feared stimuli. Modeling provides the child an opportunity to see a model learn new skills to deal with a feared stimulus, which may be particularly useful for a child who does not have the requisite skills to deal with his or her fears.

Modeling designed to enhance skills can involve either coping or mastery models. Coping models display less than ideal skills and then gradually become more proficient, whereas mastery models exhibit a "perfect" performance. Research has shown that the efficacy of modeling is improved by the use of coping models, which may be thought of as a form of shaping the model toward the desired goal (Bandura & Menlove, 1968; Meichenbaum, 1971). The child may observe the model's efforts to learn more appropriate skills. It is felt that mastery models do not, in fact model any skills for the child and are thus less likely to help the child acquire new behaviors. Graduated exposure to feared stimuli can be part of the model, so that a systematic desensitization paradigm is actually being modeled for the child. Modeling can also take many forms, including symbolic modeling, where the models, often in stories, cope with feared stimuli, or participant modeling, where the model and child directly interact, with the model guiding the child through steps to overcome fears.

Although modeling procedures have been used frequently and often successfully in treating fearful children, many of these studies have involved children with mild fears (King & Ollendick, 1997). Unfortunately, adequate studies of modeling with more intense fears and phobias have yet to be conducted.

COGNITIVE TECHNIQUES

Behavioral methods used in CBPT usually involve an alteration in activity, whereas cognitive methods deal with changes in thinking. Since maladaptive cognitions are assumed to lead to fearful behavior, it is hypothesized that changes in thinking will produce changes in behavior. The therapist helps children identify, modify, and/or build cognitions. In addition to helping children identify cognitive distortions and teaching them to replace these maladaptive thoughts with more adaptive ones, the therapist also provides children with an opportunity to test their new skills. Research suggests that cognitive interventions alone do not facilitate mastery over fear, although the combination of cognitive and behavioral interventions appears to help children cope with fearful situations and stimuli (Schroeder & Gordon, 1991).

Cognitive Change Strategies and Countering Irrational Beliefs. With adults, cognitive change strategies usually involve a three pronged approach: Look at the evidence, explore the alternatives, and examine the consequences.

Once the child and therapist have identified maladaptive beliefs, individuals can be taught to counter irrational or maladaptive beliefs through a number of different techniques. Beck, Rush, Shaw, and Emery (1979) developed the "What is the evidence" technique. This technique helps fearful children identify their negative thoughts and develop more adaptive cognitions. In combination with this, Beck et al. (1979) describe the "What if" technique. The therapist guides the child through a series of questions about the worst thing that could happen if the child's fears were to come true. Finally, teaching the child to examine alternatives (Beck et al., 1979), provides him or her with alternative explanations and solutions.

These strategies are difficult to use with children because the hypothesis testing inherent in this approach is typically beyond the cognitive abilities of most children. Helping the child change cognitions means that he or she will need assistance from an adult in generating alternative explanations, testing them, and changing beliefs (Emery, Bedrosian, & Garber, 1983). To challenge one's beliefs, it is usually necessary to distance oneself from the beliefs, a task that is beyond the grasp of most young children. Additionally, the child needs an "accumulated history of events" to understand the ramifications of certain situations (Kendall, 1991). The learning that occurs from experience is usually not sophisticated in young children, who have not gathered the life experiences necessary to help with such understanding. Despite these limitations with young children, Knell (1993a, 1993b, 1994, 1997, 1998, in press) contends that cognitive change strategies can be adapted to the developmental levels of very young children. She argues that even preschoolers can benefit from cognitive interventions if they are presented in an age-appropriate way.

Positive Self-Statements. Individuals of all ages can be helped to develop adaptive, coping self-statements. However, such positive self-statements must be adapted to the age of the child. Very young children can be taught clear, self-affirming statements that are linguistically and conceptually simple (e.g., "I am brave," "I can do this"). These statements contain an element of self-reward (e.g., "I am doing a good job"). Positive self-statements can be taught in therapy but should be modeled by the therapist and parent alike. Turning praise into self-statements is not automatic, and the child must be helped to adapt positive, self-affirming comments. Children learn the positive value of what they do through specific labeling by significant adults, with positive feedback from those adults.

Positive self-statements can teach coping strategies through active control ("I can walk past the dog whenever I feel like it"), reducing aversive feelings ("I will be able to go to school whenever I am ready"), reinforcing statements ("I am brave"), and reality testing ("There really are no monsters in our house") (Schroeder & Gordon, 1991).

Self-Control. Self-control is really not an intervention per se. Rather, it is strategy geared toward teaching the individual to use new behaviors and ways of thinking that enhance one's sense of control. Ollendick and Cerney (1981) outlined a number of reasons why teaching children to regulate their own behaviors has received increased interest. Evidence suggests that controlling one's own behavior may be more efficient (Lovitt & Curtiss, 1969) and more durable (Drabman, Spitalnik, & O'Leary, 1973) than programs initiated by significant others on behalf of the child.

Through cognitive self-control programs (e.g., Kendall, Chansky, Kane, et al., 1992), children are taught to monitor, evaluate, and reinforce themselves for using more adaptive coping skills. Silverman (1989, as cited in Eisen & Kearney, 1995) developed the STOP acronym to help children stop their anxiety (Scared, fearful Thoughts, Other thoughts (coping), Praise). Through self-control training and utilization of techniques such as the STOP acronym, fearful children can be taught to regulate their own behavior.

Bibliotherapy. Bibliotherapy is not technically a cognitive intervention, but is used increasingly as an adjunct to therapy. With children, the focus of self-help books is somewhat different than with adults. Most therapeutic books for children provide a story with a child (model) who copes with a similar situation throughout a story. Such stories may model a child's reaction to a particular situation in the hope that the listener will incorporate some of the ideas into his or her approach to the problem. A separate reference section, including appropriate published books for fearful children, is included at the end of this chapter.

At times, published materials may not be available or appropriate. In these cases, it may be desirable to create books specifically for a child. A simple therapist-created book was used in the short-term intervention of a 2-year, 5-month-old child who was fearful of fires after experiencing several fires in abandoned homes in his neighborhood. He would become upset when he heard sirens or saw fire trucks. The therapist wrote a brief story about a child who experienced similar fires. The child in the story told his family about his fears, learned to talk about his feelings, and felt safe when he went to bed at night. Although, because of the child's age, the therapist wrote the book, the child helped illustrate the book during treatment sessions, and it was read to him by the therapist over the course of several sessions, and by his parents at home (Knell, 1993a)

With older preschool and school-age children, it can be helpful to create a book with the child during the treatment session. Oftentimes, the therapist may need to model much of the problem solving and creating of positive self-statements for and with the child. The advantages of working on the book together with the child are numerous. First and foremost, the child is a more active participant in change than if a previously published or therapist-written book is brought to the therapy session. As the child actively participates in writing the book, it is possible to incorporate spontaneous material brought to treatment by the child. Furthermore, it is possible to involve the child in cognitive change strategies as the book is written; that is, if the child voices maladaptive thoughts, both child and therapist can collaboratively work on more adaptive, positive self-statements to include in the book.

A book written in therapy with a 7-year-old child who presented with depression and separation anxiety illustrates these points. The child was referred for treatment by her mother's therapist. The mother was being seen for depression and difficulty with the parenting of her two children. The child seemed to be mirroring her mother's sadness, fears, and need to be in constant contact with her child. In one session, the child expressed her concerns about being apart from her mother but was also able to express things that helped her feel safe and comfortable when her mother was not near. Among the things that helped were hugging her dog and seeking comfort from her babysitter.

The therapist helped the child write a simple book entitled "Things to Do When I Miss Mom." The child's own ideas were incorporated into the text, although new ideas and positive self-statements were added by the therapist. Each sentence was written on a separate page, which was illustrated by the child. Sample sentences included positive self statements (Say to myself, "I miss Mom but she will be back soon," "Mom's OK, I'm OK, I will see Mom really soon") and coping suggestions ("Look at a picture of Mom, look at this book") suggested by the therapist, as well as coping suggestions generated by the child ("I can give my babysitter a hug," "I can give my dog a hug").

Parent Therapy

The parent is always involved in the assessment phase of therapy. After the parents are interviewed and the child evaluation is completed, it is often best to meet with the parents again to present the findings of the evaluation and agree on a treatment plan. The plan may involve individual play therapy with the child, work with the parents, or a combination of CBPT and parent work. Such decisions are made based on the therapist's assessment of many factors, such as whether the parents will need help in modifying their interactions with the child, and whether the child will need assistance in implementing a treatment plan outside of therapy.

When the therapeutic work is primarily with the child, it is still important to meet with the parents on a regular basis. During these sessions, the therapist will gather new information about the child's progress, continue to monitor and intervene in the parents' interaction with the child, and make suggestions regarding areas of concern.

A primary focus of parent work with fearful children involves helping the parent design an approach that will not reinforce the child for his or her fears. Often, parental behavior and responses to the child have served to encourage, reinforce, maintain, or exacerbate the child's fear symptoms, as in the previous example of the almost 2½-year-old who was afraid of fire and fire-related objects and sounds (e.g., fire trucks, sirens). The therapist was able to observe the family interaction when a fire truck with siren blaring went by during a treatment session. In this unplanned but well-timed situation, the therapist observed the parents coddle the child the instant they heard a fire siren. In fact, the parents moved toward the child *before* it seemed clear that the child had even heard the siren. In this situation, it was helpful to instruct the parents not to assume that the child would react in a fearful way, and thus not to reinforce the response before it even occurred.

The parents' behavior is not necessarily one that precedes the child's; nonetheless, it can serve to reinforce or encourage the child's fear. Quite simply, a child who receives more attention for being fearful than he or she receives for a more adaptive behavior is likely to continue the fearful behavior because of the reinforcement received for the fearful response.

Generalization/Relapse Prevention

An important goal for therapy of fears is for the child to maintain adaptive behaviors after the treatment has ended and to generalize these behaviors to the natural environment. This means that if the child learns to overcome fears during treatment, he or she will maintain this new ability after treatment ends, and that the lack of fear will be evident in all settings, not just the psychotherapy setting. Promoting and facilitating generalization should be part of the therapy; it will not necessarily happen without such planning (Meichenbaum, 1977). Generalization can be dealt with by using real-life situations in modeling and role playing, teaching self-management skills, involving significant adults and caregivers in the treatment, and continuing with treatment past the initial acquisition of skills to ensure that adequate learning takes place.

In addition to generalization, therapy should be geared toward helping the child and family prevent relapse. High-risk situations should be identified, and the child and parents should be prepared for handling such potentially disruptive situations. In this way, the child is "inoculated" against failure (Meichenbaum, 1985; Marlatt & Gordon, 1985).

CASE ILLUSTRATIONS

Case 1: Laura

The treatment of a 4½-year-old girl, Laura, who was fearful of sleeping in her own room, illustrates the use of the contingency management (positive reinforcement, shaping, stimulus fading, extinction, and DRO), bibliotherapy, modeling, and positive self-statements. Laura was brought to treatment by her parents, who reported that she had not slept in her own room since moving into their new home 1½ years ago. According to the parents, Laura would fall asleep in the family room, and one of the parents would pick her up and put her in her bed. She would sleep for several hours; then, during the night, she would get up and move to her parents' bed. If the parents insisted that she return to her own room, she would scream and cry. Laura reported being afraid of monsters in her room. The child had actually slept in her own room for a brief period of time approximately 1 year before the family sought treatment. According to the father, he had taken her to her bed, told her that Mom was not allowed, read her a story, and put her to bed. She did extremely well with this until she became ill with the flu, and then the old pattern evolved again.

As part of the assessment, a Child Behavior Checklist (CBCL; Achenbach, 1991) was completed by each parent. The father's completed profile was nonclinical, with slight elevations (although still within normal limits) on the Anxious/Depressed and Social Problem scales. The CBCL completed by Laura's mother also provided a nonclinical profile, although with slight elevations (nonclinical) on the Social Problem and Thought Problem scales. The parental interview had taken place at the first appointment, and at the second, Laura was seen. A Puppet Sentence Completion Task (Knell & Beck, in press) was administered, with several of Laura's responses suggesting feelings/thoughts about her sleep difficulties. A few selections are listed below:

> I am afraid of **monsters.**
> The best secret is **that I sleep in my bed, that I should sleep in my bed.**
> I am happiest when **I wake up.**
> My biggest problem is **being afraid of the dark.**
> My room is **pretty.**

In discussion, Laura expressed her concern about monsters that are big and scary, with long teeth, who only come out at night, and only in her bedroom. She also spontaneously related that she was afraid of a poster in her room, did not like her closet door open, and was able to sleep in her own room when she was 3 years old. She remembered that she felt good about being able to sleep there. Laura and the therapist made a list of everyone who would be happy if she slept in her bed at night. The list consisted of Mom, Dad, herself, and the family cat.

Recommendations were made to Laura and her parents at the end of the second appointment. Her parents were given a list of suggestions, partly gleaned from Laura's own suggestions. They were instructed to keep her closet door closed and to remove the poster in her room that she had identified as frightening. Changing these small environmental stimuli gave Laura some control over how she wanted her room and potentially eliminated aspects of her room that she identified as frightening. The list of people who would be happy if she slept in her room was to be taped next to her bed. This provided some immediate positive reinforcement, somewhat akin to the "friends who care list" developed by Azrin and Foxx (1974) to help children with toileting. They were asked to buy a "special flashlight," one that Laura could keep next to her bed and use herself whenever she became frightened. Finally, they were given a container of (imaginary) magic monster spray that Laura had "tried" with the therapist and understood that, when used, could "magically keep the monsters away." Both the flashlight and spray offered Laura some modicum of control over her environment and, potentially, her fears. It was also decided that Laura's father would be the primary parent putting Laura to bed at night, because of the history suggesting that Laura's mother reinforced her fears at night and was unable to be firm with Laura about sleeping in her own bed. (This stimulus fading component of treatment was described in a previous section). The parents were encouraged to continue with the program, even if Laura had a difficult time the first few nights. The therapist explained to them that as the nighttime problem behavior gradually lessened, because it had been previously reinforced, they could expect to see an increase in the problem behavior before it disappeared altogether (i.e., the increase in a previously reinforced behavior while it is being extinguished). Thus, the parents were told to expect that Laura might exhibit an increase in fear and/or crying when she was not receiving attention for not being in her bed (extinction). Laura and her parents left this session eager to try the new program.

The family was seen for the third session 1 week later. They reported that Laura cried for 2 hours the first night, and 1 hour the second night. By the third night of the program, she fussed for only a few minutes, and by the fourth night, she slept in her own room without difficulty. At this session, Laura was given stickers for her positive accomplishments (reinforcement), and she and the therapist made a book (bibliotherapy) that consisted of simple positive self statements on each page:

LAURA'S BOOK

One night, Laura slept in her own bed all night.
She used her flashlight.
She used her monster spray. Dad sprayed it all.
And she slept in her bed, ALL NIGHT.
YEAH.

They also made a special sign, with stars on it, to place on her wall. The sign said, "Good job, Laura, for sleeping in your own bed" (positive reinforcement).

The family was seen for the fourth session 1 month later. At that time, Laura was sleeping in her own room, with either parent in charge of the bedtime routine. In individual play therapy with Laura, puppets were used to play out different bedtime scenarios. In response to a puppet that was fearful of the dark, Laura told him to "use his flashlight." Thus, she was able to "model" her own coping skills for the puppet. She also helped the therapist read the story they wrote at the last session and drew pictures of herself in her own bed and her parents in their bed. These activities all served to reinforce her newly gained skills and thus provide a measure of relapse prevention for Laura.

Case 2: Evan

Evan was a 6-year-old boy whose parents expressed concerns regarding a number of issues, including shyness, attention difficulties, and anxieties. During the course of treatment, Evan expressed concern regarding his fear of going into the family's playroom, which was located on a lower level of their home. His older brothers had no difficulty playing there, and Evan often felt left out when he couldn't play with them. In addressing this particular concern with Evan, a number of different books were used, including *Go Away Big Green Monster* (Emberley, 1992), *Cool Cats, Calm Kids* (Williams, 1996) and *Dear Bear* (Harrison, 1995).

Evan was familiar with the book, *Go Away Big Green Monster*, in which, during the first half of the book, the face of a monster comes into view through a series of colorful die-cut pages. The monster's features all disappear in the remainder of the book, culminating in the final lines of the book, "Go away big green monster! And Don't come back! Until I say so." With illustrations and simple words, the message of the book clearly puts the control in the child's hands. Evan wrote his own letter to the monster, stating, "Dear Big giant huge monster: GO AWAY. Signed, Evan." He drew pictures of himself and the monster, and seemed to like the sense of control his own letters provided him.

In *Dear Bear*, the child in the story is afraid of a bear that "lives" under the stairs in her house. Her mother suggests she write a letter asking him to go away. The story follows the correspondence between the child and bear (obviously penned by the child's parents). At the end, the child and bear come face to face at a tea party. After hearing this book in therapy, Evan created his own set of letters. He wrote: "Dear Monster, Meet me in the play room. Love, Evan. PS Let's have a party." His mother, apprised of the book and Evan's fear, pretending to be the "monster," left the following letter for Evan. "Dear Evan, Thanks for your letter. I saw you in the playroom playing ball. You were really good. I bet you have been practicing a lot. The playroom is a fun place with lots of things to do. Thanks for leaving some games here for me to play with. Signed, The monster." In another letter, Evan's mother (as the monster) wrote: "Dear Evan. Thanks for your letter. I am sorry that you are afraid of me, because I am a rather friendly monster. Why don't we try not to scare each other and be friends, OK? Your new friend, the friendly monster."

Finally, the book *Cool Cats, Calm Kids* was used in therapy to help Evan with some stress management and relaxation skills. The book uses nine "cat" examples, showing how cats model stress management skills (e.g., Cat Secret 5: "Hold your head high"; Cat Secret 9 "Hang in there"). The therapist and Evan came up with their own book, which Evan titled "Cool Kids, Calm Cats." Examples from his book, included Secret 1: "If someone is bothering you, ignore them"; Secret 100: "If someone teases you, you should tell an adult."

Case 3: Tina

Tina's parents sought treatment because of her disruptive and acting-out behaviors. Tina's mother, recently diagnosed with cancer, had received a number of medical interventions over the past year. Another procedure was scheduled, and for this, Tina's mom would be in the hospital for 3 weeks. Although fear was not part of the immediate presenting problem, it became clear very quickly that Tina was extremely afraid of her mother's condition, and pending separation and hospitalization. Much of treatment involved allowing Tina to voice her concerns and worries, and express her feelings. The message was clearly communicated to Tina that her acting-out behaviors might be because of her fears, that feeling afraid was appropriate and understandable under the circumstances, but that she would need to learn ways to express her fears rather than acting them out.

One of her mother's oncology nurses had given the family a book, *Mira's Month* (Weinstein-Stern, 1994), to read to Tina. This book describes the experiences of a young girl whose mother has cancer, and how she learned to deal with her situation and feelings. Tina liked the idea of expressing her own feelings in a book, and with minimal help from the therapist, she wrote the following book, which she later illustrated. The title was taken from the family, who referred to the mom's cancer as "Johnny":

Go away, Johnny

Dedicated to Mom and Dad with love and care

One time my mom found out she had cancer. And I was very upset. I think what made me upset that she had cancer. My brother made me upset sometimes. Sometimes he would tease me. He would sometimes hit me. That would hurt. Sometimes, we get punished. I would think he would get more attention when we said something out loud, he'd never get more time outs, but I would. I think it's not fair. One time he bit me on the hand, and it really hurted and I bit him back accidentally. We said sorry after were done. And we went to the hospital to see Mom. She had all these tubes in her. We were scared. Me and my brother were scared. When we came home, we started fighting again. When Mom came home we gave her presents and cards. When Mom came home from her bone marrow transplant, we were happy. I looked at all the pictures we had drawn when she wasn't here. I went back in the family room and hugged my mom. From then on, I behaved more.

About the author. My mom really had cancer, and I was scared, but now I am not. I love my mom a lot, and my brother, too.

Case 4: Cara

Cara was a 4-year, 9-month-old girl who was brought to treatment because of her difficulties separating from her mother (a more detailed description of this case is provided in Knell, 1999). She would cry and sob for hours if left at preschool and would not separate from her mother at family gatherings and birthday parties. She had no specific traumatic experiences in early childhood, although she had certainly experienced much stress when away from her mother. This case was a classic example of separation anxiety disorder, but it is being presented here because of the efforts to deal with Cara's fears associated with either the anticipation or actual event of separation from her mom.

Work with the mother included setting up a positive reinforcement chart in which Cara received stickers for every day she was able to separate from her mom and play at school without crying. Mom was encouraged to praise Cara's efforts (shaping) and ignore behaviors that interfered (extinction).

During play therapy, Cara was encouraged to express her feelings about separation fears through pictures, stories, and puppet play. In CBPT, the therapist introduced several puppets, including one that was afraid to go to school. Positive coping statements were modeled by the therapist for the stuffed bear (e.g., "I can do this," "I will have a good time at school and not miss mom too much"). Cara became interested in a puppet who seemed to "worry too much." Together with the therapist, she generated a list of things that would help the bear, entitled "Mr. Bear's List" (e.g., "Think of something happy," "Mom's coming back," "I think I can, I think I can," "Play with toys and have fun"). This list provided the bear with positive coping statements that it could use to alleviate its anxiety (modeling positive self-statements). Cara was guided through a series of discussions regarding a bear puppet's fears of being left at school. Through the "voice" of the puppet, the therapist modeled adaptive coping skills for Cara. As therapy progressed, she began to incorporate these skills into her stories, puppet play, and, gradually, into her own coping behavior at school. The book, *The Little Engine That Could*, was used to model for Cara the idea that things can be done with lots of work and effort (bibliotherapy).

Cara and the therapist wrote and illustrated several books about her fears (bibliotherapy). In one, she dictated a story of herself not crying at school and how proud she was ("Me not crying and I'm so proud of myself. One day I went to school, and I didn't even cry. At one point I started crying and then the teachers told me it's no problem to cry, and then I didn't not cry anymore [*sic*]. The end").

She also dictated a book about school, titled "Cara's Book about School." Pages from this book had statements such as "I think about the choo choo train that could. . . . I picture things in my mind. . . . I think about coloring and that makes all the tears go away. . . . Sometimes I worry about if my mom is OK. I remind myself, 'She's OK.' "

During the course of treatment, the mother expressed a new concern that Cara was avoiding playing outside because of a fear of bugs. Cara and the therapist worked on a book about bugs:

> One day, I looked at a bug and it scared me. Then it flew away, but it didn't bother me. The next day, I went outside. I walked past the bug. It saw me, but it flew by me, and didn't hurt me. It kept flying by me. One day, I went outside and I walked past a bug with a stinger. It watched me go by, and then it stinged me. It really hurt. Daddy took the stinger out. He carried me into the house, put a Band-Aid on, and fixed me up. Sometimes bugs can hurt, but it's OK, I don't need to be too afraid.

The treatment involved a total of nine sessions, which were typically spent partly with the mother, and then in CBPT. The sessions took place over the course of 6 months, with sessions purposefully spaced out in order to accommodate changes in Cara's life (e.g., entering kindergarten). At termination, her mother reported that Cara was going outside and not showing any more fear of bugs. Peer interactions were increasing. Cara had begun kindergarten, was separating from her mom, and riding on the school bus without difficulty.

SUMMARY AND CONCLUSIONS

CBPT is designed specifically for preschool and early elementary-school-age children. It emphasizes the child's involvement in therapy and addresses issues of control, mastery, and responsibility for changing one's own behavior. The child is helped to become an active participant in change (Knell, 1993a). By presenting developmentally appropriate interventions, the therapist helps the child benefit from therapy. A wide array of techniques and approaches can be incorporated into CBPT.

For CBPT to be effective, it should provide structured, goal-directed activities, while at the same time allowing the child to bring spontaneous material to the session. The balance of spontaneously generated and more structured activities is a delicate one in CBPT. Unstructured, spontaneously generated information is critical to the treatment, for without it, the therapist would lose a rich source of clinical information. On the other hand, when therapy is completely unstructured and nondirective, it is not possible to teach more adaptive behaviors, such as problem solving.

A significant component of overcoming fears appears to be gaining control over them. Developing this sense of control may mean that the child learns to deal with the feared stimuli, to manage feelings associated with the fear, or to learn specific coping skills to deal with fear. Cognitive-behavioral interventions provide such learning opportunities as well as the specific skills necessary to overcome fear. In play therapy, children may master the feared object by taking on the role of one who does not fear it. They may act in ways that suggest they are not afraid. By "pretending" and practicing, children may overcome the feared stimuli.

REFERENCES

Achenbach, T. M. (1991). *Manual for the Child Behavior Checklist 4-18 and 1991 Profile*. Burlington: University of Vermont, Department of Psychiatry.

Agras, W. S., Chapin, N. H., & Oliveau, D. C. (1972). The natural history of phobias: Course and prognosis. *Archives of General Psychiatry, 26*, 315–317.

Azrin, N. H., & Foxx, R. M. (1974). *Toilet training in less than a day*. New York: Simon & Schuster.

Bandura, A., & Menlove, F. L. (1968). Factors determining vicarious extinction of avoidance behavior through symbolic modeling. *Journal of Personality and Social Psychology, 8*, 99–108.

Beck, A. T. (1976). *Cognitive therapy and the emotional disorders*. New York: International Universities Press.

Beck, A. T., Rush, A. J., Shaw, B. F., & Emery, G. (1979). *Cognitive therapy of depression*. New York: Guilford Press.

Bedrosian, R., & Beck, A. T. (1980). Principles of cognitive therapy. In M. J.

Mahoney (Ed.), *Psychotherapy process: Current issues and future directions* (pp. 127–152). New York: Plenum Press.

Campbell, S. B. (1986). Developmental issues in childhood anxiety. In R. Gittelman (Ed.), *Anxiety disorders of childhood* (pp. 24–57). New York: Guilford Press.

Cautela, J. R., & Groden, J. (1978). *Relaxation: A comprehensive manual for adults, children, and children with special needs.* Champaign, IL: Research Press.

Cornwall, E., Spence, S. H., & Schotte, D. (1997). The effectiveness of emotive imagery in the treatment of darkness phobia in children. *Behaviour Change, 13,* 223–229.

Drabman, R., Spitalnik, R., & O'Leary, K. D. (1973). Teaching self-control to disruptive children. *Journal of Abnormal Psychology, 82,* 110–116.

Eisen, A. R., & Kearney, C. (1995) *Practitioner's guide to treating fear and anxiety in children and adolescents.* Northvale, NJ: Aronson.

Emmelkamp, P. M. G. (1982). Anxiety and fear. In A. S. Bellack, M. Hersen, & A. E. Kazdin (Eds.), *International handbook of behavior modification and therapy* (pp. 349–395). New York: Plenum Press.

Emery, G., Bedrosian, R., & Garber, J. (1983). Cognitive therapy with depressed children and adolescents. In D. P. Cantwell & G. A. Carlson (Eds.), *Affective disorders in childhood and adolescence—An update* (pp. 445–471). New York: Spectrum.

Gullone, E. (1996). Developmental psychopathology and normal fear. *Behaviour Change, 13,* 143–155.

Hampe, E., Noble, H., Miller, L. C., & Barrett, C. L. (1973). Phobic children one and two years post treatment. *Journal of Abnormal Psychology, 82,* 446–453.

Jacobson, E. (1938). *Progressive relaxation.* Chicago: University of Chicago Press.

James, J. E. (1985). Desensitization treatment of agoraphobia. *British Journal of Clinical Psychology, 24,* 133–134.

Jersild, A. T. (1968). *Child psychology* (6th ed.). Englewood Cliff, NJ: Prentice-Hall.

Kendall, P. C. (Ed.). (1991). *Child and adolescent therapy: Cognitive-behavioral procedures.* New York: Guilford Press.

Kendall, P. C., Chansky, T. E., Kane, M. T., et al. (1992). *Anxiety disorders in youth: Cognitive behavioral interventions.* New York: Pergamon Press.

King, N. J., Hamilton, D. H., & Ollendick, T. H. (1988). *Children's phobias: A behavioral perspective.* New York: Wiley.

King, N. J., & Ollendick, T. H. (1997). Annotation: Treatment of childhood phobias. *Journal of Child Psychology and Psychiatry and Allied Disciplines, 38,* 389–400.

Knell, S. M. (1993a). *Cognitive-behavioral play therapy.* Northvale, NJ: Aronson.

Knell, S. M. (1993b). To show and not tell: Cognitive-behavioral play therapy in the treatment of elective mutism. In T. Kottman & C. Schaefer (Eds.), *Play therapy in action: A casebook for practitioners* (pp. 169–208). Northvale, NJ: Aronson.

Knell, S. M. (1994). Cognitive-behavioral play therapy. In K. O'Connor & C. Schaefer (Eds.), *Handbook of play therapy: Vol. 2. Advances and innovations* (pp. 111–142). New York: Wiley.

Knell, S. M. (1997). Cognitive-behavioral play therapy. In K. O'Connor & L. Mages (Eds.), *Play therapy theory and practice: A comparative presentation* (pp. 79–99). New York: Wiley.

Knell, S. M. (1998). Cognitive-behavioral play therapy. *Journal of Clinical Child Psychology, 27*, 28–33.

Knell, S. M. (1999). Cognitive behavioral play therapy. In S. W. Russ & T. Ollendick (Eds.), *Handbook of psychotherapies with children and families* (pp. 385–404). New York: Kluwer Academic/Plenum Publishers.

Knell, S. M., & Beck, K. W. (in press). Puppet sentence completion task. In C. E. Schaefer, K. Gitlin-Weiner, & A. Sandgrund (Eds.), *Play diagnosis and assessment* (Vol. 2). New York: Wiley.

Knell, S. M., & Moore, D. J. (1990). Cognitive-behavioral play therapy in the treatment of encopresis. *Journal of Clinical Child Psychology, 19*, 55–60.

Knell, S. M., & Ruma, C. D. (1996). Play therapy with a sexually abused child. In M. A. Reinecke, F. M. Dattilio, & A. Freeman (Eds.), *Cognitive therapy with children and adolescents: A casebook for clinical practice* (pp. 367–393). New York: Guilford Press.

Lazarus, A. A., & Abramovitz, A. (1962). The use of emotive imagery in the treatment of children's phobias. *Journal of Medical Science, 108*, 191–195.

Loevinger, J. (1976). *Ego development: Conceptions and theories.* Washington, DC: Jossey-Bass.

Lovitt, T. C., & Curtiss, K. A. (1969). Academic response rate as a function of teacher- and self-imposed contingencies. *Journal of Applied Behavior Analysis, 2*, 49–53.

Marlatt, G. A., & Gordon, J. R. (Eds.). (1985). *Relapse prevention: Maintenance strategies in the treatment of addictive behaviors.* New York: Guilford Press.

Meichenbaum, D. (1971). Examination of model characteristics in reducing avoidance behavior. *Journal of Personality and Social Psychology, 17*, 298–307.

Meichenbaum, D. (1977). *Cognitive-behavior modification: An integrative approach.* New York: Plenum Press.

Meichenbaum, D. (1985). *Stress inoculation training.* New York: Pergamon Press.

Miller, L. C. (1983). Fears and anxiety in children. In C. E. Walker & M. C. Roberts (Eds.), *Handbook of clinical child psychology* (pp. 337–380). New York: Wiley.

Morris, R. J., & Kratochwill, T. R. (1983). *Treating children's fears and phobias: A behavioral approach.* New York: Pergamon Press.

Ollendick, T. H. (1979). Fear reduction techniques with children. In M. Hersen, R. M. Fisher, & P. M. Miller (Eds.), *Progress in behavior modification* (Vol. 8, pp. 127–168). New York: Academic Press.

Ollendick, T. H. (1983). Reliability and validity of the revised Fear Survey Schedule for Children (FSSC-R). *Behaviour Research and Therapy, 21*, 685–692.

Ollendick, T. H., King, H. J., & Frary, R. D. (1989). Fears in children and adolescents: Reliability and generalizability across gender, age, and nationality. *Behaviour Research and Therapy, 27*, 19–26.

Ollendick, T. H., Matson, J. L., & Helsel, W. J. (1985). Fears in children and adolescents: Normative data. *Behaviour Research and Therapy, 23*, 465–467.

Reynolds, C. R., & Richmond, B. O. (1978). What I think and feel: A revised measure of children's manifest anxiety. *Journal of Abnormal Child Psychology, 6*, 271–280.

Schroeder, C. S., & Gordon, B. N. (1991). *Assessment and treatment of childhood problems.* New York: Guilford Press.

Silverman, W. K., & Nelles, W. B. (1990). Simple phobia in childhood. In M. Hersen & C. Last (Eds.), *Handbook of child and adult psychopathology: A longitudinal perspective* (pp. 183–195). New York: Pergamon Press.

Spielberger, C. D. (1973). *Manual for the State–Trait Anxiety Inventory for Children.* Palo Alto, CA: Consulting Psychologists Press.

Strauss, C. C., & Last, C. G. (1993). Social and simple phobias in children. *Journal of Anxiety Disorder, 7,* 141–152.

Ultee, C. A., Griffioen, D., & Schellekens, J. (1982). The reduction of anxiety in children: A comparison of the effects of systematic desensitisation *in vitro* and systematic desensitisation *in vivo. Behaviour Research and Therapy, 20,* 61–67.

Walk, R. D. (1956). Self-ratings of fear in a fear-invoking situation. *Journal of Abnormal and Social Psychology, 52,* 171–178.

Wolpe, J. (1958). *Psychotherapy by reciprocal inhibition.* Stanford, CA: Stanford University Press.

Wolpe, J. (1982). *The practice of behavior therapy* (3rd ed). Oxford, UK: Pergamon Press.

BIBLIOTHERAPY

Dutro, J. (1991). *Night light: A story for children afraid of the dark.* New York: Magination Press.

Emberley, E. (1992). *Go away big green monster!* New York: Little, Brown.

Harrison, J. (1995). *Dear Bear.* Minneapolis, MN: Lerner.

Lankton, S. R. (1988). *The blammo-surprise! book: A story to help children overcome fears.* New York: Magination Press.

Lobby, T. (1990). *Jessica and the wolf: A story for children who have bad dreams.* New York: Magination Press.

Marcus, I. W., & Marcus, P. (1990). *Scary night visitors.* New York: Magination Press.

Marcus, I. W., & Marcus, P. (1992). *Into the great forest: A story for children away from parents for the first time.* New York: Magination Press.

Penn, A. (1993). *The kissing hand.* Washington, DC: Child Welfare League of America.

Piper, W. (1950). *The little engine that could.* New York: Platt & Munk.

Weinstein-Stern, D. (1994). *Mira's month.* Highland Park, IL: BMT Newsletter.

Williams, M. L. (1996). *Cool cats, calm kids: Relaxation and stress management for young people.* San Luis Obispo, CA: Impact.

2

Short-Term Gestalt Play Therapy for Grieving Children

VIOLET OAKLANDER

INTRODUCTION

Gestalt therapy is a humanistic, process-oriented mode of therapy that focuses attention on the healthy, integrated functioning of the total organism, comprised of the senses, the body, the emotions, and the intellect. Gestalt therapy was originally developed by Frederick (Fritz) Perls, MD and Laura Perls, PhD, and has at its base principles from psychoanalytic theory, Gestalt psychology, various humanistic theories, as well as aspects of phenomenology, existentialism, and Reichian body therapy. From these sources, a large body of theoretical concepts and principles have evolved underlying the practice of Gestalt therapy (Perls, Hefferline, & Goodman, 1951; Perls, 1969; Latner, 1986). A few of the most salient principles of Gestalt therapy that are pertinent to working with children are discussed in this chapter.

The Relationship

This is a particular type of relationship based on the philosophical writings of Martin Buber (1958), often referred to as the I–Thou relationship. Some of the pertinent fundamental principles of this relationship are highly significant in work with children. The therapist is cognizant of the fact that, despite differences in age, experience, and education, she is not superior to the client; both are equally entitled. It is a relationship where two people come together in a dialogical stance. The therapist meets the child however he or she presents the self, without judgment, and with respect and honor. The therapist does not play a role. She is congruent and genuine, while at the same time respecting her own limits and boundaries, never losing herself to the child, but willing to be affected by the child. The therapist holds no expectations, yet maintains an attitude that supports the full, healthy potential of the child. The therapist is involved, contactful, and often interactive. She creates an environment of safety and never pushes the child beyond his or her capabilities or consent. The relationship itself is therapeutic; often, it provides an experience for the child that is new and unique.

Contact and Resistance

Contact involves the ability to be fully present in a particular situation, with all the aspects of the organism vital and available. Healthy contact involves the use of the senses (looking, listening, touching, tasting, smelling), awareness and appropriate use of aspects of the body, the ability to express emotions healthfully, and the use of the intellect in its various forms as learning, expressing ideas, thoughts, curiosities, wants, needs, and resentments. When any one of these modalities is inhibited, restricted, or blocked, good contact suffers. Fragmentation, rather than integration, occurs. Children who have troubles, who are grieving, worried, anxious, frightened, or angry, will armor and restrict themselves, pull themselves in, inhibit themselves, and block healthful expression. Healthy contact involves a feeling of security with oneself, a fearlessness of standing alone. We make good contact with others from the edge of ourselves—from the boundary of the self. "The contact boundary is the point at which one experiences the 'me' in relation to that which is 'not me' and through this contact, both are more clearly experienced" (Polster & Polster, 1973). If the self is weak and undefined, the boundary is fuzzy and contact suffers. Good contact is fluid and involves a rhythm of withdrawal. The child who maintains a fixed contact posture, as requiring constant attention, never able to play alone, or talking constantly, shows evidence of a fragile sense of self (Oaklander, 1988).

Most children will be resistant and self-protecting to a degree. Resistance is actually a healthy response, and good contact involves some level of resistance. It is difficult to engage in good contact with someone who does not have a clear boundary, but a high degree of resistance makes achieving satisfying contact impossible. The therapist expects some resistance and recognizes it as the child's ally. She is respectful of the resistance. As the child begins to feel safe in the sessions, the resistance will soften. However, resistance comes up over and over again. When the child has experienced or divulged as much as she can handle or has inside support for, the resistance will come up again and must be honored. It is the child's signal that she has reached her limit of capability at this particular time. Resistance can be viewed as a manifestation of energy as well as an indication of the contact level of the child. When the energy fades and the contact shifts, this is evidence of resistance. Some children indicate the resistance in passive ways—ignoring, acting distracted, or appearing not to be listening. The child who can say, "I don't want to go any further with this" is making a contactful statement.

The issue of resistance is implicated in the success of brief therapy with children. The child's resistance involves his very core—his way of coping and surviving his problematic world. His resistance is an indication of his state of being. The therapist cannot push through this resistance quickly, forcefully, or mechanically. If the relationship is strong, the therapist can use all of her skill to gently override some of the resistance. It is a tenuous matter.

Inappropriate behaviors are often viewed as resistances or contact–boundary disturbances. As the child struggles to grow up, survive, and cope with life, he may manifest a variety of inappropriate behaviors and symptoms that serve to avoid contact and protect the self. He does not have the inner support, cognitive ability, or emotional maturity to express directly deep feelings. These symptoms and behaviors, the very ones that bring children into therapy, are actually the organism's way of attempting to achieve homeostasis, albeit unsuccessfully. The quest for equilibrium is unrelenting; the child has little awareness of cause and effect in his attempts to cope, get his needs met, and protect himself. The child has a powerful thrust for life and growth, and will do anything he can to grow up. Paradoxically, in the service of this quest, he will restrict, inhibit, block, and actually cut off aspects of the self. He will desensitize himself, restrict the body, block emotions, and inhibit the intellect. The consequence of this process is an increased diminishing of the self and impairment of his contact abilities, often manifesting as troublesome behaviors or symptoms.

Sense of Self

Helping the child develop a strong sense of self is a prelude to emotional expression, an important step in the healing process. When children restrict and inhibit an aspect of the organism, the self is diminished. Strengthening the skills of contact play is an important part in this process. These skills— looking, listening, smelling, tasting, touching, moving in the environment; expressing thoughts, ideas, opinions, and defining the self—give the support necessary for expressing deep emotions that block healthy functioning and integration. A variety of experiences introduced by the therapist are used to strengthen the child's self, which in turn provides the self-support required for emotional expression. This is not a linear process—the therapist presents these activities as needed.

Awareness and Experience

Gestalt therapy is considered to be a process therapy: Attention is paid to the "what" and "how" of behavior rather than the "why." When the therapist can help the client become more aware of what he or she is doing that causes dissatisfaction, the client then has the choice to make changes. Awareness encompasses many aspects of life. One can become aware of one's process, sensations, feelings, wants, needs, thought processes, and actions. As the child moves through the therapy experience, he becomes more aware of who he is, what he feels, what he needs, what he wants, and so on (Oaklander, 1982). Some older children as well as adolescents often become cognizant of unsatisfactory ways of being, experience them fully with the guidance of the therapist, and begin to make conscious choices for new behaviors. This is beyond the scope of younger children. For these children, experience is the key to awareness. Providing varied experiences for children is an essential component of the therapeutic process. These experiences may be with aspects of themselves that are blocked, such as one or more of their sensory modalities. They might be experiences that experiment with parts of the self that have been kept dormant. All of these experiences serve to strengthen the child's self and promote good contact functioning, culminating in healing emotional expression, and, in general, facilitating new, more satisfying ways of being in the world.

Many creative, expressive, and projective techniques are used to further the therapeutic experience. These techniques serve as bridges to the child's inner self and often provide the means to discover, renew, or strengthen aspects of the self. The techniques include the use of graphic arts in many forms, such as drawing, painting, and collage, as well as pottery clay, puppets, music in many forms, creative dramatics, sensory and body experiences, various games, books and storytelling, the sand tray, fantasy and imagery, and the use of metaphors. These techniques are very powerful in the context of Gestalt therapy and the relationship that develops with the therapist.

SHORT-TERM GESTALT PLAY THERAPY APPROACH

Gestalt therapy can be an ideal discipline for short-term work with grieving children since it is directive and focusing. In longer-term situations, the sessions become a sort of dance: sometimes the child leads, and at other times, the therapist does. In short-term work, the therapist becomes, for the most part, the leader. She must assess what will best serve the child's therapeutic needs to provide the best experience in the few sessions available, while being heedful of the child's developmental level, capability, responsiveness and resistance level. She must not be forceful or intrude upon the child's boundary—she must tread lightly, without any expectation.

The vitality and potency of these techniques make them particularly effective for short-term work, since they are so dynamic and particularly effective in cutting to the core of a situation.

Preliminary to doing short-term work with grieving children, the therapist must have an understanding of the issues involving loss and grief, as well as some general pointers that facilitate short-term work.

Stages of Grief

Elizabeth Kübler-Ross (1973) postulated five stages related to the reaction of the death of a loved one: denial and isolation, anger, bargaining, depression, and, finally, acceptance. Most therapists have generalized these stages to fit many kinds of loss situations. Lenore Terr, in her excellent book *Too Scared To Cry* (1990), discusses the process of mourning as presented by John Bowlby (1973–1983) in his three-volume work, *Attachment, Separation, and Loss,* as four phases particularly relating to children: denial, protest, despair, and resolution. Children, she argues, can become stuck in any one phase for long periods of time. The therapist cannot push the client through any of these stages. However, as specific issues are dealt with, movement begins to take place.

Issues

There are numerous possible issues involved that the therapist must be aware of when a child suffers a loss. Some of these issues include confusion, abandonment, loss of self, blaming the self, guilt, fear, loss of control, feelings of betrayal, feeling the need to take care of parents, unexpressed feelings of sadness, anger, shame, and misconceptions. The therapist must make an assessment regarding the issues besetting the child so that she can provide a focus to the therapy. Certain issues are particularly prevalent at various development levels. For example, the 4-year-old who loses a parent will feel responsible for that loss, since he is basically an egocentric individual. Generally, it can be assumed that every child is troubled by most of the issues mentioned.

Children suffer many different kinds of loss throughout their development. These losses affect the child deeply: The loss of a favorite toy, a friend, a neighborhood, a loved teacher, a pet, a parent through divorce, and the loss that comes about through some kind of physical impairment, all impact the child. The death of a parent, sibling, friend, or grandparent is certainly a traumatic loss. As children grow, the accumulation of these losses, without appropriate expression of grief, causes havoc to healthy development. It is not unusual for the child to develop worrisome symptoms and behaviors months, or even years, after a particular loss. The child certainly has the capacity to go through the grieving process naturally. However, he generally has introjected many messages regarding the expressions necessary for this work: It is not OK to cry. It is certainly not OK to be angry about the loss. The child feels responsible for the well-being of the adults in his life. He may be holding a secret fear that he is responsible for the loss.

In short, the child needs much support and guidance through the grieving process. When the process is encouraged, and any issues that impede his grief are addressed, the child often responds rapidly.

Short-Term Work

Often, combined with the task of helping children through the grieving process is the therapist's mandate to do it quickly, a seemingly impossible task when working with children. The therapist may feel pressured to achieve results quickly. This pressure can be a detriment to the work, and the therapist must find a way to shed this burden and trust the process, even if she is not successful. When the child suffering the loss has functioned well prior to the loss and appears to have a fairly strosng sense of self, with good support in his environment, only a few sessions can help him move through his grief. Furthermore, if the therapist can feel the thread of a relationship and the child can sustain contact when working with the therapist, good results can be achieved. Contact must be assessed periodically, since the child will cut herself off and break contact if the work becomes too intense for her—if she lacks the self-support to deal with the task at hand. The therapist must be sensitive to this phenomenon, and when it happens, she must honor this resistance and perhaps suggest that the remaining time be filled with some nonthreatening activity, such as a game of the child's choosing.

When the relationship and contact are prevalent, the therapist must then make some determinations that will best fit the model of short-term work. In spite of the goals the therapist may have, she must be vigilant in avoiding expectations. She will set the framework for each session and present the activity, but to anticipate results is a breeding ground for failure. Every child is highly sensitive to expectations that may be present; this attitude can severely affect and cloud the session. Expectations present a dynamic that becomes a living part of the encounter. The therapist must take an existential stance: Whatever will happen will happen.

Several points involving short-term work need to be considered and may be helpful:

1. See the situation as "crisis intervention." Tell the child you only have a few sessions to make things better.

2. Look at the number of sessions there are and plan what you will do (without expectation that what is planned will happen.) For example, the first session would be used to establish the relationship by getting

to know the child, engaging in nonthreatening activities and providing safety for the child. When the therapist is respectful, genuine, congruent, accepts the child however he or she presents the self, and is herself contactful, relationship and safety will be established.

3. Do not become enmeshed with the child. Often, when dealing with a child's loss, the therapist can feel she must take care of the child, make things better, feel emotional, or feel so sorry for the child that she allows him to do whatever he wants, even going beyond limits. If the therapist cannot maintain her own boundaries and have the child adhere to the limits by which she operates, the child becomes confused and anxious.

4. List the issues you determine are involved with this particular child and set priorities. Cut right to the core of the issues and feelings (examples are given in the next section). Depending on the age of the child, the therapist can share some of these items with the child, giving the child the choice to decide what he or she wants to work on.

5. Include parents in some of the sessions if possible. Explain to them the process of your work. Assess the communication level regarding the loss. For example, a child whose father lost his job felt he needed to cheer up his parents, reassure himself, and look at the "bright side" of things, totally cutting off his fears. Other symptoms, such as falling grades and inability to concentrate, cropped up. In family sessions, he admitted he was terrified about what was going to happen to the family. The parents admitted that they never showed their own fear, much less discussed it with the child, thinking that this would be detrimental. As they began to talk to each other about what they were feeling, the child's symptoms faded away.

6. Therapy is intermittent with children. Termination is generally temporary. At each developmental level, new issues arise. The child can only work at his or her particular developmental level. Parents need to understand this.

7. Be honest and clear with the child about the reason he or she is having sessions with you. Even a very young child can understand if the therapist uses appropriate developmental language.

CASE ILLUSTRATIONS

The following are condensed accounts of work with grieving children on a short-term basis.

Case 1: Jack

Twelve-year-old Jack lost his mother to cancer when he was 7. His parents had been divorced for some time and his father was remarried. Jack had a good relationship with both his parents, who had joint custody, did well in school, had friends, and appeared to be fairly well-adjusted to life in general. When his mother died, he moved in with his father and stepmother, whom he liked very much. His father reported that there had been no problems with Jack since his mother's death. When the therapist asked how Jack had handled his grief, his father realized that, actually, Jack had shown very little affect outside of some brief crying when he was first told of her death.

At his present age of 12, certainly a crucial developmental age, various symptoms appeared. Jack's grades began to fall; he preferred to stay at home rather than play with his friends, was upset when his father was not at home, and began to have trouble sleeping. His parents did not associate his symptoms with the death of his mother years earlier. However, the therapist saw this traumatic event as a red flag, particularly since the parents reported that he handled her death "so well."

SESSION 1

At the first session, Jack came in with his parents. It is during this session that the therapist learns the child's "story" and the concerns of the parents. It is important that the child be present at this session to know what his parents tell the therapist. Jack agreed that he would like to work on sleeping better, since he saw himself as somewhat of an athlete and admitted feeling too tired to do anything, presumably due to lack of sleep.

SESSION 2

At the second session, the therapist evaluated Jack's ability to make a relationship and observed his contact skills. Jack was a bright, friendly child who quickly related to the therapist and appeared to be quite contactful. From all appearances, he was a good candidate for short-term work. The first session with Jack alone was primarily a time to help him feel comfortable and to promote the relationship. After some conversation, the therapist asked Jack to draw a safe place—a place where he felt safe. Jack drew a camping scene and talked about how much he enjoyed camping outings with his Dad and stepmother. He said that he liked being with them and doing things together, and that the stresses from the regular world did not get in the way. The therapist made a list of some of these stresses as Jack dictated them. The session concluded with a game of Uno, Jack's choice from several easy, fun games.

SESSION 3

At the next session, the therapist asked Jack to close his eyes and think about his mother to see what memory might come to the fore. He was invited to draw the memory or just share it. He reported that he had very few memories of his mother but proceeded to draw a beach scene. When finished, he talked about how he remembered going to the beach with her when he was little. The therapist asked Jack to give the little boy in the scene a voice. She immediately began a dialogue with the boy, "What are you doing?" and Jack, in spite of his initial resistance to such a silly request, answered, "I'm building a sand castle." The therapist encouraged Jack to dialogue with his mother in the picture as the little boy. At the conclusion of this little exercise, Jack stated with a smile, "That was fun." Again the session was concluded with Uno.

SESSION 4

Pottery clay had been set out on two boards on the table, along with a rubber mallet and some other tools. As Jack and the therapist played with the clay, she casually asked him to tell her more about his mother and some things he remembered about her. Clay has a powerful quality of providing a nurturing, sensorial experience, along with promoting expression. Jack was surprised that he actually had numerous memories. The therapist shared with him that she believed his sleeping problems and difficulty separating from his dad were related to the loss of his mother at age 7. Jack was astonished and startled at this information. She asked Jack to make a figure of a 7-year-old boy out of clay and to imagine what it was like for this little boy to lose his mother. The therapist engaged the "7-year-old" in a dialogue, again inviting Jack to be the voice of the little boy. The therapist encouraged Jack to "make up" what he imagined a little boy would say.

THERAPIST: Were you scared when your mother got sick?

JACK: When she went to the hospital I was very scared.

THERAPIST: Yes! That's a very scary thing for a little kid.

Much to his own surprise, Jack offered lots of information in answer to the therapist's casually stated questions. The therapist told him that children at that age have difficulty grieving and need help to know how to go through the grief stages. Jack was fascinated by the various stages, and more memories of that time began to flood back for him.

"I remember that I was mad when my dad said she died! I was sure he was lying and I ran from the room and wouldn't talk to him. That's like denial I guess. My dad seemed mad at me for that. I guess he didn't know about the stages."

And Jack talked about his anger, which seemed to get him into a lot of trouble. So he suppressed it, assuming that he was very bad to feel such an emotion.

The therapist placed a large lump of clay in front of Jack and invited him to pound it with the rubber mallet. Jack did this with much gusto. When the therapist asked him to put words to his pounding, Jack stood up and hit the clay with tremendous force. He began to cry as he shouted, "Why did you leave me?", obviously now talking to his mother. The therapist articulated encouraging words, such as "Yes, Tell her!" She knew that if she remained silent, Jack would suddenly realize what he was doing and stop from his noisy outburst. Jack continued for awhile and finally sat down. Quickly, the therapist praised him for being able to allow his anger to come out. The therapist fashioned a little figure that she labeled 7-year-old Jack.

THERAPIST: Jack, this is your 7-year-old self. Imagine you could go back in a time machine and talk to him. What would you say?

JACK: I don't know.

THERAPIST: Try saying, I'm sorry you lost your mother.

JACK: Yeah. I'm sorry you lost your mother. You're just a little kid and you need her. It's not right.

Jack continued in this vein, with encouragement and suggestions from the therapist.

THERAPIST: Jack, that little boy lives inside of you. He's been quiet for a while, but now that you are 12 and can do a lot of things, I think he has been trying to get your attention. I think he's been stuck at that age because he never expressed (or even knew) his feelings. He needs you now. When you are scared, when your father goes away, it's really him thinking something will happen to his dad. It's really him keeping you from sleeping. But now he has you and, of course, you will never leave him since he's part of you. He needs you now. So every night this week when you go to bed, I want you to talk to him and tell him you will never leave him and that he's a very good kid. And maybe you can tell him a story while you're lying in bed.

JACK: My mother used to tell me stories.

THERAPIST: Now you can do it. You're good at this kind of thing so try it. This is your homework for the week!

Jack declined to practice this exercise in the therapist's office and agreed he would do it at home.

SESSION 5

At the fifth session, Jack reported that he was sleeping better but not really well yet. The therapist asked Jack to close his eyes and imagine he was in bed at night, and to report the feelings he experienced. Jack said there was still some fear but that he was not sure what it was about. The therapist asked Jack to draw the fear using colors, lines, curves, shapes.

JACK: This is how I feel. Lots of weird lines and circles, mostly black. I think I'm afraid my father will die, like you said last week.

THERAPIST: Jack, no one knows really what will happen in the future about anyone. But when a boy loses someone close, especially his mom, he can get pretty worried and anxious and naturally begins to think that it will happen to someone else close, especially his dad. You need to let the little boy in you know that it's OK to be afraid—that you understand it. Here he is (*drawing a quick stick figure*)—tell him.

JACK: Yes, it's OK to be afraid.

THERAPIST: Do you believe that?

JACK: Well, it's OK for him to be afraid. I don't think I should.

THERAPIST: That's why I'm asking you to talk to him. I think if you give him permission to be afraid, maybe it will help you not to be so afraid. Though really, Jack, it's OK if you are too.

JACK: OK, you can be afraid. It's natural. You're a little kid.

THERAPIST: Remind him that you are with him and will never leave him, and that you know how to do a lot of things he couldn't do.

Jack practiced this for awhile.

SESSION 6

At the sixth session Jack reported that he fell asleep before he finished talking to his 7-year-old self and forgot to worry about his dad. He was too busy. The therapist reminded Jack that every now and then, he would feel lonely for his mom and to remember that he needed to let himself do that, and maybe do something nice for his 7-year-old self.

SESSION 7

At this last session Jack and his parents participated. Everyone talked a bit about what Jack had learned. Jack was anxious to enlighten them, particularly about stages. Jack reported that he felt happy that he was not so tired now. A follow-up session was held 1 month later—all was well.

This work was accomplished in a total of seven sessions, including the last one. The first session involved the family, while the next two were for relationship building, as well as providing a base for focusing on the death of Jack's mother. The therapist made the assumption that this was the cause of his present symptoms, particularly because of his attachment disorder. The issues that emerged spontaneously were fear of abandonment, anger, and sadness. Learning to nurture the self and gaining skills to take care of the self are important and effective.

Case 2: Susan

Ten-year-old Susan lost her father to suicide. Her parents had been divorced since Susan, the youngest of three children, was a baby. Susan's dad was very involved in Susan's life and she was very close to him. There was an agreement that she would live with him for a year, and just prior to her move, he killed himself. Susan's mother brought her into therapy 6 months later, when Susan's behavior appeared to deteriorate into angry, aggressive outbursts and the teacher had complained that she was not doing her work and had become quite belligerent. It is common for parents to bring a child into therapy after a traumatic loss such as this after a few months have gone by and symptoms emerge and accelerate.

SESSION 1

The first session took place with mother and daughter. The mother stated that ever since the father died, Susan has been having difficulties at school, and their relationship has deteriorated. "Things are getting worse," she said, "and not better as I thought they would with time." At this session, Susan was quite withdrawn and would not participate. The therapist asked the mother to go into the waiting room, and then asked Susan to draw a house and tree and person on a single sheet of paper. Susan, relieved that she did not have to talk, worked diligently.

THERAPIST: Susan, this is really a test, but I'm not using it that way—I'm using it to get to know you better. It tells me some things about you and I would like to check them out with you to see if it's right.

SUSAN: What does it tell you?

THERAPIST: Well, for one thing, it tells me you keep a lot of things to yourself.

SUSAN: It's true. How do you know that?

THERAPIST: Your house has very small windows and dark shades and sometimes when someone draws windows like that, it could mean that.

SUSAN: (*Showing interest*) What else does it tell you?

THERAPIST: It also might show that you keep in a lot of anger because maybe you don't know how to get it out. Does that fit for you? The person looks kind of angry.

SUSAN: Yes!

THERAPIST: See how the house is tilting? Maybe you don't feel very sure about anything right now. And the girl is at this corner, far away from the house. Maybe you don't know where you belong.

SUSAN: (*Very low voice*) That's right.

The therapist noticed tears in Susan's eyes and gently told her that they would try to work these things out together in the sessions. She wrote her findings on the back of Susan's paper and read them back to her. Susan listened intently. The therapist then suggested that they spend the final few minutes of the session playing a game. Susan selected Connect Four; the relationship appeared to be taking hold.

SESSION 2

At the second session, the therapist asked Susan to make her family out of clay. Susan fashioned her two sisters and her mother. When asked to include her father, she refused. "He's not here anymore." The therapist quickly fashioned a rough figure. "This is your father," she said. "He'll be over here." The therapist placed the figure at the far corner of the clay board.

THERAPIST: I would like you to say something to each person.

SUSAN: (*To oldest sister*) You don't care anything about me. You're always off with your friends. (*to middle sister*) I wish you wouldn't tease me so much. (*to mother*) I wish you didn't have to work so much and could be home more.

THERAPIST: Now say something to your father.

SUSAN: I don't want to.

THERAPIST: OK. You don't have to. Susan, sometimes when a parent commits suicide, kids blame themselves and are ashamed to tell anyone. I wonder if that's true for you.

SUSAN: Other kids feel those things too?

THERAPIST: Yes, they are very common feelings!

SUSAN: I don't know what I did, but I was supposed to move in with him and then he went and killed himself. I thought he was glad I was coming. And I don't want anyone to know. They'll know it was because of me.

THERAPIST: It's hard for you to feel those things. I'm sorry.

Susan nodded and closed down. This was obvious by her lack of contact, her body posture, and her decreased energy. The therapist suggested they stop talking and play Connect Four again. Susan visibly brightened and took down the game with renewed energy. The therapist told Susan that her mother would be joining them at the next session.

SESSION 3

At the third session, with the mother present, the therapist asked Susan and her mother each to make something that made them angry. Susan watched her mother draw and then finally began to work on her own picture. The mother drew an incident that happened at work and talked a little about it.

SUSAN: I didn't do what you asked me to. I just drew my family.

THERAPIST: OK. I notice that you didn't draw your father. Just make a little circle up here in the corner for him. Susan, tell each person in your family something that makes you angry or you don't like that they do.

Susan complied, but again refused to talk to the father figure.

THERAPIST: (*to mother*) I wonder if you would be willing to say something to your ex-husband over here. It is hard for Susan to do it. Anything you would like to tell him.

Susan's mother immediately began to express intense anger at him for killing himself, causing so much hurt and pain to his children, especially to Susan, and leaving her solely responsible for the three children.
    Susan began to cry and said she was angry too, and that she was sure it was all her fault. The therapist directed Susan to tell this to the father figure. Susan's mother voiced astonishment and emphatically assured Susan that this was not the case, that her Dad had financial problems and that she thought that was why he probably did it, and that he loved Susan very much. But it just got to be too much for him. Susan continued to cry as her mother embraced her.

SESSION 4

At the fourth session, the therapist suggested that Susan draw a picture of something she had enjoyed doing with her father. She drew a picture of a swimming pool and talked about how much fun they used to have swimming together. She then asked if she could do a sand tray and proceeded to make a graveyard scene, announcing that one of the graves belonged to her father.

THERAPIST: Susan, I would like you to talk to your father's grave.

SUSAN: Dad, I hope you are happy where you are. I miss you a lot. I'm sorry things were rough for you.

THERAPIST: Could you tell him you love him?

SUSAN: Yes! Dad, I love you. (*long pause*) Goodbye. (*to therapist*) Do we have time to play a game?

SESSION 5

Susan and the therapist had one more session together. Her mother was unable to attend and sent a note saying that Susan was behaving appropriately. The therapist asked Susan what she would like to do at this goodbye session, and Susan opted for clay. She made a birthday cake, with toothpicks for candles, stating with much gaiety that her dad's birthday was coming up and she wanted to have a cake ready for him.

This work took five sessions. Here again, as with Jack, the relationship was established quickly and Susan was quite responsive in spite of her initial resistance. The issue of responsibility for her father's death appeared to be dispensed with quickly. Anger and sadness were expressed. The therapist called Susan's mother to tell her that Susan had worked on the loss of her father at her particular developmental level but that deeper feelings might emerge at later developmental levels, involving issues that Susan did not have the self-support to deal with now. How she functioned in her life was the best measurement for whether or not Susan needed further therapeutic work.

Case 3: Jimmy

Six-year-old Jimmy was brought in by his dad. Jimmy's sister, 2 years younger, was killed in an automobile accident, and Jimmy and his parents had sustained minor injuries. The father said that Jimmy seemed to be functioning well but he felt that Jimmy needed help to deal with his sister's death, since he never spoke of her. Jimmy's mother, extremely grieved and barely functioning, was under a psychiatrist's care. Jimmy remained stoic. The therapist assumed that Jimmy was afraid to show his grief for fear of losing his mom—he needed to be strong for her. Jimmy's dad told the therapist that the children had related quite well, played together all the time, but that Jimmy loved to tease his sister, sometimes hit her, and seemed to enjoy making her cry. Jimmy, still at an egocentric developmental level, probably blamed himself for her death, particularly in light of his behavior toward her. The therapist felt that this latter issue, plus Jimmy's fear of losing his mother's love and attention, seemed to be priorities for their work together.

SESSION 1

At the first session, as the father talked to the therapist, Jimmy refused to talk and sat at the sand tray, running his hands through the sand. The therapist could see by Jimmy's body posture that he was listening intently. The therapist asked Jimmy if it was OK with him if his father waited in the waiting room. Jimmy nodded, his back still to the therapist. The therapist drew Jimmy's attention to the shelves of miniatures, inviting him to set them in the sand to make a scene. Jimmy proceeded to put all the trees he could find in the sand, and under one of them he placed a very small rabbit. "I'm done," he said.

THERAPIST: Jimmy, could you tell me about your scene?

JIMMY: It's a forest with lots of trees.

THERAPIST: What about that little rabbit?

JIMMY: He's hiding under that tree.

THERAPIST: I'd like to talk to him. Would you be his voice, you know, as if he were a puppet? Rabbit, what are you doing?

JIMMY: I'm hiding.

THERAPIST:vWhat are you hiding from?

JIMMY: Sometimes big animals eat rabbits. I'm hiding from them.

THERAPIST: You have a good hiding place. Do you feel safe?

JIMMY: No, I'm still scared.

THERAPIST: Is there anyone around to help you?

JIMMY: (*Very low voice—body scrunched*) No.

THERAPIST: Oh, that must be hard for you.

JIMMY: Yeah.

The therapist at that point told Jimmy that they could play a game for the 5 minutes until the session ended. She asked him if it was OK if she took a picture of his scene and postponed putting the objects away so she could look at it. He readily agreed.

SESSION 2

Jimmy came in, asking if he could make another sand scene, and proceeded to make the exact scene he had made the previous week, except for another rabbit that he placed near the first one. "Now the rabbit has someone to help him," he said. It was the therapist's guess that Jimmy was acknowledging the help he might receive from the therapist.

THERAPIST: Jimmy, I am so sorry that you lost your sister. I would like it very much if you would draw a picture of her so I could have an idea of what she looked like.

Jimmy drew her picture willingly, explaining as he drew about the color of her hair, her eyes, the clothes she was wearing, and other details.

THERAPIST: Jimmy, I am going to make a list of some of the things you and your sister did together. Tell me one thing.

JIMMY: Well, we colored pictures from a book she had. We played Captain Hook and Peter Pan—I was Captain Hook. We built stuff with blocks. She was only 4 and I had to show her how to do things.

THERAPIST: I know you were a good big brother. Big brothers sometimes tease their sisters, too. Did you do that? I know my son used to tease his little sister and she would run crying to me. Now they are grown up and good friends. I bet you and Julie would have been very good friends as you got older.

JIMMY: Your son teased his sister? Yeah! I teased Julie a lot! I could make her cry easy. She bugged me sometimes, too, and I would hit her. Then, she would cry and run to my mom, who would get mad at me. I liked her really.

THERAPIST: I bet you miss her a lot.

JIMMY: (*Nodding with tears in his eyes.*)

The therapist offered to do a puppet show for Jimmy. In the first scene, two animal puppets—a dog and a cat—were playing and the dog began to call the cat silly names. The cat began to cry. In the second scene, a larger animal, an eagle, told the dog that there had been an accident and the cat had died. The dog began to cry, saying he did not mean to tease her. The eagle assured him that the cat did not die because of his teasing. In the third scene, the dog told the eagle how sad he was to lose his sister. The eagle hugged him.

Jimmy watched this simple show intently and immediately asked if he could do it himself. His show was actually more involved, with the dog telling the eagle about hitting the cat and being mean sometimes, and the eagle continuing to assure him that these actions did not cause her death. Jimmy's last statement on leaving this session was "I loved this puppet show!"

SESSION 3

The therapist asked Jimmy if he thought his mother was very mad at him, since she was so upset. Jimmy began to cry. Because of his developmental level, it was logical that Jimmy would feel that his mother's intense grief was his fault.

THERAPIST: Jimmy, I think your mom is just so sad about losing Julie that she is sick from it. I don't think she's mad at you at all. Is it OK if we ask your dad into the session so we can talk about this?

Jimmy nodded. The therapist asked Jimmy to tell his dad about thinking his mom was mad at him. Jimmy looked at the therapist, who then asked if she could tell him. He nodded vigorously. Jimmy's father was horrified at this idea, and with much emotion told Jimmy how much he and his mother loved him. Jimmy climbed on his dad's lap and sobbed.

SESSION 4

Jimmy told the therapist that his mother seemed a little better. She had smiled and hugged him that morning, he reported. The therapist guessed to herself that Jimmy's dad spoke to his mom about their last session. The therapist told Jimmy to make his sister out of clay and to talk to her. Jimmy told the clay figure that he missed her very much, was sorry she died, and that he would think about her a lot. He then spontaneously picked up the figure, kissed it, and said goodbye. "I want to play that game ('Blockhead') before I leave today."

This was actually the last session. Jimmy's dad called to say that he felt Jimmy did not need any more sessions. The therapist advised him to watch for any new symptoms that might emerge, since there were many issues that had not been addressed that might affect Jimmy. Developmentally, perhaps Jimmy had expressed as much as he could handle at this time, and that as he became stronger, some of the other issues might need to be addressed.

Case 4: Sally

Another situation involved Sally, a 9-year-old girl whose mother had been physically abused by her father; finally, she had managed to escape to a new city and there was no contact at all with him. The girl had become sullen, abusive, and aggressive toward her younger sister and mother. The mother advised the therapist that they could only come in for five or six sessions. Based on previous experiences with similar situations, the therapist felt that the child might have conflicted feelings involving the loss of her father, and anger at her mother for taking her away from him as well as her friends, her school, and her previous home.

SESSION 1

At the first session, Sally appeared quite anxious as her mother spoke, sitting with hunched shoulders and pursed lips. The therapist directed her "intake" questions to Sally, writing the answers on the pad on her clipboard. "Do you sleep OK? Do you have bad dreams sometimes? What's school like here?" and so forth. The therapist had found that many anxious and resistant children responded to a form or paper clipped to a board as she wrote the answers. This seemed to place some distance between the therapist and child, helping to reduce any apprehension the child might have. Furthermore, asking the child pertinent questions directly, in a casual, conversational manner, rather than asking the parent, involved the child immediately. Sally responded readily, visibly relaxed, and then asked why all the toys and stuff were in the room. The therapist explained that they were used, along with drawings and clay and the sand trays, to help kids express what was going on inside of them instead of just having to talk. The mother was very nervous at this session and seemed anxious to leave. The therapist invited her to wait in the waiting room while she and Sally got acquainted.

The therapist encouraged Sally to go around the room and look at everything. After a thorough examination, Sally was drawn to the dollhouse and began arranging and rearranging furniture. After some time the therapist suggested that she choose a family that would live in the dollhouse. Sally selected a mother, father, small boy, and medium sized girl, and placed them in various parts of the house. The therapist remarked that the family appeared to be a pleasant, happy one. Sally agreed, and suddenly, clearly, lost her energy and enthusiasm with the dollhouse. The therapist suggested that they play a game and Sally, with renewed contact, selected Uno.

When a child suddenly loses interest in a task, breaks contact when there had been good energy toward the task, it is generally a fairly reliable clue that something has occurred that has caused the child to close down. It seemed evident that the "happy family" in the dollhouse touched a painful spot in Sally. This type of closing down is actually a positive event in the therapeutic process, since it indicates that just behind this resistance, feelings are coming closer to the surface.

Since the mother had been emphatic regarding the limited number of sessions, the therapist mapped out a program for the therapy, always cognizant of the fact that expectations would be anathema. Her plan for Sally consisted of the following:

At the next session she would present a nonthreatening mode of expression such as the scribble technique, which is fun and easy, and can lead to important projections. At the third session, the therapist thought she might ask Sally to make figures of her family, including her father, out of clay, and request that Sally dialogue with each of them. The therapist might help her to focus on anger, self-blame, and sadness at the loss of her father, as well as her familiar home. At the fourth session, the therapist thought she might incorporate all of these feelings, including, perhaps, any confusion Sally might feel, through drawing or painting. In this way, the varied feelings became more explicit, making it easier to work through them. Furthermore, in time, the percussion instruments could be used to "play" with feelings, providing a nurturing, enjoyable atmosphere around these emotions. At the fifth session, the therapist would suggest that Sally make a sand scene about her life. Finally, at the last session, the therapist would meet with Sally and her mother and spend some time giving the mother suggestions for helping Sally to express her feelings appropriately, as well as refining their communication skills.

The following is a summary of what actually took place:

SESSION 2

The therapist introduced the scribble technique, asking Sally to make a scribble and find a picture to color within this scribble. Sally appeared to enjoy this task and found a picture of a large cat surrounded by trees. She told this story about the cat:

> "Once upon a time, there was this cat who lost her way. She was walking home from a visit to a friend and somehow got lost. She had taken a short cut through the forest and now she was lost. She didn't know where she was or which way to go to get home. It got dark and she heard all kinds of noises and got very scared."

THERAPIST: Then what happened?

SALLY: She got very tired and curled up under a tree and went to sleep.

THERAPIST: What happened when she woke up?

SALLY: When it was morning, the cat knew where she was and ran home. The family was very happy to see her and pet her and fed her. The end.

THERAPIST: That was a good story! Sally, is there anything about your story that fits for you and your life?

SALLY: I don't know. (*long pause*) Well, maybe I don't know where the home I used to have is.

THERAPIST: Tell me about the home you used to have.

Sally began to describe the house she lived in, her neighborhood, her school, and her friends. She was very animated while doing this, watching the therapist carefully (for her reaction?). The therapist realized that it was not possible for Sally to talk about these things at home, since any mention of her previous home was probably very upsetting to her mother. In the last 10 minutes of the session, the therapist decided to introduce instruments, and she and Sally played, with much gaiety, music that was happy, sad, crazy, lonely, and especially mad.

SESSION 3

At the next session, the therapist had put out the pottery clay, boards, and tools. They sat at the table playing with the clay and after awhile, the therapist asked Sally to make her family out of clay. Sally ignored this direction and proceeded to make various kinds of food. The therapist dropped her plan and joined Sally in pretending to eat the food. Sally giggled at the therapist's dramatic enjoyment of the food. In between bites, the therapist fashioned rough figures of Sally's family: mother, sister, as well as father, whom she placed some distance from the rest of the family.

THERAPIST: Sally, I want you to say something to each person here— maybe something you like about them, something you don't like, or just anything you want to say.

SALLY: (*To sister*) I like to play with you sometimes. I don't like it when you take my stuff. (*to mother*) (*long pause*) I like it when you play with me. (*to therapist*) She's always working and tired.

THERAPIST: Maybe that could be the thing you could tell her you don't like.

SALLY: Yeah. I don't like it that you are always working and tired and don't have time to play with me very much anymore.

THERAPIST: Now say something to your father over here in the corner.

SALLY: I don't want to talk to him now.

With this statement, Sally picked up the rubber mallet and began to hit a nearby mound of clay.

THERAPIST: Sally, show me how hard you can hit the clay. Stand up if you have to.

Sally began to pound the clay with all her might, holding the mallet with both hands.

THERAPIST: What are you thinking about, Sally, when you do that?

SALLY: Nothing.

THERAPIST: I bet there are a lot of things in your life that make you mad. Just hit the clay—you don't have to tell me what they are.

Sally continued to hit the clay as the therapist cheered her on. When the time was up, they cleaned up.

SESSION 4

At the fourth session, Sally's mother told the therapist that there could only be one more session, since she had changed jobs and could not bring her daughter in after that session. The therapist urged her to accompany Sally for the last session and she reluctantly agreed.

Feeling desperate because of the lack of time, the therapist decided to offer Sally a puppet show. The show consists of three scenes, which the therapist hoped would address some of the issues relating to Sally's situation. In the first scene, a mother puppet was singing to herself, "I'm cooking dinner, I'm cooking dinner." The father puppet came in yelling, "What's for dinner? I'm hungry! I hope it's ready." The mother puppet replied, "It will be ready very soon, dear. It will just be a few more minutes." The father yelled, "I want it now!!" and hit the mother squarely on the head. Sally murmured from her place in the audience, "That's just like my life." The therapist did not respond to this remark and changed scenes. Then, two furry animal puppets, a monkey and a dog, were conferring. The monkey (the smaller of the two puppets) said, "Did you see Daddy hit Mommy again? I wish he didn't do that. It scares me." The dog replied, "Yeah. It scares me too. I'm mad that he does that. Why does he have to hurt Mommy like that!" The monkey replied, "You need to tell him to stop. After all, you are the older one. You can tell him. Maybe he'll listen if he knows how we feel." The dog agreed he would try. In the next scene, the dog called Dad, who said, "Yes, son, what is it?" With a great deal of difficulty and emotion the dog said, "Daddy, you have to stop hitting Mommy. It scares me very much and it scares my little brother. And Dad, it makes me mad that you do that!!!" The father puppet acted very upset but finally said, "I guess I do lose control. I'll try to stop. I don't want you and your brother to be scared of me." "Thanks Dad," the dog said, and they hugged.

This was the end of the show and Sally immediately asked if she could do it herself. Sally repeated the show, adding her own words. The therapist offered to do another show in the remaining time of the session. This time, the dog called his mother and said, "Mommy, I have to tell you something. Don't get mad." She replied, "Honey, you can tell me anything." "OK" the dog said, "I miss Daddy." The mother puppet became very flustered. "You know we can't see him!!" The dog quickly said, "I know we can't see him. I just wanted to tell you I wish I could and that I miss him. And sometimes it makes me mad at you that you took us so far away from everything." The mother, quiet for a few seconds, then said, "I know you miss him. After all he was an OK father to you. Maybe after awhile you'll be able to see him. I know I can make you mad sometimes. That's OK. I get mad at things too." The dog said, "Thanks, Mommy. I just wanted to tell you." And they embraced.

Sally was equally thrilled with this little show and soon made it her own. The therapist was aware that Sally had been too afraid to tell her father about her anger and other feelings she had, but she wanted to at least help Sally know that her feelings were normal and acceptable.

SESSION 5

At the last session, Sally wanted to put on both shows for her mom. The therapist warned the mother that she might not like the content but that it was important to understand that Sally had hidden feelings that might be the cause of her behavior, and that expressing them through fantasy at least was very relieving and healing for Sally. Sally did the shows with great gusto and her mother applauded generously as she dabbed at the tears in her eyes. The therapist talked a little about the need for Sally to express her feelings while her mother listened without judgment.

A month later, the therapist called Sally's mother, who reported that Sally was much calmer and easier to live with, was no longer unusually belligerent, and in general was doing quite well. The mother, who seemed calmer herself, thanked the therapist profusely. The therapist advised the mother to be alert for new symptoms as Sally reached new developmental stages.

I have often used puppet shows, such as those described for Sally and Jimmy, particularly in situations where the child has much difficulty expressing feelings. Children are fascinated by such shows, and are very forgiving if they are not "perfect." Significant issues can be presented dramatically in simple scenes and the metaphorical messages are quite powerful. They seem to reach the child at a very deep level.

SUMMARY AND CONCLUSION

In this chapter, I have attempted to offer some effective methods for working with children around the issues of loss and grief on a short-term basis.

These methods have at their base the theory, philosophy, and practice of Gestalt therapy. These projective techniques (drawings, clay, and fantasy; storytelling, sand tray scenes, music, and puppetry) make it possible for children to express their deeper feelings in a nonthreatening, often fun, way. The therapist must have an understanding of the myriad issues involved in traumatic loss, and determine which ones are most essential for immediate focus in the service of brief therapy. The therapist must do this gradually, even when the time is short, to allow the child to feel safe and disclose the deeper parts of him- or herself slowly. The therapist must take care not to intrude or push the child into doing or expressing anything he or she resists. This resistance is usually an indication that the child does not have enough self-support to deal with the material presented; it must be honored regardless of the short-term requirements. Though the therapist may have goals and plans, expectations can be toxic. The therapist must be infinitely sensitive to the child.

Prerequisite to any work is establishing some thread of a relationship. This relationship will build with each session. Contact, as described in this chapter, must be present each time in order for any significant work to take place, and the therapist must carefully observe the breaking of contact in order to deflect the work into something less intimidating for the child. With practice, the therapist can anticipate the loss of contact through the child's body responses: lack of energy, deflation, glazed eyes. It is futile for the therapist to attempt to ignore this evidence that the child is not fully present in the encounter. The child must be allowed time to withdraw from contact as needed. It is the therapist's responsibility to be fully contactful with the child, regardless of the child's inability to do so. However the child presents the self, the therapist meets him or her with respect, with no anticipation for a particular response. She must be gentle, authentic, and respectful, without becoming enmeshed or confluent with the child.

In short-term work, many other issues that cry out for attention may emerge or become obvious to the therapist. If the mandate is for brief therapy, priorities need to be followed. If good results are achieved, that is, if the child appears to make some closure regarding the loss incurred, the work must be deemed successful. Often, what the child experiences in these few sessions will carry over into other areas of his or her life.

Children do not know how to grieve and often are confused about the various feelings within them. The metaphors that emerge from the projective techniques offer a safe distance to children, allowing the therapist to gently help them own the feelings that are fitting. It is through this ownership that children can move through the grief process. Therapists who work with children are privileged to have the opportunity to help them ease through difficult passages in their lives.

ACKNOWLEDGMENTS

This chapter is adapted from a forthcoming work by Violet Oaklander. Copyright by Violet Oaklander. Adapted by permission.

REFERENCES

Bowlby, J. (1973–1983). *Attachment, separation, and loss.* New York: Basic Books.
Buber, M. (1958). *I and thou.* New York: Scribner.
Kübler-Ross, E. (1973). *On death and dying.* New York: Macmillan.
Latner, J. (1986). *The Gestalt therapy book.* New York: Gestalt Journal Press.
Oaklander, V. (1982). The relationship of Gestalt therapy to children. *The Gestalt Journal, 1,* 64–74.
Oaklander, V. (1988). *Windows to our children.* New York: Gestalt Journal Press.
Perls, F. S. (1969). *Ego, hunger and aggression.* New York: Vintage.
Perls, F., Hefferline, R., & Goodman, P. (1951). *Gestalt therapy.* New York: Julian.
Polster, E., & Polster, M. (1973). *Gestalt therapy integrated.* New York: Brunner/Mazel.
Terr, L. (1990). *Too scared to cry.* New York: Basic Books.

3

Child-Centered Play Therapy with Disruptive School Students

CAROL MADER

INTRODUCTION

Brennan took the swirling clay tornado, turned it upside down, smiled a broad smile, swung it from side to side, and began a ticking sound like that of a clock pendulum. The pendulum went lower and lower until he smashed it on the tray. He reshaped the pieces into a baseball with detailed blue stitching. I reflected what I saw happening, described the student's smiling face and the carefulness used in adding the details to the ball. From this session emerged a stronger student, ready to face the challenges of his school day. What had happened to change the anxious expression of 4 weeks ago?

Brennan is one of several students I see each year whose presenting problem appears to be school phobia or separation anxiety. Schools today are beset with problems for school counselors who are limited in resources. As a counselor in a school setting, I searched for a developmentally appropriate modality for working with students in a short period of time. Child-centered play therapy (CCPT) opened a door for me into the language of the child and the world of work and form of treatment based on using play. CCPT is usually a longer-term intervention. However, based on recent research into school-based programs, it works very well in a school setting. Within 6 weeks, I may be able to determine whether outside intervention is needed, whether the student is able to move on and intervention has stopped or become intermittent, or whether a few more weeks will be beneficial and continue healing.

According to Schmidt (1991), school phobia, as in Brennan's case, is the fear of attending school, often associated with being emotionally upset, complaining of illnesses for which no physical cause is found, and having temper tantrums (p.187). School phobia presents a crisis of immediate concern but without the threat of imminent danger. Child-centered play therapy has been an effective intervention for this and other types of presenting problems including the following:

- Delayed grieving
- Chronic illness in family
- Overburden of responsibilities
- Need for assertiveness
- Need for problem-solving skills
- Speech, hearing, vision impairments
- Students on medication for attention-deficit/hyperactivity disorder (ADHD)
- Depression (mild to moderate)
- Difficulty making friends
- Oppositional behavior

We recognize that a team effort is needed to develop a plan as soon as possible that keeps the student in attendance, physically and emotionally. Three schools of thought encompass the major approaches to treating the disruptive child: psychodynamic, behavioral, and cognitive (Schmidt, 1991). CCPT is psychodynamic, develops problem-solving skills, and works well as part of a crisis team or Instructional Support Team plan.

Through a parent interview, a determination may be made as to whether the problem is chronic or episodic. A medical examination helps to rule out physical etiology. Additionally, the school principal and parent may give a clear message to the student that it is a requirement to be in school. Parents are asked to exit the building looking and feeling confident that their child is in capable hands.

The present chapter details the use of short-term play counseling with K–3 grade-level students that has made a difference in their self-efficacy, attendance, and learning behaviors. The model involves a 6-week, once weekly, half-hour play intervention.

Campbell (1993) presented issues to consider for intervention in the following way:

> When considering guidance interventions for children, the amount of time that may be given to an individual child within the context of a comprehensive de-

velopmental guidance program, the nature and severity of the child's emotional problem, and the availability of appropriate referral sources in the community, are important issues to school counselors. Some counselors question whether play therapy belongs in the schools. Their rationale is that there is a difference between a counselor and a therapist and that therapy per se, does not belong in the schools, but should take place in mental health agencies, hospitals, and private practice. Golden (1985), for example, expressed concern about the amount of time required for play therapy to be effective and questioned the clinical skills of some school counselors.

Landreth, Strother, and Barlow (1986), however, provided a convincing rebuttal, citing Guerney's (1964) description and rationale for filial therapy, thus demonstrating that play therapy enthusiasts have recognized for some time the importance of the therapeutic role receptive parents can play in their own child's mental health. They also disputed Golden's assertion that play therapy is too time consuming to be an appropriate intervention strategy for school counselors. (p. 12)

Fall, Balvanz, Johnson, and Nelson's research supports the use in schools of child-centered play therapy with positive results (1995). This study followed 62 randomly selected students: half in a control group, and half in the intervention group. School counselors asked teachers to identify children whose coping mechanisms did not facilitate learning behaviors. Examples included those who were shy, withdrawn, using self-defeating coping mechanisms, easily frustrated, acting out, unwilling to take risks, seeking attention, and not excited about learning (p. 8). Teachers reported increased learning for most children in the 6-week play therapy intervention group.

SHORT-TERM PLAY COUNSELING APPROACH

Play counseling can be beneficial because students often cannot verbalize their fears and concerns to parents and school personnel. Sometimes they seek to protect their inner world of feelings. Revealing it is too painful, and students do not have sufficiently developed coping skills. Individuals' perceptions of themselves and their relationships to their world are as uniquely their own as their heartbeats (Axline, 1955). How, then, can the school counselor create a feeling of openness, allowing for expressiveness within a safe haven?

There are two ways the student observes an atmosphere where he or she can work through problems. One is the attitude of the counselor, and the other is in the presentation of the playroom toys. A good play counselor enjoys children, is playful, has empathy, respects children and parents, sets clear, firm limits, and is flexible and creative. Axline includes these descriptions in her basic principles of play therapy.

Description of Child-Centered Play Therapy

One cannot begin to use CCPT without knowledge of Axline's (1982) eight basic principles of play therapy. Her research and writings are invaluable tools. She wrote:

- The therapist must develop a warm friendly relationship with the child, in which good rapport is established as soon as possible.
- The therapist unconditionally accepts the child.
- The therapist establishes a feeling of permissiveness in the relationship so that the child feels free to express his feelings completely.
- The therapist is quick to recognize the feelings the child is expressing and interprets those feelings for the child in an insightful manner to gain insight into the behavior.
- The therapist maintains a deep respect for the child's ability to solve problems once given an opportunity to do so. It is the child's responsibility to make choices and to institute change.
- The therapist does not attempt to direct the child's actions or conversation in any manner. The child leads the way; the therapist follows.
- The therapist does not attempt to hurry the therapy along. It is a gradual process and is recognized as such by the therapist.
- The therapist establishes only those limitations that are necessary to anchor therapy to the world of reality, and makes the child aware of responsibility in the relationship.

A variation that applies in a school setting is the necessity to use short-term play counseling to create closure within a few weeks. Principle 7, as presented by Axline, was intended to be applicable in a clinical environment. The ideas in this chapter suggest a framework within which one can work with the principal, teaching colleagues, and parents to develop an action plan that includes play counseling as a viable approach to changing behavior in disruptive students.

"Short-term" does not mean instantaneous. Play, as a means of self-expression, is an opportunity given to the child to "play out" feelings and problems just as an adult might "talk out" difficulties. Play therapy may be directive in form and combined with child-centered therapy (counseling). To build a child-centered relationship, establish trust, and display concern for the safety of the student, I observe the child in play and work, and collaborate with the teacher and parent(s). Decisions may be made to add directive approaches for 10 minutes of the session while continuing the student's 20-minute child-centered counseling. All those involved are told that the student will be dealing with feelings that may be difficult. When the door is opened, there may be spillover into classroom and home situations. Communication is important, so that I am aware when this problem occurs. Two questions that I ask when the student returns to class help reorient them in a realistic manner:

"When we are in the playroom, who is in charge?"
(Students usually respond by pointing to themselves.)
"Now, as you return to class, who is in charge?"
(Students will give the name of their classroom teacher.)

Skills

Basic skills of CCPT lend to creating an atmosphere that encourages the individual to develop necessary coping skills within safe boundaries. This inner sense of safety, developed by the student, begins with my use of short responses to follow the student's (or the toy's) lead. In order not to distract students from focusing on the work of play, I choose the proper dialog and develop insights in the meaning of their feelings. Questions are not usually asked unless students need reassurance that they are safe. When a child is playing out scary, dangerous, or unsafe actions with the toys, I do not begin with "you." Instead, I refer to the toy. In the next section specific language, toys, approximate space, and other details are discussed. Here, the skills mentioned include brief descriptions. VanFleet (1994, 1997a) describes the following four primary skills used in CCPT.

STRUCTURING SKILL

"Structuring informs children of general boundaries while maintaining an inviting atmosphere" at the beginning and end of the session (VanFleet, 1997a, p. 15). With structuring, the child understands the freedom of the special playroom, and I provide stability with the limitations. For example, I tell children upon entering the play area that they may say and do *almost* anything they want. If there is something they are not to do, I will let them know.

EMPATHIC LISTENING

This skill helps to reveal sensitivity and understanding of children's actions, feelings, and needs. I need to give undivided attention to the children's words and facial and body language, reflecting them appropriately to accurately describe feelings. Part of this skill is to be "present" with children without being intrusive. Children will usually clarify any misunderstood action/feeling and learn labels for their feelings from my vocabulary.

CHILD-CENTERED IMAGINARY PLAY

By setting goals with/for the student I readily use directive methods of interaction. In child-centered play, the student is the "actor–director" of the play, inviting me to participate, or to play out a part, at his or her discretion. So rather than saying, "Let's do this . . . ", I invite the student to choose the direction.

LIMIT-SETTING SKILL

Limit setting serves to remind children of their responsibilities to themselves, the playroom, and the counselor. Limits are kept to a minimum and are dictated by the facility. A general "rule" is to consider whether the limit is necessary for students' safety, the safety of others, or the protection of valuable toys or property. A three-step sequence of stating the limit, giving a warning, and enforcing the consequence is used during child-centered play therapy (VanFleet, 1997a).

Phases of Play Counseling

When presenting basic information to parents regarding play counseling, I use an information sheet. Sometimes I review this information during a telephone interview and, occasionally, I share it in person. One useful piece of information that helps me communicate students' progress is referencing the typical phases students go through in the counseling process.

A child's treatment tends to move in phases. Most of the time, there is an "introductory phase" during which a child settles in and forms a relationship with me. If a child's trust in people and the world has been violated, this phase may take a significant amount of time. This is the part of counseling in which the child's behavior does not represent his or her "true colors." In the short-term, the student usually moves beyond this phase after the second or third session. If the student is still in this phase after 6 weeks, I ask the parent to begin searching for an outside counselor, yet I continue to see the student regularly.

An "exploratory phase" occurs when the child begins to develop some self-awareness. A child cannot be rushed or pushed into this second phase of treatment. It takes courage for a child to reveal inner conflicts and problems and to assume that I, the counselor, will accept him or her without judgment or criticism.

A "consolidating phase" follows in which the child begins to make some lasting growth, fixing those things that have given him or her pain in the past and making them stick. As one little girl said, "It's like when you make a table, and the table's really made, but then you still have to sand it and smooth it and take care of the rough edges."

The "termination phase" involves weaning children from the counseling relationship. By using the "ticket system," described later, students are aware of how much time they will have with me. This seems to help them "plan" their work, and it gives them time to think about termination.

How Play Counseling Fits into the School Guidance Program

Through work experience in three different schools, I have created the term "play counseling." Parents and teachers are more comfortable with this term than "therapy." I try to use various forms of play media in group guidance and individual counseling. As Campbell (1993) stated, "Fun activities can motivate children to give full attention to serious thoughts" (p. 10). A letter outlining the school counseling program is sent home to all parents. This program is well on the way to becoming a K–8 Developmental Guidance Program. Interestingly enough, the goals of child-centered play therapy match the goals of a developmental program (VanFleet, 1997a):

- Develop understanding of feelings
- Express feelings to better meet needs
- Develop problem-solving skills
- Reduce maladaptive behaviors
- Work through conflicts and be heard
- Increase self-confidence

When I initially meet with parents and explain the program to them, they usually chuckle when I tell them the student may come home saying they "played" with Mrs. Mader today. I use a follow-up form to provide information to inform teachers if intervention needs to be longer than the initial 6 weeks. From needs assessments circulated to teachers, they want to know the following: What strategies are helpful in the classroom? What, if any, special allowances need to be made? What observations are of special concern to me? Dialogue is helpful for us both when dealing with any issue, especially school phobia problems. The teacher needs to know if the issues are more external or internal to the classroom. The parent(s) and teacher are my partners in supporting and encouraging the student to be an active learner. Both may be willing to help the child develop skills and focus or control, discover hope, and serve as adult anchors.

Toys

A suggested list of child-centered play therapy toys is presented in Table 3.1. I have added marbles, animal families, measuring tape, and a school bus to this list. In my playroom, marbles have been transformed into "jewels," "bombs," "treasure," "eggs," and "potion capsules." The transparent water tray placed on a bench has enabled me to make clearer observations.

TABLE 3.1. Selection of Toys for the Child-Centered Play Therapy Playroom

Family-related and nurturance toys	
Doll family (mother, father, brother, sister, baby)	Baby bottle
House or box with doll furniture	Bowl for water
Puppet family/animal puppets	Container with water
Baby doll	Kitchen dishes
Dress-up clothes	Animal families

Aggression-related toys	
Bop bag	6- to 10-foot piece of rope
Dart guns with darts	Foam aggression bats
Small plastic soldiers and/or dinosaurs	

Expressive and construction toys	
Crayons or markers with drawing paper	Blackboard/dry-erase board
Play-Doh, Sculpey, or other modeling substance	Mirror
Sand tray with miniature toys	Masking tape
Plastic telephones	Magic wand
Scarves or bandannas (pastel colors)	Masks
Blocks or construction toys	Marbles
Heavy cardboard bricks	Transparent water tray/toys

Other multiuse toys	
Cars, trucks, planes, police cars, ambulance, firetruck, school bus, etc.	Playing cards
Ring-toss or beanbag-toss game	Play money
Doctor's kit	Measuring tape
Purse, wallet	Plastic hammer, tools

Considerations when adding items
Is the item safe for children?
Does the item encourage the expression of childhood feelings or themes?
Does the item permit imaginative or projective use by children?

Note. Copyright 1998 by Play Therapy Press. Reprinted by permission.

Anne went right to the water tray and dumped the marbles. She set up a table and invited the counselor to have a party with her. While the counselor watched, she created her "secret drink" for the party. She described how each colored marble gave the drink a different flavor. She used the small teapot for mixing. This became part of a 5-week ritual. This activity seemed to calm her and help her relax so that she could talk about missing her incarcerated father. She missed having him at the dinner table.

Play Area and Adapting to Space

Often, the school counselor works in a limited space. Sand and water are very helpful and inviting for students to express feelings. They offer a medium not usually available in the classroom. I have met with counselors who needed portable toys and sometimes left a covered plastic tub full of sand at each location. Usually, even running water is not available. To compensate for this, I keep a bucket to fill daily with fresh water to pour into my transparent water tray.

Introductory Session

This model utilizes a combination playroom and counseling room in the 12′ × 6′ portion of a van. Because the room needs to travel, everything in the space needs to be covered and secured at day's end. These coverings, beach towels with Velcro over the two toy shelves, have sparked the curiosity of students. On the first visit to the playroom, only sand, water, and drawing materials are visible. I allow the student to enter the room before me and observe their reactions. There are two small stools in front of the sand and transparent water trays on a bench along one wall. The only other seating exists on the thinly carpeted floor or on the wheel wells, one of which has an old bathroom carpet on top, two big pillows, and the art box. I request that students sit where they will be comfortable. Usually, they nestle into the "artist's corner" as described earlier.

After the child is comfortable in the introductory session, I explain my responsibilities to help students discover their feelings and determine confidentiality. I might describe what their teachers and/or parent(s) have observed and ask them to share their view of the situation. Then, providing a variety of drawing materials, I ask them to draw something. Sometimes it may be "a picture you can tell me a story about" (VanFleet, 1997b), or a person doing something, or a feeling picture, usually something that happens to bring feelings of happiness. Only once have I had a student refuse to draw but created a "picture in the sand" with plastic figures instead. This was a natural introduction to our first child-centered play session the following week.

Ticket Approach

To end the introductory session, I ask the student to select a preferred color of construction paper, and we create "tickets" to the playroom. I write the student's name across the long side of a 6″ × 10″ piece of paper and cut five slits to make six tear-off tickets. I allow the student to number them. At the close of each session, the student tears one off to determine the number of remaining sessions. This has helped students with the concept of time, including how and when holidays and /or special programs interrupt the flow of weeks.

> One student, Tyson, had shut down in his first-grade classroom, was looking very sad, and droopily followed me to the van. When given the words "happy," "sad," "angry" or "afraid" in order to draw a picture, he immediately drew a sad picture of the death of his "Nan." In subsequent weeks, Tyson developed a rescue theme, turning the dollhouse into a rescue center, complete with ambulance, fire truck, and firefighters. Possibly, he wanted to be rescued from his deep sadness and confusion about death.

Of primary importance in the introduction to play therapy sessions is the creation of an atmosphere of acceptance, which I find more challenging than being direct. I hope to show students that I accept them as they are and have faith in their ability to work the problem through (VanFleet, 1997a).

First CCPT Session

In the first session after the introductory meeting, I bring the student into the playroom, where all the toys are visible. I say, "[Student's name], this is a very special room. You can do almost anything you want to do in this room. If there's something you may not do, I'll let you know. You may say anything you want." I usually only have to give this introduction one more time during that second session and the student remembers. The CCPT skill of limit setting is used as situations arise to ensure the safety of the student and the counselor. One example of limit setting usually occurs with the dart gun. (Principals are made aware that I have a plastic gun and knife in the van and have approved their use with my supervision.) During child-centered play therapy (counseling) (VanFleet, 1997a), a three-step sequence states the limit, issues a warning, and enforces the consequences.

> Darrin was referred for school phobia related to tremendous pressure from home to "get good grades or else." During our third session, Darrin invited the counselor to play "cops and robbers." His directions to me included, "You have to shoot me with the gun." The time had come for "limit setting." "Darrin, you'd like me to shoot the gun at you. Remember I said I'd let you know if there's something you may not do? One of the things you and I may not do in the special playroom is point or shoot the dart gun at someone when it's loaded. But you can shoot it almost anywhere else in the room." Darrin responded with, "OK, then we will take out the darts."

If Darrin had insisted on testing the limit further, I would have "given a warning." To do this, the limit is restated, and the consequence is described, so that the student can choose whether he or she is willing to risk this consequence. For example, if Darrin had pointed the loaded dart gun at me, I would have said: "Darrin, remember that I told you that you could not point or shoot the dart gun at me when it's loaded? If you point or shoot the loaded dart gun at me, I will have to remove it from the playroom for the rest of the session."

To "enforce the consequences," the third step in limit setting, I restate limits and carry out the consequences stated in the warning. I keep a pleasant but firm voice to help the student to understand the resolve. In a clinical setting, the completion of the session may result in a consequence. I have not had a student who needed more than two or three items removed from the session to understand that the consequence would be enforced.

When Gene lost privileges for using the dart gun, for attempting to shoot at me, he clearly heard me say, "Since you just pointed the loaded dart gun at me again, I have to confiscate it for the rest of the session." He quickly replied, "But I can have it back next week, right?" "You are hoping you will get the dart gun back next week," I empathized. "Yes, everything will be back on the shelves next week." The next week, he asked permission before picking up the dart gun. As with the first session, I stated, "You may do almost anything you want. If there is something you are not supposed to do, I'll let you know." Gene said, "I know already that I can't shoot that dart gun at a person."

Communicating with Parents

I may call the parents after meeting their child for the first time to tell them about the six play counseling sessions. I explain that I will call again after three sessions to present a progress report. I have developed an information sheet that consists of commonly asked questions by parents about child-centered play counseling. I try to obtain this information by phone, but occasionally, I mail the sheet. When giving feedback to parents, I make a point to listen to the parents' view first ("Have there been any changes at home or at school?"). Then, I relate information by possibly describing a stage of play (aggression, regression, nurturing, or mastery), or by simply stating that progress has been developmentally normal. If the child appears "stuck" in an aggressive stage, I may ask the parents if they have noticed similar behavior, or if there is any ongoing problem at home that the school might want to know about. I also reassure them that if at the end of the six sessions I feel outside counseling is necessary, I will let them know which agencies in our area offer child-centered play therapy.

CASE ILLUSTRATIONS

During child-centered play counseling in the school setting, only three levels of interpretation are used: content (what the child does), feeling (emotional expression), and intention–summary (clear intentions of play, summaries of sequences of play) (VanFleet, 1997b). I have tried several methods to record quickly, because students have appointments every half hour, or I am running to a classroom for guidance, or any number of interruptions occur. Two that work best for me are the use of a tape recorder to simply state play themes I observed and student's comments, and use of a play therapy progress note form. Progress notes help me keep track of data, including actions, behavior, and communication from the student. They also provide space for assessment and ongoing development of a student plan.

Case 1: Marcia

Marcia was the youngest of three girls. Her parents had separated in August, just 2 weeks before she came to her first-grade classroom. Her mother described Sunday evenings and Monday mornings as "a nightmare." Marcia would complain of physical symptoms, procrastinate about getting up for school, refuse to eat breakfast, and forget materials she needed in class. Marcia had once been very close to her dad and now he was inconsistent about visits with her. After her mother took Marcia for a physical, she called the school to refer her for counseling.

In class, Marcia appeared to be a mild-mannered, pleasant student. However, the teacher recognized hostility in her eyes when her mother would bring her in to school late, and her attitude toward school activities was flat, no expression. The team plan included using child-centered play counseling, the teacher greeting her with a special job each morning, her cousin calling her on Sunday evenings to encourage her to "meet me before school starts so we can talk," and her mother taking regular one-on-one time with her each week as their special time.

PATTERNS, RITUALS, THEMES

While observing a student in child-centered play, I watch for patterns and rituals as possible play themes so as not to draw far-reaching conclusions from a single play occurrence. Some common themes include control, good–evil, win–lose, problem solving, rescue, family/peer relationships, and dealing with authority (VanFleet, 1997a). Marcia's themes reflected some of the issues she was dealing with at home. She had an ongoing story in the sand tray about horses hiding gold or jewels (marbles), while other animals would try to steal them away. Another repeated theme involved different types of aggression. Puppets helped her with interpretation.

In one story, the wolf puppet was biting a pig and a rabbit. The rabbit got away and came back to shoot the wolf. In the next session, a moose took a stick and hit the "babies," held the pig in his mouth, and shook him violently. Then, the moose took weapons and money from the babies and the pig. In her last session (Session 6) Marcia was a doctor, nurturing, healing, and feeding the babies. She replayed the horses finding the jewels in the sand, which, when attacked by other animals, prevailed and won the fight. She invented her own game of building up blocks in a certain pattern and creating her own ball from clay to knock the blocks over. The nurturing, good over evil, and mastery play of creating her own game were viewed as positive signs that Marcia was progressing.

Throughout Marcia's sessions, I reflected the actions and feelings of the characters by listening to what Marcia said. I used such phrases as "The doctor is putting the Band-Aid on the baby's arm." If I make a mistake in interpretation, the students usually make the corrections, restate the facts, or shake their heads "no." Sometimes students do all three.

Following the first 6-week intervention, the classroom teacher observed that Marcia was emerging as more of a leader, arriving on time, and socializing with peers. She was expressive about her needs in class, asking questions when necessary. She became responsible for her own learning.

Case 2: Brennan

Brennan was referred as a school phobic student due to fears about the weather. He was concerned that when he came to school, something could happen to his parents if a storm came up. He was especially worried about thunderstorms and hurricanes. Even as a third grader, it was difficult for his parents and teacher to convince him that hurricane warnings were most unlikely in central Pennsylvania. Brennan's test scores bordered on the gifted range. His parents were hardworking; his mother owned her own business and had to travel some distance to work each day. Brennan had spent several years in day care facilities.

Landreth (1987) wrote that toys and materials are used by the child in the act of play to communicate a personal world to the counselor. Brennan's personal world was lost in a confusion of words from significant adults in his life at the moment. He was now feeling alienated by others feeling annoyed with him for what they viewed as unreasonable fears. Therefore, I decided on an initial 6-week nondirective play therapy approach. The primary objective was not to solve the problem, but rather to help him grow in an atmosphere of safety, understanding, and encouragement. Secondary objectives were to provide Brennan an opportunity to develop a feeling of control, as well as demonstrate his experience through behavior, words, feeling, and activity (Landreth, 1987).

I took Brennan to the counseling van, where I had left the toys displayed to help him feel more comfortable in a setting that seemed to say, "This is just for you." Since it was only a week since school began, I reassured him that I hoped to bring several students to visit the van through the course of the year. Then I let him explore freely so that I might observe his interests. I gave my usual parameters: "If there is something you may not do, I will let you know."

He was drawn to the dart gun and two games. He invited me to play the games with him. He knew the rules and did not change them at this time. I followed his lead. My sense was that he wanted to do something that he thought I would like to do. I spoke with his mother after this introductory session. She said that during special time with him at bedtime, and so on, she usually decided what activity would take place. I suggested that she give him time to decide, and that the next day, if he balked again about leaving her, she give him a token remembrance of her. I suggested this so that he might have something in his pocket to touch and hold if he missed her, and to remind him that she (and his dad) were also thinking of him throughout the day.

Brennan's mother did not have time to come in to see me and requested that I send her some information about play counseling. After our second session, she and Brennan's teacher reported "mood swings" throughout the day, again based on the weather predicted.

During Session 2, Brennan pretended that the marbles were "bullets" coming from the sky. They were buried in the sand and he had to find all of them. He perseverated until he found every one. In the third session, he repeated this activity first, then moved on to demonstrate his proficiency with the game Jenga and invented a new type of eraser for the dry-erase board. His play reflected his perfectionistic tendencies. All the marbles needed to be hidden and found, and his focus was on orderliness and cleanliness (VanFleet, 1997b). Possibly, he was working on his hidden fears and demonstrating his strengths.

Just after his fourth session, another difficulty occurred in the classroom as Brennan demonstrated an increase in confidence in the counseling playroom. His teacher wondered what he was doing, because he started to do classwork prematurely, without listening to all of the instructions, without following directions, and becoming defensive when confronted about this behavior. When the gym teacher put his class into small groups, Brennan wanted his group to do everything according to his method. He had taken his control issues to a new level. I decided to continue with the last two promised, child-centered sessions and hoped for a better outcome. Even though teachers and parents are warned that when a student is involved in counseling, difficult doors may be opened and are not easily shut, the reality of the situation may be hard to understand. Through collaboration with the classroom and gym teachers, a plan was developed to maintain the same limitations with Brennan that the other students experienced. This would hopefully allow Brennan to feel part of a secure and stable community. Because he was quick to grasp concepts, he was assigned the task of "tutor" to a couple of students who had more trouble academically. The teacher provided guided practice in his tutorials so that he would work with the students to come up with their own responses.

In his final sessions, Brennan continued with some compulsive behaviors. He needed only a certain color for drawing, certain characters carefully selected for sand tray, or created his own rules for a game. He was creating his own world. As VanFleet (1997b) stated, "Perfectionistic children who fear failure often set situations up that ensure their victory" (p. 63).

At the beginning of Session 5, Brennan came in with a broad smile and went right to work in the sand tray. There were bombs dropping from the sky on all the animals and people. An army was dropping the bombs from an airplane by remote control. In this session and the next, he seemed to change abruptly to a different activity, yet he worked through his issue in this pattern. He moved from the "bomb/airplane" story to the clay and created a "tornado," followed by the sequence of events in the introduction: turning it upside down to become a clock pendulum, smashing it up and remolding it into a baseball with detailed blue stitching. He took a pan and hit the clay baseball for, in his words, a "home run."

Then again in Session 6, Brennan opened with an aggressive piece about a sword that punished all the people. They were cut, but not dead. This time, teddy bears were "raining down" from the sky on the people and they and he laughed aloud as they fell. Once again, he turned from this scene to search the shelves for the rope. He began to demonstrate his proficiency with knot tying, trying over and over, and drawing on all of his patience to create a lasso. This he followed by creating an "original design" of a building block pyramid.

In reviewing Brennan's case and considering his therapeutic gains, I remembered Axline's (1955) original description of the child's inner world:

> When working with children in play therapy, the therapist must be able to accept the hypothesis that the child has reasons for what he does and that many things may be important to the child that he is not able to communicate to the therapist. It seems quite likely that the play therapy sessions offer the child the opportunity of experiencing affectively this relationship. Because of this present emotional experience, the child can gain much from it even though the therapist does not always know what is going on in the child's inner world—and is unable to find out.
>
> A therapist who is too literally minded and cannot tolerate a child's flight into fantasy without ordering it into adult meaningfulness might well be lost at times. (pp. 126–127)

Brennan's strengths included his natural athletic ability, especially playing baseball, and creating new ways to use simple materials. I believe that Brennan used these abilities to "turn his thinking around," just as he did the clay tornado, with regard to dealing with his fears about weather.

My follow through for Brennan included playing with and sending home, the Not So Scary Things Game for him to play with his mother and dad for a couple of weeks. His presenting behaviors had ceased. He was not afraid to leave his parents and attend school any longer. He still did not like thunderstorms, but he would sit on a parent's lap in a safe downstairs room and listen and watch as the storm passed through.

CONCLUSION

As school counselors, facing the diverse presenting problems of disruptive students, we rely on developmentally appropriate modalities that can be effective in short periods of time. CCPT has been a reliable form of treatment for over 50 years in clinical settings. I have provided a workable format for using CCPT as part of a school's comprehensive guidance program. Since the team approach to problem solving is prevalent, this strategy is also effective for communicating with teachers and parents. Recalling Campbell's (1993) words, those in the educational setting continue to need to be reminded that "fun activities can motivate children to give full attention to serious thoughts" (p. 10) and behavior change.

REFERENCES

Axline, V. M. (1955). Nondirective play therapy procedures and results. In G. Landreth (Ed.), *Play therapy: Dynamics of the process of counseling with children* (pp. 120–129). Springfield, IL: Charles C Thomas.

Axline, V. M. (1982). Entering the child's world via play experiences. In G. Landreth (Ed.), *Play therapy: Dynamics of the process of counseling with children* (pp. 47–57). Springfield, IL: Charles C Thomas.

Campbell, C. A. (1993). Play, the fabric of elementary school counseling programs. *Elementary School Guidance and Counseling, 28,* 10–16.

Fall, M., Balvanz, J., Johnson, L., & Nelson, L. (1995). A play therapy intervention and its relationship to self-efficacy and learning behaviors. *Professional School Counseling, 2,* 194–204.

Landreth, G. L. (1987). Play therapy: Facilitative use of child's play in elementary school counseling. *Elementary School Guidance and Counseling, 21,* 253–261.

Schmidt, J. J. (1991). *Survival guide for the elementary/middle school counselor.* West Nyack, NY: Center for Applied Research in Education.

Van Fleet, R. (1994). *Filial therapy: Strengthening parent–child relationships through play.* Sarasota, FL: Professional Resource Press.

Van Fleet, R. (1997a). *Child-centered play therapy training manual.* Boiling Springs, PA: Play Therapy Press.

Van Fleet, R. (1997b). Play and perfectionism: Putting fun back into families. In H. G. Kaduson, D. Cangelosi, & C. Schaefer (Eds.), *The playing cure: Individualized play therapy for specific childhood problems* (pp. 61–81). Northvale, NJ: Aronson.

4

Brief Therapy with Traumatized Children: A Developmental Perspective

JANINE S. SHELBY

> Every moment is a window on all time.
> —WOLFE (1953, p. 3)

INTRODUCTION

I have only one photograph of the children in Sarajevo. In the picture, 4-year-old Darik—who has never known life beyond the daily struggle of war—smiles exuberantly in the moment after his teenage uncle has placed him in a swing for the first time in Darik's young life.

The boy had been a toddler when soldiers forced his family out of their home in the hills above Sarajevo. Darik's mind protected him from some of what he had seen. His infantile amnesia spared him from remembering the torture and murder of his uncles; the rapes of his mother and grandmother; and the sound of his own inconsolable screaming as soldiers were assaulting his family. However, Darik's memory could not spare him the knowledge of victimization in other ways. He knew the sounds and smells of war. In his 4 years of life, Darik had learned to fear the whistles, thuds, bursts, and silences of missiles and gunfire. Because his family lived near the street so notorious for danger that it had been nicknamed "Sniper Alley," Darik had learned to play indoors, away from windows. He had learned to avoid open areas. He knew not to run, except across dangerous intersections. He had learned that his father was not coming back from the prison camp. He knew how to play funeral and burial. He knew how to pose toy armies for attack. Darik knew the play of traumatized children, but he knew nothing of the play that safe children create.

As the war finally settled into its ravaged and exhausted end, Darik and his family tentatively ventured out into the city. The adults longed to bring their children to a park, to sit with them outdoors, to begin again to live the lives that they had once known. These humiliated victims of war wanted the dignity to play again.

In Sarajevo, I worked alongside Darik's family and neighbors to reconstruct the playground that existed in a time before swing seats were firewood and slides were gunfire cover. Hour after hour, we kneaded the earth, removing glass, bullets, debris, and all of the unwanted reminders that human beings had killed and maimed other human beings there in the ultimate paradoxical place: a playground.

I encouraged the adults to allow Darik and the other children to actively participate in the project. The children had known the assault of their land. It seemed important that they also know the healing of it. We searched the impoverished city for rope and wood, and we built swings. In the wake of colossal human suffering, we did what we could do—however meager—to cleanse the earth and return joy to the place where snipers once took deadly shots from the hills.

When we finally invited the children to try the new swings, they eyed us cautiously. The adults held their breath expectantly, desperately hoping that the children could regain some sense of normalcy. For a moment, no one moved. Then, Darik boldly stepped forward, pushing his way through the older children to volunteer himself.

In my single photograph of Darik, his uncle has placed him in a swing and Darik takes his first exhilarating flight into childhood. Undoubtedly, many people died in the spot where Darik now reclaimed his youth. In the picture, the golden-haired boy dangles in midair, giggling unabashedly against the backdrop of devastated buildings in one of the most victimized cities in history. In this crucial moment, Darik has decided which of the opposing forces would influence him most. Forever suspended in memory, Darik looks in the direction of Sniper Alley and he smiles.

Some moments defy the boundaries of regular time. Traumatic as well as therapeutic moments shape and reshape young lives. This chapter can help clinicians to alter the avoidance and fearfulness of posttraumatic existence, so that young survivors can return to enthusiastic discovery of life. Below in this approach to intervention, posttraumatic therapeutic techniques are integrated into a developmental perspective on trauma. My conclusions are largely based on lessons that the children, themselves, have taught me about how they need to heal. Although not derived from systematic research, this framework nevertheless provides a tool for clinicians as they treat traumatized children of different developmental levels.

WINDOWS OF BRIEF PLAY THERAPY

I have spent a career making therapeutic moments from scraps of time, identifying the "window," or the potential, in each therapeutic instant. In treating and designing mental health programs for the children of war, gang violence, physical and sexual abuse, motor vehicle accidents, and natural disaster, I have found that posttraumatic integration and healing are not predicated entirely on the strokes of clocks. Short but meaningful therapeutic encounters—sometimes even a single moment of intervention—can produce powerful change and growth.

This therapeutic motion is influenced by two preliminary issues: "ageocentrism" and identification of psychological intersections.

The Meaning of Time and "Ageocentrism"

Single-session or brief therapy is daunting to some therapists, who experience short-term therapy as a departure from the normal approach to treatment. Granted, brief therapy is a departure from the historical precedent set by psychoanalytic treatment. However, short-term treatment is the rule of therapy rather than the exception. Cohen and Cohen (1984) coined the phrase "Clinician's Illusion," to depict therapists' belief that most patients receive long-term treatment. In truth, the number of sessions that most patients receive falls well within a short-term frame, with the median number of therapy session ranging from three to five, and the mean number ranging from five to eight (Phillips, 1989).

"Ageocentric" perspectives about time may also negatively influence the therapist's reaction to brief treatment; that is, adults and children live in different time scales, and the older of the two can impose a time scale inappropriately on the child. A limited amount of time by an adult's definition may actually be a significant proportion of a child's life. For example, a 1-month course of therapy for a 3-year-old child is proportionately equal to a 1-year course of therapy for a 36-year-old person. The child's 1 month of therapy is proportionately equal to a 2-year course of therapy for a 72-year-old person. Consider the absurdity of complaining that 2 years is insufficient time to bring about therapeutic change. Perhaps the first task of brief therapy with children is for the therapist to engage in cognitive reframing about the significance of the time spent in the process of brief therapy.

Psychological Intersections and Developmentally Informed Treatment

Although the commonly stated goal of short-term therapy is symptom alleviation, some have described the goal of posttraumatic therapy as going beyond mere symptom alleviation. Mann (1973, p. 36) writes, "Symptom relief is a by-product of the process and not its goal." The task of the brief play therapist is to seize therapeutic opportunities, or psychological intersections, where a developmentally appropriate and perfectly timed single intervention promotes progress in more than one direction.

Developmental factors may also play a role in bolstering the significance of single-session and brief interventions. Although the old-style concept of fixed critical periods of development has not been borne out in research, the notion of sensitive periods in development has received support (Rutter, 1996). Research in this area has focused on the impact of negative events during sensitive periods, but it is reasonable to assume that therapeutic interventions at certain sensitive moments may have particularly positive effects as well.

In the remainder of this chapter, a developmental perspective will be used to describe the importance of the traumatic experience, cognitive abilities, symptoms, and coping, in formulating short-term, play therapy interventions. The children described—a toddler, a preschooler, a school-age child, and an adolescent—suffered and survived horrific trauma. Through brief—but developmentally sensitive—play techniques, they integrated their traumatic events and regained normal developmental functioning.

TABLE 4.1. Developmental Chart

	Toddler	Preschooler	Primary schooler	Adolescent
Key components of cognitive functioning	Separates self from others Empathy/ empathic distress Shame	Appearance versus reality Simple perspective taking Distortions in cause–effect	Expressive language Guilt	Abstract thought Hypothetical thought
Symptoms	Shame Irritability	Loss of protection Repetitive Play Generalized anxiety	Repetitive play Somatization Omens Guilt over behavior	Adult-like PTSD; flashbacks Secondary concerns Guilt over inaction Rebellious behavior
Coping	Reliance upon caretakers Denial	Denial Wishful thinking	Projection Altruism	Intellectualization Altruism Complex problem solving Suppression
Key intervention strategies	Preset play props Soothing sessions	Preset play props Experiential mastery technique	Posttraumatic interview Self-instruction	Cognitive-behavioral therapy Blameberry pie Disclosure role play

SYMPTOMS, COPING, AND INTERVENTIONS
WITH YOUNG SURVIVORS

Symptoms

There is no doubt that a single moment of trauma can change lives for the worse. Children, like adults, experience posttraumatic symptoms and posttraumatic stress disorder (PTSD) after calamity befalls them (Vogel & Vernberg, 1993). PTSD is comprised of the following criteria: (1) exposure to an event with threat of injury or death, which is met with terror, helplessness, or horror; (2) intrusive reexperiencing, including repetitive play, nightmares, and flashbacks; (3) avoidance, including avoidance of discussion of the traumatic event; (4) arousal, including hypervigilance, startle response, sleep disturbance, and concentration difficulties. Among children with posttraumatic symptoms in the immediate aftermath of trauma, avoidance symptoms hold the highest diagnostic accuracy in predicting which children will develop PTSD (Lonigan, Anthony, & Shannon, 1998). Similarly, detachment, numbness, dissociative behaviors, and sadness are associated with chronic PTSD (Famularo, Kinscherff, & Fenton, 1990). Avoidance and numbing symptoms may then be the hallmarks of severe and chronic posttraumatic reactions. One of the challenges in providing posttraumatic treatment is that the children who are most affected by PTSD are often the most avoidant of traumatic reminders, including discussion of the traumatic event in therapy.

In the immediate aftermath of a traumatic event, children may meet criteria for acute stress disorder (ASD), which includes most of the same criteria as PTSD but adds dissociation. Dissociative symptoms include numbness, depersonalization or derealization, and amnesia for the traumatic event.

Coping

When faced with distress, children show stylistic differences from each other in their preferred modes or styles of coping. Specific coping behaviors in each child also vary across different situations and developmental levels. Thus, coping has been defined as "individual differences in children's responses to all manner of stressful events, happenings, and circumstances" (Rutter, 1988, p. 2).

The importance of attachment (Bowlby, 1977), temperament (Kagan, Snidman, & Arcus, 1995), dispositional optimism–pessimism (Scheier, Carver, & Weintraub, 1989), social support (Sandler, Wolchik, MacKinnon, Ayers, & Roosa, 1997), judgments about the stressor and the adequacy of resources with which to respond (Lazarus & Folkman, 1984), and coping behaviors themselves have been identified as significant factors that influence posttraumatic adjustment.

One factor identified here involves problem-focused or emotion-focused coping (Lazarus & Folkman, 1984). When people use problem-focused coping, they attempt to change or master some aspect of the situation itself, or their view of the situation. In problem-focused coping, the management of the stressful stimulus may be broken down into a series of tasks to be accomplished or overcome. Emotion-focused coping is aimed at feelings, not at the stressor. When people use emotion-focused coping, they attempt to manage or regulate the negative emotions connected to the situation.

If the situation can be altered, problem-focused coping is more efficacious. If the situation cannot be changed, emotion-focused coping is more beneficial. As children's cognitive skills mature, they can better differentiate between situations where they can exert some control over a stressful situation and those where they cannot (Band & Weisz, 1988). Consistent with findings among adults, children who use problem-focused coping in stressful situations perceived to be controllable, and emotion-focused coping in situations perceived as uncontrollable, evidence fewer behavior problems than do other children (Compas, Malcarne, & Fondacaro, 1988; Rossman & Rosenberg, 1992). In general, children move from reliance upon problem-focused coping to use of both problem- and emotion-focused coping as they grow from infancy to adolescence (Compas, Banez, Malcarne, & Worsham, 1991).

The specific coping and problem-solving strategies of young children are inherently bound to their cognitive abilities. There is general agreement that diversity and flexibility in the coping repertoire—regardless of age—is more important than the use of a single coping strategy in alleviating stress. Preschoolers have a relatively narrow range of coping options, and many of their coping strategies are ineffective. In contrast, adolescents have a wide range of, and access to, complex coping strategies, partly due to the emergence of sophisticated cognitive skills (i.e., abstract and hypothetical thinking) during adolescence (Compas, 1998). For example, during hide-and-seek, a young child closes his own eyes to hide from the child who seeks him. Adolescents can use perspective-taking skills to predict accurately locations where they would not be seen, and they can think hypothetically to generate strategies for concealing themselves under various conditions.

Although research regarding efficacy of specific strategies is not conclusive, there are indications that avoidance, self-criticism, catastrophizing, withdrawal, blaming others, and wishful thinking are not generally as beneficial as problem solving, emotional expression and self-soothing, distraction, reframing, and social support (Carver, Pozo, Harris, & Noriega, 1993; Epping-Jordan, Compas, & Howell, 1994; Gil, Williams, Thompson, & Kinney, 1991; Spirito, Stark, & Williams, 1988).

Interventions

Although there are numerous anecdotal reports, therapy outcome studies for traumatized children are few. In spite of the limited data, a few preliminary conclusions can be drawn. There is general consensus that early intervention is more efficacious than interventions offered long after a traumatic event. Trauma-focused treatment is more efficacious than nondirective treatment (Cohen & Mannarino, 1997; Deblinger, McLeer, & Henry, 1990). Treatment designed to induce a sense of mastery over the feared event is more efficacious than techniques designed to help children merely express their feelings (Corder & Haizlip, 1989; Galante & Foa, 1986; Shelby, 1995).

Interventions with children are more effective when clinical intervention is made with parents as well (Cohen & Mannarino, 1998; Deblinger et al., 1990). Caretakers may need to understand the normalcy of children's posttraumatic reactions. They may also need to process feelings of guilt or remorse for failing to protect the children. Adults may need to recognize that they cannot spare their children from some painful aspects of life. Children benefit most from having adults share in their subjective feelings of distress, rather than avoiding, distracting, or minimizing children's pain. When caretakers understand that they cannot detach children from painful feelings, the adults are more free to be empathic and genuine with their children.

CASE 1: INFANCY TO 3 YEARS OF AGE

> Two-year-old Mirella was brought to therapy by her maternal grandparents 1 week after Mirella's father murdered her mother, shot and wounded her maternal grandmother, and then killed himself.

On the day of the shootings, Mirella's papi had come to Grandma's house, where Mirella and Mami lived. Mirella was in her mother's arms when her parents began yelling at each other. Mirella felt afraid, so she squirmed and fussed to make them stop. She could not understand all of the words that they were speaking, but she sensed the tension between them. When Mami started crying, Mirella cried also. She saw the shiny black object in her father's hand, but she didn't know what it was. When the first loud bang struck her ears, she was confused. By the second bang, she had fallen on the asphalt driveway. Trapped under her mami's unmoving body, Mirella was bathed in blood. Mirella's knees hurt from the hard fall and her ears hurt from the loud sounds. After the third terrible noise, Mirella saw her papi fall down. Mami was very heavy. "At least," she thought, "crying will make Mami wake up." She wailed. Surely, Mami would wake up and speak to her in the low, sweet voice that always made everything good again. But, Mami did not wake up. As Mirella attempted to crawl out from underneath her, Andrew, the big boy next door, came over and picked her up. He stayed until Grandpa came home.

Key Aspects of Cognition

SELF

From the earliest days of life, human beings actively attempt to understand their world and to organize information received from it. A rudimentary concept of the self emerges between 15 and 24 months. By 2 years of age, children can generally differentiate self from others. As they do so, toddlers develop awareness of others and others' reactions. This leads to the ability to feel empathy, empathic distress, and embarrassment.

CAUSALITY

By the end of the first year, children are capable of comprehending simple cause-and-effect relationships, such as "I cry, Mother comes." Once children solidify this understanding (around the age of 2), they begin to anticipate or fear consequences. However, the toddler's understanding of cause-and-effect relationships is not sophisticated. Cause may be confused with effect and extraneous stimuli may be confused with either cause or effect. This tenuous understanding of causality may be further complicated by young children's tendency to attribute psychological causality to physical objects ("The marble went down the ramp because it wanted to"; Piaget, 1979). In Mirella's case, she seemed to believe that the gun independently caused the injuries and murders.

SELF-ESTEEM

Garbarino, Stott, & the Faculty of the Erikson Institute (1992) describe two dimensions of infant self-esteem. The first, "I know what I can do" feeling, involves gleeful excitement in self-discovery. The second dimension is Stern's (1985) notion of "self with other." This sense of self-worth is based on the belief that one is a worthy and lovable partner in an intimate relationship.

SHAME

Erikson (1950) depicted the sense of shame during this period as exposed self-doubt. Guilt, he wrote, is more prominent during the next stage of development, beginning around the age of 4. Shame involves exposure of worthlessness, powerlessness, or some other negative aspect of self, whereas guilt involves misguided behavior.

Although the child is capable of rudimentary empathy, shame—in its self-focus—interferes with the ability to direct attention to the experience of others. Shame motivates avoidance. For example, during the course of therapy, Mirella reached for a toy weapon, which she had named "bad gun." The therapist, who was initially uncomfortable with the child's preoccupation with gun-related play, said to her ruefully, "You want the gun? You want the bad gun? That gun hurt Mami. That's a bad gun." Mirella looked embarrassed as she stared downward. She turned away from the therapist and from the gun, before she attempted to return to dollhouse play. In that moment, the therapist had interfered with Mirella's need for posttraumatic play and unintentionally induced in Mirella a sense of shame.

MEMORY

Even infants have strong recognition-memory skills (Kail, 1984). Recognition memory in toddlers is more accurate than free recall because of their poor recall strategies and their limited ability to encode information symbolically (Piaget, 1979). Before the age of 3 years, long-term memory of traumatic events is thought to be primarily sensory or visual (Monahon, 1997). Children at this age are typically unable to express their memories through verbal means. However, when they acquire greater expressive language skills during a later stage of development, children may then be able to express traumatic images or sensations from this period.

UNDERSTANDING OF DEATH

Toddlers do not yet understand the irreversibility or inevitability of death.

Symptoms

The following symptoms are common among traumatized infants: (1) regressive behaviors such as clinging, increased dependency, and reemergence or heightening of separation anxiety; (2) anxious attachment behavior (Bowlby, 1977); (3) arousal symptoms, such as irritability and crying (Gaensbauer, Chatoor, Drell, Siegel, & Zeanah, 1995); and (4) a deep sense of shame.

Coping

Although they are capable of basic problem-solving strategies, toddlers rely heavily on their attachment figures for emotional soothing and problem resolution. Infants' and toddlers' ability to manage negative emotions independently is not well developed. In this respect, toddlers are extremely vulnerable to the aftereffects of stress. Denial, which is related to the toddler's not-yet-solidified understanding of object permanence and object constancy, may also be a primary coping strategy.

Intervention for Arousal Symptoms

SOOTHING SESSIONS

Mirella's grandparents developed a soothing ritual in which they held 15-minute "nice times." The grandparents were instructed to darken a room, remove distractions, make the child comfortable, and speak to her in a soothing voice. Mirella liked to be rocked and have her back rubbed, which became part of the ritual. These "nice times" were held several times a day to give Mirella respite from her own overwhelming feelings of anxiety.

INTERVENTION WITH VERBALLY IMMATURE CHILDREN

Mirella's symptoms included avoidance of the family driveway where the shootings occurred. She had intrusive reexperiences as well, such as nightmares and physiological arousal upon exposure to the driveway. However, before she could verbally express her memories and overcome her avoidance, she needed to learn the names for relevant objects, such as "driveway," and "gun."

Preset Play Therapy. Originally proposed by Levy (1939), this technique involves the use of props to facilitate children's ability to express themselves through play. Concrete retrieval cues, such as physical props, assist young children in memory recall (Goodman, 1984). So, a large dollhouse was placed on the floor of the therapy room, where Mirella could easily use it. The therapist created a driveway beside the house out of cardboard. She also stocked the room with a miniature gun, which was painted black to parallel her real-life experience. Miniature cars, dolls, and one figurine that was named "Andrew" completed the scene. When Mirella first entered the room, she was encouraged to engage in nondirective play. However, the traumatic event could be readily played out if she chose to do so.

In the first session, Mirella noticed the gun but avoided it as she explored various aspects of the room. In the second session, Mirella picked up the gun and asked, "Zis?" as if to ask, "What's this?" "Gun," the therapist taught her. Next, Mirella used miniature dolls to play out various interactions between the baby doll, the mother doll, and the father doll. Abruptly, she stopped her play, ran to the gun on the shelf, picked it up, raced to the other side of the room, opened the door of the toy oven, threw the gun into the oven, slammed the door shut, and announced, "bad gun."

Mirella apparently believed the gun, rather than her father, had caused the injuries. In every subsequent session, Mirella began by searching for the gun, throwing it into the oven, and evidencing pleasure at her ability to resolve and master the gun problem. Mirella may have been creating greater safety in the room by removing the gun from sight. She may have been punishing the gun. Whatever the case, this seemed to be Mirella's form of mastering the object that had once caused her so much pain and fear. After a few weeks, the affective intensity of Mirella's gun-in-the-oven ritual faded, although she continued to perform the act at the beginning of each session.

INTERVENTION FOR MOURNING

Conversations with Mami. During the next phase of therapy, the therapist created opportunities for Mirella to mourn the loss of both her parents. Per the therapist's request to the grandparents, Mirella brought a picture of her mami to session. When Mirella showed the portrait to the therapist, Mirella gave an unintelligible but lengthy description of Mami. The therapist echoed the reality that Mami had gone bye-bye, and that Mirella felt sad about that. The therapist then imitated a ringing telephone and handed the toy phone to Mirella, who spent the next several minutes pretending to talk to Mami. When she hung up, the therapist asked about Mirella's conversation and then encouraged her to talk to Mami again. This was repeated several times, with Mirella reporting a largely unintelligible commentary to the therapist after each call to Mami. In an attempt to help Mirella access her memories and internalized sense of her mother, the therapist asked questions such as "What is Mami doing?" and "What does Mami say?" At the end of the session, Mirella rocked back and forth gently, as she declared, "Mami loves you." In this session, Mirella was able to grasp the concept that she could continue to experience Mami without her actually being present. In short, she learned to remember Mami.

INTERVENTION FOR INTRUSIVE REEXPERIENCING SYMPTOMS

Mastering Fears. In the next session, Mirella began as usual by putting the gun in the oven. She then played with the father doll and mother doll. When she saw a miniature portrait in the dollhouse, it triggered her memory of the picture of Mami that she had brought to the last session. Mirella said, "Mami picture," and repeated, "Mami picture." She then rushed back to the oven to remove the gun, which she placed in the father's hand. Mirella interrupted her dollhouse play at that point to move to the sink. She turned on the faucet (which produced running water), handed the gun to the therapist, and put her own hands under the running water for an uncommonly long time. Her dazed brown eyes grew huge as she stared into the posttraumatic realm beyond the play room.

Finally, the therapist said gently, "It is wet, huh?" Mirella remained perfectly still under the running water. The therapist linked the traumatic event to the play by asking, "Did Mami get wet?" Mirella nodded sadly. "Did Mirella get wet?" Again, an affirmative nod. Mirella poured water on the countertop, which she then furiously wiped with paper towels. As the therapist reflected aloud how much Mirella wanted to clean it all up, Mirella's play intensified. She soon poured water on the floor and began trying to mop the water up with her body. At one point, Mirella threw a napkin over a wet area and stomped it with her foot. In the midst of the puddle, Mirella handed the therapist a pile of napkins. The therapist put the toy gun down in order to help Mirella wipe the water. The therapist repeated how Mirella wanted to clean Mami up, and how Mirella wanted to clean herself up. "Keen up," Mirella repeated often. Finally, the floor was dry and Mirella was finished reenacting the traumatic event. The therapist asked Mirella what they should do with the gun. Mirella uttered a long strain of aminated but undecipherable comments as she looked around the room. The therapist answered encouragingly, "Ah, huh." Mirella began again, and spoke a word that sounded like "clock" at the end of one of her sentences. "Clock?" the therapist asked. "Yeah, cock. My cock and your cock. Put cock!" she demanded, while pointing to the clock in the playroom. The therapist looked over at the round clock hanging high on the wall. It was the most removed object in the room. Nothing was more out of reach. The therapist, who was somewhat incredulous at the therapeutic genius of the child still in diapers, asked if Mirella wanted her to put the gun on the clock. Mirella nodded enthusiastically.

The therapist placed the gun on the clock, Mirella heaved a sigh of relief, and they were finished with posttraumatic play. Mirella never returned to gun-related play, nor did she reenact the traumatic event in subsequent sessions. Her symptoms completely remitted except for frequent inquiry about where Mami was. The "bad gun" was now forever out of reach, and she was free to return to the tasks of a grieving 2-year-old child.

THE PRESCHOOL YEARS

Tito was sleeping in bed with his mother when a stranger broke a bedroom window and entered their apartment in an attempt to rape Tito's mother (see Figure 4.1).

In a world full of mysteries, it was difficult for 4-year-old Tito to distinguish the actual from the magical. That which is true became blurred with that which is fantasy in the daily miracles of cartoons and video games, but also in reading, mathematics, science, religion, and nature. If there were guiding principles to these abilities, powers, and forces, Tito did not know them yet. In a world without clear organizing principles, there were particularly frightening aspects of life, such as nighttime and monsters. The only respite from these terrible evils was Mama and Papa. Tito knew that big boys slept in their own beds, but with his father gone to work, Tito fell asleep beside his mother. He awakened with a start to the sound of his mother's screams. In the next instant, he saw the bad man. It was a monster, actually. It was dressed like a man, except that it was more scary than a regular man. A monster was in the room, even though monsters were not supposed to come to Mama and Papa's room!

The monster said that he would kill both of them if Tito's mother didn't shut up her screaming. Tito was more scared than he had ever been his whole life. He started to cry, but the monster slapped him. Tito did not cry after that.

Tito decided to hide under the covers. Maybe, the monster would not see him if Tito were perfectly still. While he was hiding at the foot of the bed, Tito heard his mother struggling with the monster. Someone pushed him to the floor. When Tito saw the monster ripping his mother's nightgown, he closed his eyes to make the monster disappear. Tito felt his own heart jumping in his chest. He guessed that he was going to die from his jumping heart. Maybe then, he could "morphin-time," like they do on TV, so he could rescue himself and his Mama from the monster. He did not morph into anything, though. He just sat on the floor feeling scared and tiny.

He wished that his Papa, or anybody, would come home to save them. He wished and wished, until the policemen heard his wishes and pounded on the door. The monster disappeared through the window. His mother opened the door for the police. The neighbor from across the hall, Senora Espejo, came over. She told Tito to be brave and not to upset his mother.

FIGURE 4.1. "The monster came inside our house."

When Tito's mother held him later, she asked if he had been afraid. He said, "no" in his best, most brave voice.

Key Aspects of Cognition

Cognitive advances give preschool-age children a greater ability to think symbolically, to understand simple cause-and-effect relationships, and to organize, retrieve, and verbally express their memories. These children are also able to report something that they recognize as untrue. However, preschool children remain very reliant on adults for approval and have relatively little experience with information seeking apart from their parents. They are therefore apt routinely to comply with adults' commands in attempt to get approval or attachment needs met.

Donovan and McIntyre (1990) describe two particularly relevant challenges in preschool-age children's development: (1) the ability to differentiate appearance from reality, and (2) the ability to take perspectives other than their own.

The historic tradition holds that children pass through a protracted prelogical period of development. Yet children's difficulty distinguishing appearance from reality does not mean that logic is absent. "Logic is simply a relatively closed system of interrelating propositions—which may or may not be true" (Donovan & McIntyre, 1990, p. 22). Tito wished for help, assistance arrived, and he concluded that he had wished the act into reality. Interestingly, symbolic play, which is the hallmark of this period, may hold intrigue for children of this age precisely because of difficulties separating appearance from reality (a child knows that when his dad wears a Halloween mask, he is not actually a monster; yet the child may feel afraid of his masked father).

Regarding the second task, perspective taking, there has been disagreement over the degree to which preschool children are able to infer the thoughts, feelings, and sensations of others. Preschool children may take more than one perspective in familiar contexts that make human sense, but generally, they have difficulty generating perspectives others than their own.

CAUSALITY

Preschoolers may understand physical causal mechanisms (e.g., people cause guns to fire), but they are not very discriminating when selecting inclusion criteria for cause-and-effect relationships; that is, they may offer causal explanations where none actually exist or confuse cause with effect. It is common for preschoolers to provide magical and confusing explanations for events not understood. In this case, Tito believed that his wish for help (the cause) summoned the police (the effect), when, in fact, his wish was unrelated to the neighbor's call to authorities.

Memory. Preschoolers' memory capacity improves over toddlers' memory, at least in part because the older child has more schemas for organizing and retrieving specific memories. However, memories may be distorted to conform to an existing schema. For example, Tito had no knowledge of rapists. He did, however, believe in monsters. Therefore, he understood the attempted rapist to be a monster. Accordingly, his descriptions were embellished by memories of the man possessing monster-like features, such as having green hair and the ability to fly.

Guilt. Although some global feelings of guilt may emerge during this age (e.g., children may believe that they caused the traumatic event; Shelby & Tredinnick, 1995), children's linguistic and cognitive limitations inhibit them from expressing feelings of guilt (Ridgeway, Waters, & Kuczaj, 1985). Also, preschoolers are not cognitively equipped to review an event retrospectively and devise alternative actions that could have been taken. So they are unlikely to feel guilt over specific actions taken during a traumatic event. This cognitive immaturity serves a protective function, buffering young children from feelings of overwhelming guilt.

Understanding of Death. Children under 6 years of age do not generally understand the irreversibility and inevitability of death (Grollman, 1990).

Symptoms

The following symptoms have been noted among preschool-age survivors: (1) somatic complaints; (2) loss of the illusion of parental control and protection (Shelby, 1997); (3) repetitive play (Eth & Pynoos, 1995); and (4) generalized anxiety (Shelby & Tredinnick, 1995).

Coping

In general, preschool children have relatively few coping options. The options that do exist tend to be passive. Cramer (1987) describes denial as emerging early in life, peaking around the age of 2 and declining sharply by the age of 4. Fantasy peaks around the age of 4 and falls off by middle childhood. Young children's preoperational thought may result in greater reliance on wish-fulfilling strategies rather than on objectively effective strategies (Eisenberg, Fabes, & Guthrie, 1997; Eth & Pynoos, 1995).

Interventions

AROUSAL AND SAFETY

Parental Protection. Tito's world was no longer a safe one. He could no longer believe that his parents were immune from harm, and that they would protect him from danger. To restore his faith in his parents' protective abilities, the therapist instructed Tito's parents to take several steps to increase safety in their home, and to emphasize the steps that they had taken to their son. For example, after Tito's mother changed the locks on the windows, she pointed out the new locks to Tito and told him that she had done this to keep him safe. She also bought a whistle and a bedroom telephone, which she deliberately showed to Tito.

AVOIDANCE

Permission to Be Traumatized. In the moments after the assailant left their apartment, the neighbor told Tito to hide his feelings from his mother. At 4 years of age, Tito was capable of lying, and he was heavily dependent on adult approval. Thus, Tito believed that he should feel no fear or, at least, that he should not express the fear he felt. At our suggestion, Tito's mother and father told him that it was all right to feel scared, that he could not upset them with his scared feelings, and that it was all right to talk and play about what happened with "the monster" when he came to visit the clinic. Tito seemed to relax markedly in sessions following this intervention. However, his avoidance behaviors did not change at home until Senora Espejo, the neighbor, told Tito that it was now all right to show his scared feelings to his mother.

Monster Poison. Tito was, understandably, reluctant to sleep. To address his avoidance, Tito and his therapist developed several kinds of "monster poison," which was composed of water and food coloring. He also developed multiple methods for administering the poison (e.g., keeping a spray bottle by the bed, carrying a water gun in his pocket a night, and filling balloons, which could be dropped on future monsters). In one session, Tito squealed with glee when he suggested that he could leave a glass full of the "poison" by the window with a cookie, which the monster would drink unknowingly. Tito's avoidance was replaced by delight in his own ability to outsmart—even in play— the man who had once victimized him mercilessly.

Interpretations of Language. Children may have difficulty interpreting the meaning of questions and statements, although they may answer to obtain adult approval. Children may also devote particular attention to language and communication, and may misunderstand important elements of the traumatic event because of ambiguities in language. For example, following Hurricane Andrew, a number of children drew the storm as a cyclops and developed a fear of or preoccupation with eyes. Greater exploration revealed that this was because they heard adults describe the "eye of the storm." The children assumed then, that a hurricane was a creature that had some sort of giant eye. Similarly, after the Northridge earthquake, many young children heard adults discussing geologic plates. Some youngsters became fearful that moving dinner plates caused earthquakes to occur.

INTRUSIVE REEXPERIENCING

Symbolic play may be particularly powerful because of preschoolers' difficulty separating appearance from reality. Similar to treatment with toddlers, therapeutic reenactment among preschoolers is facilitated by the use of props in the playroom.

The Experiential Mastery Technique (EMT). This technique is designed to elicit posttraumatic feelings (Shelby, 1997). In this technique, children draw pictures of the thing that frightened them. They then tell what it did to them. Reticent children are prompted by therapists who speak to the drawing themselves. For example, Tito's therapist said to the drawing, "Hey you monster. We don't like what you did. We don't like you because you . . . (the therapist paused to wait for Tito to respond) you came in the window and you scared me and my Mama." Children are encouraged to verbalize all of their feelings about the assailant (or disaster) to the drawing. Following their descriptions, the children are instructed to do anything they want to the drawing. Tito scribbled on the drawing, poked holes in it, slapped it, put it under a blanket, ripped it, and then flushed it down the toilet. He delighted in his ability to dominate the previously overwhelming "monster."

The Lie in Therapy. Tito told his therapist that, during the attack, he took a baseball bat and chased the monster out of the room. When the therapist reflected that he must have really *wished* that he could make the monster run away, Tito insisted that it had *really* happened. Although therapists often make interpretations about the child's lie, or they may correct young children's lies or fantasies, it is important to realize that the child's first successful lie is important as a function of separation from parents (Goleman, 1989). As children learn that they can report believable false information, they realize their power as separate individuals; that is, adults are not omnipotent beings, with access to or control over children's thoughts. This allows for more realistic views of themselves and of adults. Lying itself is sometimes a form of mastery. Instead of focusing on Tito's imagined heroic attack of the man, his fabrications, or his beliefs about the "monster," interventions were focused on solving the problems he perceived in ways that made sense to him, given his position in the course of development.

THE ELEMENTARY SCHOOL YEARS

Eight-year-old Kadeesha and her 7-year-old sister, Pauletta, were waiting for their school bus when they were struck by a truck with faulty brakes. Pauletta's sister was killed instantly, and Kadeesha suffered severe internal injuries and multiple fractures to her left leg (see Figure 4.2).

She remembered red. One second there was the regular early morning hum in the city, the school bus stop, and her sister's laughter. The next second, the big, red blur roared at them. A face peered down. A horn screamed in the midst of the red wave. There was time neither to think nor to move. Excruciating pain arrived a moment before the world went silent and dark.

From the darkness, she heard a lady asking her name. Kadeesha did not understand that her spleen was rupturing and that her left leg was almost severed, but she could feel her body dying. She heard someone say, "This one is dead," but Kadeesha could not make the enormous effort required to ask if it was her sister. Kadeesha's consciousness retreated.

She awakened in the hospital, where she received the medical care that saved her life. Her leg was also spared, albeit with significant injury and disfigurement.

Kadeesha's guilt consumed her. She easily recognized the bitter fact that if she had been standing on the other side of her sister, her sister would have been the one who lived. Kadeesha thought of a hundred ways that she could have changed the situation. Kadeesha was usually careful to stand far from the street corner. She usually watched for the bus. She had behaved differently this time.

Kadeesha's emotions threatened to overwhelm her. She was furious at the driver of the truck. She wanted him thrown in jail forever. She told the nurse that she would kill him if she ever saw him. Kadeesha missed her sister more than anything in the world, and she thought that by dying herself, maybe she could see Pauletta again.

Kadeesha saw how sad her mother was, and she did not want to cause her mother more pain. When the psychiatrist came to ask Kadeesha if she wanted to die or to kill anyone, Kadeesha's mother was in the room, so Kadeesha said that she did not want to die and that she was not so mad after all. Her silenced pain created a prison that she struggled to survive.

FIGURE 4.2. "The day of the big red truck."

Key Aspects of Cognition

Around the age of 7, children can mentally step back from, reflect on, and attend to their thoughts and language. Children in this developmental era generally can evaluate their actions from their own perspectives, separate self from behaviors, take the perspective of another, preoccupy themselves with rules and order, and view peers as a significant means of social support. Between the ages of 5 and 8, children's narrow focus on the outcome of an action (i.e., good or bad), moves to a consideration of others' reactions to a behavior (approval or disapproval) and then to a yet more sophisticated consideration of the self's own reaction (approval or disapproval) to the behavior (Harris, 1989). Children's ability to evaluate themselves from their own perspective, and not just from perspective of adult approval, means that, unlike with the younger child, the therapist cannot merely reassure by saying, "It wasn't your fault."

By 8, children distinguish fundamental aspects of self from discrete behaviors. For example, Kadeesha knew that she usually stood away from the street, but that she had behaved differently in this instance. This ability is helpful in separating her specific behavior from her global sense of self.

The ability to take the perspective of another is well in place by the elementary school years. In this case, Kadeesha was well aware of her mother's feelings and of how her mother might react in the hypothetical situation that she constructed (i.e., "If I share my sadness and anger, my mother will feel worse"). In addition, children may shield their parents from their adverse trauma reactions. Following a ferry disaster, Yule and Williams (1990) observed that children revealed more about their symptoms when they were interviewed away from their parents than when their parents were present.

During this developmental stage, it is common for children to hold preoccupations with rules, order, and justice. Whereas Tito wanted the assailant in jail because of safety concerns, Kadeesha wanted the driver in jail because of her ability to conceptualize justice. Also during the elementary school years, peers become more important, and the child's social circle expands. For Kadeesha, losing her sister meant losing her best friend, which dealt a significant blow to her social support system.

MEMORY

Children at this age are likely to have detailed, long-term memory for the traumatic event. They are capable of holding factually accurate memories, but the memories may contain embellishments or distortions (Terr, 1991). Kadeesha remembered a number of accurate details about the event, but she also recalled that the driver had "teeth like a vampire," and that "the truck was as tall as the Empire State Building."

GUILT

Some rudimentary form of guilt may be present around age 2 or 3, but children are not able to identify or express it until elementary school. Ridgeway et al. (1985) found that the word "guilt" is not part of children's active lexicon until about 5½ or 6 years of age. Tangney (1998) found that children in this age range feel guilt over concrete types of events (hurting someone, breaking something), whereas adolescents and adults feel guilty over more abstract notions (inaction, or failure to attain an ideal) or over a combination of concrete and abstract issues. In this case, Kadeesha felt guilty that she had not traded places and that she had not stood further away, rather than experiencing guilt over the more abstract notion that she had failed to live up to her sense of responsibility.

Shame, in its self-focus, interferes with empathy. In contrast, guilt motivates corrective action (Baumeister, Stillwell, & Heatherton, 1994; Tangney, 1991). In formulating intervention approaches, it may be important, then, to help channel the child's feelings of guilt toward actions that promote empathic expressions.

UNDERSTANDING OF DEATH

The concept of death as irreversible is typically understood between 8 and 10 years of age (Garmezy, 1983). By 9, most children also understand the notion of death as inevitable. Unlike Mirella in her expectation that her mother would return, Kadeesha knew that her sister was truly gone.

Coping

Children at this developmental level have more realistic self-perceptions than younger children. As a result, they may be more vulnerable than younger children to internalization of negative experiences (Thompson, 1990). Elementary-school-age children's more realistic appraisals of their failures break down the protective barriers used by younger children. Also, the older child is able to generate multiple alternatives to a problem. This skill, which is enhanced into adolescence, makes the child vulnerable to intense self-blame and guilt for not taking alternative actions. Whereas Tito never thought about what he could have done differently, Kadeesha ruminated on such thoughts every day.

Symptoms

In addition to the PTSD and Acute Stress Disorder symptoms described earlier, children of this developmental level may demonstrate the following symptoms or issues: (1) elaborate posttraumatic play, with possible involvement of friends in the reenactment; (2) inner plans of action (i.e., retrospective wishes about remedies to the traumatic moment; Eth & Pynoos, 1995); (3) somatic complaints and concerns about bodily integrity; (4) guilt over actions taken; (5) the effortful shielding of distress from parents (Yule & Williams, 1990); and (6) omens (i.e., the belief that something foretold the traumatic event; Terr, 1991).

Interventions for Avoidance

THE JIMMY BOOK

For many children, the first focus of posttraumatic therapy is on overcoming avoidance of play or discussion about the traumatic event. A therapeutic activity book, which I named the "The Jimmy Book," is useful in understanding and addressing children's avoidance, although these books can be tailored to suit the needs of each client, here are sample pages of my Jimmy Book (see Figure 4.3). These pages are helpful in identifying the reasons why children are reluctant to discuss their traumatic experiences.

INTERVENTION FOR INTRUSIVE REEXPERIENCING

Semistructured Interview. At this stage of development, children have a better developed capacity to verbalize their posttraumatic experiences and feelings. Pynoos and Eth (1986) developed a posttraumatic interview in which children are encouraged to draw a picture and then to tell a story about the drawing. The clinician points out the inevitable reference to the traumatic event that occurs in the drawing and asks the child to recount the traumatic event in detail (including the child's sensory experiences and the worst moment). Following the child's account, the therapist encourages the child to fully express "revenge fantasies." The authors of this technique recommend separating fantasy from reality by commenting that it feels good to do something now in play, whereas there was nothing that the child could do then. They conclude by acknowledging the child's bravery either during the traumatic event or in recounting it.

INTERVENTION FOR AROUSAL

Self-Instruction. Cognitive-behavioral techniques have been used with children and adolescents to reduce arousal symptoms and intrusive reexperiencing symptoms (Saigh, 1989). Kadeesha's therapist used a variation of Meichenbaum and Goodman's (1971) self-instruction, in which Kadeesha identified her responses (physical sensations, emotions, and self-talk) when a vehicle approached. Rather than having Kadeesha imagine a vehicle approaching (which involves a hypothetical thought) the therapist made the intervention more developmentally appropriate by moving a large red cardboard box past Kadeesha. The therapist and Kadeesha practiced deep breathing and positive self-statements, such as "I am scared, but I will get through this." At first, the therapist both reminded Kadeesha to breath deeply and verbalized the positive statements as the box moved past her. Later, Kadeesha inhaled and verbalized the statements aloud. Ultimately, the child engaged in silent self-talk. Kadeesha's aunt also learned the procedure and practiced it with Kadeesha at the bus stop.

This is Jimmy.
Something awful happened to him, but . . .

he can't talk about it.
Draw what would happen if Jimmy talked about it.

If Jimmy talked about it, he thinks that what would happen:

☐ His Mom or Dad wouldn't like it

☐ He would get too scared

☐ His therapist wouldn't want him to tell

☐ Some other reason

If Jimmy could talk about what happened, I wonder how he would feel:

FIGURE 4.3. *The Jimmy Book* is useful in understanding and addressing children's avoidance.

INTERVENTION FOR PERCEPTION OF JUSTICE

Law and Order Games. Because children this age are commonly concerned with justice and fairness, opportunities for them to pretend to be in the role of adjudicator can be especially beneficial. A judge's robe and gavel, or sheriff's badge and handcuffs, with a pretend jail nearby, are useful tools to help children play out their desire to see justice rendered. Kadeesha spent a great deal of time pretending to be the judge during the weekly hearings that took place in the playroom. As she forced the driver to testify during session after session, Kadeesha eventually understood that he had not maliciously hurt her and her sister. She reduced his sentence but revoked his drivers' license. As a termination gift, the therapist gave Kadeesha a gavel and told her that it could always remind her of her power.

INTERVENTIONS FOR MOURNING

Therapeutic Funeral. Kadeesha had many reasons to mourn. Hospitalized when Pauletta's funeral took place, Kadeesha was denied the opportunity to ritualize her sister's death. In the session, Kadeesha planned and held her own funeral for her sister. Kadeesha's favorite dolls and her sister's dolls were invited guests. Kadeesha brought a picture of Pauletta and buried in it a shoe box full of sand, which she then took home to bury in the family's backyard.

Memory Boxes. Kadeesha also created a special box full of pictures and memorabilia of her sister. She decorated the box in her sister's favorite colors and filled it with movie stubs, special coins, and her sister's favorite earrings, drawings, and pictures. This box remained in Kadeesha's room as a tangible reminder of her sister.

Commemorating Losses. Kadeesha's favorite purse was destroyed during the accident. When she described it longingly during several sessions, the therapist asked her if she wanted to have a funeral for the purse. Kadeesha enthusiastically agreed. She and the therapist discussed various attributes of the purse, such as what it looked like, how she acquired it, all of the places that the purse had gone with her, what was inside the purse, and where she imagined the purse to be now. Kadeesha participated in the descriptions with an intensity that signified a loss much greater than the loss of a purse. At the end of the session, the therapist and Kadeesha concluded that it had been a good purse, that it would be missed, that nothing could ever replace it, but that one day it would be all right to get another. A couple of months after her last session, Kadeesha mailed a school picture to the therapist. In the photograph, Kadeesha's beaming smile pressed her cheek against a new, pink purse.

INTERVENTIONS FOR GUILT

Parental Permission. To deal with Kadeesha's guilt, the therapist actively involved Kadeesha's mother in the treatment. In the session, the mother reassured Kadeesha that their family would survive their grief and that Kadeesha did not have to hide her sadness and anger.

Altruism. Because of Kadeesha's persistent feelings of guilt, the therapist looked for altruistic outlets for her feelings. With her mother's assistance, Kadeesha became a school safety officer, where she helped to direct children safely across the street.

ADOLESCENCE

Julie was raped by a stranger who had agreed to transport her to a party in his car.

Julie and Laura smiled to each other as they climbed out Laura's bedroom window. Within a few minutes the 14-year-old girls had walked to a classmate's house for the first party of the school year.

Judd, the bomb, was there. He was even better looking up close. He told Julie that he and his friends were relocating the party to an abandoned beach house. When he winked at her and asked her if she would like to come along, Julie happily agreed as long as Laura could come also.

Julie failed to find Laura in the crowded house. After about half an hour, someone told Julie that Judd and his friends had left in a caravan of several cars and that Laura had gone with them. "Judd must have found Laura, and they must think that I am in one of the other cars," Julie thought. She walked outside to see if she could still catch a ride from one of Judd's friends, but everyone was gone.

Julie had told everyone inside that Judd had asked her to his exclusive party. She could not go back inside and face everyone. She finished her third beer as she walked toward the bus stop. A car pulled up beside her. The driver introduced himself as Larry. He was an older guy, probably 20. As they talked, Julie decided that he was nice, but really geeky, like a computer nerd. "A goof like this guy has to be harmless," she thought. So, she accepted Larry's offer to drive her to Judd's party. Finally, her problems were solved.

On the way to the party, Larry said that he needed to stop by his house to pick up some money for gas. Julie was bummed about the delay. When Larry invited her inside, she initially declined but went inside after about 15 minutes so that she could use the bathroom. Larry said that he was still looking for his wallet and gave her another beer. Julie was really wasted. It was hard for her to stand up. Larry seemed weird now, and Julie felt uncomfortable. When she tried to leave, he dragged her back inside. When she refused his sexual advances, he raped her.

The phone rang, and Julie asked to use the bathroom. Larry agreed as he hurried toward the phone. After she had safely locked the bathroom door, she removed the screen from the bathroom window and escaped.

Larry had her purse, her money, and Judd's phone number. As she wandered through the unfamiliar neighborhood, Julie considered calling her parents, but she knew that she would be in major trouble for what she had done. She was not even fully dressed. She would die of embarrassment if someone from the party saw her like this. Julie felt guilty for tricking her parents. She felt guilty for going with the goof. She felt guilty for not doing something sooner to escape. She also felt ashamed and dirty because of the sexual acts that she had been forced to perform.

Julie finally retraced the path to Laura's house, where Laura was waiting and worried. She told Laura what happened, and the girls pledged not to tell anyone else. A couple of months later, Julie learned that she was pregnant. She told her mother at that point, and they agreed that Julie would terminate the pregnancy. She also filed a report with her local law enforcement agency, but the detective was reluctant to believe her because she had not revealed the rape until she learned that she was pregnant. Julie entered therapy following the termination of her pregnancy and her subsequent report to police.

Key Aspects of Cognition

Although adolescence is often characterized as a tumultuous period, research has failed to support the idea that universal or dramatic stress and disorganization occur during adolescence. With their increased cognitive maturity, adolescents are typically able to engage in abstraction, complex perspective taking (including third-person perspectives), and retrospective or prospective hypothetical thought.

GUILT

Recognition of wrongdoing intensifies from earlier childhood through adolescence (Bybee, Merisca, & Velasco, 1998), in part because improved cognitive reasoning abilities increasingly enable self-blaming attributions. Furthermore, adolescents may negatively evaluate their behavior in terms of inaction or the inability to attain an ideal. In this case, Julie felt guilty not only for what she did, but also for what she did not do.

DEATH

By adolescence, young people generally understand the irreversibility and inevitability of death. They may continue to underestimate the risk of their own death, however.

Symptoms

Adolescents may demonstrate the following symptoms: (1) adult-like PTSD symptoms, including flashbacks; (2) preoccupation with concerns secondary to the traumatic event (e.g., parental punishment); and (3) rebellious, antisocial, or risk-taking behaviors, such as substance use or promiscuity (Eth & Pynoos, 1995).

Coping

Because of their increased cognitive maturity, adolescents may engage in intellectualization, altruism, complex problem solving, and suppression (Bybee et al., 1998). They also have greater capacity than younger children to use emotion-focused coping and to manage negative emotions without necessarily making attempts to change the problem.

Interventions

AVOIDANCE

Embarrassment Reduction. Adolescents' acute awareness of their feelings of embarrassment may impede the therapy process. The therapist might reassure the teenage client in the following way: "It is perfectly understandable that *you* feel uncomfortable talking about what happened, but it is not embarrassing to *me*. Teenagers tell me things like this every day. So, even though it might feel a little embarrassing to you, this is my job and it is not embarrassing for me at all."

"Would I Blame Her?" Activity. To address self-blame, the therapist can ask victims if they would blame someone else who had experienced a similar trauma (reacted the same way, made the same choices). Many adolescents report that they would not blame another victim in the same situation. The therapist and client can then explore the disparity in the client's reaction to self and others. If the adolescent reports that she would, in fact, blame someone else, the therapist can use this as an opportunity to further explore the victim's attributions and beliefs about culpability.

Blameberry Pie. For survivors who believe that the sexual assault is their fault, one tactic is to bring several pie tins into the session and introduce the first (largest) pie tin as the "Blameberry Pie." This pie can be described as a special pie that will help clarify why the victim believes he or she was responsible for the traumatic event. The client is given different pieces of colored paper on which he or she, or the therapist, write the reasons why the victim feels responsible for the victimization ("Because I got in the car with him," or "Because I was drinking"). After an exhaustive list has been written, the items are all placed in the pie tin. "No wonder you feel so awful," the therapist might respond. "Look at all of those reasons in there, but this is supposed to be a pie about the rape. Let's see if the reasons all fit into this pie. Let's take one of these." The therapist or teenager selects one of the items inside the pie. "This says, 'Because I trusted him.' OK, you trusted him. You wish you hadn't trusted someone who hurt you. That belongs in a different pie, not in a pie about who is responsible for raping you. Let's make a trust pie for that." The therapist asks the client to place the paper in a separate, smaller pie dish or bowl and label it "trust." The therapist and adolescent select another item from the large pie tin, discuss it, and label a different bowl ("drinking," "accepted a ride," "waited so long before escaping"). Eventually, there will be nothing left in the "blame" pie tin. "So," the therapist can conclude, "you wish you had not trusted, not been drinking, not accepted a ride from him, and not waited so long before escaping. You feel responsible for these things. But, this is a pie about who is responsible for the rape, not who is responsible for trusting and drinking. Whose fault is the rape?" It is usually clear to teenagers by that point that they are not at all responsible for the traumatic event itself. The therapist can use the labels assigned to the other bowls as the targets of future interventions (to help clients feel more secure in their judgments and to assist them in making safe decisions about alcohol consumption).

INTRUSIVE REEXPERIENCING

Global Alleviation of Symptoms. A number of methods have been empirically validated for treating intrusive reexperiencing in adolescent and adult trauma survivors. Most of these methods involve cognitive-behavioral techniques, including repeated exposure to (i.e., retelling) the traumatic stimuli, some form of cognitive reprocessing, or education about the traumatic event and common symptoms (Cohen & Mannarino, 1997; Deblinger et al., 1990; Foa & Rothbaum, 1998; Saigh, 1989; Veronen & Kilpatrick, 1983).

These methods can be made more adolescent-friendly by offering the young person the opportunity to draw, play, or otherwise nonverbally depict what happened. Typical tools in the playroom may seem too infantilizing for teenagers. Therefore, therapists can present other media for reenacting traumatic scenes. Julie used a shoe box and pieces of cardboard (rather than a dollhouse) to depict the assailant's home and the rooms inside. She could then demonstrate, using both verbal and nonverbal methods, what happened to her. Even when using cognitive behavioral repeated exposure techniques, the therapist can offer comforting and familiar items to teenagers during the session (nail polish, or music from a favorite radio station).

Flashback Management. To alleviate the panic accompanying flashbacks, a grounding technique is often helpful. Clients are instructed to remind themselves when flashbacks occur that they know the flashbacks are a result of the traumatic event, and that they will pass. Clients can then focus on the chairs in which they sit or the ground on which they stand. They can squeeze the chair, or stomp the ground, and remind themselves that they are here and safe now, not back in the past.

Nightmare Management. To manage troubling nightmares, adolescents can be instructed to think about a more positive ending to the dream as soon as they awaken. Many people fall back asleep and integrate the new material into the dream. To crystallize these new endings, teenaged clients can draw, describe, or act them out in therapy.

INTERVENTION FOR AROUSAL

To help adolescent survivors deal with arousal symptoms directly related to the trauma, relaxation training and positive imagery are useful. Survivors may also experience arousal symptoms indirectly related to the traumatic event, such as anger over feeling damaged or victimized. To treat this aspect of arousal, the therapist used the following story:

> There is a special tree near the bayous in the South. The tree was deprived of the sunlight that it needed to grow straight. Because it was hurt from not getting what it needed, it grew horizontally for a few feet before finally curving upward toward the sky. There was a little girl, who played on the bench that its crooked trunk made for her. She knew, and thought that the tree knew, that it would never be like the other trees. It was horribly disfigured. She remarked to herself how unfair it was that an innocent tree would always have to be so different from other trees because of its misfortune.
>
> After she had grown into a woman, she returned to the place where the tree grew. She looked in the right part of the bayou, but she could not find the horribly damaged tree. As she was giving up, she noticed a tree with a slight bend in its upper trunk. That was it! Yet, the tree before her now had changed almost beyond recognition. Its green branches elegantly draped from the sky to the bayou floor. It had largely straightened itself. The slight curve in its upper trunk would always exist, but the tree that was once defined by its calamity was now remarkable for its strength, beauty, and ability to survive with grace.

INTERVENTION FOR DEALING WITH PEERS

Because of the importance of the adolescent's social network, these survivors benefit from a therapeutic focus on integrating the traumatic event into their social contexts. Sometimes, this means developing a plan for whom will be told, and how others will be told about the traumatic event.

When appropriate, the therapist might also help the adolescent prepare for victim-blaming responses or otherwise unsupportive responses by doing role-playing activities.

INTERVENTIONS FOR GRIEF

Therapeutic Funeral. Julie's posttraumatic work involved finding some sense of closure to the loss that she sustained. In therapy, Julie tearfully described her unresolved feelings about terminating her pregnancy. With the therapist, she planned a funeral. She set a date and chose a site in a nearby park. With Laura at her side, Julie held a funeral. First, she read a letter to her unborn child. Then, she buried the baby shoes that Laura had given her when Julie first learned of her pregnancy. Finally, Julie and Laura each left flowers over the "grave." This ritual provided a sense of completion that would have been difficult to obtain through verbal therapy alone. Julie was then emotionally free to return to the tasks of regular teenage life.

Intervention for Integration. Particularly during the final stage of treatment, altruism is a useful method for solidifying posttraumatic therapeutic gains. Adolescents may be particularly interested in offering lessons from their experience to other young people. They can write letters or prepare a handbook for other teens who might experience a similar traumatic event. Similarly, adolescents can audio record their messages for others. These interventions give teenagers the opportunity to view themselves as experts giving information to others. The therapist might keep a library of tapes to share with future survivors. Julie wrote: "What I learned [in therapy] was that you just have to forget about it. I mean, you can't get sucked down with all of the thoughts about it. You just have to go with the flow. It's like the ocean. When you are in the ocean, you should just float with it. Don't let it pull you under. Just say that you can do it and relax in the ocean until you come on in."

CONCLUSION

When the fruit has served its full term, drawing its juice
from the branch as it dances with the wind and matures in
the sun, then it feels in its core the call of the beyond and
becomes ready for its career of a wider life.
—TAGORE (1956, p. 82)

When my time came to leave Sarajevo, I gave a farewell gift to a boy named Manul. Because Manul had been the most tenacious worker of all the children who helped rebuild the playground where Darik first learned to swing, it was to be his task to maintain the park after I left

Bosnia. As an 11-year-old orphan, Manul was also the quietest child. He had seen horror too terrifying for words. In the days that we worked together to build the playground, Manul was always by my side. Often, he spoke of the profound disappointments thrust upon him by 4 years of war. Other memories, he said, he could not speak. With a stick, he drew on the ground the faces of those he had seen die. I stayed with him through his suffering, trying to honor the silent way in which he grieved his losses.

Manul was fascinated with my silver ring, which depicted the eye of Horus. I told him the myth of Horus, who—in Egyptian mythology—provided protection to his loved ones. Manul identified himself with Horus, whose father was also murdered. Horus' vigilant eye symbolized watchful protection from harm and love strong enough to endure great self-sacrifice.

On the day before I left, I gave Manul the ring as a farewell gift. I wanted him to keep a symbol of the safety and warmth that we had shared together. Manul said that the eye on the ring would remind him of my eye watching over him. The myth had been meaningful to Manul, and he cherished the gift.

On the day that I left Sarajevo, Manul came to the bus station along with six other boys from his neighborhood. As my overcrowded bus began to drive away, Manul's sadness called out to me. I instinctively moved toward him, placing my hand against the window pane. He matched his hand to my hand. For a moment, the reflection in the glass gave the illusion that we each wore the ring. In my last memory of him, he is trying to look stoic. He waves goodbye until he has to wipe a tear from his eye. The silver ring reflects the sun for an instant before he disappears from me.

A few days later, I was surprised when a NATO soldier returned the ring to me in Zagreb. Manul had pleaded with the man to find me before I left the Balkans. Manul reasoned that if he kept the ring I would not return to Sarajevo, but if I had the ring, I would be bound by obligation to return "his ring" to him in Bosnia. I could not return to Manul, though. My time with him had ended. I did not expect to see him again.

For years, Manul remained present for me, as a disquiet memory. I regretted that I had given him something that he believed he could not keep. I wished that he could have allowed himself to hold the comfort the ring might have brought him.

Five years later, after the end of a different relief mission to Albania, ironically, I was able to return the ring. Manul had become a man. "At last, I have returned to bring you your ring," I said as I greeted him. "From the moment I gave it to you, it has belonged to you," I told him fondly. After we talked about his many satisfactions with life in the post-war city, he paused to give me a long, pensive stare. He had become wise. He had long since learned to value his strengths of endurance and recovery. A symbol of protection was no longer essential to him, and he had found more love than he needed to sustain him.

Manul and I each realized that he no longer needed the ring that he had once so desperately valued. "When you were younger, it was a symbol of protection and caring," I explained. "Now, the eye is not a protector, it is a witness. Long ago, Horus and I watched your suffering and now we see the ways in which you have healed." "And with that eye," Manul added mischievously, "will you watch as I become rich and have many girlfriends?" "Yes," I assured him as we laughed together. "It will be my privilege to watch as your life unfolds before you." As he left, he put the ring in his pocket. I resisted stoicism; the tears fell freely as I observed his departure. This time, there was no doubt, he would keep the ring.

In posttraumatic therapy, young clients come to terms with their horror and survival. The therapist momentarily walks with children through the extremes of human existence. Then, the therapist steps aside as children find their way though the rest of life.

This chapter provided developmentally appropriate interventions to assist therapists who deliver short-term treatment to traumatized children. Until empirical studies of intervention strategies with traumatized children are more forthcoming, the lessons taught by children, themselves, must be the guideposts of treatment. As for the children described, Mirella is now in the first grade, Tito is a little-league soccer star, Kadeesha helped name her new baby brother Daniel, and Julie is a high school class officer. Manul is working in Sarajevo, where he is actively searching for his next girlfriend. Perhaps the most notable and wonderful thing about them now is that, compared to other children, they are utterly unremarkable. They are uniquely ordinary.

As for Darik, I do not know where he is. His family, along with hundreds of other families, was forced to relocate as part of the last peace agreement. Wherever he is, and whatever he has faced since that spring day, I am convinced that he remembers how to swing.

REFERENCES

Band, E. B., & Weisz, J. R. (1988). How to feel better when it feels bad: Children's perspective on coping with everyday stress. *Developmental Psychology, 24,* 247–253.

Baumeister, R. F., Stillwell, A. M., & Heatherton, R. F. (1994). Guilt: An interpersonal approach. *Psychological Bulletin, 11,* 243–267.

Bowlby, J. (1977). The making and breaking of affectionate bonds. *British Journal of Psychiatry, 130,* 421–431.

Bybee, J., Merisca, R., & Velasco, R. (1998). The development of reactions to guilt-provoking events. In J. Bybee (Ed.), *Guilt and children* (pp. 185–214). San Diego: Academic Press.

Carver, C. S., Pozo, C., Harris, S. D., & Noriega, V. (1993). How coping mediates the effect of optimism on distress: A study of women with early stage breast cancer. *Journal of Personality and Social Psychology, 65,* 375–390.

Cohen, P., & Cohen, J. (1984). The clinician's illusion. *Archives of General Psychiatry, 41,* 1178–1182.

Cohen, J. A., & Mannarino, A. P. (1997). A treatment study for sexually abused preschool children: Outcome during a one-year follow-up. *Journal of the American Academy of Child and Adolescent Psychiatry, 36,* 1228–1235.

Cohen, J. A., & Mannarino, A. P. (1998). Interventions for sexually abused children: Initial treatment outcome findings. *Child Maltreatment: Journal of the American Professional Society on the Abuse of Children, 3,* 17–26.

Compas, B. E. (1998). An agenda for coping research and theory: Basic and applied developmental issues. *International Journal of Behavioral Development, 22,* 231–237.

Compas, B. E., Banez, G. A., Malcarne, V., & Worsham, N. (1991). Perceived control and coping with stress: A developmental perspective. *Journal of Social Issues, 47,* 23–34.

Compas, B. E., Malcarne, V. L., & Fondacaro, K. (1988). Coping with stressful events in older children and young adolescents. *Journal of Consulting and Clinical Psychology, 56,* 405–411.

Corder, B. F., & Haizlip, T. M. (1989). The role of mastery experiences in therapeutic interventions for children dealing with acute trauma: Some implications for treatment of sexual abuse. *Psychiatric Forum, 15,* 57–63.

Cramer, P. (1987). The development of defense mechanisms. *Journal of Personality, 55,* 597–614.

Deblinger, E., McLeer, S. V., & Henry, D. (1990). Cognitive behavioral treatment for sexually abused children suffering post-traumatic stress: Preliminary findings. *Journal of the American Academy of Child and Adolescent Psychiatry, 29,* 747–752.

Donovan, D. M., & McIntyre, D. (1990). *Healing the hurt child: A developmental–contextual approach.* New York: Norton.

Eisenberg, N., Fabes, R. A., & Guthrie, I. K. (1997). Coping with stress: The roles of regulation and development. In S. A. Wolchik & I. N. Sandler (Eds.), *Handbook of children's coping: Linking theory and intervention* (pp. 41–72). New York: Plenum Press.

Epping-Jordan, J. E., Compas, B. E., & Howell, D. C. (1994). Predictors of cancer progression in young adult men and women: Avoidance, intrusive thoughts, and psychological symptoms. *Health Psychology, 13,* 539–547.

Erikson, E. H. (1950). *Childhood and society.* New York: Norton.

Eth, S., & Pynoos, R. S. (1995). Developmental perspective on psychic trauma in childhood. In C. R. Figley (Ed.), *Trauma and its wake: The study of treatment of post-traumatic stress disorder* (pp. 36–52). New York: Brunner/Mazel.

Famularo, R., Kinscherff, R., & Fenton, T. (1990). Symptom differences in acute and chronic presentation of childhood post-traumatic stress disorder. *Child Abuse and Neglect, 14,* 439–444.

Foa, E. B., & Rothbaum, B. O. (1998). *Treating the trauma of rape: Cognitive-behavioral therapy for PTSD.* New York: Guilford Press.

Gaensbauer, T., Chatoor, I., Drell, M., Siegel, D., & Zeanah, C. H. (1995). Traumatic loss in a one-year-old girl. *Journal of the American Academy of Child and Adolescent Psychiatry, 34,* 520–528.

Galante, R., & Foa, D. (1986). An epidemiological study of psychic trauma and treatment effectiveness for children after a natural disaster. *Journal of the American Academy of Child Psychiatry, 25,* 384–392.

Garbarino, J., Stott, F. M., & the Faculty of the Erikson Institute. (1992). *What children can tell us: Eliciting, interpreting, and evaluating critical information from children.* San Francisco: Jossey Bass.

Garmezy, N. (1983). Stressors of childhood. In N. Garmezy & M. Rutter (Eds.), *Stress, coping, and development in children* (pp. 43–84). New York: McGraw-Hill.

Gil, K. M., Williams, D. A., Thompson, R. J., & Kinney, T. R. (1991). Sickle cell disease in children and adolescents: The relation of child and parent pain coping strategies to adjustment. *Journal of Pediatric Psychology, 16,* 643–663.

Goleman, D. J. (1989). What is negative about positive illusions? When benefits for the individual harm the collective [Special Issue: Self-illusions: When are they adaptive?]. *Journal of Social and Clinical Psychology, 8,* 190–197.

Goodman, G. S. (1984). The child witness: Conclusions and future directions for research and legal practice. *Journal of Social Issues, 40,* 157–175.

Grollman, E. A. (1990). *Talking to children about death.* Boston: Beacon.

Harris, P. L. (1989). *Children and emotion: The development of psychological understanding.* New York: Basil Blackwell.

Kagan, J., Snidman, N., & Arcus, D. (1995). The role of temperament in social development. In G. P Chrousos, R. McCarty, K. Pacak, G. Cizza, E. Sternberg, P. W. Gold, & R. Kvetnansky (Eds.), Stress: Basic mechanisms and clinical implications. *Annals of the New York Academy of Science, 771,* 485–490. New York: New York Academy of Science.

Kail, R. (1984). *The development of memory in children* (2nd ed.). New York: Freeman.

Lazarus, R. S., & Folkman, S. (1984). Coping and adaptation. In W. D. Gentry (Ed.), *The handbook of behavioral medicine* (pp. 282–325). New York: Guilford Press.

Levy, D. M. (1939). Release therapy. *American Journal of Orthopsychiatry, 9,* 713–736.

Lonigan, C. J., Anthony, J. L., & Shannon, M. P. (1998). Diagnostic efficacy of posttraumatic symptoms in children exposed to disaster. *Journal of Clinical Child Psychology, 27,* 255–267.

Mann, J. (1973). *Time-limited psychotherapy.* Cambridge, MA: Harvard University Press.

Meichenbaum, D. H., & Goodman, J. (1971). Training impulsive children to talk to themselves: A means of developing self-control. *Journal of Abnormal Psychology, 77,* 115–126.

Monahon, C. (1997). *Children and trauma: A guide for parents and professionals.* San Francisco: Jossey-Bass.

Phillips, E. (1989). Early studies of mental health delivery systems. *Perceptual and Motor Skills, 68,* 1129–1130.

Piaget, J. (1979). Comments on Vygotsky's critical remarks. *Archives de Psychologie, 47,* 237–249.

Pynoos, R. S., & Eth, S. (1986). Witness to violence: The child interview. *Journal of the Academy of Child Psychiatry, 25,* 306–319.

Ridgeway, D., Waters, E., & Kuczaj, S. A. (1985). Acquisition of emotion-descriptive language: Receptive and productive vocabulary norms for ages 18 months to 6 years. *Developmental Psychology, 21,* 901–908.

Rossman, B. R., & Rosenberg, M. S. (1992). Family stress and functioning in children: The moderating effects of children's belief about their control over parental conflict. *Journal of Child Psychology and Psychiatry and Allied Disciplines, 33,* 699–715.

Rutter, M. (1988). Stress, coping, and development. In N. Garmezy & M. Rutter (Eds.), *Stress, coping and development in children* (pp. 1–42). Baltimore: Johns Hopkins University Press.

Rutter, M. (1988). The role of cognition in child development and disorder. In S. Chess, A. Thomas, & M. E. Hertzig (Eds.), *Annual progress in child psychiatry and child development* (pp. 77–101). New York: Brunner/Mazel.

Rutter, M. (1996). Transitions and turning points in developmental psychopathology: As applied to the age span between childhood and mid-adulthood. *International Journal of Behavioral Development, 19,* 603–626.

Saigh, P. (1989). The use of an *in vitro* flooding package in treatment of traumatized adolescents. *Journal of Developmental and Behavioral Pediatrics, 10,* 17–21.

Sandler, I. N., Wolchik, S. A., MacKinnon, D., Ayers, T. S., & Roosa, M. W. (1997). Developing linkages between theory and intervention in stress and coping processes. In S. A Wolchik & I. N. Sandler (Eds.), *Handbook of children's coping: Linking theory and intervention* (pp. 3–40). New York: Plenum Press.

Scheier, M. F., Carver, C. S., & Weintraub, J. K. (1989). Assessing coping strategies: A theoretically based approach. *Journal of Personality and Social Psychology, 56,* 267–283.

Shelby, J. S. (1995). Crisis intervention with children following Hurricane Andrew: A comparison of two treatment approaches. *Dissertation Abstracts International, 56,* 1121.

Shelby, J. S. (1997). Rubble, disruption, and tears: Helping young survivors of natural disaster. In H. Kaduson, D. Cangelosi, & C. Schaefer (Eds.), *The playing cure* (pp. 143–169). Northvale, NJ: Aronson.

Shelby, J. S., & Tredinnick, M. G. (1995). Crisis intervention with children following natural disaster: Lessons form Hurricane Andrew. *Journal of Counseling and Development, 73,* 491–497.

Spirito, A., Stark, L. J., & Williams, C. (1988). Development of a brief coping checklist for use with pediatric populations. *Journal of Pediatric Psychology, 13,* 555–574.

Stern, D. N. (1985). *The interpersonal world of the infant.* New York: Basic Books.

Tagore, R. (1956). The world of personality. In C. Moustakas (Ed.), *The self: Explorations in personal growth* (pp. 76–85). Northvale, NJ: Aronson.

Tangney, J. P. (1991). Moral affect: The good, the bad, and the ugly. *Journal of Personality and Social Psychology, 61,* 598–607.

Tangney, J. P. (1998). How does guilt differ from shame? In J. Bybee (Ed.), *Guilt and children* (pp. 1–17). San Diego, CA: Academic Press.

Terr, L. (1991). Childhood traumas: An outline and overview. *American Journal of Psychiatry, 148,* 10–20.

Thompson, R. A. (1990). Vulnerability in research: A developmental perspective on research risk. *Child Development, 61,* 1–16.

Veronen, L. J., & Kilpatrick, D. G. (1983). Stress management for rape victims. In D. Meichenbaum & M. E. Jaremko (Eds.), *Stress reduction and prevention* (pp. 341–374). New York: Plenum Press.

Vogel, J., & Vernberg, E. M. (1993). Psychological needs of children in the aftermath of disasters: Children's responses to disasters and intervention strategies with children after disasters. *Journal of Clinical Child Psychology, 22,* 485–498.

Wolfe, T. (1952). *Look homeward angel.* New York: Charles Scribner.

Yule, W., & Williams, R. M. (1990). Post-traumatic stress reactions in children. *Journal of Traumatic Stress, 3,* 279–295.

5

Structured Short-Term Play Therapy for Children with Attention-Deficit/ Hyperactivity Disorder

HEIDI GERARD KADUSON

INTRODUCTION

Attention-deficit/hyperactivity disorder (ADHD) is one of the most researched childhood disorders. Numerous types of therapies have attempted to manage this condition with limited success. Play therapy has been a successful technique because it involves the child in the process while it teaches the clients life management techniques.

Childhood cognitive and behavioral problems categorized as disorders of attention, impulsiveness, and hyperactivity present a challenge for the play therapist. These problems constitute the most common chronic behavioral disorder (Wender, 1987) and the largest single source of referrals to adolescent mental health centers (Barkley, 1990). The cluster of problems includes inattention, excessive stimulation, hyperactivity, impulsiveness, irritability, and inability to delay gratification. These conditions are diagnostically referred to as attention-deficit/hyperactivity disorder (American Psychiatric Association, 1994), one of the most complex disorders of childhood. These problems affect children's interactions within their own environment and result in an inability to meet situational demands in an age-appropriate manner (Routh, 1978). Children with

ADHD typically experience behavior difficulties at home, in school, and within their community. Peer interaction, academic achievement, and overall adjustment are affected. Children with ADHD are frequently enigmatic to their parents and teachers. Their sporadic, unpredictable behavior creates additional stress, leading to the erroneous belief that these are problems of motivation and desire rather than physically driven disabilities.

ADHD symptoms typically cause significant pervasive impairment to a child's daily environmental interaction. Although this condition begins at birth, prognosis at an early age is impossible. The familial, social, and academic demands placed on children are determined primarily by the adults in their lives (Goldstein & Goldstein, 1990). While adults can minimize the negative impact of these problems on their lives, children cannot do so. They feel different and do not understand the reason. ADHD appears to impact significantly the child's emerging personality and cognitive skills. These skills deficits result in negative feedback in various areas of their environment. For example, the child may feel he or she never does anything right, sense the family's displeasure with negatively exhibited behavior, and experience unreciprocated positive relationships while feeling helpless to remedy the situation. Skills deficits result in years of suffering negative feedback and lack of positive reinforcement, as well as an inability to meet the reasonable demands of family, friends, and teachers. As a result, the child is affected for life. Play therapists must be concerned with both the core symptoms of this disorder and the significant secondary impact they have on the child and associated family members.

ADHD confronts many practitioners, including physicians, psychologists, educators, social workers, speech pathologists, and play therapists. For years, each discipline worked in isolation, developing its own set of definitions and ideas for assessment and intervention. The short-term approach introduced in this chapter is a combination of various techniques with multimodal approaches to give the ADHD child the most effective treatment possible.

This multimodal approach requires parental education regarding facts about ADHD and prognosis whenever possible, parent training on a weekly basis, medication referrals when necessary, classroom intervention, social skills training, and individual play therapy. These approaches help the child take ownership of the disorder and develop coping skills.

In this structured, short-term approach, parents of the child become cotherapists, capable of continuing treatment when the short-term intervention is completed. For a variety of reasons, this is not always possible. It is imperative to educate parents about the significance of their participation. When a child is referred, the therapist is frequently confronted with complex problems that are further complicated by a variety of social and nonsocial problems.

Parental Issues

It is extremely important to realize that parents of children with ADHD are dealing with several issues at the same time. First, they have to mourn the loss of the "normal" child. This is a process that requires support and guidance. Although the child's physical appearance is normal, a good deal of the child's behavior is not. Paralyzed children require a wheelchair for mobility and are not expected to walk. Children with ADHD possess a behavior disorder—a conceptual "wheelchair" mandatory that keeps the brain from functioning in a normal fashion. Therefore, one cannot expect the child to behave.

The therapist might encounter a variety of issues when dealing with parents. These include denial and false hopes. Parents must recognize that ADHD is not a temporary problem that the child will outgrow. They must be trained effectively to improve their child's behavior. This process is quite possible. Therapists should advise parents to maintain a realistic attitude and stay open-minded to additional approaches. Difficulties prevail with a child with ADHD, but there are numerous coping techniques. Parents need to be open to all possible strategies to treat ADHD (medication, child and associated family therapy, and communication with school personnel). Parents must learn all they can about ADHD in order to teach coping skills to other family members. In addition, the therapist should teach child development skills to parents in order to help them adjust their expectations of the child with ADHD.

Parents of children with ADHD should understand that feelings of guilt and inadequacy are natural. They must accept negative and ambivalent feelings, and gain a better perspective of the child by avoiding perfection as a goal. The child must be educated to accept this as well. Working to accept mistakes and exercising the courage to be imperfect will help parents to function effectively in the face of daily problems. Therapists must try to help parents recognize and appreciate small gains and improvements in the child's behavior to develop a stronger parent–child relationship. Unconditional love should be displayed toward the child at all times and not just as a reward for positive behavior. Parents should learn to create situations for positive interaction with the child. These productive steps should incorporate positive feedback for the parents, resulting in a stronger sense of confidence and self-worth. Parents of children with ADHD tend to be excessively critical of themselves as people. The therapist should continue to stress to parents the importance of self-appreciation of themselves as people and not just as parents.

Another prevalent issue with the current population of parents is their tendency toward overinvolvement. When the child neglects to follow through with chores, and so on, parents tend to take on the responsibility for life experiences. Instead, they should back off somewhat and enjoy sharing in the child's life experience. Allowing the child the freedom to accomplish something on his or her own produces a sense of competency that cannot otherwise be taught. Once the child assumes responsibility for experiencing his or her own life, the parents should express faith in the child's ability to handle difficult situations. If problems occur, parents can *assist* children in generating solutions to these difficulties rather than solving them for the child. It is beneficial for the child to deal with the natural consequences of his or her behavior to a certain degree. Displaying sympathy for the child causes the child to experience negative feelings about his or her own situation. Parents must strive to overcome feelings of pity for their child. It is vital for them not to dramatize the situation, and to organize events in the proper perspective in order to help the child to handle difficult situations more effectively.

The therapist must remember parents of children with ADHD have many fears and worries. Some will ask for guarantees that they are not raising a juvenile delinquent. While guarantees cannot be made, the therapist can teach parents to distinguish between concern (a warm expression of interest in potentially dangerous or stressful situations) and worry (a weak, nonproductive state of anxiety about someone's ability to contend with difficulties). Concern may be helpful; worry is not. Guide parents to analyze situations to determine the best course of action. Past experiences cannot be changed, so parents should concentrate on the future.

Parents of children with ADHD experience ridicule and criticism from people with no exposure to the condition. Therapists can help parents understand that there may be some credibility in the advice they receive from others. They should anticipate the advice and consider it harmless. Usually, they have heard these opinions before, and while they may not be constructive, they are well intended. Parents may misinterpret the advice as criticism. Guide parents to sift through the words of advice to discover substance. This process will alleviate resentment and defensiveness. Advise parents to accept suggestions based on empathy and insight, and ignore all others.

Parents will come into your office full of anger and resentment. They never expected to give birth to or adopt a child with ADHD. They can spend a lifetime questioning why it happened, but there will be no answer. Help parents avoid anger displacement toward others, especially the child with ADHD. No one can force another person to feel angry. People *choose* to feel and express anger. When parents acknowledge this fact, the power to control and channel their anger is possible. It is also important for parents to realize that anger is a secondary reaction to some other primary emotions such as stress, disappointment, anguish, and sadness. It is more productive to decrease the effects of the primary emotion rather than the anger. When embarrassment transforms to anger because of a misbehaving child, parents should not attempt to control their child. In addition, they must not fault themselves for the child's negative behavior, which is not a reflection of the parents' personal worth or value as parents. "I" statements can help parents locate the source of their anger. In many instances, the anger is self-directed against what they consider to be ineffective and impulsive behavior. Have them explore and discuss their frustration. Educate them to differentiate between their relationship with the child and their reaction to the child's behavior. Usually, the behavior is ADHD related and may not be intentional. The source of the primary distress is the disorder, not the child. Parents should look beyond the behavior to the child's experiences and provide unconditional support.

Parents must be prepared to accept the toll that years of living with ADHD will have on their child as an adult. There are a number of general variables that predict adult outcomes. These predictors are generally independent of specific types of childhood problems.

SOCIOECONOMIC STATUS

The higher the parents' socioeconomic status, the better a child's chances. These parents are more likely to be aware of behavior problems, may receive better pre- and postnatal care, and may be more likely to be able to afford professional help.

INTELLIGENCE

Higher intelligence levels can help children with ADHD compensate for their distraction and lack of self-control. However, the gifted child with ADHD seems to live with the burden of feeling that he or she should know something more but cannot retrieve, visualize, or define it. In general, anyone with a higher intelligence level makes a better adjustment to adult life.

AGGRESSIVENESS

Often, the controlling attitude of the child with ADHD will moderate as years pass. However, aggression is closely related to parenting style and socioeconomic status (Conners & Wells, 1986). One of the best single predictors of antisocial behavior and poorly adjusted emotional status in adolescence is a history of aggressive behavior in younger childhood (Loney, 1980). It is a very stable characteristic, and once established, it is very difficult to extinguish.

ACTIVITY LEVEL

Certain studies have suggested that there is an inverse relationship between the degree of hyperactive behavior in elementary school and academic achievement in high school. The more hyperactive the elementary school child, the more likely high school achievement will be negatively affected

(Loney, Kramer, & Milich, 1981). However, since nonhyperactive children with ADHD are easier to control, they may slip through the cracks of the educational system; therefore, they are not likely to be seen at an earlier age.

SOCIAL SKILLS

Milich and Landau (1981), have reported that the best single predictor of adequate emotional adjustment in adulthood is the ability to develop and maintain positive social contacts and friendships during childhood. While many children with ADHD have social problems, children who have a history of positive social interaction frequently adapt better to their attentional handicap and to daily frustrations in the home and at school.

DELAY OF GRATIFICATION

It is suggested that children who are more competent at delaying rewards tend to develop into adolescents who perform more effectively on intelligence tests, resist potentially problematic temptation more successfully, demonstrate more appropriate social skills, and have higher achievement desires (Mischel, Shoda, & Rodriguez, 1989). Certainly this delay can be taught, but it is not intrinsic in many children with ADHD.

FAMILY MENTAL HEALTH

In many families of children with ADHD, one of the parents exhibits the syndrome. Families with multiple generations of ADHD tend to be difficult to treat in therapy. While they certainly want their child to change his or her behavior, their follow-through is weak. Sometimes they lack the skills, persistence, and ability to stick with therapy and a treatment program. A history of psychiatric problems in a family increases the likelihood that the child with ADHD will be presented with a similar or related set of problems in adulthood (Weiss & Hechtman, 1986).

Acquainting parents with these predictors can assist in motivating them. It is rare for a child not to exhibit some of these variables that predict positive outcomes in adulthood.

STRUCTURED SHORT-TERM PLAY THERAPY APPROACH

The basic assumption of this program is that children with ADHD need intensive treatment in order to learn skills to manage their world better and enhance relationships with others. In this managed health care, it is important to find ways to help the child with ADHD within a short-term format. This multimodal approach includes the combined use of play therapy and participation by school personnel and parents to create a more rounded treatment protocol. Empirical research has revealed that children who participate in a multidisciplinary intervention program demonstrate better adjustment than children receiving no intervention or singular intervention (Satterfield, Satterfield, & Cantwell, 1981).

The following 10-week program presents the treatment protocol. This protocol includes meeting with the parents separately for 15 minutes, and then meeting with the child separately in the playroom for 35 minutes or the balance of the 50-minute session. The procedure is very direct and teaches both parents and child improved ways of handling ADHD.

The treatment focuses on the primary components of ADHD, namely, attention (short attention span, approximately one-third of agemates; Barkley 1990), hyperactivity (restlessness, fidgeting, difficulty staying seated, etc.), and impulsiveness (acting before thinking, poor planning ability, and low frustration tolerance, etc.). Treatment goals focus building children's self-confidence in specific areas of deficiency, increasing their ability to stay focused on tasks, encouraging them to demonstrate self-control, and teaching them to consider consequences before acting.

Session 1: Intake

Probably one of the most important aspects of treatment is the process of the intake session. The therapist should take a complete family developmental history. Appendix 5.1 displays a genogram that is used at the time of intake. Asking the names and ages of everyone is also important. In a classic interview, one would ask the names and ages of the child's siblings, parents, grandparents, aunts, uncles, and cousins. Once the information is obtained, the following questions are asked of maternal and paternal relatives:

- Has there been any drug or alcohol abuse?
- Has there been any physical or sexual abuse?
- Has anyone had emotional disorders—diagnosed or otherwise?
- Has anyone had any learning problems or attention-deficit disorders?

In most cases, one or more of the foregoing scenarios have occurred. In the case of an adopted child, there may not be any biological history available. The therapist should seek out this information, because it gives insight into the parents' upbringing, any learning disabilities, and their importance in the treatment protocol.

Discipline is an important part of parenting, and the therapist needs to explore (nonjudgmentally) disciplinary techniques in the home. Time-out, spankings, yelling, and so on, tend not to work with the child with ADHD. Once disciplinary techniques are established, the therapist should determine from the parents if these methods are successful.

The therapist must obtain specific information about the child:

- *School, teacher, grade, academic problems.* Determine learning problems (mathematics, reading) and homework issues, and so on.
- *Biological habits.* Establish if there are sleep disorder problems (trouble falling asleep, staying asleep, or nightmares, etc.), eating pattern problems (finicky eater, overeater, etc.), unusual toilet patterns (late toilet training, bed-wetting, primary or secondary enuresis, encopresis, etc.), or self-care issues (dressing self, brushing teeth, etc.).
- *Social problems.* Determine relationships in the child's environment (inability to make or maintain friendships, controlling play, etc.).
- *Gross motor abilities.* Gather insight into the child's physical abilities (sports oriented, fear of sports or organized sports, problems riding a bike, etc.).
- *Fine motor abilities.* Gather insight into the child's finer physical skills (trouble drawing and/or writing, pencil grasp, etc.).

After obtaining this information, the therapist conducts a play history with the parents. Appendix 5.2 is a Play History Questionnaire that reveals some of the questions the therapist might ask to determine the child's response in the playroom and in other parts of the treatment protocol.

The parents are then given the following rating scales to obtain baseline data on the child.

CONNERS PARENT RATING SCALE

This scale, developed by Conners (1989), is the most widely used rating scale of parental opinion concerning ADHD (Barkley, 1990). It lists 48 items that rate the child using descriptors such as excitability, impulsiveness, excessive crying, restlessness, inability to complete tasks, and so on. The scale is simple for parents to complete. The items are rated on a 4-point scale (0 = *Not at all*, 1 = *Just a little*, 2 = *Pretty much*, 3 = *Very much*).

ACHENBACH CHILD BEHAVIOR CHECKLIST

This scale, created by Thomas M. Achenbach (1978), was revised in 1982. While this is a more lengthy scale of 113 items, it helps with differential diagnoses since it asks questions regarding internalizing (depressed, anxious) or externalizing (hyperactive, aggressive) behaviors. Parents rate their child's behavior on a 3-point scale (0 = *Not true*; 1 = *Somewhat, or sometimes true*; 2 = *Very true, or often true*).

HOME SITUATIONS QUESTIONNAIRE

This questionnaire was developed by Russell Barkley (1987) as a means of assessing the impact of the child's attentional and related deficits on home and community-based situations. This also gives the therapist qualitative data, as opposed to quantitative data, to use in the assessment of the child.

CHILD AND FAMILY INTERVIEW QUESTIONNAIRE

Appendix 5.3 displays the questionnaire that is given to parents to take home to complete. It gives a more detailed accounting of the child's developmental history and family problems. This reduces the time needed by the therapist to obtain this information, and allows parents time to analyze occurrences within the family that are the result of the child's participation.

Session 2: Child Intake

In the second session, the child is seen alone. The therapist greets the child in the waiting room and asks if he or she wants to play in the playroom. The child most likely will enter the playroom without hesitation. If the child is cautious, the parents can walk him or her to the door, where the therapist engages the child in conversation, and the parents depart.

In the first part of the session, the child draws a person. If the child has fine motor problems and cannot draw, this part must be eliminated. While the child draws, the therapist can praise the work or ask questions regarding the picture ("How old is this person?," "What is this person doing?," "Does this person go to school or work?," "What does this person like to do best?," or "What does this person like the least?," etc.). Since the first drawing of a person is usually representative of the child, the therapist can thus gather information without directly asking the child.

After the "person" drawing exercise, the therapist asks the child to draw a house and tree. According to Lord (1985), the following questions can be asked at this time:

1. What's the one special thing about this house?
2. What's the worst thing about this house?
3. What kind of tree is this?
4. What's the one thing you would change about the house?
5. Is there a scary place in this house?

The last drawing would be of the entire family. The child is asked the following questions about the drawing of a family (Lord, 1985):

1. What is each family member's name?
2. What is this family doing?
3. What is the one best thing about this family?
4. What is the one bad thing about this family?
5. Does this family have any secrets?
6. What kinds of things does this family do together?
7. Who is the favorite person in this family?
8. How does everyone get along?

It is important to keep all questions in the third person, which is less threatening to the child. If there is no answer to a question, the therapist should just move on to the next question.

Following the drawings, a Puppet Sentence-Completion Test (Knell, 1993) is given. Many children with ADHD find this to be fun and will participate willingly. The therapist allows the child to choose a puppet. Then, the therapist chooses two puppets, one for each hand. Puppet A and Puppet B are on the therapist's hands, and Puppet C is on the child's hand. After puppets A and B state their names, the child is prompted to have Puppet C give its name. After these introductions, several nonthreatening stems are presented. When the child understands the task, more stems are presented to access the child's thinking on various issues ("I am saddest when . . . ," "I am happiest when . . . ," etc.). The stems can be modified to fit each client's issues based on the initial input from the parents ("I get yelled at when . . . ," "I need more self-control when . . . ").

It is important to perform a play observation with the child to analyze his or her interaction style with play materials. During this free, unstructured play session, the therapist notes the child's attitude and approach toward the toys, any response latency, frequent changes, creativity, aggressive style, or inability to play without structure. It is important to determine if the child's play age is appropriate for the diagnostic criteria, since children with ADHD tend to play at a more immature level than their peers. The therapist should determine if there are any repetitious themes in the play, and whether the child has trouble initiating or finalizing play.

The last portion of the session is structured with several games to check the child's ego stability, concentration, self-control, and auditory processing. Guess Who is a very useful tool in assessing the child's ability. Many children with ADHD respond impulsively to board games and will not wait for the answer to the question before proceeding. The therapist can intervene and assist the child when that occurs. However, during the assessment process, it is better to allow the child to continue to play without intervening.

The games Trouble and Sorry measure the child's response in taking turns, winning, and losing. Once again, it is best not to intervene during the intake session. Gathering the information will help focus on therapy for its short-term course.

Session 3: Meeting with the Parents

When meeting with the parents, several important factors must be noted. The therapist must keep parents focused on the personal training in order to achieve the skills necessary to manage their child. Parents may insist that the therapist recommend another type of punishment because previous methods have been unsuccessful. The therapist should emphasize that parents know best which disciplinary actions work best. The positive parenting program is recommended, because it focuses on positive reinforcement, which encourages better behavior and stronger relationships.

The therapist should teach the parents the four reasons children misbehave (Barkley, 1990) and present to them a Characteristic Sheet, which requires them to respond to the following topics about their child and themselves:

- Activity level
- Attention span
- Stimulation response
- Impulsiveness
- Emotional response
- Sociability
- Habit consistency
- Physical characteristics
- Developmental abilities

While parents cannot change the "wiring" of the child (Reason 1), the "wiring" of themselves (Reason 2), or family stresses (Reason 3), they do have the ability to change the learning history of the child and parent (Reason 4). Behavior patterns that have developed over time can be changed by focusing on the positive.

"The Good Behavior Book" is then presented (Kaduson, 1993). This is a stenographer's pad in which the parents record all of their child's good behavior. All good behavior is defined as behavior that is not "bad." The therapist illustrates using a sample page and tells the parents to verbalize and record behaviors such as "got up, undressed, put on underwear, put on shirt, put on shorts, put on socks, put on shoes, went to bathroom, combed hair," and so on. Positive behavior is communicated and listed on a separate line, so that by the end of the day, a full page of good behaviors has been recorded. Each entry should be only two to four words. The parent recording this information should share it with the significant other in the child's life, either after school or at dinnertime. "You won't believe the day Joey had today! He got up. He got undressed!" Whenever possible, children should overhear the parents praising their positive behavior, which will reinforce its importance. More sharing and positive reinforcement occur at bedtime, when the parent again reads the book outlining the positive behaviors of the day. The parents know the child is hooked when he or she makes a statement such as "I picked up my clothes. Did you write that in the book?"

Session 3: Meeting with the Child

In the playroom, the therapist should have the child play the *Feeling Word Game* (Kaduson, 1993). The therapist needs four pieces of 8½" × 11" blank paper—torn in half to create eight pieces, a marker, and a bag of bingo chips. Then the child is asked, "What feelings does a [age of child] have?" Each feeling is written on a piece of paper and placed in front of the child. A feeling word poster should be placed on the wall so that the child can refer to it. Many times, children resist contributing specific words. In order for the therapist to model this technique, basic feeling words such as "happy," "sad," "mad," and "scared" must be introduced. If the child does not produce these, the therapist asks "Do you think they would be happy?" This allows the therapist to write the word on the list.

Once all the feelings are listed, the therapist tells a personal, nonthreatening story that produces several of the feelings listed by the child. After telling the story, the therapist discloses that the bag of Bingo chips is a bag of feelings, and discusses feelings about the story being told. For example:

> "I went to the mall to get my favorite book. I got the book and then came outside and my car was missing.
> "I might feel happy because I got the book I wanted. But I might also feel scared because my car was missing, and mad because someone might have taken it. I could have different feelings all at the same time, and different amounts of those feelings [represented by the amount of Bingo chips put down].
> "Now let me tell you a story and you put your feelings down."

The therapist should tell a nonthreatening story that includes both negative and positive feelings represented by the child's list of feeling words. After the child sets down the Bingo chips, the therapist explores the associated feelings.

The last part of this process requires the child to tell a story while the therapist associates feelings with Bingo chips. This story project is a valuable therapy tool that can be repeated several times to encourage verbal expression of what is in the child's unconscious mind.

The second process introduces the Beat the Clock game (Kaduson, 1993), in which the child is taught to focus on a project without interruption, to increase his or her attention span. The therapist gives the child 10 poker chips, a paper to color, and the following instructions:

> "We are going to play the Beat the Clock game. I am giving you 10 poker chips. You must keep your eyes on your work for 2 minutes" (or whatever the baseline attention span is of the child), "without looking up and without paying attention to anything else. If you do that, you will earn an additional 10 chips. If you look up, however, I will have to take a chip away. After we have done this three times, and you have accumulated 25 chips" (allowing for five mistakes), "you can pick from the treasure box" (simple, inexpensive toys from a dollar store or warehouse sale).

The child must be successful in all the techniques and interventions performed in the play session. The Beat the Clock session is timed by wristwatch, so that if the child is having significant difficulty, the therapist can shorten the time and begin again. After successful completion of the game, the child can choose from the treasure box immediately.

The last part of the session is a strategic board game. Suggestions include Trouble, Sorry, Connect Four or checkers, all commercially available games. During these games, the therapist performs all the moves while discussing strategy out loud. This allows the child to observe the therapist problem solving, taking turns, decision making, and using strategies to win. Once the child is willing, the therapist helps him or her make appropriate strategic moves and learn the "stop and think" method.

Session 4: Meeting with the Parents

This session reviews "The Good Behavior Book" and corrects inappropriate entries. These would be negative statements. "He didn't hit his sister," would be replaced with "kind to his sister." Since the book is read to the child, only positive statements are helpful. The next portion of parent training involves a nondirect, client-centered approach to playtime. While this is certainly not as extensive as filial therapy (Van Fleet, 1994), this training teaches parents to play with their child without giving directions, making demands, or initiating commands. The therapist can demonstrate this technique to the parents by allowing them to play on the floor while he or she therapist models the tracking of the play skills. This is a difficult task, and the parents should know this, so that their expectations are not unrealistic. It is helpful if they spend 15 minutes per day doing this special play. The only question asked is "What do you want to play?" The parents can guide the child to figures, dolls, blocks, drawings, and so forth. This will promote creative play by the child so that the parent can narrate.

During this session, parents are taught the Beat the Clock game so that they can start playing it at home.

Session 4: Meeting with the Child

The therapist reads "The Good Behavior Book" to the child, with heavy emphasis on how terrific the behavior has been. The child is asked whether it is hard to display good behavior all the time. Whatever response is given, the therapist guides the child into another Feeling Word Game with different stories based on the initial intake and information provided by parents via subsequent telephone calls.

The next technique introduced to the child is the "garbage bag technique." The child and the therapist have a brown paper sandwich-type bag, and both begin drawing whatever they want on the outside. While drawing, the therapist describes how garbage is gathered in the house, the smell and look of the garbage, and the growths all over the garbage; hooking the child on the subject. The therapist dramatizes:

> "Garbage uncollected would gather into huge piles. These piles would be so heavy they would have to be carried around on people's backs from our house to our friend's house, from home to school, and so on. If we could never dispose of the garbage, we would always have to worry about where to store it."

This metaphor is then compared to the type of garbage that people carry around:

> "Garbage is all that yucky stuff that we think about all the time, that bothers us when we try to go to sleep, that interferes with our thinking pleasant, happy thoughts. So let's get some of that garbage out of ourselves and stick it in the garbage bag."

The child is then given four slips of paper to jot down personal "garbage"—one item per piece of paper. The therapist writes four items as well, and they both place the papers into the garbage bag and close it. These remain with the therapist for each subsequent meeting.

The Beat the Clock game is played again, increasing the time to 5 minutes that the child does not look up. Prior to the start of the game, the child is given the instructions and rules again. Three trials are played again. The child is told that this game will be played at home also.

The end of the session is given to playing Rebound, a game of self-control. The competitive nature of the child with ADHD is directed toward teaching self-control capabilities in order to win the game. Throwing the game pieces quickly will result in a loss, but demonstrating self-control will result in a win. The therapist must play this game well enough to win or lose at will. The object is to keep the game relatively even until the last move.

Session 5: Parents and Commands

In this session, review of special playtime between parents and child is conducted to determine any problems. Parents are helped to understand the needs of the child and to create positive interaction scenarios as examples. After review, parents are taught how to give effective commands. Many parents of children with ADHD have been "asking" the child to do chores, rather than commanding. When parents ask the child to perform a task, he or she may assume that "no" is an acceptable response. Some parents believe that "commanding" violates proper etiquette because it is discourteous. When parents give effective commands to children with ADHD, they help them by utilizing the following specific guidelines:

1. Present the command directly and effectively, not as a question or favor.
2. Give one command at a time.
3. Follow through is necessary. Consequences, either negative or positive, should be presented to the child.
4. Be sure to have the child's attention. There should be no distractions. Sometimes it may be necessary to gently turn the child's face toward the parent's face.
5. When comprehension is questionable, have the child repeat the command.

The parents practice giving three "easy" commands per day to the child. Each time the child completes the command, the parent replies, "I love when you do what I ask." Some easy commands include "Pass the fork," "Hand me the napkin," and so on.

Parents are asked for one behavior that they would like to see changed, and the therapist contracts with the child to accomplish this choice. This concept teaches children the meaning of contracting with their parents and how to have successful results. Therefore, if a parent says, "He should behave in the morning," this is not operationally definable as one behavior, but as many. Parents should be taught to choose "one" behavior for contracting.

Session 5: Contracting with the Child

Read "The Good Behavior Book," reemphasizing all of the pages listing the child's good behavior. This process serves as a segue to the contracting procedure. The therapist tells the child about the reward system and the potential to earn a toy. If the child is interested in earning a toy (almost always a positive response), the therapist draws a contract with the child.

"Sample Contract"

Joey will brush his teeth every
morning without complaints or reminders, and
[therapist's name] will give him a
package of baseball cards.

Both the therapist and the child sign the contract, and each keeps a copy.

The therapist and child review special playtime. The child's perspective and feedback are very important to determine if the play is successful. Following this review, the child picks one piece of personal "garbage" from the garbage bag. The therapist should be prepared to help play out (either through role play or miniatures) the problems in the "bag." By helping the child play out the problem, solutions are explored utilizing the child's experience. It is nonthreatening for the child to play out problems "as if" they are real. The therapist remains focused and helps the child work through solutions to these problems utilizing dolls or other toy choices.

After playing out one problem, the therapist directs the child to play Beat the Clock again for a prize. The time is increased by 2 minutes. The directions for a game need to be reiterated at the onset (even if the child claims ability).

Following this game, the therapist and child finish the session playing another self-control game (Trouble, Sorry, pick-up sticks, Connect Four, checkers). The therapist models moves using verbal descriptions. The child listens attentively and pays more attention to the therapist's moves than to his or her own. Additionally, the child models the therapist.

Session 6: Train Parents to Focus on Child

Review of the compliance training should be accomplished first to see if any problems exist. Working through the parental issues will help with further parental compliance.

The next training segment teaches parents to pay attention to their children when they are *not* bothering them. In the case of children with ADHD, the more attention given to them, the more positive behavior will be exhibited. Therefore, when the child is doing exactly what the parent wants, the parent is to reward him or her with hugs, praise, a soft touch, or other positive feedback. Parents must be reminded to make the time to focus wholeheartedly on the child's independent play. As a result, parents will notice longer stretches of positive behavior by their child, resulting in fewer interruptions. The parents should test this new behavior while pretending to read a book, talk on the telephone, and so on).

The therapist has another item to add to the child's contract, thereby increasing compliance and positive feelings in the child.

Session 6: Continue Positive Feedback with the Child

Read "The Good Behavior Book" first and then review the contract item. In most cases, the child has accomplished the initial task and will be excited to receive his or her prize.

The child then takes another piece of "garbage" out of the garbage bag and plays out solutions to that problem. The therapist once again directs the play either through miniatures or role play. In directive play therapy, the therapist remains active in the play to help the child resolve psychological problems.

By this session, the Beat the Clock game is played again, with a 5-minute increase. Each week, the child will be able to focus more on independent work, and homework should now be the focus. As the therapist holds the timer, repeats instructions, and administers praise for concentration and successful focus, the child feels successful and deserving of the prize.

This session ends with a game to teach self-control as well as "closing down" the child regarding underlying "garbage" issues.

Session 7: Parental Review and Feedback

Review of the homework assigned to the parents in the previous week is performed by the therapist while reemphasizing the lessons. The therapist must keep the parents focused on the training and not allow them to discuss every problem encountered during the week. This enables them to practice the positive parenting approach while deemphasizing the punishment routines that have been set in motion as a regular course of business in the household. For children with ADHD, the punishment does not help to stop the behavior. Punishments only engage the parent and child in negative interactions. However, it is recognized that praise and attention alone are rarely sufficient to motivate better compliance in children with ADHD. The therapist requires the parents to implement a highly effective motivational program that enlists a variety of rewards and incentives easily accomplished at home. This "token" reward system encourages compliance with commands, rules, codes of social conduct, and school behavior. For children ages 4 through 10, poker chips are used as the tokens. Older children may use a bank book format that utilizes debits and credits.

A sample of the token economy system is illustrated in Appendix 5.4. The parents list five "easy" tasks worth 1 to 5 chips per chore, five "moderate" tasks worth 5 to 10 chips, and three "difficult" tasks, worth 25 chips per successful completion. These tasks and concepts can be taken from "The Good Behavior Book." The therapist guides the parents through this process by researching the repetitive behaviors (easy), the rare behaviors (moderate), and those not yet discussed (difficult). The "buying chart," which monitors the child's earnings from good behavioral accomplishments, must now also monitor spending for activities such as a half-hour of television viewing. Most children enjoy control of the chips and seek to earn more and more so they can buy what they want. The premise is to have the child spend 80% of the chips earned for desired activities and save 20% of the chips for a longer-term reward. The child should save for at least a week or two. Even if the children have never saved money before, they may hold all their chips for a long-term (delay of gratification) reward.

After establishing the token economy concept during the office session, the therapist allows the parents and child to finish it together at home. This creates a more effective goal-setting system.

The parents' portion of this session takes about one half of the session this week. However, the therapist will motivate the child to earn 100 or more chips to win a prize, as part of the therapist–child contract.

Session 7 with Child: Introduction of Token Economy

This week is the last time "The Good Behavior Book" is read. The therapist introduces the token economy concept using a very positive format. The child is, in most cases, very willing to participate at this time. The therapist signs another contract with the child, adding to the original contract a requirement that the child must earn 100 or more chips during the week to earn a prize.

After signing the contract, the child chooses the last piece of "garbage" out of his bag and plays it out with the therapist, who actively helps either to solve the problem or teach coping skills during this play time.

The Beat the Clock game is played using homework for at least 10 minutes. These games are practiced at home, and the child becomes very proficient at increasing his or her attention span by the seventh week of treatment.

If a child has trouble falling asleep at night (this information was obtained during the intake), the Bubble Blowing Game is introduced. This game teaches the child the art of deep breathing using a fun format so that the body relaxes before bed, during homework, or while taking a test. The therapist uses two bottles of bubbles: one for the child and one for the therapist. The therapist models how to blow bubbles; if one takes a short breath and blows fast, there will be no bubbles; if one takes a deep breath and blows fast, there are many bubbles; but if one takes a deep breath and blows slowly, then one can blow a very big bubble. The object of the game is to compete with the child five successive times to determine who can blow the biggest bubble. The therapist encourages the child to use deep breathing to blow the biggest bubble. They practice this technique during the session, and the child takes the bubbles home so that parents and child can practice the game five times before bed each night. (If the therapist believes that there will be a problem getting this accomplished, it can be added to the behavioral contract).

Session 8: Parent Feedback

The token economy is reviewed to determine any problems, and the therapist helps the parents modify the program to work better.

During this session, the concept of time-out is explored with the parents. This is the first week that a negative reinforcement will be performed. Time-out should be used sparingly—usually, only when a child is violent or swears. If parents were to use the time-out procedure for all instances of noncompliance, the child with ADHD would spend the majority of the day in the time-out room! It is recommended that the time-out location be chosen by the parents, and that the same place be used every time. Many parents use the bedroom. This is sufficient so long as it does not have luxuries that would be attractive to the child. A bathroom (with all items removed) or a utility room is more aversive and still safe. Time-out is done for 1 minute per year of life, and the timing is performed by an electronic or kitchen timer. The child needs to be quiet before coming out of time-out. The therapist can guide the parents in the proper use of this method. If the parents have been compliant during the weeks of parent training, most of the aversive behaviors have been reduced, so that time-out is not abused.

Session 8: Child Feedback

The poker chips are counted and the child reports all good behaviors. Many children remember all of the positive things they have accomplished, because the chip rewards are highly motivational. This session focuses on the child's successes, and a board game about the child is created. Appendix 5.5 is a sample of the board game. The therapist and child document all the successes the child has experienced both in the playroom and at home. The therapist guides the child to create squares, and the child writes each success inside the square. If there are still problem behavior areas, they can also be listed on the game board as reminders. For example:

> In square two, Joey brushes his teeth without complaints—go ahead two. In Space 5, Joey gets dressed by himself—go ahead three spaces. In Space 7, Joey is late for the bus—go back two spaces, and so on.

Session 9: Releasing the Child into the Parents' Care

This session is used to empower the parents to take over management of the child in all respects. By this time, they have attained the skills needed to manage their child. They may feel cautious and want to stay in therapy, but it is helpful to assure them that they can manage on their own now. Several successes have been demonstrated by the parents. The therapist reiterates those in detail (keeping "The Good Behavior Book," having special playtime with the child, giving better commands, and following through). The parents are also ready to take over contracting with the child. While there is no one answer to ADHD, they now have the ability to engage with school personnel because of the training and education they have received in therapy.

The therapist should also issue parents a Conners' Parent Rating Scale and an Achenbach Child Behavior Checklist to see posttreatment measures. This is helpful if the client returns at any time, since it measures their ratings as they change over time.

Parents should be advised to examine their own behavior if their child seems to be regressing. The therapist recalls the reasons for misbehavior, and how the parents' focus may have changed during a family stressor. The importance of positive parenting to maintain the child's compliance and self-esteem is reemphasized.

Session 9: Releasing the Child

The ninth session focuses on termination. The child will feel some loss when play therapy in the office is discontinued. The therapist must empower the child by completing the Board Game, and they play the game during this session. Emphasis is on the child's accomplishments. Any new adjustments can be managed using the same techniques the child learned during the therapeutic relationship (staying on task; problem-solving one thing at a time; self-control; stopping, thinking, and then acting; increased concentration with a motivator, etc.).

In the last portion of the session a "List of Good Me" is created with the therapist's help. The therapist asks the child if he or she is a good swimmer; then, the therapist lists "good swimmer"; if the child is a good friend, the therapist lists "good friend." This "List of Good Me" is typed, laminated, and given to the child during the last session.

Session 10: Termination of the Parents and Child

The therapist invites the parents and child into the room together. They talk about only the good changes that have occurred in the family. Credit is given to the parents and the child for their active participation in all the changes. A Drawing Game then begins, in which all the parties, including the therapist, sit around a table and participate in the termination drawing.

On a piece of 11″ × 17″ paper, the therapist starts drawing while discussing all of the wonderful successes in the family. Then, each person draws individually for 3 minutes, then passes the markers to the next person. For a family in which mother and father are both present, this requires approximately 12–15 minutes. A theme is not necessary, but the therapist may draw a picture in which a rainbow shows a transition from pretherapy to this final session. The child follows that theme while the parents draw whatever they desire. It is the last positive interaction involving the therapist. After this meeting, the family continues independently to produce successes.

The child is given the "List of Good Me" and the Board Game produced by the therapist and the child. These transitional objects are left with the child to reinforce successes and accomplishments during times of doubt. The "List of Good Me" or the Board Game can be revisited with the parents.

CASE ILLUSTRATION

Rita P, a 9-year-old girl, was referred for treatment by her school and parents. They were not able to handle her noncompliance, hyperactivity, and impulsiveness. School personnel were complaining about her lack of attention and incomplete, late work.

Session 1: Intake

At the intake session, several important points were brought up. Since Rita was the oldest of two children (her younger sister was 6 years old), the family had spent an excessive amount of time involved in Rita's life. To avoid Rita's temper tantrums over daily personal hygiene routines, her parents dressed her each day. All of the negative attention had encouraged and increased Rita's negative behavior, which was mimicked by her younger sibling. Family history showed learning problems in two cousins, and Mr. P thought that he had been hyperactive when he was young. He had been physically punished as a child and did not want to do the same to Rita. Therefore, while there was a lot of arguing, there was little follow through from either parent. Rita was taking 10 mg of Ritalin two times per day, and the family could not manage her before the medicine took effect or after it wore off.

Both parents attended the intake session and were very open about their problems with Rita. While they were angry about her behavior, they were not placing blame on each other. They were advised to read several books on ADHD, specifically, *Taking Charge of ADHD* by Russell A. Barkley (1995). After explaining the motivation for ADHD children's misbehavior, they seemed to understand how they lost control of Rita. They were given all of the rating scales to complete before the next session. Both Mr. and Mrs. P started "The Good Behavior Book" immediately before Rita came in for her play session.

Session 2: Evaluating Rita

Rita's first session was very productive. She was clearly hyperactive and impulsive. She complied with all the therapist's instructions and found enjoyment in drawing her pictures and performing the Puppet Sentence-Completion Task (Knell, 1993). Her pictures illustrated the power she held in her home and the insecurity she felt about it. In her drawing, the female person was smiling, but her hands were reaching outward. She said the girl was trying to get someone to pay attention to the fact that she needed something. The family drawing illustrated that her mother was very important to her, but her father was somewhat removed. She said the family was trying to have a good time at the beach, but it kept raining on them. During her puppet task, she said she was happiest with her friends, afraid when it was dark, hated reading, and loved to play. Many of her answers followed the same theme. She stated, "Mommy is nice when she reads to me, and Daddy is nice when he smiles." She had trouble finishing the stems: "Mommy and/or Daddy is mean when. . . . " This resistance is not unusual.

Her ability to play *Guess Who* was somewhat impaired. She had an impulsive style when asking and answering questions that confused her. She would ask, "Does your person have blue eyes?" The therapist would answer "no," and she would look confused and say that none of her remaining pictures had blue eyes. With encouragement and direction, she was able to understand the game better.

When playing Trouble, she impulsively took her turn and the therapist's turn without realizing it. She quickly wanted to quit when the therapist began to win. This inability to stay on task or finish games with her family was reported at intake. Again, with encouragement, Rita stayed with the game until it was finished.

Session 3: Meeting with the Parents

Mrs. P attended all the sessions with Rita. "The Good Behavior Book" required a few minor revisions. Mrs. P wrote more than two to four words per line and had some listings that were negative. After retraining, she clearly did the job well. By the third session, Rita performed additional positive tasks, so that her mother recorded them in the book. Mr. P's responsibility was to put Rita to bed. He read a book to her at night, and she enjoyed their time together.

Session 3: Meeting with the Child

In Rita's first play session, she was introduced to the Feeling Word Game During the game, it became clear that Rita felt her parents favored her sister, and that she experienced a general sense of anxiety and felt school was a difficult place. Rita did not seem to have any social problems (which is unusual for children with ADHD), but she felt somewhat alienated from certain people. She loved being with her friends and found that to be a great reason to go to school.

The Beat the Clock game had a baseline time of 4 minutes. Rita kept her eyes on her drawing without ever looking up. Toward the end of the 4-minute session, she was more fidgety and used all her resources to "win" the game. After three trials, she did pick a prize from the treasure box. She wanted to play Beat the Clock again, but the therapist insisted that they play Connect Four. She followed the therapist's lead without resistance.

During Connect Four, a game of self-control, Rita was quite impulsive. The therapist began verbalizing move strategies and cued Rita to look around the board before moving. With this stopping technique, Rita was able to slow down her responses and comment before making her move.

Session 4: Meeting with the Parents

In the next session, Rita's parents commented on her progress with chores and accomplishments in previously difficult areas. The therapist commented on the parents' positive change of style and Rita's responsiveness.

The "Special Playtime" technique was introduced next. At first, Mrs. P felt that this would not be a problem because she always liked to play with Rita for short periods of time. The therapist then modeled the narrating behavior and playtime tracking, but Mrs. P was hesitant. She was asked to perform these tasks every night with only Rita. Her younger sister would have to focus on something else or play with Mr. P.

Session 4: Meeting with the Child

Reading "The Good Behavior Book" to Rita was a pleasure because she was excited about all that she had accomplished. She even remembered accomplishments Mrs. P forgot to record. After playing the Feeling Word Game, more positive stories were produced by Rita. She seemed to feel more confident about "being good" and told stories reflecting this. The therapist explored fears affecting Rita and, once again, generalized anxiety seemed pervasive.

Rita began the "Garbage Bag" technique with some resistance. She would not agree to the garbage descriptors used by the therapist. She finally related to piles and piles of garbage and said, "You would walk around like the Hunchback of Notre Dame if you carried all of that around with you." Rita recorded her three garbage items: (1) "My sister always gets me in trouble"; (2) "Math homework takes all night"; (3) "My friends don't call me much." The therapist recorded three items also: (1) "A lot of stuff scares me"; (2) "My body won't stay still"; (3) "No one wants to do things my way." The three items were confirmed by Rita, who nodded her head.

After putting the "garbage" in the bag, Rita began the Beat the Clock game. That week, Rita reached 5 minutes and held it easily. She received all 30 chips for the three trials. Rita was asked to practice this at home with her mom as homework for 5 minutes per trial to determine her ability to cope in the "real world." She was excited about trying this.

The next self-control game was called Rebound. Rita threw the pieces so fast that they jumped off the board. With some modeling of the game and a great deal of verbal instruction, she slowed down her moves, was able to play, and gained more points each trial. The therapist kept the game even and then won in the end to measure Rita's ability to lose. She said she would challenge the therapist again the following week under these same conditions.

Session 5: Meeting with the Parents

Special playtime was hard for Mrs. P. She felt she had no time to do it. Since Rita still took baths, the therapist advised Mrs. P to play during that time. Rita loved to play in the bath, and Mrs. P could narrate.

The "Compliance" training was then introduced. Mrs. P said that she seemed to always "ask" her children to do things, because she felt it was rude to command. With her other daughter, the "asking" worked, but with Rita it did not. She was willing to try this new technique but asked if she could say "please" to make it sound less demanding. It was agreed that she would perform the commands with both children so that there would be consistency.

When the therapist asked for a contractual item, Mrs. P responded immediately. She wanted Rita to get dressed by herself by 7:30, so that Mrs. P could have a portion of her morning back. This seemed like a reasonable request, since Rita was certainly capable of dressing herself on weekends when there was no school. The therapist told Mrs. P to set a timer and prompt Rita with "On your mark, get set, go," the first two times. Then, she was to remark how well Rita was doing from time to time.

Session 5: Meeting with the Child

Rita's session started again with "The Good Behavior Book." The therapist then told Rita that sometimes children worked for larger prizes by performing one specific behavior all week. Rita was excited and wanted to do that. It was agreed that she would get dressed by herself and finish by 7:30. Her mom would set a timer to guide the time. Rita seemed very willing to go along with this, and a contract was signed. Rita wanted to earn some arts-and-crafts prizes.

The first piece of "garbage" Rita pulled from the bag was "Math homework takes all night." Rita and the therapist set up miniature people and created a small math homework sample. The mother doll told the child to look at how much homework was on the page. Then, the mother doll folded the paper in half and told the girl to do just that portion before taking a break. The girl doll had trouble sitting down; she wanted to play instead. The mother doll explained how this would take less than 10 minutes, and then she could play for the same amount of time. The mother doll used a clock to show the time. If the girl doll decided to do all the work at once, it would only take another 5 minutes, and then playtime would be longer. The girl doll questioned this, then decided to do all the homework at once to get more playtime. Rita commented, "Hey, that was easy."

The Beat the Clock game was going well at home because Rita's baseline time was 8 minutes that week. Rita and the therapist played twice, and she was able to pick a prize. (When the game is played at home, the child increases his or her attention span at a faster rate.)

The session ended that week with Rebound and the Trouble game. The therapist modeled each move and talked about the process she was incorporating. Rita focused on the therapist's moves and mimicked with her own. That week, she also verbalized her move strategies, indicating that planning capabilities were developing.

Session 6: Meeting with the Parents

Compliance training went very well for Rita. She easily completed the tasks, and Mr. and Mrs. P were amazed at her follow through. Mrs. P was congratulated for following through with Rita as well. Previously, they had told her what to do, leaving it up to Rita to complete the tasks (which rarely happened). Rita also got dressed alone and was ready on time every day for the previous week. Mrs. P was truly proud of her.

Mrs. P was taught how to pay attention to Rita and her sibling when they were not bothering her. She had reported that she felt they never played quietly without a fight, but with encouragement, she was willing to give it a try. She chose to pretend she was reading the paper and would frequently break away to comment on the sisters' good behavior.

Rita's next contractual item was to complete homework without complaints. Mrs. P was practicing Beat the Clock with Rita (coloring only). It was decided that she would motivate Rita to do her homework in one sitting, without complaint, through use of the contract.

Session 6: Meeting with the Child

Rita was excited about receiving her prize as a reward for completing her homework. "The Good Behavior Book" seemed overshadowed by her excitement. She asked if she was going to earn another prize; a contract was drawn up: Rita would do her homework, without complaint, in one sitting. The therapist reminded Rita that she was already exceeding her expectations at Beat the Clock, so this would be simple. Rita was motivated to try.

The next piece of "garbage" chosen was "My sister always gets me in trouble." This was played out with both parents and sisters using miniatures. Rita illustrated through her play that her sister tattled on her whenever Rita made a mistake or struck her sister. The "mom doll" helped Rita practice a technique in which Rita went to her mom first to report any trouble, thereby thwarting her sister's efforts to make her look bad. Rita was able to problem-solve without anger once she realized she had some control over the situation. Rita also showed jealously toward her sister in play, which was understandable under the circumstances. Things came easier for her sister. The "mom doll" started listing all the good things the older sister could do faster and better in order to level those negative feelings.

Rita's play took more time than usual, so the Beat the Clock game was skipped. Mrs. P was working on the game at home, and Rita had reached 15 minutes of attending without lifting her head or becoming distracted.

At end of the session, Rita and the therapist played pick-up sticks in order to focus more on developing self-control. Rita was certainly working hard at trying to control and quiet her body as she played the game. She fidgeted when the therapist took a turn, but Rita took a deep breath before taking her turn and said "OK" as if to prepare herself for the trial.

Session 7: Meeting with the Parents

Mrs. P was as excited as Rita to tell the therapist that not only was Rita dressing herself, but also she did homework without complaints for the entire week. However, Mrs. P said that focusing on her children when they were not bothering her was difficult. She felt they were misbehaving more than usual. While this might have been true, the therapist told her that when a change is noticed by children, their behavior tends to get worse before getting better. This information encouraged Mrs. P to stay with it.

The token economy was then introduced, and Mrs. P was told that she no longer had to keep "The Good Behavior Book" up to date; she was re-lieved. The token economy used poker chips, and each child participated. Competition concentrated on good behaviors rather than bad. Mrs. P grasped the system quickly, and she and Mr. P developed it together the fol-lowing weekend with the girls. It would be easy for Rita to earn 100 points, so that was added to her contract.

Session 7: Meeting with the Child

During Rita's session, the therapist introduced the concept of the token economy. The therapist brought in poker chips and started giving her enough of them to illustrate the following items:

- Got up   2 chips
- Got dressed   5 chips
- Brushed teeth   4 chips
- Packed backpack   5 chips
- Took pill   3 chips
- Put clothes away   10 chips
- Set table   8 chips
- Made bed   8 chips
- Fed dog   5 chips
- Walked dog   10 chips
- Homework without complaints   25 chips
- Played nicely with sister   25 chips

Rita was excited about earning the chips, and agreed in the contract that she would earn 100 chips before the next week.

Rita played out her last piece of "garbage"; "My friends don't call me a lot." This play session was performed with role play. The therapist and Rita dressed as different girls. The play focused on girlfriends who were very busy with homework, gymnastics, and so on. Then, the therapist's character, Rita, called her friend once a night to see how she was doing. "Rita" asked the friend many questions, answered questions, and felt very involved. After the role play, Rita explained what she experienced as the friend. She said she felt the therapist cared a great deal about what she was doing, and she would try that technique with her friends. She finished by stating: "I guess that problem is solved."

The Beat the Clock game was now a regular item at home, so the ther-apist introduced the Bubble Blowing Game. Rita was very good at taking deep breaths, but she held them instead of slowly blowing out. After ap-proximately 10 trials, she began to perform correctly and was given both bottles to practice this at home. She would compete with Mom five times before homework, and with Dad five times before bed.

Session 8: Meeting with the Parents

The token economy was working well with both children. Mrs. P felt that this was a lifesaver, because the girls were trying to do more and more (tasks and good behaviors) to get more chips. There was less hitting going on between the girls, and more positive playtime. The girls were rewarded with chips for each hour they played nicely together.

The therapist reviewed the time-out procedure with Mrs. P. She agreed to use it sparingly and felt that it really had not been necessary to use it in weeks. Mrs. P thought the utility room would do, because Rita could not harm herself with anything there. The concept of taking away chips was discussed. The therapist advised her that after Rita obtained a long-term reward, chips could be deducted when she did not accomplish what was on the list; however, the removal could not be random.

Session 8: Meeting with the Child

Rita showed the therapist her poker chips in the playroom and immediately wanted her prize. The prizes were given at the end of the session, so she had to control herself. She did so very well. The therapist then introduced her to making her own board game.

Rita's Board Game was created, listing all her successes; then, she felt that there were some things she had not accomplished yet. She listed her successes: got dressed alone, played nicely with sister; completed homework without complaints, finished homework without getting up, called friends once per night, made bed, felt happy. She listed her goals: get a C on a spelling test, pick up clothes, watch more television, have private time with her mom. She wanted to work on accomplishing these things. Therefore, her Board Game included spaces representing these items. In a couple of spaces, the therapist just put a happy face that said, "Smile because you are you."

Session 9: Meeting with the Parents

All of Mrs. P's successes were listed for her. She really felt that she was doing a good job. She said it was the result of the therapist's help that made it possible. But the therapist said, "I was the director. You did all the work." Mrs. P was prepared to take over the contracting, especially because the token economy was the contract medium.

Mrs. P was then given the rating scales to complete while Rita had her session. Mr. P would fill them out and return them the following week. This last session required that both parents be present. Mrs. P was advised on managing future problems by examining her own behavior or family stressors and determining whether Rita was reacting to a change *before* calling. The door is always left open for clients to call or come back when needed.

Session 9: Meeting with the Child

Rita was then informed that there were two sessions left in therapy. Rita did not want to stop, but the therapist focused on how successful she had been, and began the "List of Good Me." Rita recalled many of her accomplishments, and the therapist helped her finish the list with "Good Daughter," "Good Sister," "Wonderful Student," and "Genuine Friend."

The session ended with Rita and therapist playing her Board Game, which she thoroughly enjoyed. When she landed on the "Smile," she displayed a huge grin that revealed how she felt about herself.

Session 10: Transition to Parents

Both Mr. and Mrs. P joined Rita and the therapist for the last session. Everyone was happy to report that the token economy was going well, and Rita had attained her long-term goal of having two friends spend the night.

The therapist began the Drawing Game by drawing a bridge connecting a cloudy sky to a rainbow sky. Rita went next and colored in the entire rainbow very carefully (paying attention to her work the entire time as she was praised by both parents). Mrs. P added a golden pot at the end of the rainbow filled with candy and prizes. Mr. P added a sun and singing birds. No one added anything to the cloudy-sky side of the bridge (the transformation was complete, and the family focused on the future with new beginnings.)

Rita was given her "List of Good Me" and Board Game to take home. She asked the therapist for a hug. She was happy to leave with positive personal representations.

SUMMARY AND CONCLUSION

ADHD is a chronic disorder that baffles many therapists and teachers alike. However, through the use of play therapy and parenting changes, families can function and manage the problem so they achieve the normal criteria society sets for raising children. Many families have not been able to understand the disorder well enough to know where to start. Once motivated and directed, many of these families function better and better. There will always be setbacks and tough days. But to see the smile on children's faces, and hear how terrific they feel, makes all the hard work worthwhile. As a therapist, it is so fulfilling to join a family in this process.

REFERENCES

Achenbach, T. M. (1978). The child behavior profile. *Journal of Consulting and Clinical Psychology, 46,* 478–488.

American Psychiatric Association. (1994). *Diagnostic and statistical manual of mental disorders* (4th ed.). Washington, DC: Author.

Barkley, R. A. (1987). *Defiant children: A clinician's manual for parent training.* New York: Guilford Press.

Barkley, R. A. (1990). *Attention-deficit hyperactivity disorder: A handbook for diagnosis and treatment.* New York: Guilford Press.

Barkley, R. A. (1995). *Taking charge of ADHD: The complete, authoritative guide for parents.* New York: Guilford Press.

Conners, C. K. (1989). *Conners Parent Rating Scales.* Toronto: Multi-Health Systems.

Conners, C. K., & Wells, K. C. (1986). *Hyperkinetic children: A neuropsychosocial approach.* Beverly Hills, CA: Sage.

Goldstein, S., & Goldstein, M. (1990). *Managing attention disorders in children.* New York: Wiley.

Kaduson, H. G. (1993a). Play therapy for children with attention-deficit hyperactivity disorder. In H. G. Kaduson, D. Cangelosi, & C. Schaefer (Eds.), *The playing cure* (pp. 197–227). Northvale, NJ: Aronson.

Kaduson, H. G. (1993b). The Feeling Word Game. In H. G. Kaduson & C. Schaefer (Eds.), *101 favorite play therapy techniques* (pp. 19–21). Northvale, NJ: Aronson.

Knell, S. M. (1993). *Cognitive-behavioral play therapy.* Northvale, NJ: Aronson.

Loney, J. (1980). Hyperkinesis comes of age: What do we know and where should we go? *American Journal of Orthopsychiatry, 50,* 28–42.

Loney, J., Kramer, J., & Milich, R. (1981). The hyperkinetic child grows up: Predictors of symptoms, delinquency and achievement at follow-up. In K. D. Gadow & J. Loney (Eds.), *Psychosocial aspects of drug treatment for hyperactivity* (pp. 243–252). Boulder, CO: Westview Press.

Lord, J. (1985). *A guide to individual psychotherapy with school-age children and adolescents.* Springfield, IL: Charles C Thomas.

Milich, R. S., & Landau, S. (1981). Socialization and peer relations in the hyperactive child. In K. D. Gadow & I. Bailer (Eds.), *Advances in learning and behavior disabilities* (Vol. 1, pp. 283–339). Greenwich, CT: JAI Press.

Mischel, W., Shoda, Y., & Rodriguez, M. L. (1989). Delay of gratification in children. *Science, 244,* 933–938.

Routh, D. K. (1978). Hyperactivity. In P. R. Magrab (Ed.), *Psychological management of pediatric problems* (Vol. 2, pp. 131–140). Baltimore: University Park Press.

Satterfield, J. H., Satterfield, B. T., & Cantwell D. P. (1981). Three-year multi-modality treatment study of 100 hyperactive boys. *Journal of Pediatrics, 98,* 650–655.

VanFleet, R. (1994). *Filial therapy: Strengthening parent–child relationships through play.* Sarasota, FL: Professional Resource Press.

Weiss, G., & Hechtman, L. T. (1986). *Hyperactive children grownup: Empirical findings and theoretical considerations.* New York: Guilford Press.

Wender, P. H. (1987). *Minimal brain dysfunction in children.* New York: Guilford Press.

APPENDIX 5.1. FAMILY EVALUATION FORM

FAMILY
NAME

FATHER'S
NAME

MOTHER'S
NAME

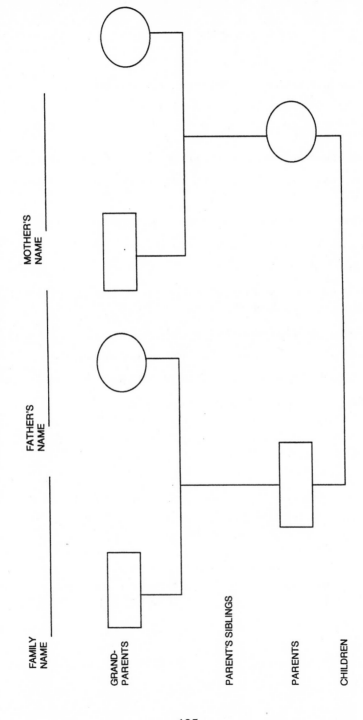

GRAND-
PARENTS

PARENT'S SIBLINGS

PARENTS

CHILDREN

APPENDIX 5.2. PLAY HISTORY QUESTIONNAIRE

1. What is the child's favorite plaything?

2. How long does the child play with one toy?

3. Is your child responsible for keeping his toys in order?

4. Does the child play with the toy or take it apart?

5. Does your child collect anything?

6. Does your child have a favorite game?

7. How does your child play the game; can she/he finish the game; can she/he lose without getting upset?

8. If your child is given a choice, what would she/he choose to do?

9. How much time does your child watch TV?

10. What is his/her favorite program?

11. Does your child play Nintendo/Sega/Play Station/Game Boy? How much time does she/he spend doing it?

12. Does your child like to draw or color?

13. Does your child join in with others when at a playground?

14. Would your child prefer to play alone or with others?

15. What sports, if any, does your child enjoy?

APPENDIX 5.3. CHILD/FAMILY QUESTIONNAIRE

Date: _____

Child's name: _____ Date of birth: _____
Present address: _____
_____

Home phone: _____ Business phone: _____
Race: _____ Religion: _____
Sex: M_____ F_____ Birthplace: _____
Annual income: _____
No. of persons dependent on this income: _____
School attending: _____ Grade: _____

Name(s) of adult(s) completing this form: _____
_____ Relationship to child: _____
Who referred you?
_____ Address: _____
How long has child had problem for which you are seeking help? _____

What is the main problem for which you are seeking help? _____
_____

Why did you seek help at this time? _____
_____
_____

Has child been seen previously for psychological or psychiatric consultation?
                Yes _____   No _____
If yes: Name of professional: _____
           Dates of service: _____
           Place of service: _____
           For what purpose: _____
Is the child adopted: Yes _____ No _____ Date: _____
Is the child a twin? Yes _____ No _____ Identical? _____

(continued)

137

APPENDIX 5.3. (*continued*)

Was the child ever placed or boarded away from the family?

Yes _____ No _____ If yes, with whom?

_____ Dates: _____

Has child ever had difficulty or contact with police?

Yes _____ No _____ If yes, describe circumstances:

_____

_____

_____

List all those living in child's home:

Name	Relationship	Date of birth	Occupation

List other persons closely involved with child but not living in home (e.g., older brothers and sisters, grandparents, sitter, teacher, religious leader, etc.).

Name	Place of residence

If child is not currently living with both natural parents.

Is either natural parent deceased? _____

If so, when? _____

Were natural parents married? _____

Explain briefly any special living circumstances (foster care, custody arrangements, visiting rights, etc.).

_____

_____

_____

Who financially supports child? _____

(continued)

APPENDIX 5.3. (*continued*)

How long have you resided at present address? _____

With whom does child share a bedroom, if anyone? _____

How would you describe the child as a person? _____

_____

_____

_____

Has your child had problems in school? Describe briefly: _____

_____

_____

_____

Has your child repeated any grade? _____

Briefly discuss progress and behavior in school: _____

_____

_____

Does your child have many friends? _____

Does your child have difficulty making or keeping friends? _____

_____

Difficulty with brothers and/or sisters? _____

Family concerns (× if appropriate):

Marital difficulties _____ Death in family _____

Aging grandparents _____ Drug addiction _____

Alcoholism _____ Financial problem _____

Serious illness _____ Single parent _____

Birth of new child _____ Job loss _____

Other: Please specify: _____

Describe briefly any special interests, hobbies, and recreational activities in which family members participate.

Child	Mother	Father

(*continued*)

APPENDIX 5.3. (*continued*)

Check (×) one in each column to show when child showed development in each area.

Early childhood

Child walked:	Child spoke words:	Child spoke sentences:
__ < 12 months	__ < 12 months	__ < 12 months
__ 12–24 months	__ 12–24 months	__ 12–24 months
__ 24–36 months	__ 24–36 months	__ 24–36 months
__ > 36 months	__ > 36 months	__ > 36 months
__ has never walked	__ has never spoken words	__ has never spoken sentences

Child first trained for urination:	Child first trained for bowels:
__ < 12 months	__ < 12 months
__ 12–36 months	__ 12–36 months
__ 3–5 years	__ 3–5 years
__ > 5 years	__ > 5 years
__ not yet trained	__ not yet trained

Since initial toilet training:	Since initial toilet training:
__ frequent wetting during day	__ frequent soiling during day
__ frequent wetting during night	__ frequent soiling during night

Puberty

Onset of puberty (breast development, menstruation, pubic hair, facial hair):
__ < 10 years   __ 14–16 years
__ 10–12 years   __ > 16 years
__ 12–14 years   __ no development

Illnesses and diseases

Place a check next to any illness or disease which your child has had.

__ asthma	__ tuberculosis	__ dizziness
__ eczema	__ head disease	__ meningitis
__ arthritis	__ influenza	__ broken bone
__ diabetes	__ pneumonia	__ others (write name of illness)
__ cancer	__ migraine headaches	_____
__ anemia	__ undescended testicles	_____
__ measles	__ high blood pressure	_____
__ mumps	__ low blood pressure	_____
__ chickenpox	__ sinusitis	_____
__ Diptheria	__ appendicitis	_____
__ scarlet fever	__ heart surgery	_____
__ polio	__ tonsillectomy	_____

(*continued*)

APPENDIX 5.3. (*continued*)

__ cerebral palsy   __ convulsions
__ lead poisoning   __ brain injury
__ encephalitis   __ fainting

Hospitalizations

List any hospitalizations your child has had. Give age at which hospitalization took place and length of hospitalization.

Condition for which hospitalized	Child's age	Length of hospitalization

APPENDIX 5.4. TOKEN ECONOMY
(©1997 Heidi Gerard Kaduson, PhD)

GOOD BEHAVIOR CHART		BUY CHART	
Got up	2	Snack	5
Got dressed	3	Soda	2
Brushed teeth	2	15 min. Nintendo	10
Ate breakfast	1	1/2 hr. TV	15
Dish in sink	4	Ice cream	10
		Alone w/Mom	25
		Alone w/Dad	25
Put clothes in hamper	5	Rent movie	25
Took out trash	10	Got to movie	100
Made bed	10	Sleepover	100
Packed backpack	5	Dinner of choice	50
Made lunch	5	Dessert	20
		Lollipop	5
		Candy	15
		Stay up 15 min. later	50
Nice talk			
Morning	25		
After school	25		
After dinner	25		
Go to bed at 9	25		
Homework done	25	————	
		Great Adventure	1,000
		Toy ($10)	1,000
		Go to . . .	500

APPENDIX 5.5. BOARD GAME

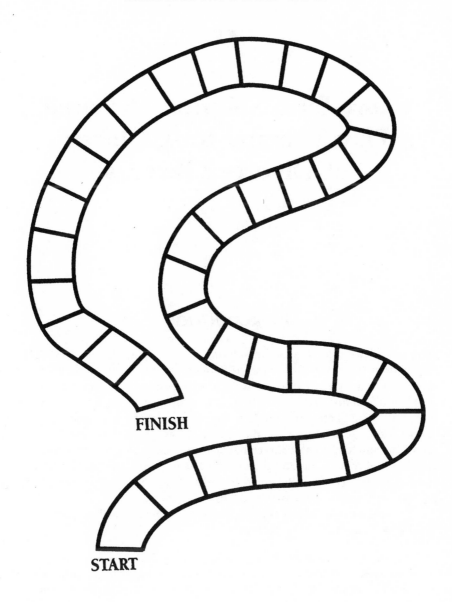

FINISH

START

6

Short-Term Solution-Oriented Play Therapy for Children of Divorced Parents

JULIA A. TREBING

INTRODUCTION

Why should we offer short-term solution-oriented play therapy (STSOPT) for children (ages 3–10) of divorced parents? Mainly because there are so many children to reach and so few child therapists to go around. STSOPT is time efficient and there are only so many hours in a day. In addition it is less costly, so it better fits the limitations imposed by managed care. Of course, there are also the societal pressures. However, perhaps most importantly, because children's character structure is more flexible, their personalities are more resilient, and their outlook is more positive and health oriented, STSOPT is naturally suited to them. There are many reasons why, but the best reason is *because it works*.

For the purpose of this chapter, short-term therapy will be defined according to Shapiro (1994). He states:

> The therapist and child are usually best served when short-term therapy is broadly defined. The aim of short-term therapy is not to "cure" children, but rather to simultaneously stimulate their internal resources for growth and development and make their environment responsive to their needs. Short-term therapy is rarely an end in itself, but rather a transition point in a child's journey towards adulthood. (p. 5)

There is no exact number of sessions that delineates short-term therapy from long-term treatment, but research reports a range of 12–18 sessions as the norm. Creative Therapies™ reports an average of 8–12 sessions, with a gradual increase in the time between sessions. Many cases require fewer sessions, especially the younger children who tend to achieve the goals quickly, provided their parents implement the recommendations and engage in effective, consistent parenting.

Poinsier and Laurin (1995) support brief psychotherapy for children with mild problems and report that this psychotherapeutic treatment prevents various pathologies that would otherwise require medical follow-up. Furthermore, they report that children treated through short-term therapy will benefit from a better quality of life. When treated at a young age or as soon as initial symptoms manifest themselves, the benefits increase throughout their life. The cost sustained by the health care system is significantly less than with traditional treatments.

According to Klar and Coleman (1995), short-term solution-oriented therapy is particularly efficient because of six solution-focused techniques: It concentrates on the present and the future; builds on strengths; focuses on clear, realistic goals; uses tasks; and develops client cooperation and efficacy.

Though the literature on short-term therapy is limited, it dates back over 70 years. The reader is referred through time to the work of Ferenczi and Rank (1925), Alexander and French (1946), and Barten and Barten (1973). Marmor (1979) states that we are now dealing with a more contemporary philosophical shift in the mental health professions toward greater pragmatism, eclecticism, and a systems orientation. Most recent are Selekman's (1997) book *Solution-Focused Therapy with Children* and Shapiro's (1994) book, *Short-Term Therapy with Children: A Multi-Modal Approach to Helping Children with Their Problems.*

Long-term therapy is often deemed appropriate in cases of prolonged abuse and trauma, parent psychopathology, attachment and severe personality or character disorders. Castelnuovo-Tedesco (1971) reports that briefer therapies are especially useful for the basically intact person who possesses at least a modicum of ego strength, for someone who, for instance, adapted reasonably well in life but became the victim of an unfortunate predicament that unduly taxed his or her endurance or rekindled a previously dormant internal conflict. Such treatment can be aimed at relieving the most pressing symptoms and restoring the person to the state that existed before the acute difficulties.

Many therapists are biased against short-term therapy. One study found that at the end of a 12-week program, therapists felt that the children had to continue to be seen for a greater number of sessions over a longer period of time, to be considered improved. Conversely, the parents were satisfied with the length of the program, and they overwhelmingly stated that their parenting had improved and their children's symptoms were relieved (Kissel, 1974). The researchers went on to suggest strongly that when it comes to evaluating effectiveness of psychotherapy, therapists, in general, have a built-in bias toward long-term care.

This controversy over short- and long-term therapy divides professionals. However, with a clear understanding of short-term therapy, one realizes that both types of care are very much needed. It is the intent of this chapter to demonstrate the efficacy of short-term therapy for children of divorced parents. Laymen's terms have been used to support parents, teachers, and other caregivers in gaining a greater understanding of this innovative approach.

SHORT-TERM PLAY THERAPY

At Creative Therapies, five categories make up the success of STSOPT with children of divorced parents:

1. Assessment, FEEDBAC 2™, and the collaborative approach to the treatment plan
2. Components of STSOPT
3. Play space and materials
4. Involvement and participation of both parents
5. Ongoing support and the 6-month follow-up

ASSESSMENT FEEDBAC 2, AND THE COLLABORATIVE APPROACH TO THE TREATMENT PLAN

Early intervention is most important since children experience high levels of stress during the first year of their parents' separation, as well as during the years before the divorce when there is a high level of parental conflict. During this period, parents usually are so involved in their own needs that they are unavailable to address the needs of their children. The roots of the divorce and the postdivorce circumstances are far-reaching and affect children in complex ways. Ideally, this means getting children into treatment even before the physical separation of their parents.

The assessment is a thorough examination of the child and his or her environment to determine appropriate treatment. For short-term, solution-oriented therapy, a comprehensive and individualized treatment plan with outside collaboration from the "child's system" (the parents, school professionals, and community caregivers) is developed to maximize the child's well-being. Specific goals, techniques, and schedules are created to organize the individualized care. The people within the "child's system," are provided with techniques to move the child toward the therapeutic goals of the treatment plan.

The theoretical framework of FEEDBAC 2 formulates the assessment and choice of techniques while removing subjective eclecticism. FEEDBAC 2 is an acronym that stands for

F—Family and getting the dysfunctional family unstuck
E—Everyone else/social/community
E—Emotional
D—Developmental
B—Behavioral
A—Academic
C—Cognitive

The "2" in FEEDBAC 2 is a reminder to look at a parallel acronym with other variables for the most comprehensive and effective use of the therapy time.

F—Food (including diet, nutrition, height, weight, supplements and substances)
E—Environmental (such as air and noise)
E—Everything else (a catchall category containing an ever-growing list including self-esteem, interests, etc.)
D—Diagnostic (intellectual, mental, and physical, such as otitis media and its treatment through ear candles, before surgical tubes)
B—Background information (including details of treatment history, what worked, what did not, etc.)
A—Altruism (What is their concern for the well-being of others, and how will values be taught?)
C—Consciousness (religion, spirituality, faith, and trust)

Every person in the child's system is held responsible for the implementation and follow through of their part of the highly individualized treatment plan, in accordance with observable and measurable criteria. By the end of the short-term therapy, a variety of services, such as tutoring, weekly visits with a guidance counselor, and community services, will have been put into place to provide the child with whatever ongoing support he or she may require.

Components of Short-Term Solution-Oriented Therapy

NONDIRECTIVE AND DIRECTIVE PLAY THERAPY

Creative Therapies uses both nondirective and directive play therapy, with a delicate balance of the two, ideally offering maximum effectiveness. For example, children gravitate to where they need to go in the playroom to work on whatever their (not the parents' or therapist's) is-sue(s) may be. It must be the child's therapy. This is extremely important in play therapy. In one initial parent session, though, the issue of mom returning to work was mentioned, and their choice to use the older brother as the young girl's caretaker was discussed. The parents focused primarily on their belief that their daughter had become increasingly "withdrawn since, and because, her father moved out." However, nondirective play therapy revealed a much greater issue. By allowing the girl to go where she needed to go and not where her parents thought she should go, in play, the girl set up the two houses: (1) the mother's office building, and (2) her home. She showed her mother busily working and ignoring the phone ringing while she was home being sexually abused by her older brother. This may not have been discovered so easily, if at all, without nondirective play therapy.

An example of when play therapy shifts to become directive would be when a child is repeatedly engaging in the same play over and over again. The therapist interrupts the pattern with something as simple as a snap of the fingers to something as directive as an alternative. Alternatives are of-fered in the belief that only when the child is ready and the alternative is meaningful to him or her that the option will be accepted.

For example, Sara, a 6-year-old girl, while engaging in nondirective play, repeatedly had a child doll die in a hospital bed while her divorced parents fought over possession of her. Switching to directive play, the thera-pist entered into the play a judge figure who became the decision maker, thus alleviating the child's role of being in the middle. The judge, miniature figurine, also taught her to say, "Don't put me in the middle," "Don't fight in front of me," and "Ask Mom yourself." Without this direct intervention, the dying theme, along with the accompanying array of physical symptoms and avoidance behaviors, such as school absences, would likely have con-tinued for weeks. However, being empowered by the judge with education and words, this girl no longer needed her symptoms to speak for her. All symptoms were released.

HOMEPLAY™, INCLUDING BIBLIOTHERAPY

Teachings are reinforced by the family's agreement to participate in the assigned Homeplay. Homeplay was chosen as a friendlier concept than homework. Homeplay may include signed out therapeutic material, books and games, and behavioral management strategies such as "Feel Better Time." "Feel Better Time" is discussed in a later section. Home-play is goal oriented, time-limited, and beneficial to both children and their families.

Bibliotherapy is the use of books in the therapeutic process. Children are loaned books on issues specific to their treatment plan. (see the list at the end of the chapter for a sampling and description of some of the available children's books on divorce.)

IN-HOME CARE™

In-Home Care is a custom-tailored program to match each family's specific needs when additional support is required. It may be twice per week for an hour-long visit to support the child's individual challenges, or it may be as wide-ranging as around the clock, including family programming, house meetings, and coordination with the child's school to prevent (re)-hospitalization. Often, staff members work as liaisons with schools and various public agencies. If the child is having "behavioral problems" in class, a staff member may accompany the child as an intermediary that can calm both the student and the teacher.

The In-Home Care staffing consists of professionals, students interning in psychology, and other Creative Therapies–trained and supervised adults. The effectiveness of this programming and its staffing is supported by: Mosher and Burti (1989), who described the Soteria House Project in California and found that the home environment with a nonprofessional therapist outperformed the traditional mental health system and medication; the Harvard–Radcliffe Mental Hospital Volunteer Program, in which college students became case aides and even psychotherapists for individual mental patients on the back wards of a state mental hospital; and Jerome Miller, president and founder of the National Center for Institutions and Alternatives (NCIA) in Alexandria, Virginia, who used volunteer advocates to work with families as part of an overall strategy that eventually emptied and closed Massachusetts Juvenile detention centers.

GROUPS

Upon the completion of individual and family work, sometimes a child will be referred into a confidential psychosocial, educational divorce group, called the Feelings Group. The themes from these groups include different kinds of families, why people get divorced, feelings, managing anger, coping strategies, taking care of yourself, and saying goodbye. Follow-up on these 8-week programs has consistently demonstrated significant improvement in adjustment behaviors. This observation is supported in the research of Stolberg and Mahler (1994) and Garvin, Leber, and Kalter (1991).

Two professional resources for working in groups with children from divorced homes are *Building Trust, Making Friends: Four Group Activity Manuals for High Risk Students, Thomas Barker Talks about Divorce and Separation* (Schmidt & Spencer, 1991), and a new group program currently being tested, *Helping Your Kids Cope with Divorce the Sandcastles Way* (Neuman, 1998).

Play Space and Materials

A description of Creative Therapies at the Playroom™ follows, with attention to details including materials and ambience.

Creative Therapies at the Playroom is located in a Victorian-style professional building in the downtown business district of Stamford, Connecticut. You know you are there when you open the door and everything turns warm and fuzzy. Feng shui decorating creates the affect of balance, peace, and harmony. Feng shui was selected for the creation of the healthiest, most comfortable space for play and healing. Plush pink carpeting, soft-colored walls, and the calming effect of a wind chime invite you in.

A heart-shaped welcome sign greets you as you walk in. What would traditionally be called a waiting room is called and feels more like a cozy home's "Family Room." Family Time happens in this room, though mostly it is the place where parents relax while their children are in the other therapy rooms. This room includes peaceful music, velvet beanbag chairs, a child's rocking chair, cooperative games, drawing materials, an ever-expanding bibliotherapy lending library, and audiotapes for both children and parents. There is also audio equipment, directions, and scripts (for guidance) so parents may make a relaxation or bedtime tape for their child. These scripts have been created for specific issues such as separation or fear. Other scripts are also available, with general messages of peace, love, and positive affirmation.

Children returning to this room after their individual sessions might find a parent sprawled out, fast asleep on one of the couches—his or her only free time all week. Other parents are discovered to be engaged in play with the child's sibling, in a concentrated, pleasurable manner, which is often not experienced at home, where there are sibling rivalry, phone interruptions, television, and other distractions. Still other parents take notes while watching a 10- to 12-minute recommended video. Each video is on a specific, relevant parenting skill (Boys Town National Training Center, 1990). The television/VCR is used only for teaching purposes.

The next room is the "Water Room." It also feels home-like, with the appliances and conveniences of a kitchen. There is adult- and child-scaled furniture to offer safe exploration and mastery of both child and adult environments. The room also includes a large, two-seated rocking chair for calming and soothing.

Children over 5 years of age who repeatedly void urine into their bed or clothes (enuresis) and children who have had traumatic births seem to gravitate toward water play. The "Water Room" offers children opportunities such as exploring water without rules about spilling or making a mess, and feeling and controlling water on their bodies. Frequently, boys with enuresis often elect to play with large tubs of water and phallic, parallel objects that hold and squirt liquid, such as eye droppers or a turkey baster. They will often progress in the play to include holding and drying objects such as sponges.

Transparent drawers, cabinets without doors, and a stepping stool invite children to select from a large array of art materials. These materials, like everything throughout the playroom, are categorized for organization, consistency, and predictability. Supplies include sand, clay and finger paints, which often invite regression, papier-mâché for the creation of structures such as the metaphorical raging volcanoes, and just about all other art supplies imaginable.

For further symbolic expression, there are hundreds of miniatures, in drawers classified by categories including (1) houses, buildings, and other structures; (2) trees and bushes; (3) fences and gates; (4) wild and domestic animals; (5) sea animals; (6) transportation vehicles; family, community helpers and other people; (7) fantasy, folk-lore, "good guy" and "bad guy" characters; (8) food and serving objects; (9) sand and water equipment; (10) multi-purpose equipment. These miniatures are for use in the sandtray or in and around the two small, wooden houses. The houses are deliberately not called dollhouses, because this tends to make them gender specific. Having the two houses allows children to express their feelings about different issues, such as school, grandparents, church, and, most often, about Mom's and Dad's separate homes.

This powerful technique that was developed and tested at Creative Therapies is called "Two House Therapy." It has been found to enhance the symbolic play of children of divorce. Aside from Kuhli's (1983) work, which is not about divorce, no other references were found in the literature regarding the use of two houses. Given the opportunity in nondirective play therapy, children will quite literally play out what is troubling them in Mom's and Dad's homes. The play is a microcosm of life, offering opportunities to work through conflicts and challenges, reconnect to feelings, or learn to resolve issues that are blocks to learning, growth, and development.

During an initial assessment, one divorced couple said their daughter has become increasingly anxious since the divorce. Rather than creating programming only around this specific concern, she was given the opportunity to enter into nondirective play. The girl then demonstrated in "Two-House Therapy" that it was not the divorce per se that created anxiety in her, but the "mean, mean" nanny that was now "in charge."

A 5-year-old boy focused on the kitchen and bathroom exclusively, ignoring all other areas of Mom's home. With minimal nondirective play, it became evident that Mom had bulimia nervosa. Another boy showed the difficulty of the transition from one home to the other. During the "Phone-In," a telephone conversation with the parents that occurs on the business day following the child's session (for further explanation see later in this chapter), ways to develop a smooth transition from home to home were explored. The parents found a release of their son's symptoms when they provided him with increased understanding, downtime and private time before leaving one home and upon arriving at the other.

As previously mentioned, a vast assortment of miniature furniture, people, and other objects is available to the child in order to stimulate therapeutic play. However, if the therapist observes children getting caught up in the details of the miniatures and their placement then the therapist may choose not to use the miniature and just have the children use their imagination, so the process is not lost. This allows for natural fantasies not to get contaminated.

The final therapeutic room is the "Sun Room," a bright, cheery room with no furniture. A multifaceted crystal in the window projects an array of rainbows as it sparkles in the afternoon sun. This warm, yellow room encourages the safe exploration, expression, and ventilation of strong feelings, such as scary thoughts from fantasy or reality. There are over 100 quality puppets used for safety and distance in the projection of children's inner emotional world. These puppets were carefully selected for their projective value (e.g., ferocious, innocent, pregnant), while many others were rejected because of where the hand enters the puppet and how that might be translated.

The room also includes anatomically detailed dolls, a gym mat, a full-length mirror, a pull-up bar, foam wedging, huge velvet pillows, a big body ball, and a giant, cuddly, stuffed bear that is both nurturing and doubles as a wrestling partner. The room was specifically designed so that active children can safely explore boundaries and develop sensory integration and centering within their bodies. Hidden from view inside the closet is a vast assortment of therapeutic toys (such as aggression and throwing toys that provide for safe discharge of emotional energy and tension), therapeutic games, and costumes that offer additional tools conducive to healing. A child's choice of materials, the manner in which they are used, and his or her accompanying words provide insight into the child's anxieties, defense structures, and restrictive or loose drives.

As one exits the playroom, he or she walks under a child's painting of a giant rainbow. This is a powerful symbol known to most as sunshine after rain. In therapy, it is often spontaneously drawn by children, representing their healing after pain.

Beyond the play space and materials, Creative Therapies recognizes that what matters most is the REAL-ationship. The therapeutic relationship between client and therapist is considered the most important aspect. The unseen energy between the child's heart and that of the therapist contains the conditions for healing.

Involvement and Participation of Both Parents

Short-term solution-oriented therapy requires motivated parents. They are asked for their commitment to be involved and participate fully in the creation, implementation, and follow through of the treatment plan. Parents who say, "Just fix my kid," and are not willing to follow recommendations and policies are referred elsewhere. In a comprehensive review of brief psychotherapy literature, in addition to motivation, there are three other factors listed by Mackenzie (1991) that require clinical assessment before considering a recommendation of short-term solution-oriented therapy. These factors are (1) a capacity to relate, (2) psychological mindedness, and (3) evidence of adaptational strength. These traits should be looked for in the parents first, before considering short-term, solution-oriented therapy with their child.

The healing process for children is not separate from their parents' recovery process. The therapist must educate parents regarding the impact that conflict and divorce have on children—with a focus on what is best for the children. To minimize the negative effects and maladjustment of their children and to develop positive parent–child relations, parents must not only be involved in treatment but also must be ready to acknowledge that their children come first. Parents' frequent conversations with their children, in which they invite questions, normalize strong reactions, and provide a nurturing, secure environment for the children's optimal well-being are essential. Equally important are creating and maintaining the calendar that each child keeps, which includes visitation details, routines, and other plans to enhance parent–child communication and decrease children's confusion as to when and where they are seeing each parent. With younger children this calendar is simplified to a day, or part thereof, and the mode of information is in pictures—drawn photographed, or cut-out. Establishing and maintaining new rules, roles, and routines is important to help everyone recognize that chaos is temporary and adjustment is possible. Clear and consistent boundaries must be set and communicated within both homes. Children must be kept out of the middle, and arguments should never be witnessed or overheard by children. Engaging in cooperative, respectful, patient, and supportive coparenting is the key. Disagreements should be settled through listing problems and solutions, give and take, and compromise. Agreements are important in developing trust between the parent partners. Kelly and Wallerstein (1977) report that short-term, supportive, educational, crisis-oriented work with recently divorced parents can significantly reduce the negative effects of divorce on children.

And finally, near the end of the child's first session, he or she is invited to come back and work on feeling better. Most children not only want to come back, but they also want to know how soon they can come. The rare child who says, "I don't want to," and resists the treatment is most likely not a candidate for short-term, solution-oriented therapy.

CONFIDENTIALITY, "CHECK-IN," AND "PHONE-IN"

"Confidentiality" is redefined to extend beyond the therapist to include the parents. In this capacity, the therapist is "the middleman," the goal being that with improved communication, family participation, solution-oriented care, and follow through on recommendations, parents will be able to "cut out the middleman" and work directly with one another and their child. This type of care is clearly not for everybody. It would not be appropriate to accept into this program parents who would use the information in harmful ways, such as using session information against the child or the other parent. Fortunately, this type of person is usually revealed at intake and referred out for a different mode of care.

Parents are instructed to leave a private "Check-in" message on the therapist's answering machine the morning of their child's appointment to bring him or her up to date on the challenges and successes of the week. This allows for the therapy time to be used most efficiently and effectively, with no initial therapy time used on talking about the child in front of the child. Additionally, parent–therapist phone time is no longer an infrequent, telephone-tag-like, haphazard or crisis-oriented experience. It is now a mandatory 10- to 15-minute appointment scheduled for the next business day after their child's session, often in a conference-call format with both parents. "Phone-in" time includes discussions about the child's session and the teaching of effective parenting skills and behavioral-management strategies. In addition, they cover training to deal successfully with the child's symptoms, techniques to apply for the next week, review, support, and reinforcement.

"FAMILY TIME"

At the beginning of the session, and often near the end, "Family Time" is spent with the child and parent (and siblings where applicable.) Burdsal and Buel (1980) found that treatment programs must include the child's family. If the child changes but the natural environment to which the child returns remains the same, the likelihood of lasting results are minimized. Burdsal and Buel's reason for specifying family involvement was fourfold:

- To provide the parents with coping skills (such as tools for dealing with their child).
- To attempt to produce an attitude of change on the part of the parent toward the child.
- To provide a positive, supportive environment in which the parents can share challenges that they are having with their child.
- To provide information.

"Family Time" is a solution-oriented approach to here-and-now challenges. This can include reaching agreements on alternative means of handling situations, teaching new parenting skills, modeling, and role-playing a new way of interacting. The focus is on choices and solutions, with an emphasis on the positive. Strategies are then implemented and followed until the next appointment, at which time they are reviewed and, if necessary, reworked. By the end of therapy, "Family Time" has become "Family Meetings" taught, then held, once a week at home. The meetings teach about sharing, caring, and problem solving. The social skills benefits are so great that Creative Therapies is working to get "Classroom Meetings" into school curriculums.

"FEEL BETTER TIME"

A special space is created with the child specifically for "Feel Better Time." It is a kinesthetically soothing space that the child is supported in creating. The child chooses what the space will contain (e.g., a fuzzy blanket, a velour beanbag, or a fluffy teddy bear). One important element is that the child has designed it according to his or her growing knowledge of what is soothing.

"Feel Better Time" is a positively oriented, feeling-focused version of "Time-Out." When a child misbehaves, he or she is given two warnings. If the misbehavior continues, the parent leads the child to the designated "Feel Better" space. 1:1:1 means this is done within 1 minute of the "behavioral infraction." One sentence or less is said to the child and a timer is set for a period of 1 minute for each year old the child is. For more serious misbehaviors such as hitting, the child has been told in advance that there will be no warnings, and that he or she immediately has to go to his or her "Feel Better" space. Parents model by taking their own "Feel Better Time." After the "Feel Better Time," the parent implements the "4:1 Rule" for behavior shaping by recognizing, over a short period of time, 4 positive behaviors for every 1 that was corrected.

Usually, when a behavioral program like this does not work, it is not the fault of the technique but the administration, often either because the directions were not followed or the parents were inconsistent.

U 'N' ME TIME™

Patterson and his associates (Patterson, 1974; Patterson & Reid, 1973) verify in their research that parents of "problem" children can be trained to deal successfully with their children. U 'N' Me Time builds on that belief. It is a 20-minute, daily, uninterrupted, nondirective playtime for the child with the parent at home. The parent is taught to refrain from questions, suggestions, and commands. Within broad limits, the child decides what to do. The parent observes and narrates the ongoing play in positive terms while ignoring mildly inappropriate behaviors. This allows the parent and child to reconnect and strengthen their relationship. Parents discover that with the focus on the positive, children become calmer, listen more, and demonstrate positive feelings of self-worth, confidence, competence, and security.

This technique is demonstrated during "Family Time," built up during the "phone-in" and expanded upon in a flyer given to the parent on the child's third visit. Many of the common, nondirective play therapy curative factors are used, such as empowering, reflecting, returning responsibility to the child, pacing, crediting the effort, tracking, accepting the silence, setting limits, and open-ended questioning. U 'N' Me Time has often been the successful technique parents say they return to when times get challenging and they want to reconnect with their child.

INVOLVEMENT IN COURT PROCEEDINGS WAIVER

According to Johnston and Roseby (1997), the fundamental agenda of each parent is to win the therapist's alliance. The pressure is put on the therapist to unilaterally support one parent as the good parent and the other as bad. Although parents may not acknowledge or even be conscious of this covert intent, it is likely to be experienced quite forcefully by the therapist. Often, parents want to blame their child's challenges on the other parent and to use the therapy information in their requests for custody and visitation schedules. Chances are that if the therapist feels this, then the child most likely experiences it as well. This type of behavior in parents is usually at least part of the reason their child is struggling emotionally. Parents have to be taught to reframe their agendas. When indicated, parents are referred to a psychologist who specializes in divorce mediation.

To see and understand the child as an individual separate from the parental conflict, play therapists must stay in their role. They should avoid becoming involved in litigation. Once therapy has begun, changing their role back to assessor or detective is countertherapeutic. The Creative Therapies policy form that the parents sign during the first parent session is adapted from Gardner (1976) and states:

> The undersigned will neither individually nor jointly involve (name of company) or (name of therapist) in any litigation. The undersigned will neither request nor require that (name of company) or (name of therapist) provide testimony in court. The reason for this is so that treatment is not compromised, the therapeutic relationship with the family is maintained, and the child experiences his or her play therapist in a clear, consistent, therapeutic role and not as an assessor or detective. If the services of a mental health professional are desired for court purposes, the services of a person outside of (name of company) or (name of therapist) must be enlisted. (p. 152)

This policy allows the therapist to remain consistent in the role of being supportive and reliable in keeping the best interests of the child foremost. Treatment would be compromised if information revealed during therapy were subsequently brought to the attention of the court. Moreover, this policy tends to weed out parents looking for a therapist to join forces in a custody battle.

Ongoing Support and the 6-Month Follow-Up

A very specific discharge plan of objective from Creative Therapies lists who will be continuing to support the child and in what fashion. The plan may include the school psychologist checking in with the child on a particular schedule, the child's placement in an enrichment program, tutoring for identified learning difficulties, and so on.

Parents are informed that even after their child has completed treatment at Creative Therapies, they may phone in for up to three complimentary 10- to 15-minute scheduled consultations. This is a quality control service commitment to the family's ongoing success.

Six months after the date of discharge, parents know that the standard practice of Creative Therapies is to follow-up with a phone call. This is a marvelous opportunity to review successes and explore challenges with the parents and sometimes with the child, too. Furthermore, the therapist may recommend a book to a parent, inquire about the treatment plan and the effectiveness of the "child's system," and, if indicated, suggest a "tune-up" session.

This follow-up service benefits not only the family but also the therapist and the field. Follow-up provides opportunity for professional insight, program improvement, and personal growth. Additionally, a blank copy of the same questionnaire the parent completed on the day of discharge is mailed out with a self-addressed, stamped envelope and a reminder of the upcoming follow-up phone call. The return of this completed questionnaire and its comparison to the one completed on the day of discharge give valuable research information for continually improving services. Through this kind of follow-up, Creative Therapies provides colleagues and the field with documentation of STSOPT successes and limitations.

CASE ILLUSTRATIONS

Case 1: The Angry Child—Jay, Age 4 Years, 9 Months

INITIAL PARENT INTERVIEW

The mother complained, "He is nasty to me. He will not listen or do as I ask, and recently he started hitting me." She explained that she divorced when Jay had just turned 2. He was toilet trained at 2 years, 11 months. In this initial intake, she also reported no history or current signs of depression. Jay's dad lived in California and flew in every other weekend to see his son. Mom signed out the first in a series of parenting audiotapes from Empowering People (800-456-7770). She also signed out the book *Time-Out: Abuses and Effective Uses* (Nelson & Glenn, 1992).

Developmental challenges are seen as the paramount issues of children from divorced families. In the preoperational stage (ages 2–7), children need to develop insight into the divorce and understand that it was not their fault. The therapist must explore misconceptions and correct them. During this stage, there may be regression, enuresis, clinging, deep longing for the other parent, insomnia, nightmares, temper tantrums, fears, abandonment issues, sadness, excessive neediness, denial, attempts to be perfect, and fantasies of reconciliation.

SESSION 1

Jay went directly into play, and took out a miniature boy, man, woman, and hospital bed. He placed the woman in the bed and moved the boy around the bed continuously. At this point in the play, the therapist kneeled in something wet and quickly realized Jay had wet his pants. The play continued. Once a child has repeated the same play three times, the therapist offers an intervention, trusting that it will be rejected if the timing or idea is off.

The therapist asked if the woman would like some food which represented nurturance. Jay said she doesn't eat anything but because he didn't say, "No, she doesn't want anything," the therapist, sensing the situation from the play, chose to explore medication. Jay informed the therapist that his mother had already had too much. Jay was demonstrating a depressed, possibly overmedicated mom and a neglected, approximately 2-year-old boy. In an attempt to contain the intensity before the end of the session, the therapist and Jay spent some time with Mom.

The therapist asked the Mom if she was sad, mad, or glad. The Mom indicated that she was glad because Jay was with the "feelings doctor." Mom was asked to share a variety of glad stories about her day. For the Homeplay, Mom was asked to tell a sad, mad, then glad story to Jay as part of their afterschool ritual, and then have him tell her one of each from his day. The goal was to increase communication between mother and son, to help Jay identify and express his feelings, and let Jay see that his mother experienced an array of feelings. Three instant photos were taken of Mom and Jay, demonstrating what sad, mad, and glad looked like. They signed out the Angry Monster Games from Childswork/Childsplay (800-962-1141), whereby Jay would learn 10 alternative ways of handling his anger. A written list with drawings of the 10 choices was given to them. Jay colored it in, and his mother told the therapist that it was posted on the refrigerator door.

"PHONE-IN"

This had been scheduled as a conference call with both Mom and Dad. However, given the content of the play, the therapist chose to speak with Mom and Dad separately. Mom reported that Jay was continuing to uri-nate in his pants. This suggested that the play had not been successfully contained before he left. In a review of the session, Mom was amazed and saddened by her son's regression to a younger age, complete with report-edly "accurate" memories she had not shared at the initial intake. She ac-knowledged that she was "devastated" by her husband's sudden request for a divorce. She had used sleeping pills to cope. She reported that since that time, she had formed a "new life," including a "fun boyfriend" and a "re-warding job," with an "ideal schedule" that allows her to be home when her son got in from school. She denied use of all substances except an occa-sional glass of wine when out to dinner. She agreed to emphasize in the Homeplay the stories from her day that made her feel happy/glad. She re-ported that she and Jay had put the sad, mad, and glad photos on his bed-room wall. The U 'N' Me Time handout was reviewed. Mom planned to start that day. She inquired about taking a parenting class. This was ar-ranged through her son's school.

"CHECK-IN"

Both Mom and Dad reported, separately, that Jay had completely stopped hitting. They both believed this was because Jay knew, without warning, that he would be sent to his "Feel Better Place." They recognized that con-sistency was the key to this success. Also, Mom noted that verbal identifica-tion of sad, mad, and glad had created an outlet that significantly dimin-ished the angry outbursts. She was able to support Jay in selecting alternative ways of expressing his anger like he learned in the Angry Mon-ster Game, and as was posted on the refrigerator. Mom said she noticed a stronger connection to her son since they started the U 'N' Me Time. Jay's wetting had reportedly stopped.

SESSION 2

During the "Family Time," Jay sang, "I love U 'N' Me Time." When asked how he thought his mom felt right then, he yelled, "Glaaaaaaaaad." When asked how he could tell, he said, "She's smiling and has cracks" (smile lines). Both Jay and his mom seemed calmer and happier. Sad, mad, and glad were reviewed, along with alternative ways of handling anger.

Jay then returned to the same play from the last session, with less in-tensity. When the therapist offered Jay a "feelings doctor" for the woman in the hospital bed, he sat the woman up and said, "She's all better now."

At this point, Jay seemed to be saying metaphorically, "Mom is okay now." He had evidently successfully reworked the trauma, because he then said he was "all done" and asked to go out to his mother. It is common that children let you know when their therapy is complete.

"PHONE-IN"

The mother said that because Jay was so young at the time of the divorce, he probably did not remember his parents living together. Therefore, she decided it was not the divorce, but her reaction to the divorce, that had created this situation. She agreed that with her newly developing, assertive parenting skills and the cessation of all Jay's symptoms, the work left now was her own.

6-MONTH FOLLOW-UP

Mom recognized that when she was consistent with her parenting, Jay did well emotionally and behaviorally. She said, "When I'm happy, we're all happy." She reported that she had changed to a male therapist to explore her issues with her father, former husband, partner, and son.

Case 2: "The Y-Home-Rec?!"—Three Sisters, Ages 7 Years, 3 Months; 9 Years, 2 Months; and 10 Years, 10 Months

INITIAL PARENT INTERVIEW

The parents reported that they both had told the girls that they were getting a divorce. The therapist's impression was that the girls had been told very matter-of-factly that Mom and Dad did not love each other any more. They would be visiting Dad every other weekend in his New York City apartment, where he would now live full time, instead of just on weeknights when he was working there. The parents said that they did not provide the girls with an opportunity to ask questions, and that the girls surmised that Dad was a "home wrecker," and that they "hated" him and "never" wanted to see him again.

In the concrete operations stage (ages 7–11), children need to know as much about the cause of the breakup as they can understand. This age group is more likely to grieve openly, place blame, and show anger or hatred toward one parent. There may be issues of hypermaturity, low self-esteem, and confused sexual identity. It is important to recognize that while some sources break down children's issues by age at the time of the divorce, the trauma rarely begins with the physical separation/divorce of the parents. Therefore, look for children to undergo developmental delays and arrests in various areas and stages of growth.

SESSION 1

By the time they arrived for therapy, each girl was symptomatic. They wanted some process to help them grieve, heal, and accept the new situation. They decided upon a rite of passage, which they titled "The Y-Home-Rec?!", a near reversal of the word "ceR-emoN-Y" and an actual undoing of their parents' marriage ceremony. It was scheduled for the third session. Much of the first session was "Family Time" in which information was provided to the girls about the divorce, and myths dispelled to help release shame and stigma. Some of the myths that were corrected with truths included the following:

- We, as a family, are getting divorced. (Actually, it is only Mom and Dad who are getting divorced.)
- It's my fault. (The divorce has nothing to do with you children; it is a result of our incompatibility as husband and wife.)
- I have to pick between my Mom and Dad. (You are a product of both of us. You do not have to be good or bad. We do not have to be good or bad. We can all love each other.)

The girls saw their father cry, reportedly, for the first time as he heard the girls express their pain at being apart from him. This seemed to have a warming effect on all. The children's book *The Un-Wedding* by Cole (1997) was signed out for their Homeplay in preparation for the rite of passage.

"PHONE-IN"

The parents processed the session. Mom and Dad agreed to a variation of U 'N' Me Time. They said that, depending upon whom the children were with, that parent would spend 20 minutes of quality time with each daughter before her bedtime, during which they would make time for questions and even suggest concerns the girls might have. They would use the All the Basic Facts list from Schmidt and Spencer (1991) to guide them. Mom agreed to purchase a white board for the kitchen, so everyone could add to the agenda for a weekly "Family Meeting." Mom and Dad agreed to neither defend nor badmouth each other, but, rather, to encourage the girls to speak directly to the person with whom they took issue. Also, they agreed to keep the children out of their disputes, including not letting them overhear half of a phone conversation.

"CHECK-IN"

Mom reported that the girls had read the book together every day and were planning for the rite of passage. Furthermore, Mom said they were more expressive, supportive of each other, and understanding of why Mom and Dad were divorcing. She reported significant improvement in all the girls symptoms.

Dad reported that he had "only" had phone contact with his daughter since the last session, but he felt much more "connected" to them. He made arrangements to come into town on Tuesdays to take the girls out to dinner, in addition to his every-other-weekend arrangement. He said he felt happier than he had been in years.

SESSION 2

The girls discussed happy and sad memories from their pasts to explore why their parents were divorcing. There was laughter and tears. Each discussed what was most difficult for her about their parents' getting a divorce, and then they worked together to create rituals they would like for the new family structure. They signed out the book *My Life Was Turned Upside Down, But I Turned It Right Side Up* by Blitzer/Field and Shore (1994).

"PHONE-IN"

Mom and Dad were asked to think about an appropriate story they would be willing to lovingly share to help their daughters put the impending divorce into perspective. They were advised that they were welcome to bring to the ritual ideas or objects that would help support the process.

"CHECK-IN"

Mom and Dad reported separately the improvement in themselves and the girls. Apparently, everyone was excited about the event.

SESSION 3

This session was attended by both parents and the girls. The girls decided to change the appearingly accusatory, hostile name of the ceremony to "The Friendly Divorce." The girls each told one of their fun, sweet, positive memories, followed by one that helped them put into perspective why Mom and Dad were divorcing. Each of them then suggested a ritual. Mom and Dad told stories and, also, suggested rituals. The therapist added recommendations about family meetings and increased communication, including the ongoing combating of myths. During the ceremony, the parents forgave themselves and each other. Dad gave each girl a heart-shaped locket that had a photo of her on one side and him on the other. As he put the locket around each daughter's neck, he said, "You are always in my heart and I am always with you."

6-MONTH FOLLOW-UP

Dad said he was spending more time than ever with his girls and truly enjoying their company. Mom reported being more relaxed, enjoying parenting and new freedoms. Both parents reported that "The Friendly Divorce" had significantly helped not only their children but also themselves. They agreed the most powerful piece for them was to forgive themselves and each other. The parents also stated that each of the girls was continuing to do well.

Case 3: The Systematic Desensitization of Elevators in Own Apartment Building—Patty, Age 7 Years, 7 Months

This case history demonstrates the effectiveness of the program and techniques used by In-Home Care, which can often facilitate tremendous healing in a fraction of the time of traditional office visits. Appointments were more frequent and at the time of day considered most therapeutically beneficial (including early morning before school).

INITIAL PARENT INTERVIEW

According to Mom, Patty was an artistic, mature, 7-year-old, only child. Shortly after her father "abandoned" Patty and her mother, Patty refused to take the elevator up and down from her family's 15th-floor apartment. Mom described herself as a grief stricken, financially stressed, and harried mom, with no energy, patience, or time to walk the stairs with her daughter. She reported that she was "dragging" a "hysterical" Patty into the elevator "kicking and screaming" at least twice a day.

Mom signed releases giving the therapist permission to talk with the schoolteacher and school psychologist. The school psychologist agreed to put Patty in a group for children of separated/divorced parents and see her individually two times a week.

SESSION 1

The therapist went to Patty's home and after easily establishing rapport, taught Patty deep-breathing and relaxation techniques. Patty then used the techniques while looking at Polaroid instant photos the therapist had taken on the way to the session of the inside and outside of the two elevators. By the end of the session, Patty was playing in the doorway of her apartment, pretending that the elevator was coming.

"PHONE-IN"

Mom was referred for care at a Center for Separated and Divorced Women. She was educated about the deep-breathing and relaxation techniques her daughter had been taught.

SESSION 2

Patty and the therapist talked about elevators and why they were scary. Patty reenacted how her sobbing mother had told her that her father had left them, while the two of them were riding in the elevator. A negative association apparently had been created in that instant. The therapist reviewed the deep-breathing and the progressive muscle relaxation technique, and then Patty drew a picture of her mother telling her the sad news. The elevator was heavily shaded with a large black crayon. The picture portrayed the blackness engulfing the two tiny people. The therapist and Patty read *A Boy and a Bear: The Children's Relaxation Book* by Lori Lite (1994). Patty signed the book out until next session.

"PHONE-IN"

Mom reported that she had read the book and practiced the deep-breathing and relaxation techniques with Patty. She said she was enjoying their time together, planned to do the techniques with Patty daily, and that she was feeling more positive in general. She and the therapist reviewed the Boys Town video for parents, "Catch 'Em Being Good," that she had out on loan. They discussed effective encouragement instead of praise. Mom was to look for and report concerns provided on a list which included Patty fearing her mother would abandon her, general loss themes, and Patty needing to take care of her mom while constricting her own feelings and needs.

"CHECK-IN"

Mom reported no additional concerns from the list given to her the previous week and discussed during the phone-in.

SESSION 3

The therapist and Patty stood in the hallway and counted the times they heard the elevator go up or down, past the floor she lived on. Patty pushed the button and the elevator soon came. She repeatedly did this and greeted and waved to many neighbors. Then, the therapist and Patty discussed the "different kinds of families" leaving for school. Patty knew, and told the therapist, who were single parents, stepfamilies, and blended families. She waved to friends on the elevator. Throughout the experience, Patty was cued to use deep breathing and various relaxation techniques. She reported that it was "better" and "quieter" now that her father was gone. Patty was given the Homeplay of using the Galvanic Skin Resistance Biofeedback Device (Thought Technology Ltd., [514-489-8251], Montreal, Canada) frequently to learn to recognize and take charge of her anxiety.

"PHONE-IN"

Mom reported that she, herself, was feeling much calmer. She agreed to begin the U 'N' Me Time.

"CHECK-IN"

Mom reported a significant improvement in her relationship with her daughter and credited the U 'N' Me Time.

SESSION 4

Just as planned, Patty pushed the elevator down button. When the elevator stopped and opened, the therapist held the door as Patty got in and walked to the back of the elevator, then came out. She repeated this many times, becoming more playful over time. She explored getting in, running around, spinning, and peekaboo from the hidden corner and even sitting while the therapist continued to hold the door. Patty pushed the button for the other elevators to come then go after she played in it.

"PHONE-IN"

Mom and the therapist discussed using the curative factors in U 'N' Me Time and beginning "Family Meetings" at home.

"CHECK-IN"

Mom requested to borrow two Creative Therapies videos, one on using the curative factors and the other on "Family Meetings."

SESSION 5

The therapist and Patty went down in the elevator one floor at a time, got out, got in, then went down another floor. Next, they went down two floors at a time, then three floors. When they got to the bottom, Patty decided they would go all the way back up to the 15th floor together. Patty raced in to tell her mother, who then went all the way down and up with them. She then practiced going down an agreed upon number of floors at a time, on her own. The therapist had gone down ahead so as to greet Patty when her elevator doors opened. Then, Patty went all the way down by herself, to where the therapist was standing, waiting for her. Patty and the therapist laughed and laughed. It seemed to be an incredible release of pent up energy. Patty made a book with magazine cutouts, drawings from some of the sessions and instant photos of her therapy story. She planned to finish it for the final session the following week.

"PHONE-IN"

Mom decided it would be helpful to have a final session with the therapist to review the parts of the programming for which she would be responsible.

SESSION 6

The therapist buzzed Patty's apartment from the lobby and asked her over the intercom to come down in the elevator and get her. Without hesitation, Patty agreed. The therapist showed Patty the cupcakes that she had brought for Patty's graduation from therapy and suggested that they take separate elevators up to Patty's apartment and race to the door. (They had a celebration, iced cupcakes that had to be refrigerated!) Patty then spent the next 30 minutes going up and down in the elevator. This was followed by a graduation celebration, in which they read the story Patty had made of her six sessions. This book was an ongoing representation of her healing process.

SESSION WITH MOTHER

This session was held to reinforce teachings and review programming.

6-MONTH FOLLOW-UP

Mom reported that Patty had read the book over and over for weeks. She had a sheet of common divorce myths and their truths to keep herself and Patty in check. Mom reported that, to date, while Patty occasionally mentions her father, she continues to describe his departure as a relief. Patty has no symptoms of anxiety. Per the arrangement set up with the school, the school psychologist checked in with Patty occasionally and reported that she was doing "better than ever" in school. Mom continued to be involved in her own therapy.

SUMMARY AND CONCLUSION

Bradshaw (1995) says that "divorce is a fact of modern life and yet many couples don't divorce and many who do continue the dysfunction they had when married." Arguably, the main reason children may require psychological care before, during, and after their parents' divorce may be due to the ugliness, fighting, yelling, deception, and litigation. We usually hear about this type of divorce and not about the children who are doing better, as a result of divorce, because they are now living in a functional, calm home. Furthermore, children who grow up in high-conflict families with both parents can have more challenges than children from low-conflict, divorced families. What about the divorces that maintain family ties and provide children with four parents and two happier homes? These parents can model, assist, and guide other divorcing parents. Communication that would help normalize blended families would significantly decrease the stress these families experience.

It is time to change the thinking about divorce. One could start by getting rid of problem language such as "ex," "illegitimate," "living in sin," "broken home," then move on to eliminate all those hyphens that separate out stepfamily members. After all, demographers project that between 40% and 60% of all marriages in America will end in divorce in the 21st century, although many of the partners will remarry (Bradshaw, 1995). Divorce is on the verge of becoming acceptable, with serial monogamy becoming the lifestyle and blended families becoming the more common statistic. It is projected that between 50% and 60% of children born in the 1990s will live, at some point, in single-parent families (Hetherington, Bridges, & Insabella, 1998; Furstenberg & Cherlin, 1991; Wallerstein, 1991). Even children of stable marriages are now aware of divorce and its effect on children by observing their friends and classmates who are from divorced households.

Given the statistics, one could say that divorce has become the norm. Increased awareness and an improved attitude can better support and guide our children. A focus away from family structure and onto family process would be a helpful start. It is not the divorce per se but the events surrounding it that often seem to determine children's challenges.

Acknowledging divorce as normal would assure children that emotional security and social acceptance are not dependent upon their parents being married. With this social stigma removed, children's self-esteem could remain intact. They would know that despite their parents' marital status, they are still within the norm.

In summation, Creative Therapies has identified five categories that make up the success of STSOPT with children of divorced parents: (1) assessment, FEEDBAC 2, and the collaborative approach to the treatment plan; (2) components of STSOPT; (3) play space and materials; (4) involvement and participation of both parents; and (5) ongoing support and the 6-month follow-up.

An extensive description of the playrooms and their contents was included to emphasize the importance of the environment and to increase professionals' attention to details, supplies, and equipment.

"Two-House Therapy" was described as a powerful technique to offer children from divorced homes. Every playroom is incomplete without them.

Three cases were listed to support the theory, practice, and effectiveness of short-term, solution-oriented therapy for children of divorced parents with ongoing success reported in the 6-month follow-up with the parents.

REFERENCES

Alexander, F., & French, T. M. (1946). *Psychoanalytic therapy.* New York: Ronald Press.

Barten, H. H., & Barten, S. S. (Eds.). (1973). *Children and their parents in brief therapy.* New York: Behavioral Publications.

Boys Town National Training Center. (1990). *Boys Town Videos for parents.* (800) 545-5771. Boys Town Center, Boys Town, NE 68010.

Bradshaw, J. (1995). *On surviving divorce* [Audio]. Houston, TX: Sagebrush Productions.

Burdsal, C., & Buel, C. L. (1980, January). A short term community based early stage intervention program for behavior problem youth. *Journal of Clinical Psychology, 36*(1), 226–241.

Castelnuovo-Tedesco, P. (1971). Decreasing the length of psychotherapy: Theoretical and practical aspects of the problem. In S. Arieti (Ed.), *The world biennial of psychiatry* (pp. 55–71). New York: Basic Books.

Childswork/Childsplay. (800) 962-1141 c/o Genesis Direct, Inc., 100 Plaza Drive, Secaucus, NJ 07094-3613.

Creative Therapies. (1998). *How to use the curative factors: A video for parents.* Stamford, CT: Musical Dog Studio.

Creative Therapies. (1999). *Family meetings* [Video].

Empowering People. (800) 456-7770. P.O. Box 1926, Orem, UT 84059.

Ferenczi, S., & Rank, O. (1925). *The development of psychoanalysis.* New York: Nervous and Mental Disease.

Furstenberg, F. F., Jr., & Cherlin, A. J. (1991). *Divided families: What happens to children when parents part.* Cambridge, MA: Harvard University Press.

Gardner, K. (1976). *Psychotherapy with children of divorce.* New York: Aronson.

Garvin, V., Leber, D., & Kalter, N. (1991, July). Children of divorce: Predictors of change following preventive intervention. *American Journal of Orthopsychiatry, 61*(3), 438–447.

Hetherington, E. M., Bridges, M., & Inabella, G. M. (1998, February). What matters? What does not? Five perspectives on the association between marital transitions and children's adjustment. *American Psychologist, 53*(2), 167–184.

Johnston, J. R., & Roseby, V. (1997). *In the name of the child: A developmental approach to understanding and helping children of conflicted and violent divorce.* New York: Free Press.

Kelly, J., & Wallerstein, J. S. (1977, January). Brief interventions with children in divorcing families. *American Journal of Orthopsychiatry, 47*(1), 23–39.

Kissel, S. (1974, July). Mothers and therapists evaluate long-term and short-term child therapy. *Journal of Clinical Psychology, 30*(3), 296–299.

Klar, H., & Coleman, W. L. (1995). Brief solution focused strategies for behavioral pediatrics. *Pediatric Clinic of North America, 42*(1), 131–141.

Kuhli, L. (1983). The use of two houses in play therapy. In C. E. Schaefer & K. J. O'Connor (Eds.), *Handbook of play therapy* (pp. 274–280). New York: Wiley.

Mackenzie, K. R. (1991). Principles in brief intensive psychotherapy. *Psychiatric Annals, 21,* 398–404.

Marmor, J. (1979). Short term dynamic psychotherapy. *American Journal of Psychiatry, 136,* 149–155.

Mosher, L., & Burti, L. (1989). *Community mental health.* New York: Norton.

Nelson, J., & Glenn, H. S. (1992). *Time-out: Abuses and effective uses.* Fair Oaks, CA: Sunrise Press.

Neuman, M. G. (1998). *Helping your kids cope with divorce the Sandcastles way.* New York: Random House.

Patterson, G. R. (1974). Interventions for boys with conduct problems: Multiple settings, treatment, and criteria. *Journal of Consulting and Clinical Psychology, 42,* 471–481.

Patterson, G. R., & Reid, J. A. B. (1973). Intervention for families of aggressive boys: A replication study. *Behaviour Research and Therapy, 11,* 383–394.

Poinsier, B., & Laurin, A. S. (1995). Economic evaluation of a simulated program of brief psychotherapy for children with mild problems. *Sante Mentale au Quebec, 20*(2), 203–218.

Schmidt, T., & Spencer, T. (1991). *Building trust, making friends: Four group activity manuals for high-risk students. Thomas Barker talks about divorce and separation (Grades K–6).* Minneapolis, MN: Johnson Institute.

Selekman, M. D. (1997). Solution-focused therapy with children: Harnessing family strengths for systemic change. New York: Guilford Press.

Shapiro, L. (1994). *Short-term therapy with children: A multi-modal approach to helping children with their problems.* King of Prussia, PA: Center for Applied Psychology.

Stolberg, A., & Mahler, J. (1994, February). Enhancing treatment gains in a school-based intervention for children of divorce through skill training, parental involvement, and transfer procedures. *Journal of Consulting and Clinical Psychology, 62*(1), 147–156.

Thought Technology, Ltd. (514) 489-9251, 2180 Belgrave Avenue, Montreal (QC) Canada H4A 2L8.

Wallerstein, J. S. (1991, May). The long term effects of divorce on children: A review. *Journal of the American Academy of Child and Adolescent Psychiatry, 30*(3), 349–360.

BIBLIOTHERAPY

Blackstone-Ford, J. (1995). *My parents are divorced, too: Book for kids by kids.* Washington, DC: Magination Press.

Blakeslee, S., Fassler, S., & Lash, M. (1996). *The divorce workbook: An interactive guide for kids and families.* Burlington, VT: Waterfront Books.

Blitzer/Field, M. (1992). *All about divorce.* King of Prussia, PA: Center for Applied Psychology.—The book comes with a doll family and back drop scenes to allow children to play out their concerns.

Blitzer/Field, M., & Shore, H. (1994). *My life turned upside down, but I turned it right side up.* King of Prussia, PA: Center for Applied Psychology.—A story about a girl who lives in two places. On every page, we learn about a problem, and when we turn the book upside down it tells how she solved it.

Blume, J. (1972). *It's not the end of the world.* New York: Bradbury.—Ages 10–12. A first person, humorous, narrative about a child's experiences at home and school. The child does not want her parents to divorce, but deep down knows it is inevitable. Includes the confused emotions experienced during divorce.

Cole, B. (1997). *The Un-wedding.* New York: Alfred A. Knopf, Inc.—A silly story about why divorce can be a good thing for parents and children.

Coleman, W. (1998). *What children need to know when parents get divorced: A book to read with children going through the trauma of divorce.* Minneapolis, MN: Betany House.—Ages 6–12.

Evans, M. D. (1986). *This is me and my two families: An awareness scrapbook/ journal for children living in step-families.* Washington, DC: Magination Press.

Fassler, D., Lash, M., & Ives, S. (1996). *Changing families: An interactive guide for kids and grown-ups.* Burlington, VT: Waterfront Books.

Gardner, R. (1970). *The boys and girls book about divorce: For children and their divorced parents.* New York: Bantam.—Ages 9–12. Discusses the fears and worries common to children of divorce and offers advice on how to handle these challenges.

Heegaard, M. (1991). *When mom and dad separate.* Minneapolis, MN: Woodland Press.—Ages 6–12. A facilitators' guide is also available.

Heegaard, M. (1993). *When a parent marries again.* Minneapolis, MN: Woodland Press.

Hogan. (1996). *Will dad ever move back home?* Ages 5–8.

Johnston, J., & Breunig, C. (1997). *Through the eyes of children: Healing stories for children of divorce.* New York: Free Press.—15 metaphoric stories to help children understand and cope with their parents' separation and living apart. Ages 5–8.

Kimball, G. (1996). *How to survive your parents' divorce: Kids' advice to kids.* Chico, CA: Equality Press.

Krementz, J. (1984). *How it feels when parents divorce.* New York: Random House.—By children ages 7–16 from highly diverse backgrounds.

Lindsay, J. W. (1996). *Do I have a daddy?* Buena Park, CA: Morning Glory Press.— Ages 3–6. Contains a special section for single parents, including the never-married parent and the totally absent father.

Lite, L. (1994). *A boy and a bear: The children's relaxation book.*

Prestine, J. (1996). *Mom and Dad break-up*. Parsippany, NJ: Fearon Teacher Aids.—Preschool–second grade. A practical resource guide is also available.

Stinson, K. (1997). *Mom and Dad don't live together anymore*. Buffalo, NY: Annick Press.—Ages 4–8.

Thomas, S., & Rankin, D. (1998). *Divorced but still my parents: A helping-book about divorce for children and parents*. Longmont, CO: Springboard Publications.—Contains workbook activities for children ages 6–12.

PART II

FAMILY PLAY THERAPY

7

Short-Term Play Therapy for Families with Chronic Illness

RISË VANFLEET

INTRODUCTION

Advances in medical technology have dramatically reduced mortality from illness, and many devastating diseases have been eliminated or controlled. Even so, 15% of children in the United States are estimated to have chronic illnesses that require some lifestyle adaptation or ongoing medical management (Hobbs & Perrin, 1985). That number rises to 25% of people between the ages of 45 and 60 (Shuman, 1996). When one considers the number of parents who live with chronic illnesses, the number of children whose lives are directly affected by chronic illness becomes substantial.

For the purposes of this chapter, the term "chronic illness" refers to a long-lasting illness that requires ongoing medical supervision or treatment and/or results in physical debilitation or lifestyle alteration. Illnesses such as cancer, diabetes, asthma, cystic fibrosis, renal disease, heart disease, and others fit this description. With the vast improvements in the treatment of AIDS, it is now considered a chronic disease.

While the quality of life for chronically ill children and parents has improved, these illnesses and their treatments still demand much of families, often in the form of ongoing and sometimes unpleasant medical treatments, periodic hospitalizations, special diets, anxiety, loss of time with each other, financial pressures, and the need to dispel others' misunderstandings about illness. With changes in the health care system, families are carrying the responsibility for medical management to a greater extent than ever before. While many families cope admirably, these demands can result in psychosocial difficulties for children and their parents, and place them at risk for adjustment and mental health problems.

The current contribution outlines the impact of chronic illness on families and describes a short-term play therapy intervention that can help families live fulfilling lives despite the demands of illness. General use of filial play therapy with this population has been described elsewhere (VanFleet, 1992), but a short-term application of filial play therapy is introduced here.

The Impact of Chronic Illness on Families

Chronic illnesses can impact families in several ways: the illness itself, the treatment or management of the illness, and broader, family lifestyle disruptions. Detailed descriptions of the impact of chronic illness are available elsewhere (Eisenberg, Sutkin, & Jansen, 1984; Hobbs & Perrin, 1985; Hobbs, Perrin, & Ireys, 1985; Bigbee, 1992; VanFleet, 1985, 1992; McCue, 1994; Shuman, 1996), so the impact is only briefly outlined here.

IMPACT OF THE ILLNESS

Chronic illnesses can be painful and/or uncomfortable. Many illnesses result in loss of energy. Some illnesses restrict a person's movement or sleep patterns or diet. For example, to remain healthy, diabetic children or adults must restrict sugar intake and eat other foods in carefully controlled portions at regularly scheduled times. Illnesses can result in changes in outward appearance as well as mood and behavior. The course of the illness can affect family emotions and lifestyle: Some illnesses are steadily progressive; others stabilize for long periods; still others are characterized by a series of remissions and recurrences.

Everyone in the family needs to understand the illness and its likely outcomes. Young children often misunderstand and fear that they have caused the illness by their misbehavior or anger. It is not uncommon for children to assume that diabetes (i.e., *di*-abetes) means that the person will *die*. Siblings of ill children can fear that they, too, will get sick. Parents must learn complex medical language about the illness and its treatment.

All family members have emotional reactions to the illness as well. Anxiety, fear, anger, and depression are common in ill children and ill parents. Siblings can feel resentful and guilty. Emotional withdrawal and denial are also common.

The presence of chronic illness can alter family members' social interactions within the family and with extended family members, neighbors, teachers, employers, and so on. Children commonly report feeling "different" when they have chronic illnesses. A 9-year-old diabetic girl won a chocolate candy bar in a Halloween costume contest. After she was given the candy bar, which she planned to give to her siblings, the contest judge returned and asked her to give back the candy, saying, "You're diabetic and can't have this." Others may tease chronically ill children or refuse to interact with them. Parents of ill children report that well-meaning extended family members can give restricted foods to children, even when parents protest, saying, "Just this once, it won't hurt." This inadvertently undermines the parents' efforts to help the child comply with medical requirements. Within the family, roles can change. Siblings of ill children or children of an ill parent may become caregivers and protectors. Family recreational activities can be reduced (Quittner, Opipari, Espelage, Carter, & Eid, 1998).

IMPACT OF THE TREATMENT

The treatment of chronic illness brings its own stresses to the family. Treatment procedures can be painful, invasive, or frightening. Daily injections and blood testing can be a nuisance at best; renal dialysis can be time-consuming and result in energy loss. Restrictive diets can be extremely hard to follow and sometimes result in the entire family altering its eating habits. Medication side effects can be worse than the illness itself. Chemotherapy and radiation treatments for cancer can result in prolonged nausea, loss of hair, and so on. Hospitalizations can separate family members when they most need each other. For example, an 8-year-old with cystic fibrosis had to be hospitalized for 2 weeks. She and her family lived in a rural community, 150 miles from the hospital. The girl and her mother stayed at the hospital while her father and siblings remained at home to attend work and school. She and her mother reported feelings of isolation, and her father and siblings said they constantly worried about what was happening at the hospital.

Family members often must learn complex medical management procedures to carry out at home (Quittner, Opipari, Regoli, Jacobsen, & Eigen, 1992; Siminerio & Betschart, 1986). This can be especially problematic if the ill child or parent fails to comply with the treatment or has difficulty following the diet. Medical professionals can exacerbate family tensions surrounding treatment adherence with comments that are blaming or that place responsibility on the wrong person. For example, a chronically ill father was having difficulty complying with strict fluid intake restrictions while on hemodialysis for end-stage renal disease. His doctor, frustrated with his medical condition, called the man's wife and told her, "You really need to keep an eye on everything he drinks. It's your job to make sure he does better." This displaced advice infuriated the wife and led to increased arguments between herself and her husband.

FAMILY LIFESTYLE DISRUPTIONS

Chronic illness and its treatment can disrupt family life in many other ways. It is common for at least one parent to reduce his or her employment in order to care for an ill child or spouse. Interference with school attendance or the necessity for special schedules or considerations at school occurs frequently (Rynard, Chambers, Klinck, & Gray, 1998; VanFleet, 1985). Financial pressures are substantial for many chronic illnesses. As family members tackle the medical management, they must learn to give injections, prepare specialized diets, reschedule their lives around the illness, and generally live less spontaneous lives. Most families report that, while they adjust to new routines, they never feel "normal" again. Misunderstandings and prejudices by family and community members can hurt. A teenage boy who mowed lawns after school lost one of his longtime customers when she discovered he had diabetes.

All of these factors complicate the lives of families with chronic illness. While many families cope admirably with these additional demands (Barbarin, Hughes, & Chesler, 1985; Drotar, Crawford, & Bush, 1984; VanFleet, 1985), some do not. As one mother of an ill child put it, "We've been able to adjust to all this, but it's not easy. It definitely complicates our decisions (as parents), we get pretty stressed sometimes, and planning family activities can be a nightmare with all the extra things to consider." In this chapter, families dealing with chronic illness are viewed as being "at risk" for psychosocial difficulties.

SHORT-TERM PLAY THERAPY APPROACHES

Short-term play interventions for families dealing with chronic illness can serve three primary purposes: (1) provide support to families experiencing the stresses of chronic illness, (2) strengthen family relationships and increase the chances that families become closer rather than more distant in response to family chronic illness, and (3) assist families who are experiencing difficulties. This section details a short-term intervention that effectively combines play therapy with family therapy: filial (parent–child) play therapy.

Short-Term Filial Play Therapy

Filial play therapy, developed by Bernard and Louise Guerney (B. Guerney, 1964; L. F. Guerney, 1983), combines play therapy and family therapy in a highly effective intervention that can be very beneficial for families experiencing chronic illness (VanFleet, 1992). In filial play therapy, the therapist trains and supervises parents as they conduct special child-centered play sessions with their own children. With appropriate training and supervision, parents usually are able to conduct these special play sessions at home without the therapist's direct supervision.

The goals of filial play therapy are to help the parents create an accepting, safe environment in which their children can express their feelings fully, gain an understanding of their world, solve problems, and develop confidence in themselves and their parents. The therapy process is designed to help parents become more responsive to their children's feelings and needs, to become better at solving child- and family-related problems, and to become more skillful and confident as parents. Families who participate in filial play therapy are expected to emerge with better communication skills, problem-solving and coping skills, and stronger family relationships. Furthermore, filial play therapy is usually enjoyable for the entire family, and many families incorporate it into their lifestyles after formal therapy has ended (VanFleet, 1998).

Filial play therapy is particularly useful for families dealing with chronic illness for several reasons:

1. It is designed to strengthen family relationships, which can be strained by the illness and its treatment. It can provide a positive focus that balances the illness-related stresses. It permits family members to provide real support for each other.
2. It provides parents of an ill child with something *proactive* to do at a time when they might feel quite helpless. As one mother put it, "We were very focused on the illness. Everything seemed heavy and serious. The illness was running our lives. Filial gave us a big sense of relief because we felt we were doing something positive and fun for all of us."
3. When a parent is ill, filial play sessions can provide "quality time" that might be in short supply otherwise.
4. Filial play therapy provides chronically ill children, as well as healthy siblings, with a safe, effective outlet for their feelings and a supportive atmosphere in which to develop coping and problem-solving skills.
5. While illness-related losses may leave families feeling helpless, filial play therapy can restore a sense of control to all family members.
6. This approach provides parents with an accepting climate in which to discuss and work through their own feelings and issues.
7. Filial play therapy provides parents with skills that can help them outside the play sessions and in the future.

Because of its educational nature, filial play therapy has never been a lengthy therapeutic approach. Families presenting with mild to moderate problems typically require 17–20 one-hour sessions before discharge. For families experiencing chronic illness, however, even this amount of therapy might seem overwhelming. Their lives may seem filled with medical appointments, the management of the illness, or the lifestyle restrictions imposed by the illness. In an attempt to adapt filial therapy to the special concerns of these families while keeping the therapy as brief as possible, this chapter outlines a 10-session (11-hour) program that maintains the integrity of filial play therapy, minimizes actual therapy contacts, and provides families with real, lasting benefits. The following sections outline the process of filial play therapy and this short-term adaptation of it.

THE PROCESS OF FILIAL PLAY THERAPY

VanFleet (1994) has detailed the methods and process of filial play therapy, which are outlined below.

1. The therapist explains the rationale and methods of filial play therapy, answering parents' questions and engaging them as partners in the process.

2. The therapist then demonstrates the play sessions individually with the children in the family as the parents watch and record their observations and questions. The therapist fully discusses the play session demonstrations with the parents afterward.

3. The therapist trains the parents in the four basic play session skills: structuring, empathic listening, child-centered imaginary play, and limit setting. A variety of training approaches can be used, but this phase of therapy culminates in mock play therapy sessions in which the therapist pretends to be a child and the parents practice the four basic skills. The therapist and parents then discuss the experience fully, including skills feedback and anticipation of what to expect from the parents' children.

4. The parents begin play sessions with their own children under the supervision of the therapist. The play sessions involve one parent and one child at a time, and the sessions can be alternated to include all family members (VanFleet, 1994). The therapist observes the initial play sessions that parents have with their children, then discusses them fully with the parents afterward. The therapist provides feedback to the parents on their play session skills, helps them understand their children's play, and discusses a variety of family dynamic issues that inevitably arise.

5. After parents feel comfortable conducting the play sessions, they begin to hold play sessions independently at home. The therapist and parents meet periodically to discuss the play sessions, problem-solve family issues that arise, and generalize the skills beyond the play sessions to everyday life.

SHORT-TERM ADAPTATION FOR FAMILIES DEALING
WITH CHRONIC ILLNESS

This short-term adaptation of filial therapy has been used successfully by the author with families dealing with a chronically ill member in several settings: medical centers, mental health centers, independent practice offices, and in the families' homes. Child chronic illnesses have included diabetes, cystic fibrosis, cancer, congenital heart disease, end-stage renal disease, growth disorders, and asthma. Parental chronic illnesses have included AIDS, cancer, diabetes, autoimmune liver disease, end-stage renal disease, and multiple sclerosis.

Session-by-Session Outline of Short-Term Filial Play Therapy

SESSION 1 (1 HOUR, PARENTS ALONE): INTRODUCTION

After discussing the parents' concerns, the therapist recommends filial therapy along with other interventions. It is extremely important for the therapist to explain *explicitly* how filial play therapy can help with the parents' concerns and presenting problems. All questions are discussed.

Discussion of everyone's understanding of the illness and its impact is also important at this early stage of therapy, and the therapist can recommend activities or reading materials to help the children and parents understand their family member's illness fully. Most illness-related organizations, such as the American Cancer Society, American Diabetes Association, and the American Heart Association, have available information pamphlets, books, coloring books, and so on, appropriate for children and adults. McCue (1994) has written a comprehensive guide for helping children through a parent's illness. Increasing numbers of children's books about their own, their siblings', or their parents' illnesses are available (Krisher, 1992; Mills, 1992; Mulder, 1992; Peterkin, 1992; Kohlenberg, 1993; Carter & Carter, 1995) and gain meaning when families read them together.

Before concluding, the therapist shows the parents the playroom and discusses the selection of toys. The therapist explains that a variety of toys can be used imaginatively and are included to permit expression of a wide range of feelings. The therapist encourages the parents to ask questions and answers them as fully as possible.

SESSION 2 (1 HOUR, ENTIRE FAMILY):
PLAY SESSION DEMONSTRATION

During this session, the therapist demonstrates the child-centered play sessions that parents will eventually learn to conduct. Ideally, the therapist holds individual brief play sessions with each 3- to 12-year-old child in the family. If there is only one child, the play session can last approximately 30 minutes; time is lessened when more children are involved. For example, if there are two children, the therapist holds a 15-minute play session with one child, then a second 15-minute session with the other. The parents observe the play session demonstrations from a corner of the room, preferably set off by a desk or other piece of furniture. The therapist provides parents with paper and clipboards so they can record their observations and questions.

After the play session demonstrations, the therapist shows the children to a separate waiting area and meets with the parents alone to discuss the play sessions. The therapist asks the parents to share their comments first, listens carefully, and then shares his or her own reactions to the play sessions. Often, the therapist can point out various skills that were used, as well as some basic themes of the children's play.

The session concludes with the therapist providing an overview of the four play session skills that the parents will learn and provides a handout about filial therapy, such as *A Parent's Guide to Filial Therapy* (VanFleet, 1998).

SESSION 3 (1½ HOURS, PARENTS ALONE): TRAINING

Before starting the training phase of filial therapy, the therapist inquires about the educational interventions that were suggested in the first session. Then, the therapist discusses in depth the rationale and "mechanics" of the four play session skills: structuring, empathic listening, child-centered imaginary play, and limit setting (VanFleet, 1994). Wherever possible, the therapist reminds the parents of the various skills used during the play session demonstrations.

The next step of training involves practice of the empathic listening skill. Parents remain in their seats while the therapist gathers some toys and plays with them, asking the parents to describe aloud what the therapist is doing (behavioral tracking) and what the therapist seems to be feeling. The therapist ensures that parents are successful by showing obvious feelings, prompting or modeling for parents, and reinforcing their efforts. For example, the therapist might pile up the blocks while parents reflect, "You're adding another block. . . . You're making it very tall. . . . It's hard to get it the way you want . . . ," in response to the therapist's behaviors and facial expressions. The therapist then might knock over the tower of blocks with a big laugh, helping the parents to reflect the feeling, "You really liked knocking that over" or "It's fun to watch the blocks tumbling." The key throughout the training is to ensure that the parents are successful.

After each parent has had the opportunity to practice the empathic listening skill briefly, the therapist holds one or two mock play sessions with each parent. The therapist plays the role of the child and assists the parent as he or she practices the four basic skills. Again, therapist prompting, modeling, and reinforcement are used to ensure success. The therapist provides the parent with constructive feedback on his or her use of the skills during the mock play session, going into more detail at the end of the mock session. The therapist uses behavioral shaping with the parents, reinforcing their steps in the direction of skills acquisition. If both parents are involved, they observe each other's mock play sessions but do not critique each other. All feedback is provided by the therapist.

It is preferable for the therapist to hold two mock play sessions with each parent to help build confidence and refine the use of the skills. Time factors may not always permit this, however, but at least one mock play session should be conducted with each parent.

The training phase of filial play therapy is critical, and because time is limited, it is essential that the therapist keep the focus of this third session on skills acquisition. If parents can apply the four basic skills, even if imperfectly, without much difficulty during the mock sessions, then the therapist prepares them for having play sessions with their own children during the next session.

SESSION 4 (1 HOUR, PARENTS AND CHILDREN): FILIAL PLAY SESSION 1

For the first half-hour of this session, the therapist observes as the parent holds a play session with one of the children. If two parents are involved, each holds a 15-minute play session with two of the children (or with the same child, if only one child is involved). The therapist then discusses these first filial play sessions with the parents alone, while the children wait in a separate waiting area.

The feedback portion of the session consists of (1) asking the parents for their reactions and questions about their play sessions, (2) providing the therapist's feedback about parents' use of the skills, and (3) discussing play themes and possible meanings of their children's play.

At the close of this session, the therapist provides parents with a list of toys that they can begin to acquire or set aside to use eventually in their special play sessions at home. The therapist explains that separate toys help accentuate the special nature of the child-centered play sessions and provide a range of emotional expression and problem solving. The therapist suggests that parents look over the list and return with any questions about acquiring toys inexpensively.

SESSION 5 (1 HOUR, PARENTS AND CHILDREN): FILIAL PLAY SESSION 2

The therapist supervises the parents' second play sessions with their children, following the same format described for the fourth session. Play sessions occupy the first half of the session; skills feedback and play theme discussion occupy the last half.

During the discussion period, the therapist helps the parents understand how their children's play may be relating to real-life events. If needed, other problems and interventions can also be covered.

At the close of this session, the therapist asks how the parents' assembly of their special play session "toy kit" is coming and helps troubleshoot any problems.

SESSION 6 (1½ HOURS, PARENTS AND CHILDREN): FILIAL PLAY
SESSION 3 AND TRANSITION TO HOME SESSIONS

The third filial play sessions and their discussion occur as before. If there are no significant problems, the therapist uses the final half-hour to discuss the transfer of the filial play sessions to the home setting. The therapist guides the parents as they decide where, when, and how they will have their special play sessions at home, without the direct supervision of the therapist. This involves selecting a location, scheduling these one-to-one play sessions, and deciding how parents will handle potential interruptions and the special limits they may need to set to protect their furniture, and so on. The therapist indicates that he or she would like the parents to hold only one home play session with each of their children and return to discuss them before proceeding.

SESSION 7 (1 HOUR, PARENTS ONLY): DISCUSSION OF FIRST HOME
PLAY SESSIONS AND OTHER ISSUES IN CHRONIC ILLNESS

Parents report on their first home play sessions with their children, indicating what went well, what difficulties arose, and the primary play themes they recognized. The therapist assists them with recognizing and understanding play themes as necessary. Usually, parents are quite skillful by this point, and children's play reflects real issues, problem solving, and coping. Often, parents report improvements in the presenting problems by this phase of therapy.

The therapist invites parents to share their own reactions to the children's play. This frequently elicits parents' own feelings about the illness, their family life, and so on, and gives the therapist an opportunity to help parents problem-solve their own issues. In this way, the therapist can significantly impact parents' feelings and behaviors.

SESSION 8 (1 HOUR, PARENTS ONLY): DISCUSSION OF SECOND AND
THIRD HOME PLAY SESSIONS AND OTHER ISSUES

The therapist meets with the parents after they have completed their second and third home play sessions. Again, the session begins with a discussion of those home sessions and what can be learned from them about the children and the parents. Additional problem solving for issues that arise is encouraged by the therapist as needed.

More attention is now given to the special family and parenting issues created by the illness and its treatment. As parents gain confidence and learn more about their children through the play sessions, they become more active as partners in the therapeutic process. Problem solving can be applied to many issues, ranging from ways to determine if children's maladaptive behavior is a result of the illness or of more "normal" developmental/behavioral factors, to helping their children deal with others' misunderstanding the illness, to easing parents' guilt because their lives are "different" from those of other people.

The therapist helps parents learn to generalize to everyday life the skills they have mastered in the playroom. For example, the therapist helps parents discover ways to use the listening skills when discussing school or friends or illness-related matters with their children. The use of limit setting is adapted to daily situations.

At this time, the therapist can share other interventions such as family storytelling (VanFleet, 1993), drawings (McCue, 1994), behavioral counseling (Schaefer & Eisen, 1998), or other short-term play techniques (Kaduson & Schaefer, 1997) that help children with illness-related and other concerns.

SESSION 9 (1 HOUR, PARENTS ONLY): DISCUSSION OF FOURTH AND FIFTH HOME PLAY SESSIONS AND OTHER ISSUES

The therapist discusses the family's fourth and fifth home play sessions as described for Session 8. Skills generalization and other issues and interventions are also covered in much the same manner.

If therapeutic goals are being met and all is going well, the therapist prepares the family for discharge, which will occur after one more session. The therapist explains that play sessions may continue at home after the formal therapy sessions have concluded and that this will be discussed in more detail in the next and final session.

SESSION 10 (1 HOUR, PARENTS ONLY): DISCUSSION OF SIXTH AND SEVENTH HOME PLAY SESSIONS AND DISCHARGE

After discussing the most recent home play sessions and issues, the therapist focuses attention on the discharge process. The following topics are covered: how to continue having home play sessions and what to look for, how to determine when children are ready to end the play sessions, how to shift from play sessions to "special times" with the children, and how to involve the entire family in fun activities.

The therapist reminds parents that they may contact him or her at any time with future questions or problems but focuses upon their competence and confidence in their newly acquired skills and parenting abilities. The primary message is one of empowerment: The parents are capable of carrying on. The therapist can discharge the parents in a celebratory manner once the discussion of the future is completed, such as by awarding "diplomas" or clown noses, or some other playful symbol of their time in filial play therapy.

Summary of the Short-Term Filial Play Therapy Model

This 10-week, 11-hour model for families with chronic illness is summarized in Table 7.1.

Flexibility with This Model

This short-term model is intended as a guide. Much flexibility is needed when working with this population. For example, when two elementary-school-age girls with cystic fibrosis were hospitalized for 2 weeks, their parents stayed nearby at a relative's home. The hospital-based psychologist worked with the family on a daily basis, covering the training and supervised sessions of filial play therapy during that hospitalization. When the girls were discharged, the parents continued with the play sessions and kept in touch with the psychologist by telephone. Follow-up sessions were held 9 months later, when one of the girls was hospitalized again for 1 week.

The spacing and number of sessions are likely to vary depending upon the family's needs and circumstances.

CASE ILLUSTRATION

Kim, a 34-year-old wife and mother, had been living with a chronic pain problem for 6 years. It had limited her mobility periodically. Recently, she had been diagnosed with an autoimmune liver disorder that might eventually necessitate a liver transplant. She initially requested help in coping with her fears and depression surrounding her illnesses. She described her husband as very supportive, but his work often took him out of town. She also reported that she was not as playful or as active with her 7-year-old daughter, Sami, as she wished for fear of aggravating her medical symptoms. The time frame for therapy was limited because the family was relocating in 10 weeks.

The initial treatment consisted of individual psychotherapy for Kim. Two 1-hour sessions were spent discussing her limitations and fears about

TABLE 7.1. Summary of the Short-Term Filial Play Therapy Model

Session	Activity	No. of Hours
1	Recommendation of filial play therapy Information about chronic illness Discussion of toys for filial therapy	1
2	Play session demonstration Discussion of play session(s) Overview of skills; handout	1
3	Training—full discussion of skills Practice of empathic listening 1 to 2 mock play sessions/parent	1½
4	First filial play session(s) Feedback and discussion	1
5	Second filial play session(s) Feedback and discussion	1
6	Third filial play session(s) Feedback and discussion Discuss transition to home setting	1½
7	Meeting after first home session Other chronic illness issues Other interventions, as needed	1
8	Meeting after third home session Other issues/interventions, as needed Generalization of play session skills	1
9	Meeting after fifth home session Other issues/interventions as needed Generalization of play session skills	1
10	Meeting after seventh home session Discussion of continuing home sessions Discussion of eventual transition to "special times" Discussion of family fun activities Discharge	1

her health. Together, the therapist and Kim identified her losses and made a list of things she could still do. The therapist encouraged her to grieve for the "things she has lost" but to focus simultaneously more on the "things she had left."

It became clear that most of her anxiety and depression surrounded the many "unknowns" of her recently diagnosed life-threatening liver disease. The therapist helped Kim determine a list of questions for medical professionals and several strategies to educate herself about her illness, treatment options, and transplantation.

During these initial meetings, Kim also reported that her perfectionism led to significant stress that interfered with her health and relationships. The next three sessions were spent working directly on her perfectionistic attitudes and the problems they seemed to cause. Using an educational cognitive therapy approach, the therapist taught Kim to recognize and modify her distorted perfectionistic thought patterns. She read selected chapters from the cognitive self-help book *Feeling Good: The New Mood Therapy* (Bums, 1980) for homework, and together, the therapist and Kim applied cognitive therapy principles to real-life problems until Kim learned to do so independently. During sessions, Kim identified her automatic thoughts, and she and the therapist discussed more rational responses, recording them on a card she kept for reference. They covered problem areas such as Kim's exaggerated fears of imminent death from liver disease, anxiety (and negative prediction) about poor quality medical care in her soon-to-be new home, and her inability to play freely with children for fear of appearing "foolish" or "inept" in front of extended family members.

Kim quickly learned to apply cognitive therapy principles during these three sessions, as demonstrated by her "homework assignments." She reported feeling much more relaxed and "in control" after this brief intervention.

After these five individual sessions, five more sessions focused on Kim's relationship with Sami. Kim and Sami already had a good relationship. They had shared activities and Kim had straightforwardly educated Sami about her illnesses and their treatment. The therapist recommended filial play therapy for several reasons:

- To strengthen Kim and Sami's relationship despite Kim's chronic medical conditions; to permit them to play and have fun together.
- To provide Sami with an opportunity to express and work through her feelings and concerns about her mother's illness.
- To give Sami a greater sense of control and security during a time of many changes and uncertainty (i.e., Kim's illnesses and a major family move).
- To give Kim a greater sense of satisfaction in her parenting and restore her sense that she was giving something positive to Sami.

The filial play therapy with Kim and Sami approximated the 11-hour model outlined earlier. The five sessions concluded prior to the family's move are outlined below.

Session 1: Play Session Demonstration (1 Hour)

The therapist described filial play therapy in more detail for Kim, discussed the play session toys, and provided a 20-minute play session demonstration with Sami while Kim watched from the corner of the room.

Sami played quite aggressively during the first 15 minutes of the play session. She punched and kicked the bop bag using elaborate "wind up" moves and martial arts–like spins. The therapist empathically reflected her obvious enjoyment of "showing him who's boss" and set one limit for safety. Sami complied with the limit without protest. She also created a hideout behind the kitchen set and pretended to shoot the "bad guy" (the bop bag). Sami played with the water and dishes during the remaining 5 minutes.

After the demonstration, the therapist discussed the play session with Kim alone, while Sami played with some other toys in a separate waiting area. Kim had never seen Sami play so aggressively and asked if that was "normal" and healthy for her. The therapist discussed the general nature of aggression with Kim, pointing out how well Sami had responded to the limit setting when her aggression became unsafe. The therapist also drew Kim's attention to Sami's quieter play during the latter part of the session. Kim reported that she usually felt uncomfortable with the expression of anger and aggression, but she could see the benefits of discharging some of it. The therapist listened empathically to Kim's concerns and responded that she would learn two skills in filial play therapy that would help ensure Sami's healthy expression of aggression: (1) empathic listening, which would convey acceptance of aggressive and control themes, allowing Sami to release them; and (2) limit setting, which would keep that expression within safe and socially acceptable bounds. Kim recognized that Sami had very little control over the current events in her life and admitted seeing value in Sami's being able to express her feelings about it.

Session 2: Training (1½ Hours)

The therapist used the training format described earlier with Kim. This included a review of the skills, practice of empathic listening, and two mock play sessions. Kim learned quickly and without incident. The therapist gave her feedback as they went, and she improved with each try. During the second mock play session, they worked a bit longer on limit setting, which the therapist had identified as a weak area for Kim. The goals were to give Kim a working knowledge of the four play session skills and prepare her to handle Sami's potentially aggressive play. At the end of the session, Kim and the therapist both thought she was ready to start with Sami.

SESSION 3: FIRST FILIAL PLAY SESSION (1 HOUR)

For the first half-hour, Kim and Sami had a play session while the therapist observed. Sami began with aggressive play, similar to that in the play session demonstration. She punched and kicked the bop bag. After several minutes of this, her play became more regressive in nature. She pretended she was a baby, sucking from the baby bottle, scribbling pictures, and talking baby talk. She told Kim specific things to say to the baby (herself), such as "Baby, do you need your ba-ba (bottle)?" and "Baby, that's a very pretty picture." Kim handled the play session very well, allowing Sami to play the way she wanted, reflecting Sami's actions and feelings, and playing the mothering role as Sami instructed her.

During the last half-hour, Kim and the therapist discussed the play session. The therapist praised her use of the skills and suggested that she simply use the empathic listening skill a bit more frequently. Kim reported that it had seemed easy for her overall but that it was still difficult for her to tolerate fully the aggressive play. They discussed her discomfort and fears that Sami might become uncontrollably aggressive at home as a result of this play. Kim said she had seen no sign of such changes in Sami following the play session demonstration, and the therapist reminded her of the role of the limit-setting skill, explaining that such "fallout" from the play sessions is rare, but that if she saw more aggression in Sami at home, she was to contact the therapist. The therapist also suggested that Sami's aggressive play had turned to other thematic play in both of the play sessions thus far. They then discussed the regressive and nurturance themes in Sami's play and what those themes might tell them. Kim seemed very interested in the things she had already learned about Sami and said she was eager for their next session.

Session 4: Second Filial Play Session (1 Hour)

Kim and Sami had their second play session during the first half-hour of the session. Sami's play was much less aggressive and more exploratory in nature. She played with a variety of toys, rolled on the bop bag, made food items with the play dough, and asked her mother to play a card game with her. Kim had to set one limit when Sami tossed the rubber knife aside and it hit the ceiling, but Sami accepted it without resistance.

Kim and the therapist discussed the session alone afterward, as before. The therapist highlighted Kim's excellent use of the limit-setting skill and how Sami had responded. Kim said she was feeling more comfortable with her own ability to manage Sami's aggressive play should it recur. They also discussed how Sami had picked up the doctor's kit and the stuffed bear that was dressed as a doctor but had put them aside. Kim had hoped Sami would engage in some medical play. The therapist reinforced Kim for refraining from such suggestions to Sami and reassured her that Sami would likely play her medical-related concerns in her own way in time, and had in fact already been expressing control issues. Sami had been very excited about returning for a play session, and Kim already felt that they were sharing something special.

As Kim and Sami left, Sami noticed some toys the therapist had gathered for use in an upcoming professional training workshop. She asked about a small container with amber-colored gooey material in which a plastic lizard was embedded. The therapist explained that it would be used in a workshop, and Sami asked her to put it in the playroom the next time she came.

Session 5: Third Filial Play Session, Wrap-Up (1½ Hours)

Immediately upon arriving, Sami asked if the therapist had put the "lizard-thing" in the playroom and was told that she had. At the start of their half-hour play session, Sami pulled the lizard out of the amber gooey material, rolled the amber material into a ball, and played "tricks" on her mother. She reinserted the lizard and told Kim to pretend to eat the amber material and then to act disgusted when she discovered she had eaten (pretending) a lizard. Kim played this role out very well. After 10 minutes of this play, Sami removed the lizard, rolled out the amber material, and began cutting it into small balls. She then said that she was "making livers." Sami then enacted a factory scene in which she was the boss and the factory people were making livers. She stood up and yelled loudly for them to make lots of livers, not just for themselves, but for others. She continued yelling at the workers for 5 minutes. Kim reflected the boss's feelings of frustration with the workers and enjoyment of yelling very well, and Sami told Kim it felt good to yell. Sami then took the little pile of "livers" and handed them to her mother, telling her to "put them in," which Kim pretended to do. Sami then removed the imaginary "bad liver" and then said to Kim, "Now you're all better, so get down on the floor and play with me." Sami ordered Kim to play several times and then joined her at the dollhouse. They played quietly together with the doll family and dollhouse for the rest of the session.

During the debriefing afterward, little skills feedback was needed because Kim had handled the session beautifully. Kim was very touched by Sami's play. She quickly saw how Sami was trying to make her better with the livers and that Sami really wanted to play with her very badly. Kim was extremely motivated to continue with the play sessions.

The therapist would have preferred several more sessions to help Kim and Sami transition to their home play sessions and for follow-through, but their moving date had arrived, so she spent the remaining time of the session discussing with Kim how to continue. They discussed setting up their special play area, what to watch for, and how to reach the therapist by telephone or confidential e-mail to discuss anything that might arise with their home sessions. Kim and Sami were very motivated to continue their special play sessions. Kim had learned the skills and principles of the play session very well. A follow-up contact about 2 months later revealed that they were continuing to do very well in spite of some serious stresses with their move.

SUMMARY

Families experiencing chronic illness have many psychosocial needs that can be complex and stressful. The illness has an impact on everyone in the family and complicates the daily challenges faced by most families. Filial play therapy involves the entire family in a systematic yet enjoyable experience designed to strengthen family bonds and coping abilities. It helps everyone in the family express their feelings and work through problems that arise because of the illness. Although short term, its psychoeducational methods, a blend of play therapy and family therapy, provide families with tools to help them cope effectively for many years to come.

REFERENCES

Barbarin, O., Hughes, D., & Chesler, M. (1985). Stress, coping, and marital functioning among parents of children with cancer. *Journal of Marriage and the Family, 47*, 473–480.

Bigbee, J. L. (1992). Family stress, hardiness, and illness: A pilot study. *Family Relations, 41*, 212–217.

Burns, D. D. (1980). *Feeling good: The new mood therapy.* New York: New American Library.

Carter, J., & Carter, A. (1995). *The little baby snoogle-fleejer.* New York: Times Books.

Drotar, D., Crawford, P., & Bush, M. (1984). The family context of childhood chronic illness: Implications for psychosocial intervention. In M. G. Eisenberg, L. C. Sutkin, & M. A. Jansen (Eds.), *Chronic illness and disability through the life span* (pp. 103–129). New York: Springer.

Eisenberg, M. G., Sutkin, L. C., & Jansen, M. A. (Eds.). (1984). *Chronic illness and disability through the life span: Effects on self and family.* New York: Springer.

Guerney, B. G., Jr. (1964). Filial therapy: Description and rationale. *Journal of Consulting Psychology, 28,* 303–310.

Guerney, L. F. (1983). Introduction to filial therapy: Training parents as therapists. In P. A. Keller & L. G. Ritt (Eds.), *Innovations in clinical practice: A source book* (Vol. 2, pp. 26–39). Sarasota, FL: Professional Resource Exchange.

Hobbs, N., & Perrin, J. M. (Eds.). (1985). *Issues in the care of children with chronic illness.* San Francisco: Jossey-Bass.

Hobbs, N., Perrin, J. M., & Ireys, H. T. (1985). *Chronically ill children and their families.* San Francisco: Jossey-Bass.

Kaduson, H., & Schaefer, C. (Eds.). (1997). *101 favorite play therapy techniques.* Northvale, NJ: Aronson.

Kohlenberg, S. (1993). *Sammy's mommy has cancer.* New York: Magination Press.

Krisher, T. (1992). *Kathy's hats: A story of hope.* Morton Grove, IL: Albert Whitman.

McCue, K. (1994). *How to help children through a parent's serious illness.* New York: St. Martin's Griffin.

Mills, J. C. (1992). *Little tree: A story for children with serious medical problems.* Washington, DC: Magination Press.

Mulder, L. (1992). *Sarah and Puffle: A story for children about diabetes.* Washington, DC: Magination Press.

Peterkin, A. (1992). *What about me? When brothers and sisters get sick.* New York: Magination Press.

Quittner, A. L., Opipari, L. C., Espelage, D. L., Carter, B., & Eid, N. (1998). Role strain in couples with and without a child with a chronic illness: Associations with marital satisfaction, intimacy, and daily mood. *Health Psychology, 17,* 112–124.

Quittner, A. L., Opipari, L. C., Regoli, M. J., Jacobsen, J., & Eigen, H. (1992). The impact of caregiving and role strain on family life: Comparisons between mothers of children with CF and matched controls. *Rehabilitation Psychology, 37,* 289–304.

Rynard, D. W., Chambers, A., Klinck, A. M., & Gray, J. D. (1998). School support programs for chronically ill children: Evaluating the adjustment of children with cancer at school. *Children's Health Care, 27,* 31–46.

Schaefer, C. E., & Eisen, A. R. (Eds.). (1998). *Helping parents solve their children's behavior problems.* Northvale, NJ: Aronson.

Siminerio, L., & Betschart, J. (1986). *Children with diabetes.* Alexandria, VA: American Diabetes Association.

Shuman, R. (1996). *The psychology of chronic illness.* New York: Basic Books.

VanFleet, R. (1985). *Mother's perceptions of their families' needs when one of their children has diabetes mellitus: A developmental perspective.* Unpublished doctoral dissertation, The Pennsylvania State University, University Park, PA.

VanFleet, R. (1992). Using filial therapy to strengthen families with chronically ill children. In L. VandeCreek, S. Knapp, & T. L. Jackson (Eds.), *Innovations in clinical practice: A source book* (pp. 87–97). Sarasota, FL: Professional Resource Press.

VanFleet, R. (1993). Strengthening families with storytelling. In L. VandeCreek, S. Knapp, & T. L. Jackson (Eds.), *Innovations in clinical practice: A source book* (pp. 147–154). Sarasota, FL: Professional Resource Press.

VanFleet, R. (1994). *Filial therapy: Strengthening parent–child relationships through play.* Sarasota, FL: Professional Resource Press.

VanFleet, R. (1998). A parent's guide to filial therapy. In L. VandeCreek, S. Knapp, & T. L. Jackson (Eds.), *Innovations in clinical practice: A source book* (pp. 457–463). Sarasota, FL: Professional Resource Press.

8

Theraplay for Enhancing Attachment in Adopted Children

PHYLLIS B. BOOTH
SANDRA LINDAMAN

INTRODUCTION

Theraplay is an active, playful, short-term treatment method that uses attachment-based play to create better relationships between parents and their children. Parents are involved in treatment, first as observers and later as cotherapists. Theraplay is modeled on the playful, engaging, physical interaction of parents with their young babies and includes all the elements of that interaction that are so important in establishing a secure attachment and a healthy self-image: structure, engagement, nurture, and challenge.

A secure attachment leads to a strong sense of self and self-confidence, the ability to deal with stress, the ability to trust, and the capacity to form relationships throughout life. The goal of treatment for a child who is adopted is to create or strengthen the attachment between the child and her adoptive parents. The most important factor in this process is helping parents recognize and meet their child's younger needs and helping the child accept these attachment-enhancing interactions. The child should be able to accept her parents' direction, to turn to her parents for comfort, security, and assistance with emotional regulation, and to use them as a secure base from which to explore the environment. In order to develop this secure attachment with an adopted child, parents must provide the attuned, responsive caretaking, the playful engagement, and the structure that is part of the healthy parent–infant relationship.

Attachment is not something that happens quickly but is a process that develops between parents and children during the first years that they are together and continues to be strengthened throughout life. Theraplay, as a short-term treatment, can start the process of attachment and give parents and children the tools to carry on after the direct treatment is completed.

In describing Theraplay, Jernberg and Booth (1999) say:

> The goal of treatment is to enhance attachment, self-esteem, trust and joyful engagement and to empower parents to continue on their own the health-promoting interactions learned during the treatment sessions. . . .
>
> The Theraplay therapist, like the "good enough" parent, takes charge while remaining carefully attuned and responsive to the child's needs. Whether the emphasis in a given session is on structuring, engaging, nurturing, or challenging, . . . the sessions are always intended to be playful and fun. . . . Although most children who come for treatment are beyond the infant stage, they still need the nurturing touch, the focused eye contact, and the playful give and take that are such important parts of the healthy parent–child relationship. These are the elements that help children learn who they are, what their world is like, who the important people in their world are and how they feel about them. (pp. 3, 4–5)

Theoretical Foundation

In its focus on the parent–infant relationship, Theraplay is closely aligned with interpersonal theories of human development, especially self psychology (the work of Kohut, 1971, 1977) and object relations theory (particularly the work of Winnicott, 1958, 1965, 1971). It also is strongly based in attachment theory (Bowlby, 1969, 1973; Ainsworth, 1969; Karen, 1994) and the work of Stern (1985, 1995).

In order to understand the principles underlying the Theraplay method and its concept of attachment-based play, it is helpful to call to mind the kind of play that is typical of healthy parents with their infants and toddlers. Parents take charge, set limits, and make things safe. They play engaging interactive games such as peekaboo, patty-cake, and This Little Pig Went to Market. They babble and sing to their babies. They hold and rock and cuddle them. They feed, bathe, and comfort them. Throughout all these interactions, they show a sensitive responsiveness to their baby's needs and convey a sense of joy and shared pleasure. As a result of these many kinds of activities, a strong, secure attachment is formed between the baby and his parents. The baby learns that he is lovable, special, and competent, that his parents are loving, attentive, and dependable, and that the world is a safe, interesting place where good things can happen.

The many activities that take place between parent and child can be seen as falling roughly into four dimensions: structure, engagement, nurture, and challenge.

• *Structure*. Parents take charge, structure the child's world, and make the baby feel safe and secure. They move with confidence and assurance as they respond to their infant's needs. They are trustworthy and predictable. They define and clarify the child's experience. This aspect of care conveys the message: "You can depend on me. You are safe with me. I will take good care of you."

• *Engagement*. Parents provide excitement, surprise, and stimulation in order to maintain an optimal level of alertness and engagement. In this way, they convey the message: "You are fun to be with. The world is full of interest and excitement. You can interact in appropriate ways with others. You can enjoy being close to people."

• *Nurture*. As they care for their infant, parents are warm, tender, soothing, calming, and comforting. They convey the message: "You are lovable. You can count on me to respond to your needs for care, affection, and praise."

• *Challenge*. Parents provide just the right amount of challenge to encourage their child to move ahead, to strive a bit, and to become more independent. The message conveyed by this aspect of the interaction is: "You are capable of growing and of making a positive impact on the world."

Each of these dimensions provides support to different aspects of healthy growth. And as will be shown, each can be used in treatment to address the emotionally younger needs and the characteristic behavior problems of older adopted children.

Evidence for Its Effectiveness

Theraplay is effective with a wide variety of behavior problems, ranging from withdrawal, depression, and passivity to aggressiveness and hyperactivity. Many of these behavior problems have their origins in disturbances in the relationship between children and their parents. Whether the disturbance is due to problems stemming from the parent, the child, or the environment, or whether the problem is that a new relationship must be formed (as is the case with adopted children), Theraplay works quickly to create a change in that relationship.

There is a great deal of anecdotal evidence describing the successful outcome of Theraplay treatment with individual clients (Jernberg & Booth, 1999; *The Theraplay Institute Newsletter*, 1980–1999). In addition, several empirical research studies demonstrate its effectiveness in a number of ways. Morgan (1989) evaluated the outcome of Theraplay treatment using pre- and postassessments completed by parents, teachers, observers of the program, and the program therapists. For over two-thirds of the study sample (68%), the Theraplay program had a positive impact on the development of self-confidence, self-control, trust, and self-esteem.

Ritterfeld (1990), in a controlled study comparing the effectiveness of speech therapy and Theraplay, found that language-delayed preschool children who received Theraplay treatment showed greater improvement in their language skills than those who had only speech therapy or no intervention at all. These children improved not only in their language-processing abilities, but also in their expressive ability. The self-concept of children who had received Theraplay treatment also improved, and kindergarten teachers rated the children as happier.

Koller (1976) found increases in performance IQ scores of Indiana schoolchildren following Theraplay treatment. Munns, Jenkins, and Berger (1997) found a decrease in aggressive, acting-out behavior following Theraplay treatment. Bernt (1990) found Theraplay a helpful approach in working with failure-to-thrive infants and their parents.

Adopted children have always constituted a significant proportion of those brought for Theraplay treatment. Since 1992, when the first child adopted from a European orphanage came to the Theraplay Institute for treatment, an increasing number of "postinstitutionalized" children have been treated using this method. Mahan (1999) found that Theraplay facilitated a more secure attachment and decreased behavior problems in twin children adopted from a foreign orphanage.

Characteristics of Theraplay That Make It Effective with Adopted Children

This chapter describes how Theraplay is used as a short-term treatment for families with adopted children. The focus is on children who have experienced caretaking inconsistencies, failures, or losses that have disrupted or prevented the development of a secure attachment. Children adopted at birth or shortly after experience some degree of discontinuity in their caretaking experience and later may need help to come to terms with their feelings about being given up for adoption. Forming an attachment with an infant, however, is much easier than with an older child. As a result, most families adopting infants do not find that they need extra help. If they do, Theraplay techniques described in this chapter can be useful.

Although the process of forming an attachment to an older child involves all the same steps as with an infant, the challenge is to take a child who has lost his first caretaker (and perhaps many more), who therefore is wary of trusting anyone, and entice him into a trusting relationship. Lindaman (1999), in describing how Theraplay can help this process, says:

We face special challenges when we try to form an attachment with a child whose hopes have been shattered. Given this disappointment, forming an attachment takes time, patience, energy, and commitment on the part of adoptive and foster parents. The normal attachment process has an eager and trusting child participant. The adoptive . . . attachment process has a wary child participant who readily reverts to the tactics she developed to survive on her own. Because it is so much more difficult, adoptive and foster parents need a great deal of support throughout the process.

Whatever the age of the child, Theraplay dramatizes that the child is special and lovable, that the world of the child is now a place of responsiveness, lively experiences, and growth, and that the child can count on others. Rather than talking about these assurances, the parent and child enact the assurances in the session. With its emphasis on the child's emotionally younger needs, Theraplay recreates the early attachment process for the parent–child pair. Just as a biological child comes to rely on and trust her responsive parents, so adopted children begin to experience their new parents as reliable and trustworthy. (p. 294)

Theraplay's emphasis on enthusiastic engagement with the child and on replicating the pleasurable interactions that are an essential part of the healthy parent–infant relationship are the elements that make it possible to set the family on the road to a better relationship and a more secure attachment. Adoptive parents need to do everything they can to make their children fall in love with them: spending time with them, responding to their needs, appreciating their special characteristics, and enticing them into playful interactions. Families stuck in negative patterns, where bad feelings have developed, learn to have more fun together. Parents learn to respond to their child's younger emotional needs, and they learn the strategies and the focus required to carry on the Theraplay approach once treatment ends.

Theraplay helps parents provide the structure that will make the child feel safe and secure. It models for parents (and then gives them practice in establishing) the energetic, playful engagement that is characteristic of parents with their infants and essential to forming a strong attachment with a newly adopted child. Children who have never learned to play, and parents who are struggling to reach those children, are shown how to play together. Because it involves active physical interaction, parents can practice the affectively attuned give and take that leads to empathy and awareness of feelings which is so characteristic of parents with their young biological children. They can also gain experience in understanding and modulating their child's activity level and emotional state. Adoptive parents are helped to respond to their child's younger emotional needs, and to provide the same responsive nurturing care to their older adopted child that comes so naturally to parents of infants. And finally, they learn when and how to challenge their child in ways that enhance the child's self-esteem and ultimately lead to greater independence.

Characteristics of Theraplay That Make It Effective as a Short-Term Treatment

In addition to the aspects of Theraplay that make it particularly effective for adopted children, Theraplay shares with all effective short-term treatments the following characteristics:

- *Intervention begins immediately.* The process of helping parents understand their child's needs begins during the initial evaluation period. Many parents report that they gain new insight about their relationships and behaviors even during these first contacts.
- *Treatment is direct, active, and positive.* Even during the assessment period, the parents and their child interact directly as they perform the simple tasks of the Marschak Interaction Method (MIM), which will be described later. Treatment itself involves energetic physical interactions between child, therapist, and parents.
- *Caretakers are included.* Parents are actively involved in treatment right from the beginning.
- *A working alliance is established from the beginning.* In Theraplay, the working alliance is formed most explicitly with the parents. Parents are unlikely to choose a treatment that requires as much involvement and follow through as Theraplay does, unless they are ready to play a large role. The therapist and child form a "playing alliance," which ultimately facilitates the goal of forming a secure attachment between the child and parents.
- *Homework assignments are given.* As soon as the interpreting therapist feels that the parents understand the purpose of the activities and feel comfortable with the approach, she gives homework assignments. Specific activities are suggested and parents are helped to schedule times for carrying out the activities at home.
- *Optimism about success is conveyed.* Starting with the intake interview, parents are supported and given hope for a positive change. Based on their experience, Theraplay therapists believe that the treatment process can result in changes in parent and child behavior in a short period of time. They are therefore able to convey optimism about the possibility for change.
- *Strengths are built on.* Feedback following the MIM focuses on strengths in the parent–child relationship. Parents are helped to continue and expand the successful approaches they are already using. Activities in treatment are upbeat, positive, and fun, in order to ensure that both parents and child will feel successful.
- *Treatment is goal-oriented, structured, and focused.* Goals are clearly defined in consultation with the parents. The goals can be as specific as increased eye contact, comfort with touch, and reduction of temper tan-

trums, or as global as accepting nurture, relinquishing the need for control, or more secure attachment. Throughout the sessions, treatment is planned and focused toward the established goals. If additional issues arise during treatment, the goals can be renegotiated, but the key issues generally remain the same.

• *Time limit is set from the start.* From the beginning, there is an agreement between parents and therapists on the proposed number of sessions. Depending on how treatment goes, however, this number can be renegotiated. The therapist keeps parents informed of how he thinks treatment is progressing.

Factors That Determine Successful Outcome

Successful treatment for adoptive families depends on many factors related both to the child's and the parents' experience. For the child, outcome depends on the length and severity of neglect, abuse, trauma, and deprivation, on the presence or absence of medical problems, neurological problems and developmental delays and disorders, as well as on the child's resilience. In general, the younger the child at the time of adoption and the earlier the intervention, the more rapidly treatment progresses. If parents adopt a Theraplay philosophy when planning for adoption and begin the interactions immediately on bringing the child home, the chances for a successful outcome are better.

The ability and willingness of adoptive parents to do the necessary work in Theraplay treatment can depend on the following:

• *Their history with the child.* How much and what have they already tried? How tired, burned out, hopeless, or angry are they? If they have done many of the things Theraplay recommends, were those things done properly, at the right time, or for long enough?

• *Their own history.* What is their knowledge about and experience with children with attachment problems? How comfortable are they with taking charge, nurturing older children, initiating interactive play, or accepting their child's regressive needs? How were they parented?

• *Other environmental factors.* Have they adopted several children at once? Do they have other biological children? Are they single parents? Are they struggling with marital, work, or other family problems? Is there illness or other stress in the family?

All of these issues will determine the level of parental involvement in Theraplay sessions and their ability to carrying on the work at home. A combination of problems in the child and parents will affect outcome and determine whether Theraplay or other types of treatment should be used. In general, the older the child at the time of adoption or when he comes for treatment, the greater the possibility that he has suffered ongoing trauma, that the family has struggled for a longer time with attachment and behavior problems, and that the child's parents will have more difficulty understanding and responding to their child's younger needs. Progress in treatment with these children is likely to be slower, requiring more sessions over a longer time, perhaps 20 sessions over a 6-month period. Theraplay treatment may need to be combined with other treatment modalities to deal with the child's experience of trauma, to set up a supervised, therapeutic milieu at home, or to deal with other family and marital issues.

Needs of Adopted Children and Their Parents That Require Other Kinds of Treatment

Although Theraplay can be very effective in treating the attachment and relationship problems of adopted children and their parents, it is not designed to address all the important problems that adoptive families face. Theraplay does not focus on helping the child deal directly with issues of loss, abandonment, abuse, or trauma. It does not attempt to manage severe behavior problems in which there is actual or potential injury to self or others requiring supervision in a hospital setting. The ongoing effects of medical problems and learning problems must be dealt with in other settings. Although an improvement in the parent–child relationship may help peer relationships, Theraplay does not directly address problems with peer relationships. The treatment of significant marital issues or parental mental health problems and the provision of much needed support services are outside its scope.

There are many other activities and techniques that can help children handle the transition from one family to another, form a coherent narrative of their lives, and understand the process of adoption. These can be an important adjunct to Theraplay treatment. Rituals and ceremonies that legitimize the new relationship, allow children to say goodbye to earlier caretakers, and receive permission to transfer their affection to their new parents and become part of the family, can play a very important role in starting the new relationship out well. Parents can be taught techniques that facilitate their connection to a newly adopted child (Hopkins-Best, 1997). Children can be helped to make "Life Books" or create life stories in order to fill in unremembered gaps in their life experience and create narratives that are positive and coherent. Children can read, or have books read to them, about the experience of adoption to help them understand that they are not alone and that they can share their feelings with others. Group therapy can also be helpful in this regard. Children adopted from foreign countries can benefit from learning about their birth culture as part of developing a clear identity.

Adopted children have a need to talk about and come to terms with the meaning to them of being given up for adoption. While adoptive parents can play an important role in helping children with this need, many adopted children will require professional help at some point in their lives to come to terms with all the issues that adoption raises. A number of treatment modalities are available to help children understand and come to terms with their feelings about the experience of being adopted: sand-tray work, art therapy, dollhouse play, puppet play, or other ways of playing out their experience with a therapist or with their adoptive parents.

Many children who are available for adoption have suffered neglect as well as physical, sexual, or emotional abuse; consequently, their problems are severe. Some children will need focused trauma or grief work. Others will need more comprehensive programs that include an opportunity to address their attachment–trauma problems directly. There are a number of therapies that concentrate on helping children understand the connection between their early experiences of neglect or abuse and their current difficult behaviors and intense feelings of anger (Welch, 1988; McKelvey, 1995; Hughes, 1997, 1998; James, 1994).

Adoptive parents may need help to provide the therapeutic parenting that these children often need (Hage, 1995). Teachers and other professionals who work with adopted children may need help to understand their special needs. Adoptive parents may need counseling to deal with their own issues surrounding the adoption. They may benefit from adoptive parent support groups.

When to Use Theraplay

Decisions about when to use these other approaches, alone or along with Theraplay treatment, depend on the child's most pressing need at the moment and must be made on a case-by-case basis. Techniques designed to foster a smooth transition, to help parents provide the care their child needs, and to help the child understand about adoption can be useful from the very beginning of the adoption process. At times, the issues of loss or abuse are so urgent that they must be addressed before it is possible to do effective work with Theraplay.

For most adopted children, however, the first priority is to build a better, more trusting relationship with their new parents. Theraplay is especially useful in the early stages of adoption because it allows parents to "check out" the child, get to know his preferences and learn what he enjoys. Whatever the stage of the child's understanding and acceptance of being adopted, Theraplay can be helpful in the crucial task of building a relationship between parents and their adopted child. The development of trust and security in his relationship with adoptive parents can be a source of comfort and stability that will free the child to come to terms with his experience.

This chapter describes how Theraplay can be tailored to meet the needs of adopted children and their parents. It begins with a step-by-step description of how Theraplay treatment works, how a single session is structured, and how parents are included in the treatment, and it describes the typical difficulties encountered in the course of treatment. It outlines the behavior problems characteristic of adopted children and shows how the Theraplay dimensions can be used to address the underlying issues that lead children to behave in these ways. Finally, it presents a case study to illustrate the method.

THERAPLAY TREATMENT

Logistics

SETTING AND MATERIALS

In order to keep the focus of treatment on the relationship between the child and the adult, the Theraplay treatment room is simple, comfortable, and uncluttered. There are no toys to invite the child into symbolic play or into a private fantasy world. Rather, the therapist and the parents are the most attractive "toys" in the room. A few comfortable pillows and a blanket help set the stage and are the props for some activities. The materials that might be needed for the planned activities of a particular session, such as food, cotton balls, lotion, or a bean bag, are out of sight in a bag or basket.

This simple focus on the playful interaction between the child and the adults makes Theraplay treatment flexible enough to be used in almost any setting. Theraplay can be taken into homes or schools, where a sheet or blanket placed on the floor defines the uncluttered space within which the adults and child can interact. This flexibility makes it especially adaptable to homework assignments for parents. In the more formal setting, it is helpful to have a two-way mirror behind which the parents and the interpreting therapist can observe.

NUMBER AND TIMING OF SESSIONS

Theraplay treatment includes an assessment period of three or four sessions; the treatment itself, which ranges from 10 to 20 sessions; and a follow-up period of from four to six sessions, spaced out over a year. Because there are often many complicating factors for adopted children, treatment will be longer than the minimum 10 sessions. Sessions are 30–45 minutes in length and are typically scheduled once per week. In order to make a more powerful impact, sessions can be scheduled more frequently for the first 2 weeks before settling into the once-a-week pattern.

PARTICIPANTS

Whenever possible, all Theraplay treatment includes parents in the sessions. In work with adopted children, this is absolutely essential. Parents observe a few sessions before joining their child in the playroom.

The ideal pattern is to have two therapists: one to work with the child and one, the interpreting therapist, to work with the parents. If a second therapist is not available, a single therapist can adapt the method to work with both the child and the parents. Parents can observe the session from behind a two-way mirror, or if one is not available, they can sit in the room to observe. The therapist can discuss the session with the parents later on the telephone or while the child sits in the waiting room. Another alternative is to videotape the session and discuss it with the parents at another time.

Assessment

The assessment procedure includes an intake interview, an observation session with each parent and the child, and a feedback session.

INTAKE INTERVIEW

In the intake interview, information is gathered about the child's current functioning (with emphasis on how each parent sees the problems), the child's history (with emphasis on experiences that might affect the development of attachment), the parents' experiences growing up and their current marital relationship (both of which affect how they relate to their child), and the extent of the family support systems. This interview may need to be quite lengthy because adopted children often have very complex histories. The child is not present for this interview.

THE OBSERVATION SESSION

The child's relationship with her adoptive parents is assessed using the MIM (Marschak, 1960, 1967), a structured observation technique designed to assess the nature of the relationship between a child and each of her caretakers. The MIM gives information about the child's emotional level of development and her readiness to accept what her adoptive parents have to offer in terms of structure, engagement, nurture, and challenge. The parents' ability to provide these elements of healthy caretaking in the face of whatever difficulties the child may present can also be seen. For more details about how to do an assessment, see Jernberg and Booth (1999), and Lindaman, Booth, and Chambers (1999).

THE FEEDBACK SESSION

In the feedback session with the parents, the clinician presents an initial evaluation of the problem and shows segments of the videotaped MIM sessions to illustrate particular points. This is an opportunity to help parents understand their child's particular needs and their own behavior in response to the child. The nature of treatment is explained and parents are prepared for what will go on in the sessions. This includes what response they might expect of their child and what their role will be. Based on this evaluation and the discussion with the parents, a decision is made whether to proceed with Theraplay treatment. Goals are set in consultation with the parents.

Treatment

Theraplay sessions are designed to be engaging and fun. The therapist approaches each session with a plan based on an understanding of the needs of the particular child. This plan is subject to change in response to the child's behavior at the moment.

Although children respond in their own fashion to the experience of playing with the new therapist, most children follow a sequence from hesitant acceptance through resistance, to final enthusiastic engagement. Some adopted children are very charming and engaging with their new therapist at first, but their fear of forming an attachment leads them to show resistance at some point in treatment before they move on to more comfortable acceptance of the therapist and of their parents.

In the typical Theraplay treatment plan, parents observe their child with his therapist during the first four sessions and are guided in their observations by the interpreting therapist, whose job it is to help parents understand what is going on and to prepare them to join their child in the Theraplay room. After four sessions, parents come into the playroom for the second half of each session, where they are coached to interact in ways that are specifically designed to engage their child and to meet her needs. Because the formation of an attachment to adoptive parents is such a high priority, adoptive parents may join their child in the playroom as early as the end of the first session in order to begin the process of focusing on the parent–child relationship. The parents of an infant or toddler, or a child who is very frightened about being separated, may stay with the child from the beginning. Parents are given assignments to carry out some of the Theraplay activities at home between sessions.

CHECKUP SESSIONS

Checkup sessions are scheduled at monthly intervals for the first 3 months and then at quarterly intervals for a year. These sessions follow the pattern of sessions in the second half of treatment. The child and the Theraplay therapist play together in the treatment room while the parents and the interpreting therapist observe and have an opportunity to discuss any problems or issues that have arisen during the intervening weeks. For the second half of the session, the parents come into the playroom and are able to demonstrate new activities that they have enjoyed with their child.

SEQUENCE OF A SINGLE SESSION

The Theraplay therapist brings the child into the session in an engaging, playful way that conveys the message that the session will be fun, interactive, and well structured by the therapist. Entry activities can include the following: picking up and carrying a very young child; giving the child a piggyback ride; helping the child be a wheelbarrow; doing a three-legged walk together; hopping, tiptoeing, or taking giant steps together; or carrying the child in a special chair made by joining the therapist's and the parent's arms.

The child is helped to settle in a beanbag chair or on pillows with the therapist sitting in front of him. There should be a definite place to sit and a well-defined play area. The initial activity is a "checkup" in which the therapist focuses exclusive attention on the child. She may count his freckles, put lotion on his hurts, check how warm his cheeks are or how soft his hands are. She establishes eye contact, appreciates all his special qualities, and makes him feel very much attended to.

Following this initial get-acquainted period, a series of playful activities are planned to alternate between active and energetic and calm and quiet. Specific activities within sessions are chosen to meet the particular child's needs for structure, engagement, nurture and challenge. The way in which the dimensions are used to address the characteristic behavior problems of adopted children is discussed later.

When it is time for parents to enter the playroom, activities are designed to help the child look forward to and accept the entry of his parents. The child and his therapist may hide under a blanket for the parents to find, dots of powder may be hidden on the child for the parents to find, or the child may be wrapped in ribbons as a present for his parents to unwrap.

The last third of each session is a time for calming, soothing, and nurturing activities such as feeding a snack and a drink. If the child accepts this care, the therapist simply feeds him as a parent would a young child. If the child says he can feed himself, the therapist responds, "I know that you can do it for yourself, but when we're together, I like to do it for you." Older or more resistant children may need the challenge of eating a donut held on a parent's index finger or of being fed pieces of watermelon prior to a seed-spitting contest in order to accept the nurture. The therapist may offer the treat to the parents, allowing them an opportunity to be nurtured as well.

The session ends with a special song about the child or a recounting of all the things the therapist discovered about the child in that session. Rather than allowing the impact of the session to become diffused, the family is helped to leave the treatment room in some connected way, for example, holding hands all the way to the elevator or having one parent give the child a piggyback ride.

WORKING WITH PARENTS

The interpreting therapist's work with parents is a crucial part of effective Theraplay treatment for adopted children. The work with parents has many facets. The interpreting therapist must help parents achieve an empathic understanding of their child's needs, help them learn how to maintain the Theraplay approach with their child at home, teach them about developmental issues and how to handle behavior problems, and provide support and meet the parents' unmet emotional needs.

Empathic appreciation and understanding of their child's needs begins as parents observe the Theraplay therapist with their child and see how much the therapist appreciates and values the child. By pointing out and enjoying the child's unique and special qualities, the therapist helps parents see their child as more appealing and more lovable. The interpreting therapist guides the parents' observations to help them understand how their child might be feeling and what her responses indicate about her needs. Special role-playing sessions can be set up to give parents an opportunity to experience how it might feel to their child to be comforted or to have out-of-control behavior stopped.

The goal of helping parents carry on the Theraplay approach after treatment ends is achieved through a series of increasingly active steps. The first step takes place in the feedback session, when the therapists share their understanding of the child and her problems. During the early treatment sessions, parents observe the Theraplay therapist with their child and are encouraged to model their own behavior with their child on that of the therapist. Once they enter the treatment room, they are given guided practice in carrying out the approach. When parents seem ready to try the new activities at home, they are given homework assignments. The interpreting therapist helps them plan when, where, and how to carry out the assignments and checks at the next session on how the assignment went. In preparation for the parents' taking charge of activities during the final sessions, a special role-playing session is scheduled to give them practice in leading a whole series of activities. The final sessions of treatment are largely under the guidance of the parents, with the therapists providing a supportive cheering section.

Teaching parents appropriate developmental expectations and how to manage behavior problems is an important component of parent work. As noted elsewhere, adopted children often have emotional needs at a much younger level than their physical or cognitive development. Since attachment is fostered by attuned responses to infantile needs, parents must be helped to adjust their expectations to meet their adopted child's younger needs. Management of behavior problems is based on providing clear structure and simple rules, and following through in a calm, consistent manner. Parents are helped to understand the importance of providing this firm, clear structure for their adopted children and of providing an increase in nurturing and caretaking interactions to support the attachment process.

A final and very important part of the work with adoptive parents is providing support and finding ways to meet the parents' own unmet needs. Support includes acknowledging how hard it is to work with their difficult adopted child and accepting parents' negative feelings about the child. Helping parents find support groups, organize their lives so that they have time to themselves, and find respite care for their child are also important. Parents who have not been well parented themselves may need Theraplay experience for themselves. This can be provided in role-playing sessions in which they play the role of their own child, or in sessions designed just to meet some of their own needs. Because adopted children put so much strain on the relationship, parents often need help reconciling differences and understanding the feelings of their partners. Some of this work can be done by the interpreting therapist behind the two-way mirror or in separate sessions set aside for such work. When the problems are severe, parents should be referred for marital or individual treatment.

TYPICAL DIFFICULTIES IN THE COURSE OF TREATMENT

Most adopted children will fend off or resist Theraplay treatment in some way because the attachment-enhancing activities make them feel uncomfortable and/or vulnerable. Sometimes the resistance comes immediately, in the form of refusal and opposition, or passive sabotage of activities; at other times, there is an initial "honeymoon" period and resistance heightens after several sessions. The Theraplay therapist persists in offering an empathically attuned engagement, acknowledging discomfort but not going away. Older children, particularly, may be able to sustain a façade of superficial engagement; therapists must be alert to this, monitoring for engagement of the "real" child. As children come to trust the therapist and parents, they begin to accept small periods of playful engagement or soothing nurture.

Parents frequently have difficulty accepting the concept of their child's younger needs for structure, engagement, nurture, and challenge. The interpreting therapist reinforces this concept through the discussions, guided observations, and active participation described earlier. Some parents may feel that "playing" will not help their problems, or they may be so tired and angry with the child, or so stressed by other demands on their time, that they do not have the energy to meet the child's younger needs. These parents may be encouraged to sit back and rest for a while as the therapist does the majority of the interaction until the parents feel more able to join the sessions.

Using the Theraplay Dimensions to Respond to the Characteristic Behavior Problems of Adopted Children[1]

Many adopted children have significant delays or arrests in emotional development as well as many behavior problems that reflect their efforts to cope with an unpredictable, unresponsive, and often hurtful and neglectful world. Their "difficult" behaviors may include the following: refusal to accept adult authority; insistence on having their own way; a compulsive need to control others; aggressive or oppositional defiant behavior; lying, stealing; avoiding eye contact or physical contact; clinging or indiscriminate friendliness; lack of empathy for others; little evidence of guilt and remorse; disturbances in eating, sleeping, urinating, and defecating; intense, often meaningless talk or questions; difficulty understanding cause and effect; poor planning and/or problem solving; and impulsivity, hyperactivity, frequent emotional outbursts, and temper tantrums. These behaviors fall roughly into five clusters:

- Problems accepting structure and adult control
- Problems forming trusting relationships
- Problems accepting care
- Problems with self-esteem and feeling competent and worthy
- Problems regulating and expressing emotions

The following section describes how the Theraplay dimensions can be adapted to respond to the younger emotional needs underlying each of the characteristic problems.

PROBLEMS ACCEPTING STRUCTURE AND ADULT CONTROL

Many adopted children have experienced their world as unpredictable, overwhelming, untrustworthy, and frightening. Their common response to these experiences is to take control and insist that everything be done in a predictable, "safe" way. They impose this structure on their environment through temper tantrums and aggressive outbursts, or through withdrawal

---

[1]An earlier version of the following section appeared in Lindaman (1999, pp. 296–305). Copyright 1999 by Jossey-Bass. Reprinted by permission.

into their own world. They may run away or refuse to follow the family rules. These problems are so prevalent among older adopted children that they are at the top of the list of concerns for most parents who seek help for their adopted children. They say, "She has to have everything her way. No matter what I tell her to do, she will do just the opposite." "He argues about everything. He won't listen to me."

"It is as though the child says 'I must take charge of things or no one will. . . . I must make others do what I want so that they won't do the abusive, neglectful things that I fear' " (Lindaman, 1999, p. 297).

Addressing Control Issues. The Theraplay dimension of structure is designed to address these issues of control by helping parents take charge, set limits, and keep the child safe. Parents need to understand the importance of structure and predictability in the home setting. This involves simple rules, clear limits, careful monitoring and supervision (even to the extent of keeping the child close to an adult at all times, as one would a 2-year-old), and recognizing the impact of transitions and change. Parents need to learn to ignore distractions, stick to their guns, and complete activities so that clear structure can be maintained. They must help their child learn to relax in the safety of their dependable caretaking.

Since Theraplay is a structured therapy and the therapist plans activities and gives the child practice in following her lead, it provides the child an experience of accepting adult authority in a setting where following an adult's lead can be satisfying and fun. Specific activities that help the child accept adult control and help parents provide it include follow the leader, "Mother, May I?" Red light–green light, three-legged walk (Standing beside the child, tie your two adjacent legs together with a scarf. With arms around each other's waist, walk across the room), and having the child wait for a signal before doing an activity.

PROBLEMS FORMING TRUSTING RELATIONSHIPS

Adopted children often have difficulty establishing a trusting relationship. They may be indiscriminately friendly, going eagerly to each new stranger they see, but resist the advances of their new mother for fear of being let down once again. In their efforts to ward off a committed relationship, they may avoid eye contact, shrug off or resist physical contact,

> display a superficial friendliness, appear distracted, and even seem not really "there" with you. They may be impulsive, unpredictable, hard to get along with, and have difficulty making and keeping friends. Hughes (1997, p. 3) points out that they often "avoid reciprocal fun, engagement, and laughter" and that they have limited skills for engaging with others.
>
> It is as though the child says to herself, "I'm not comfortable with peo-

ple—I don't know how to enjoy myself with others, I can only do so on my terms." (Lindaman, 1999, p. 298)

Addressing Relationship Issues. Theraplay's extensive repertoire of engaging activities and novel ways of enticing a child into a relationship make it an ideal approach to help families with this problem. It encourages parents to persist in their attempts to woo the reluctant, untrusting child and to maintain their self-confidence in the face of their child's rejection of their efforts to engage him. They also need a good repertoire of engaging activities to counter the child's resistance. This includes using physical contact, eye contact, interactive play, affect attunement, and emotional state regulation, as parents do with infants. At first, the child may be engaged for only a short time, but repeated experiences of authentic connection will add up to greater comfort and trust.

As parents watch their child's therapist and then follow suit themselves, they learn new, special characteristics of their child. They find special freckles and new scratches and bruises that must be kissed, lotioned, and watched daily for the progress of healing. They kiss his old scars and tell him they wish they had been there to take care of him and see that he didn't get hurt. The wary, newly adopted child may brush off this kind of close attention at first, but most children cannot resist for long this special attention, with its accompanying appreciative comments. Children who have never let anyone get close to them, often return to the next Theraplay session pointing out some new freckle or special attribute to their therapist eagerly anticipating their therapist's pleasure.

Theraplay activities that engage the child in a relationship include hand-clapping games in which the child and adult can enjoy the shared excitement of rhythmic chanting and clapping, peekaboo, This Little Pig Went to Market, hide and seek, marshmallow free-for-all, and tug-of-war (in which the parents pull the child over to their side).

PROBLEMS ACCEPTING CARE

Many adopted children have great difficulty allowing others to take care of them. If they hurt themselves, they are likely to say, "It doesn't matter. I'm OK," as they brush off their parents' offers of help. Some children are quite self-sufficient in caring for themselves and may even become caretakers to others. Other children, in contrast, are reckless and accident-prone, while being unable to accept comfort for their hurts. Some children will accept comfort if they initiate the request, but only on their own terms. Hughes (1997) describes these children as trying to avoid being loved, feeling special to someone, or needing anyone.

"The child seems to be saying to himself, 'I can't count on anyone to take care of me so I will do it myself' " (Lindaman, 1999, p. 300). The child who is reckless and accident-prone may be saying in addition, "I'm not worth taking care of."

Addressing Caretaking Issues. A major emphasis in Theraplay treatment is on finding ways to nurture and comfort children. Since it is responsive caretaking that forms the basis of the attachment process, the emphasis is on noticing the child's facial and bodily cues, acknowledging feelings, and making attuned responses that mirror the child's reactions.

While providing nurturing care is easier and comes more naturally with a young child, it is essential that adoptive parents provide it for a child of any age. This includes taking every opportunity to respond to their children's needs; holding, feeding, bathing, and dressing them; responding in the middle of the night to their need for food or comfort; and explicitly keeping them safe and reassured.

Parents may find it difficult to provide the nurturing care that an older adopted child needs because it seems strange to cuddle and comfort a large child the way they would a small baby. Such care often makes adopted children feel very vulnerable, because in the past, the very people who might have cared for them have let them down. They therefore resist it in many ways, including being very grown-up and self-sufficient. Adoptive parents who want to nurture and comfort their newly adopted child are hurt and frustrated by their child's unwillingness to let them take over the caretaking role. Some parents, however, may welcome this self-sufficiency as a sign that their child is doing well. To add to the difficulty, "parents who have the impulse to nurture their older adopted child as they would a newborn are often ridiculed by friends and family members who say the child is 'too old for that baby stuff' " (Lindaman, 1999, p. 302). For all these reasons, it is easy to pass up opportunities to provide the nurture that will gradually make it possible for their child to relax into a relationship in which she can allow herself to feel vulnerable and count on her parents to take care of her. However, being able to take over the nurturing aspect of caretaking is crucial to successful adoptions. Theraplay can help parents find ways to provide the responsive caretaking and nurturing that adopted children need.

Caring for hurts, rocking in a cradled position, swinging in a blanket, and feeding favorite foods and drinks are activities that *directly* replicate the early parent–infant relationship and quickly establish the relationship that is needed for the child to feel part of the family. Theraplay also has many *indirect* ways of nurturing the child who will not allow direct caretaking. These include activities such as making painted hand- or footprints, decorating the child with crepe paper bows as a present for the parents to unwrap, hiding a cotton ball on the child for the parents to find, and having a parent put three kisses on the child's foot and get the shoe on before the kisses fly away.

PROBLEMS WITH SELF-ESTEEM AND FEELING COMPETENT AND WORTHY

"Many . . . adopted children feel incompetent, bad, and unworthy. These feelings stem partly from a conviction that they deserved the bad things that happened to them and partly from not having experienced themselves as the object of loving, attentive caretaking" (Lindaman, 1999, p. 302). Some adopted children, particularly if their early years were marked by neglect and lack of stimulation, may also have cognitive and developmental problems. These children seem to define themselves as unworthy and act as if they do not deserve any good fortune or success they achieve.

"It is as though the child says, 'I'm no good. I can't have been worth much if they hurt me, of if they didn't want me' " (Lindaman, p. 302).

Addressing Competence and Self-Esteem Issues. In order to counteract the child's low self-esteem, it is essential that parents' expectations of the child be geared to the level at which the child can be successful. This includes encouraging activities that are noncompetitive and confidence building, and accepting inconsistencies in performance due to fluctuations in the child's emotional state.

Many older adopted children are unable to maintain self-control in situations that other children their age can handle. They may be able to do good schoolwork when they are rested, well fed, and feeling connected and secure. When any of these supports are missing, they can no longer perform well. The child forgets to do his homework, cannot concentrate, breaks the rules, and falls apart under pressure. The parents' temptation is to say, "He knows better. He's deliberately doing this to make me mad." In fact, at that moment, the child did not know better. He was overwhelmed by feelings that he could not control.

Parents must learn to expect inconsistent performance, differences between intellectual ability and emotional self-control, and differences between school performance and behavior at home. They need to be reminded, "At times Joan is more like a 2-year-old. Would you leave your 2-year-old unsupervised and expect her to exert self-control in the face of that temptation?" Parents are helped to shift from teaching, reasoning, and waiting for their child to behave appropriately, to understanding, anticipating, and actively meeting the child's younger needs. Once they become more responsive to their child's emotional needs, the episodes of babyish, out-of-control behavior diminish.

Theraplay activities must be geared to the younger emotional needs of each child. This means providing more nurturing and caretaking than challenge. Challenging activities that are cooperative rather than competitive, and that assure the child's success, help make children feel more self-confident.

PROBLEMS WITH REGULATION AND EXPRESSION OF EMOTIONS

Adopted children have great difficulty regulating and expressing emotions. Out of the blue, and for no apparent reason, they may suddenly "lose it." They may have temper tantrums, impulsively hit or hurt others, or run away. At other times, they may appear unfeeling and unresponsive emotionally. It is as if they are so out of touch with their feelings that they suddenly burst through in uncontrolled ways. These children often seem to experience their emotions as frightening. Many of them are so out of touch with their feelings that they have difficulty naming their feelings.

"The child seems to experience his emotions as frightening. He may say to himself, 'I can only handle feelings in certain limited ways or they will spill out; even feeling good can be scary' " (Lindaman, 1999, p. 304).

Addressing Problems in Regulation and Expression of Emotions. It is difficult to calm children who have missed the early experiences that lead to self-regulation and the ability to concentrate, and to respond to stress. The experience of being cared for, soothed, and nurtured provides the template for children later to be able to focus, concentrate, control impulses, and recognize their feelings.

> Faced with an out-of-control child, parents often panic, fearing that their child will grow up to be violent. Or they may become angry and feel out-of-control themselves. . . . Even less violent emotions such as the child's sadness and grief can stir up parents' own feelings of grief and make it hard to respond to the child's needs.
>
> The child's difficulty regulating and being in touch with his own emotions can be addressed through the dimension of nurture and through multiple experiences of affect attunement and acknowledgment of the child's feelings by therapist and parent. (Lindaman, pp. 304–305)

Games designed to help children learn to modulate their excitement (doing activities slow and fast, loud and soft, waiting for the signal) all give the child practice in self-control and self-regulation.

The Theraplay therapist helps the child become more accepting of his feelings by acknowledging them ("You're having a hard time today . . . seems like you're feeling a little sad," or "I can see a sparkle in your eye and you've got a big smile. . . . You look happy today") and validating them ("That must have made you really mad! I'd be upset if that happened to me"). The following game in which the parents and child identify the meaning of facial expressions can help the child become more aware of her own and others' feelings. The child and her therapist agree on a feeling that the child can express with her face and her body. Her parents must try to identify what the feeling is. Parents take turns as well. Once the feeling is identified, both child and parents can tell what kinds of things make them feel that way.

The following case study illustrates how Theraplay treatment is carried out with a young adopted child.

CASE ILLUSTRATION

Summary of Intake Information

Carlos was a 3-year-old boy who lived with his adoptive mother and father, the Js, and their two biological children, ages 5 and 7. Carlos was placed in foster care shortly after his birth, when his biological mother abandoned him. Carlos spent 1 year in this foster home, which was ultimately found to be neglectful. He then was placed in the Js foster home, and his adoption was finalized when he was 30 months old.

Mrs. J sought help for Carlos, describing him as bright, charming, and engaging, but also very independent and very difficult to manage at times. She said that Carlos did not seem to care about limits and that he did what he pleased, despite adult guidance, redirection, rule setting, or discipline. It especially concerned her that Carlos would do dangerous things, for example, leaving the house on his own despite locked doors. He also repeated certain activities in a driven manner, for example, throwing objects in the toilet.

Mr. J was on active military duty and was unavailable when the mother sought treatment. Because he would be gone for 2 months, the assessment and treatment were conducted without the father with the plan that he would join the sessions at a later time.

The Marschak Interaction Method

The interaction between Carlos and Mrs. J was observed using the MIM. The MIM tasks included: playing with toy animals, playing a familiar game, teaching Carlos something, putting lotion on each other, leaving Carlos alone for 1 minute, telling Carlos about when he joined the family, putting hats on each other, having Carlos copy Mrs. J's block structure, and feeding each other.

Their interaction on three tasks from the MIM is described to illustrate the assessment and treatment planning process:

1. *Play a game with the child that is familiar to both of you.* The mother quickly initiated a rhythmical clapping game. She clapped in a pattern and Carlos sometimes connected with her hands, but it was clear that

the fun was the important task and that the mother was not concerned about having Carlos clap precisely. At first, the mother clapped a little too fast for Carlos to be able to catch up with her; she then slowed and simplified her clapping so that they were clapping together at the end of the song. Carlos wanted to do it again and again, and Mrs. J complied. At one point, she led a very fast and vigorous clapping game that ended with both yelling the words and Carlos leaning back to lie on the table. The mother pulled him up and said, "One more time, we'll do it very slowly and very softly." Carlos began to speed up immediately. Mrs. J tried to slow him down, and then sped up even faster than Carlos could manage. The game ended with a bear hug from mother and a kiss to Carlos's neck while he laughed excitedly.

2. *Adult leaves the room for one minute without the child.* Mrs. J expressed her reluctance to leave. Carlos's expression was sober and he rubbed his face. Mrs. J reassured him, saying, "Carlos, Mama's going to go over there for 1 minute. . . . Mama's going to go over there like this [snaps fingers] and come back like that [snaps fingers again]." As soon as his mother left the table, Carlos got out of his chair and explored the envelopes of MIM materials, finding the one containing food. He glanced questioningly at the camera several times while holding the food in his hand. Mother returned and Carlos asked if he could eat the pretzels. The mother responded, "I don't know. . . . Lets' see if we get to the card that says, 'Carlos eats pretzels.' Maybe I'll just find that card," which she did.

3. *Adult and child feed each other.* At first, Mrs. J played "the baby" and had Carlos feed her. When she attempted to feed him, Carlos resisted and fed himself. She persisted and offered to feed him four times before he agreed to take a bite from her pretzel. He was ready again to take care of himself and eat from his own pretzel, but she successfully persuaded him to accept two more bites from her.

SUMMARY OF OBSERVATIONS

From this interaction, it is clear that Carlos and Mrs. J enjoyed being together; they have developed familiar, pleasant play and conversational patterns. Carlos sometimes tested the limits of the situation or wanted to do activities by himself and without help. He fended off nurturing and seemed to be more comfortable lotioning and feeding his mother than receiving this care. Mrs. J was playful and engaging. She delighted in Carlos's accomplishments and gave enthusiastic praise. She was empathic when she knew an activity might be difficult, such as leaving Carlos, telling him about joining the family, or waiting to be fed, and she tried to be extra helpful at these times. Sometimes she escalated Carlos's excitement by becoming louder or more physically intrusive. Mrs. J then used verbal directions or explanations to structure and calm Carlos. She seemed ambivalent about setting limits and often gave in to Carlos's desire to do things his own way.

Feedback Session

In the feedback session, the clinicians sat with Mrs. J and reviewed and discussed portions of the MIM videotape. They acknowledged the obvious affection that Mrs. J and Carlos have for one another. They pointed out many instances of Mrs. J's skillful, playful, and engaging manner, and her persistence even when Carlos sometimes rebuffed her. They also pointed out exchanges in which Mrs. J had structured or set limits to which Carlos had responded well.

In the review of the familiar clapping game, the mother noted that she did not feel that getting too excited was a problem for Carlos, so if he wanted to go fast, she would let him. Mrs. J said that she allows Carlos to make his own choices when possible. This exchange gave the clinicians the opportunity to talk about the importance of structure in attachment formation, and the young child's view of the adult caregiver as someone who can be counted on to keep him safe. The mother responded, "That's what Carlos has a problem with, me as an authority figure. He just does what he pleases."

When "Parent leaves the room" was reviewed, Mrs. J spoke about her own discomfort in leaving Carlos, because she felt he was apprehensive and somewhat confused. The therapists pointed out how helpful she had been by making it very clear she would be back quickly and giving Carlos something to do in her absence. Rather than being mischievous, Carlos's exploration of the materials was interpreted by the clinicians as a way of taking care of himself in his mother's absence. Carlos's glancing at the camera and waiting for his mother's return before eating the pretzel were interpreted as first steps toward the development of inner control and a conscience. Mrs. J disagreed, however, saying that if Carlos really felt he was alone, he would have eaten the pretzels. This led to a discussion of Carlos's wandering and leaving the house. The clinicians described the typical secure-base behavior of toddlers. They suggested that Carlos's wandering from his mother or leaving his house might be triggered by the lack of a feeling of connection at those moments. Mrs. J said that she found this information very useful—that Carlos, rather than being noncompliant or oppositional at those moments, was responding to a momentary lack of connection to her.

When looking at the feeding task, Mrs. J said, "Did you see that he wouldn't let me feed him? I thought I'd die." She related how Carlos toilet trained himself before the age of 2, saying, "Now I know it was a way of putting me off—he was too young for all of that." Mrs. J acknowledged that sometimes Carlos's fierce independence was helpful to her, presenting "one less child to take care of." On the other hand, Mrs. J stated she always took the opportunity to feed Carlos when he asked for it, and she saw Carlos's love of being messy as a window into the baby part of him. The clinicians supported Mrs. J's awareness of the importance of nurturing Carlos, and her persistence in finding a way to help him accept being fed during the MIM. Mrs. J. responded, "I hear that I should be the caretaker, not Carlos."

Based on the information from the intake interview, the MIM observation, and the feedback discussion, the clinicians recommended Theraplay treatment. They felt that the personally engaging, structuring, and caretaking aspects of Theraplay treatment would address Carlos's emotional needs. Carlos, like many adopted children, needed to control his environment and take care of himself in order to be comfortable. This kind of control and self-care is a heavy burden for a 3-year-old, and it disrupts the attachment process and interferes with other age-appropriate developmental tasks. The immediate goals of treatment were to help Carlos become more comfortable (1) following the therapist's lead in playful, interactive activities (structure) and (2) accepting nurturing care (nurture). Additionally, it was important to increase age-appropriate engagement and to reduce challenge. Because some of Carlos's skills were precocious, it was tempting to his mother to treat him as an older child, and to use teaching and reasoning as ways to get him to accept her limits, rather than more personal, physical ways of relating and of getting him to accept care. It also was a goal to have Mrs. J enter into a more parent-initiated, direct structuring and nurturing role as quickly as possible. Two 30-minute sessions were scheduled for the first week, with weekly sessions thereafter.

Treatment

SESSION 1

A path of three large pillows a few inches apart on the floor led to a beanbag chair. The therapist held Carlos's hands and squatted down in front of him.

THERAPIST: Carlos, I want to see if you can jump on these pillows all the way to the beanbag chair; here's my signal, jump when I say "Go" . . . One-two-three—Go! (*Helps Carlos jump safely to pillow, continues to hold his hands and keeps eye contact.*) Let's do that again!

CARLOS: (*Begins to move away from the beanbag. Therapist helps him sit in the beanbag. Both sit cross-legged, facing each other.*)

THERAPIST: Now, let's see what you brought with you today. You brought your hair (*touches lightly*), you brought your big brown eyes.

CARLOS: (*At the mention of eyes, Carlos puts his hands up to his eyes.*)

THERAPIST: Oh you know that game. Let's do this, "peekaboo." Let's do it together. (*Several instances of synchronous movement, each covering and uncovering their own eyes.*) I have a funny way to play; I'm going to pick up your feet. (*Holds Carlos's feet in front of her eyes, peeks again. Carlos holds back from saying, "Boo" but with prompting, they say it together one final time.*) Now I want to look at your thumb because I know you bumped it on the way into the room. Is this the one? (*Carlos nods.*) Oh, I'm so sorry that your thumb got hurt. Let's get some lotion and take care of it.

CARLOS: (*Lies back in the beanbag, appears relaxed, watches with interest as therapist takes care of his thumb.*)

THERAPIST: I'm going to be very careful not to rub it too hard. (*Begins to sing "Oh lotion, oh lotion on Carlos's hand . . . "*)

CARLOS: (*Scrunches up his face, looks questioningly at therapist.*)

THERAPIST: Let's do your other thumb too, the one that didn't get hurt. (*Sings again.*) I think you're wondering about my lotion song.

CARLOS: Want more!

THERAPIST: Oh, you want more.

CARLOS: I want to put some on my—I can put some on.

THERAPIST: Let's see if I can give you a slippery hand. (*Applies more lotion to one of Carlos's hands, puts own hands on either side and pulls away, saying, "Slip, slip, slip, slippery hand." Carlos's hand slides through. Therapist falls back a little. Carlos sits forward, offers other hand. Therapist does slippery hand with both hands, then leans back.*) Can you reach my hands and pull me back up? (*Carlos pulls her up.*) Oh, good. Look, we can make a stack of hands. (*Carlos has difficulty following directions for stacking hands, even with physical assistance. Therapist decides it's worth a second try with simpler directions, saying, "Up, up, up" with each hand movement and looking for Carlos's eyes. This goes better, but the therapist ends the activity before it is completely done, because it is difficult and Carlos is losing interest. Carlos sticks a foot out toward therapist.*) Carlos, how about your feet? You have an "owie" on your toe. I'll put a little lotion on it.

CARLOS: Big lotion.

THERAPIST: Oh, you like lots of lotion. (*Carlos begins to wiggle around in beanbag and looks restless.*)

THERAPIST: Let me help you get settled in the chair. (*Carlos makes a face.*) Does it feel funny? It makes noise doesn't it? Make it make more noise like this. (*Shows Carlos how to rock from side to side to make the beanbag filling scrunch. He copies her. Therapist takes large pillow and puts it across Carlos's lap as a surface for the next activity and to settle him.*) Carlos, I'm going to take big lotion and put it on your hand. We're going to make a special picture of your hand.

This interaction lasted approximately 10 minutes, or one-third of a typical Theraplay session. The therapist continued to lead Carlos through a number of engaging activities, such as catching a bean bag off of her head on the count of three or playing Stop and Go as he wiggled his toes on command. Carlos mostly lay back in the beanbag in a relaxed, babyish position and gazed with a smile at his therapist. He offered minimal resistance in this first session. When he was restless or wanted to do something on his own, the therapist encouraged him to do the activity "one more time." The therapist found that it was not necessary to use more complicated activities to engage Carlos; he appeared content to play the very young games he probably did not experience as an infant. When it was time to feed Carlos, the therapist had a butter cookie ready. With a wary look on his face, he accepted the first bite. He tried to hold the cookie for a second bite, but let the therapist hold it when she redirected the activity by developing a routine of listening for Carlos's chewing. Carlos said that he bit his tongue, so the therapist checked but saw no evidence of a bite. She then talked about feeding him carefully so no hurts could occur. As the therapist sang Carlos a special "Twinkle Song" (What a special boy you are), put on his shoes and socks, and talked about how they would play together next time, he looked relaxed again. Carlos's mother and the interpreting therapist were called in to look at his handprint and to lift Carlos up with a one-two-three signal.

Behind the Mirror with Mother and the Interpreting Therapist. The interpreting therapist and Mrs. J observed the beginning of the session silently. When Carlos became a bit restless, the interpreting therapist pointed out how Carlos's therapist handled it by gently helping him settle down and by varying the activities, or by suggesting, "One more time." Since Mrs. J had a policy of letting Carlos "make up his own mind" about things that were not harmful or dangerous, she questioned this policy of taking charge: "Shouldn't he be allowed to practice deciding what he wants?" The interpreting therapist reminded her of what was said in the feedback session: "The development of a secure attachment depends on the child's experiencing the adult as able to take charge and keep things safe and well structured. Once he is more securely attached, he will be ready to handle being more independent. Right now he is practicing being independent without having an inner connection to you."

As they observed how the therapist's intense focus on his body and on taking care of him captured Carlos's attention, the interpreting therapist commented, "These very simple baby games and activities work best to capture his interest and keep him focused. He seems to welcome being snuggled in the beanbag chair. As if it provides some level of security and comfort. These are the kinds of activities that will help him begin to feel more connected to you."

SESSION 2

The second session began with Carlos crawling through a tunnel made of pillows to get to the beanbag. He accepted and enjoyed the checkup activities that were becoming special rituals: wiggling his toes, playing peekaboo, and allowing the therapist to check and care for his hurts. The therapist had Carlos push her over with his feet on a signal and then pull her up with his hands. He did this two times with pleasure, but the third time, he pulled back and said, "Not gonna bring you up." The therapist used a bit of challenge to get past this resistance, saying, "Oh, Carlos, I want to play with you—see if you can pull me up with those strong arms of yours." Carlos pulled her up with a smile. The therapist helped Carlos follow her structure and practice modulation by singing and swaying to "Row, Row, Row your Boat," moving backward and forward, side-to-side, fast and then slow. She commented, "Wow, you can go fast and you can go slow. That was really neat." Several other activities focused on waiting for signals before doing an activity. This time, Carlos was ready to resist direct nurturing. When the cookie was offered to him, he said several times, "I want to hold it." The therapist responded, "I know you can hold it, but in here, I like to do it for you." Carlos refused. She said, "Oh, you want to hold it so bad, don't you?" He nodded. "If I put it on my finger like this, can you take a bite?" Carlos responded to the challenge and took the whole cookie on one bite. She responded, "Oh my gosh, you took the whole cookie—it's making your mouth very full. Go ahead and chew it up. I can see where it is in your mouth." The therapist decided not to pursue the battle over the cookie any further. She and Carlos hid under a blanket and called his mother and the interpreting therapist into the room. When she found him, Carlos excitedly told his mother about the games he had played.

Since it was nearly time to end the session, the therapist brought out a juice squeeze bottle and held Carlos in her lap. She asked his mom to sit close and listen for the sound of his swallowing and watch for the bubbles as he drank. Soon Carlos began to tease, biting the bottle top and pointing out what he was doing. Then, Carlos asked to sit in his mother's lap. The therapist had not put him there initially because she knew that he might refuse to allow his mother to feed him. To everyone's surprise, however, he cuddled in his mother's lap and accepted the bottle. The session ended with his mother joining the therapists in singing the Twinkle Song and putting kisses on Carlos' feet before she put his shoes on.

Behind the Mirror. The interpreting therapist pointed out that Carlos was now showing more deliberate resistance: "Not gonna bring you up," or "*I* want to hold it." She told Mrs. J that children who are used to calling all the shots typically will test in increasingly direct ways whether the therapist, and their parents, really will stick to their guns. Notice how the therapist redirects the activity rather than confronting his resistance. Later, there may come a time when directly confronting it might be needed, but right now, simply making the activity more interesting is all that is necessary to keep Carlos willing to stay engaged. As Carlos and his therapist played the rowboat game, the interpreting therapist commented on how the therapist was helping Carlos modulate his activity level and excitement. She went on to say that the regulation of activity level and arousal is an important part of parenting for very young infants. It is essential in working with adopted children that their new parents provide some of those experiences that they missed. Although Mrs. J had not experienced Carlos as too easily excited, he still needed to learn that she could help him feel calm and regulate his impulsiveness.

During a telephone call to Mrs. J between the second and third sessions, she reported that she had been thrilled at Carlos's being able to accept the bottle from her in the session. He had also allowed her to feed him a baby bottle of juice while she rocked and sang to him before putting him to bed.

SESSION 3

The session began with the checkup and gentle play routines developed in the first two sessions. Then, in order to increase his comfort with close contact and holding, the therapist cradled Carlos in her lap while playing games of "blowing" each other over and making funny sounds when she touched particular parts of his face. Carlos was given turns so that he also was the initiator of activity.

When his mother joined the session, she led the same activities with coaching from the therapists. Carlos's therapist held him in her lap facing his mother and helped him wait his turn. Next, Carlos was placed in his mother's lap and they played the blow over and funny sounds games he and his therapist had enjoyed earlier. The mother was encouraged to do it one more time or redirect if Carlos started to take control. With Carlos cradled on her lap, she fed him a baby bottle of juice. At first he accepted this; then, he became quiet and looked sad. He moved his hand to control the bottle and the therapist intervened to remove his hand. He began to move about, finally saying, "I want to hold my little bottle," and later, "Put it in my back pack." He allowed "one more sip before you go" and was reassured his mother had juice at home to drink. The therapists and his mother sang the Twinkle Song to Carlos.

Behind the Mirror. The interpreting therapist pointed out that Carlos seemed more comfortable being held. She had also told Mrs. J that she would be asked to do some of the same activities with Carlos when she entered the playroom.

SESSION 4

The therapist gave Carlos a piggyback ride in to the session while his mother was directed to watch Carlos's face to check for his safety and comfort. As the therapist took Carlos's shoes off and pulled out her lotion, he remembered his earlier hurt and reported, "My thumb don't hurt." The therapist responded, "Good, I think we took really good care of it." She sang the lotion song many times while caring for Carlos's hands and feet, imitated his facial expressions, looked at his strong teeth, and played patty-cake with his feet. During these activities, she was positioned about 12–15 inches from Carlos's face, giving him exclusive attention, and noticing and appreciating him as a parent would a newborn. Carlos drank in this attention, anticipating favorite activities ("Are you gonna play this?" placing his hands over his eyes for peekaboo) and telling his therapist when she forgot an important part of the routine ("You gonna sing 'Oh lotion'?") The therapist had Carlos close his eyes and tell her where she had gently touched him with a cotton ball; she then hid three cotton balls on Carlos for his mother to find. His mother joined the session, and to Carlos's delight, found the cotton balls and gave him a gentle touch as well. They then played a more active game of blowing the cotton ball back and forth between them; the therapists cued the mother to remain in charge of this activity. The mother fed Carlos from a bottle and there was no resistance. The therapists and mother swung him gently in a blanket while singing "Rock-a-bye Carlos." He laughed and cooed, saying, "That was fun." After the Twinkle Song and putting on shoes and socks, Carlos was helped to stand up. He immediately went to his mother and lifted his arms to be held by her.

Behind the Mirror. The therapist pointed out that Carlos was very responsive to the quiet, comforting, attentive, physical activities of his therapist and that they seemed to have a profound effect on him. "He is like a small baby as he lies there and looks into her eyes. These are the kinds of activities that he missed out on before he came to you. Can you do them with him at home? They will make a big difference in how connected to you he feels."

In a telephone call between the fourth and fifth sessions, Carlos's mother reported that he seemed very different. He asked his mother to take care of him in ways he had not allowed in the past. He had not wandered from the house since the beginning of treatment. The frequency and driven nature of repetitive activities had also been reduced. Mrs. J was structuring Carlos's time better, so that he did not have time or access to prohibited materials.

Carlos had two more sessions that used the kinds of activities described earlier and included the mother in a leadership role for more of each session. Her homework was to initiate time each day to hold, rock, or feed Carlos, to engage him in as many of the playful games of the treatment sessions as possible, and to provide an overall increase in the amount of structure and adult control of his environment. Because she was able to carry out these suggestions at home and Carlos responded so positively, the therapist suggested that four or five additional treatment sessions be saved for use in the future, when the father was available, or to deal with issues as they emerged.

Therapeutic Gains

The progress that Carlos and his mother displayed is typical of Theraplay outcomes. Most parents report that they feel closer and more connected to their child, that they have a better understanding of the child's feelings and actions, and that they feel heard, understood, and supported themselves. There usually is a reduction in the child's behavior problems of opposition, tantrums, anger, and withdrawal, and an increase in cooperation and acceptance of parental guidance. As with Carlos, one of the best indicators of improvement is the child's turning to the parent for comfort and care.

Although Carlos was only 3 years old, the activities described are appropriate for children as old as 6 or 7. Children older than that need to be engaged by tasks that have more variety, challenge, and complexity, but the therapeutic emphasis is still on appreciating, enjoying, engaging, guiding, and caring for the child, and on helping the child accept those interactions.

SUMMARY

Theraplay is an effective, short-term treatment method for helping adopted children and their parents develop better relationships and more secure attachments. It does this by replicating the playful, engaging, physical interaction typical of healthy parents and their infants and includes all the elements of that interaction that are so important in establishing a secure attachment and a healthy self-image: structure engagement, nurture, and challenge. Although forming an attachment takes a long time, Theraplay, as a short-term treatment, can start the process of attachment and give parents and children the tools to carry on after direct treatment is completed.

The most critical aspect of Theraplay for adoptive families is helping parents to recognize and meet the child's younger needs and helping the child accept the attachment enhancing interactions offered by the parents. The Theraplay dimensions are used in treatment to address these younger emotional needs that account for the five clusters of behavior problems typical of adopted children.

- The child's difficulty accepting structure and adult control is addressed through the dimension of structure. Parents are taught to provide limits and structure as they would for a younger child: using simple rules, setting clear limits, keeping the child close, monitoring behavior, and recognizing the impact of transitions.
- The child's difficulty forming trusting relationships is addressed through the dimension of engagement. Parents learn to use a variety of activities adapted from baby games to entice the child into a relationship: using physically interactive games, seeking eye contact in playful ways, and engaging in give-and-take activities that allow for affect attunement and emotional-state regulation.
- The child's difficulty accepting care from his parents is addressed through the dimension of nurture. Theraplay activities include feeding, holding, and rocking. At home, parents can add bathing, dressing, managing comforting sleep arrangements, responding to the child's needs during the night, and keeping the child safe and reassured.
- The child's problem with feeling competent and worthy is addressed through the dimension of challenge. Parents are helped to adapt challenging activities to the child's emotional level of development so that he can feel successful and competent. Parents also learn to allow for inconsistencies in self-control and performance.
- Finally, the child's problems regulating and expressing emotions can be addressed through the dimensions of nurture, and through many experiences of affect attunement and acknowledgment of the child's feelings.

Successful treatment depends on the age of the child at the time of adoption, how soon after adoption treatment begins, the severity of the attachment–trauma problems, and the child's resilience. It depends also on the energy, commitment, and availability of parents for this difficult work. Theraplay cannot do it all, however, and other treatments may be needed either before, after, or during Theraplay treatment.

Theraplay's special role is to build a better, more trusting relationship between parents and their adopted children. The development of trust and security in their relationship with adoptive parents can be a source of comfort and stability that will free children to come to terms with all aspects of their experience.

REFERENCES

Ainsworth, M. (1969). Object relations, dependency and attachment: A theoretical review of the infant–mother relationship. *Child Development, 40,* 969–1025.

Bowlby, J. (1969). *Attachment and loss: Vol. I. Attachment.* London: Hogarth Press.

Bowlby, J. (1973). *Attachment and loss: Vol. II. Separation, anxiety and anger.* London: Hogarth Press.

Bernt, C. (1990). *Theraplay as intervention for failure-to-thrive infants and their parents.* Unpublished doctoral dissertation, Chicago School of Professional Psychology, Chicago, IL.

Hage, D. (1995). Therapeutic parenting: Part I. A personal journey. Part II. The ACE Philosophy of Parenting. In C. A. McKelvey (Ed.), *Give them roots, then let them fly: Understanding attachment therapy* (pp. 177–212). Kearney, NE: Morris Publishing.

Hopkins-Best, M. (1997). *Toddler adoption: The weaver's craft.* Indianapolis, IN: Perspectives Press.

Hughes, D. (1997). *Facilitating developmental attachment: The road to emotional recovery and behavioral change in foster and adopted children.* Northvale, NJ: Aronson.

Hughes, D. (1998). *Building the bonds of attachment.* Northvale, NJ: Aronson.

James, B. (1994). *Handbook for treatment of attachment–trauma problems in children.* New York: Lexington Books.

Jernberg, A. M., & Booth, P. B. (1999). *Theraplay: Helping parents and children build better relationships through attachment-based play* (2nd ed.). San Francisco: Jossey-Bass.

Karen, R. (1994). *Becoming attached: Unfolding the mystery of the infant–mother bond and its impact on later life.* New York: Warner Books.

Koller, T. J. (1976). *Changes in children's intelligence test scores following Theraplay.* Paper presented at workshop for Comprehensive Mental Health Center, LaPorte County, IN.

Kohut, H. (1971). *The analysis of the self.* New York: International Universities Press.

Kohut, H. (1977). *The restoration of the self.* New York: International Universities Press.

Lindaman, S. (1999). Theraplay for children who are adopted or in foster care. In A. M. Jernberg & P. B. Booth (Ed.), *Theraplay: Helping parents and children build better relationships through attachment-based play* (pp. 291–333). San Francisco: Jossey-Bass.

Lindaman, S., Booth, P. B., & Chambers, C. (1999). Assessing parent–child interactions with the Marschak Interaction Method (MIM). In C. E. Schaefer, K. Gitlin-Weiner, & A. Sandgrund (Eds.), *Play diagnosis and assessment* (Vol. 2). New York: Wiley.

Mahan, M. (1999). *Theraplay as an intervention with previously institutionalized twins having attachment difficulties.* Unpublished doctoral dissertation, Chicago School of Professional Psychology, Chicago, IL.

Marschak, M. (1960). A method for evaluating child–parent interaction under controlled conditions. *Journal of Genetic Psychology, 97,* 3–22.

Marschak, M. (1967). Imitation and participation in normal and disturbed young boys in interaction with their parents. *Journal of Clinical Psychology, 23*(4), 421–427.

McKelvey, C. A. (Ed.). (1995). *Give them roots, then let them fly: Understanding attachment therapy.* Kearney, NE: Morris Publishing.

Morgan, C. E. (1989). *Theraplay: An evaluation of the effect of short-term structured play on self-confidence, self-esteem, trust, and self-control.* Unpublished research, The York Centre for Children, Youth and Families, Richmond Hill, Ontario, Canada.

Munns, E., Jenkins, D., & Berger, L. (1997). *Theraplay and the reduction of aggression.* Unpublished research, Blue Hills Child and Family Services, Aurora, Ontario, Canada.

Ritterfeld, U. (1990). Putting Theraplay to the test: Evaluation of therapeutic outcome with language delayed preschool children. *Theraplay Journal, 2,* 22–25.

Stern, D. N. (1985). *The interpersonal world of the infant: A view from psychoanalysis and developmental psychology.* New York: Basic Books.

Stern, D. N. (1995). *The motherhood constellation: A unified view of parent–infant psychotherapy.* New York: Basic Books.

The Theraplay Institute Newsletter. (1980–1999). Chicago: The Theraplay Institute.

Welch, M. (1988). *Holding time.* New York: Simon & Schuster.

Winnicott, D. W. (1958). *Collected papers: Through paediatrics to psychoanalysis.* London: Tavistock.

Winnicott, D. W. (1965). *The maturational processes and the facilitating environment: Studies in the theory of emotional development.* London: Hogarth Press.

Winnicott, D. W. (1971). *Playing and reality.* London: Tavistock.

9

Involving and Empowering Parents in Short-Term Play Therapy for Disruptive Children

CHERYL B. MCNEIL
ALISA BAHL
AMY D. HERSCHELL

INTRODUCTION

In this chapter, we discuss a 12-session model for conducting play therapy with disruptive children (McNeil, Hembree-Kigin, & Eyberg, 1996, 1998). Sessions 1–7 focus on individual therapy with the child, while Sessions 8–12 focus on teaching play therapy to parents. We believe that parents are the key to accomplishing goals in a short time because they can support our efforts outside the therapy hour. Parents are incorporated into this model in three ways: (1) by structuring time so that we check in and check out with them in each session, (2) by giving them weekly homework assignments to support the therapy goals, and (3) by coaching them to use play therapy skills at home to accomplish such goals as enhancing the parent–child relationship and improving child self-esteem (McNeil et al., 1996). In addition to parental involvement, this 12-session model is unique in that it focuses on productivity. Treatment goals are carefully articulated and weekly objectives are established prior to sessions, so that they build on each other. These session objectives are met by structuring each session so that there is a therapist-directed, task-oriented portion that precedes the child-directed play. Additionally, powerful behavior management strategies are used to help prevent disruptive behavior from interfering with session objectives (McNeil et al., 1996).

Parent–Child Interaction Therapy: The Empirical and Theoretical Foundation for This Approach

The play therapy model described in this chapter is based in part on a parent-training program called Parent–Child Interaction Therapy (PCIT; Eyberg, 1988; Eyberg & Boggs, 1998; Hembree-Kigin & McNeil, 1995). PCIT is an empirically supported treatment for children with disruptive behavior and conduct problems (e.g., Eisenstadt, Eyberg, McNeil, Newcomb, & Funderburk, 1993; Eyberg, Boggs, & Algina, 1995; Eyberg & Robinson, 1982; Schumann, Foote, Eyberg, Boggs, & Algina, 1998). Research has suggested that children whose parents participate in PCIT have clinically significant improvements in disruptive behavior problems, from outside of normal limits to within normal limits (e.g., McNeil, Capage, Bahl, & Blanc, in press). In addition, outcome studies suggest that the behavior improvements gained in clinical settings generalize to the home (Boggs, 1990; Zangwill, 1984), to the school (McNeil, Eyberg, Eisenstadt, Newcomb, & Funderburk, 1991), and to untreated siblings (Brestan, Eyberg, Boggs, & Algina, 1997).

PCIT is based on the two-stage Hanf (1969) model of parent training. The two stages of PCIT are (1) the child-directed interaction, and (2) the parent-directed interaction. During the child-directed interaction, parents are taught to follow their child's lead by using behavioral play therapy skills (Capage, Foote, McNeil, & Eyberg, 1998). These skills, sometimes referred to as the PRIDE skills, are designed to strengthen the parent–child relationship and include the following: (1) Praise, (2) Reflection, (3) Imitation, (4) Description, and (5) Enthusiasm. Parents are taught to praise positive behavior and attributes in a very specific way, which is called "labeled praise." They also learn to listen actively to their children using reflection, a verbal statement that repeats back or paraphrases what the child says. As the essence of play therapy involves following the child's lead, parents are taught how to imitate the child's play. They also learn to describe the child's activities. The description becomes like a running commentary of behavior. By being enthusiastic in the use of these skills, the parent increases the likelihood that the child will remain interested and behave appropriately during play. In addition to the PRIDE skills, parents are taught to use selective attention and ignoring to manage minor disruptive behaviors. For example, if a child is playing roughly with the toys, the father would be instructed to turn his back away from the child and play enthusiastically by himself. When the child begins behaving again in an appropriate manner, the father returns his attention to the child and praises prosocial behaviors.

During the parent-directed interaction stage of PCIT, sometimes referred to as the discipline stage, parents are taught to be consistent in dealing with noncompliant and aggressive behaviors. Parents learn to give effective instructions to their child, to praise compliance, and to provide choices when the child does not comply. For example, the parent might provide a two-choices warning for noncompliance such as the following: "You have two choices: You can either pick up the toy or you can go to time-out." Parents are taught step by step how to implement an effective time-out as a consequence for noncompliance.

Rather than relying solely on didactic training, PCIT employs a coaching model of teaching; that is, the therapist actively directs the parent's interactions with the child. (In two-parent families, each parent is coached separately while interacting with the child.) Many clinics that use PCIT are equipped with a one-way mirror and a bug-in-ear microphone system. This allows the therapist to unobtrusively observe the parent–child interaction and communicate directly with the parent during this interaction. In this way, parents can benefit from immediate feedback, and children learn to respond to their parents rather than to the therapist. When the one-way mirror and bug-in-ear system are unavailable, the therapist can coach the parent from within the room.

Relationship between PCIT and This Short-Term Play Therapy Model

The 12-session model described in this chapter is based in part on PCIT. For example, a portion of the first seven sessions is devoted to the therapist using the child-directed interaction (or PRIDE) skills from PCIT. Among other benefits, these skills are helpful for establishing rapport, making the session fun for the child, and helping to improve child self-esteem. Then, in Sessions 8–12, these nondirective play skills are taught to parents using the coaching model from PCIT. Again, this model assumes that parents are the key to success in short-term treatment. Thus, parents are taught the child-directed play skills as a way for them to (1) enhance their relationship with their child, (2) help their child deal with anger and frustration, (3) manage disruptive behaviors, and (4) improve child self-esteem. The principal difference between this 12-session model and PCIT is that this is primarily a play therapy model, whereas PCIT is a parent-training model. In PCIT, the therapist does not typically work individually with the child. Another important difference is that PCIT involves teaching parents a discipline program (i.e., compliance training, time-out) in addition to the child-directed play skills. In our 12-session play therapy model, only parents are taught and coached in the child-directed play skills.

SHORT-TERM PLAY THERAPY APPROACH

Structure of the Play Therapy Session

In order to use time efficiently and minimize disruptive behavior, a great deal of structure (e.g., predictable routines, clear limits, and transition rituals) is incorporated into this approach. In fact, each of the sessions has a predictable, four-part structure: (1) Check-In with the caregiver—approximately 10 minutes, (2) Child's Work (therapist-directed activities)—approximately 20 minutes, (3) Child's Play (child-directed activities)—approximately 20 minutes, and (4) Check-Out with the caregiver—approximately 10 minutes. In contrast to typical, stimulating play therapy rooms that have many toys in the open (e.g., sand trays, pretend kitchens, dollhouses, etc.), our playroom contains only those toys and materials that the therapist brings in for that particular part of the session. The purpose of structuring the room is to prevent children with disruptive behavior from becoming overactive and overstimulated. With only 12 sessions to obtain treatment goals, every attempt is made to minimize disruptive behavior and keep the child on-task.

CHECK-IN

Each session begins with a 10-minute Check-In period with the child's caregivers. In most cases, the child is present during this time so that the child (1) does not become concerned that the therapist is revealing confidential information, (2) can participate, and (3) can be adequately supervised. The purpose of Check-In is to provide parents and children with the opportunity to share information that might contribute to the therapeutic process. They are asked about progress on weekly homework assignments and problems that occurred during the week, as well as familial stressors and significant events. This Check-In time is also a valuable opportunity for the therapist to build rapport with parents and help them feel like powerful contributors to their child's progress in treatment.

CHILD'S WORK

Child's Work is the therapist-directed portion of each session, which incorporates planned activities to address preestablished therapeutic goals. Examples of activities conducted during Child's Work include therapeutic games, role plays, presentation of educational materials, and thematic drawings. Child's Work always precedes Child's Play for several practical and therapeutic reasons. The first is that disruptive children will be more cooperative with planned activities if they know a "free play" will follow. In contrast, disruptive children will be less cooperative if they are required to transition from a "free play" activity to a structured activity chosen by the therapist. In terms of therapeutic benefits, beginning with thematic activities allows conflictual issues and emotional responses to be triggered early in the session. The child then is likely to carry these issues and responses into the Child's Play portion of the session, providing rich, therapeutic material for nondirective play therapy. Placing Child's Work before Child's Play also allows ample time for the child to work through strong reactions before leaving the session.

CHILD'S PLAY

In Child's Play, the therapist follows the child's lead and provides a supportive atmosphere in which the child can work through difficult issues. A primary goal of this portion of play therapy is to build a strong relationship between the therapist and child. Other goals, such as building self-esteem, improving communication skills, and improving social skills, are also part of Child's Play. Through careful use of some very specific skills, the therapist works towards these goals.

These specific skills are used throughout the hour session but are more concentrated during Child's Play. In addition to the PRIDE skills that were discussed earlier (i.e., Praise, Reflection, Imitation, Description, and Enthusiasm), the therapist uses questions and interpretations to make Child's Play a rich, therapeutic time. Questions make an explicit demand on the child to provide specific information and are therefore used in moderation. Examples of questions include "When does your daddy come visit you?" and "How do you feel about visiting your dad?" In the beginning sessions of therapy, questions are often anxiety-arousing to children and yield little information; however, questions tend to become more productive with time. Questions also are more productive when they are open-ended, used sparingly, and accompanied with pauses long enough to let the child respond.

Interpretations are therapist statements that make a link between the child's behavior and his or her motivations or feelings. Interpretations are used to make the child more aware of this link. Because interpretations are "educated guesses" or hypotheses, they should be stated hesitantly, so that the child may agree or disagree. Often, interpretations are stated with tentative beginnings such as "I wonder," "Perhaps," "Maybe," or "Sometimes." An example of an interpretation to a child's statement, " I hate my dad's girlfriend because she's always talking to him" could be "Maybe you're feeling angry at her because she gets so much of your dad's attention."

CHECK-OUT

Similar to Check-In, Check-Out is a time when the therapist meets with the child as well as his or her parents. During this 10 minutes, the therapist informs parents of the therapeutic nature of the play therapy work. This helps to facilitate communication between the parents and therapist, as well as keep the parents invested in their child's therapy. An important consideration is the child's right to confidentiality. This right must always be balanced with the parents' need to know about the content of therapy. Thus, at the end of Child's Play, the therapist and child should discuss what material should be shared with the parents. Typically, sensitive material regarding the child's feelings and thoughts is not shared with the parents. Another important goal of Check-Out is to promote generalization of treatment gains. Through homework assignments, parents can prompt and reinforce skills acquired during Child's Work. Homework assignments are given each week and are specific to the session's content. If Child's Work involved helping the child express anger though acceptable channels, the homework assignment might be for the parent to prompt and reinforce appropriate ways of expressing anger, such as hitting a pillow, scribbling on a piece of paper really hard, or writing an angry letter and tearing it up. Similarly, if Child's Work involved prompting the child to recognize accomplishments, the homework assignment might include having the child keep a chart of things he or she did well each day.

MANAGING DISRUPTIVE BEHAVIOR DURING SESSIONS

While some play therapies view disruptive behavior as rich therapeutic material from which valuable information can be gleaned and interpreted, this approach views disruptive behavior as an impediment to treatment progress. Little energy can be focused toward circumscribed therapeutic goals when a child is engaged in off-task and oppositional behaviors. Therefore, throughout all four portions of the session, managing disruptive behavior is a priority. This management is accomplished though proactive structuring that inhibits disruptive behavior, as well as controlled responses to disruptive behavior when it occurs. Proactive structuring of each session includes established rules, consistent routines for transitions, careful attention to precedents, choosing appealing Child's Work activities, and requiring work before play. Even with these preventive features in place, strategies such as praise, tangible reinforcers, rules for being a good listener, contingent attention, effective directions, the "When–Then" strategy, special game rules, and the "Turtle Technique" are used for managing disruptive behavior during play therapy. A summary of these procedures is provided in Table 9.1.

A 12-Session Model for Short-Term Play Therapy

This play therapy approach follows a 12-session model in which the first seven sessions are focused around the therapist working individually with the child. The remaining five sessions emphasize joint therapy with the

TABLE 9.1. Skills for Managing Disruptive Behavior

Management skill	Explanation and example
Establishing rules	Establishing rules clearly indicates to the child what is acceptable versus unacceptable behavior. Before Child's Work begins, the child is told he or she must stay in the playroom, play gently with the toys and materials, and not do anything that would endanger him- or herself, or the therapist. Rules are typically reviewed at the beginning of each session as a reminder to the child.
Develop transition routines	Transitions are often times when a disruptive child will become overly active and distracted. One way to minimize misbehavior is to provide the child with a warning that the transition is about to occur. Approximately 5 minutes before the end of Child's Play, the child should be given a transitional statement such as "In just a few minutes, it will be time to stop playing and clean up." Singing special songs also can make transitions easier.
Pay careful attention to precedents	If the child is allowed to engage in any minor problematic behaviors during the first sessions (e.g., running from the waiting room to the playroom, demanding choice of toys, running out of the session to visit parents), these behaviors will continue throughout sessions and become larger issues. It is best to establish clear, strict boundaries early on.
Use unlabeled and labeled praise	Unlabeled praise is a general comment indicating approval (e.g., "Good job"), whereas labeled praise is a specific statement that tells the child exactly what he or she did that the therapist liked (e.g., "Good job using your words to tell me how you feel"). To manage disruptive behavior using praise, the therapist should identify a problem behavior, identify behaviors that are incompatible with the problem behavior, and then praise the incompatible behavior. For example, the problem behavior might be screaming. A behavior incompatible with screaming is talking in an indoor voice. So the therapist would give a labeled praise for talking in an indoor voice.
Incorporate tangible reinforcers	The best systems for tangible reinforcers involve immediate rewards for specific behaviors. For example, a hand stamp could be used for good listening. Also, a star chart could be used, such that the child earns a reward once a certain number of stars has been achieved.
Develop rules for being a good listener	Because one of the greatest challenges in doing play therapy with disruptive children is maintaining their attention, children are taught three "good listening rules" early in treatment: (1) "Look in my eyes when you talk"; (2) "Hold your body very, very still," and (3) "Think hard about what I am saying" (McGinnis & Goldstein, 1990a, 1990b).

TABLE 9.1. (*continued*)

Use strategic ignoring and contingent attention	Many disruptive behaviors are a child's attempt to gain attention and therefore can be managed by ignoring. The therapist explains and models in advance that he or she will turn and ignore disruptive behavior (e.g., aggressive play, hiding from the therapist). For example, if the child is playing roughly with farm animals, the therapist can ignore the rough play, model appropriate play, and then praise the child for engaging in more gentle, appropriate play.
Give good directions	Directions are defined as specific instructions the child is told (rather than asked) to follow. When it is important for the child to comply, the direction should be positively stated, polite, and specific. For example, if a child began to run ahead during a transition time, the therapist could say, "Please come back and walk with me."
"When–Then" strategy	Children are told that a pleasant, rewarding activity will be provided once they engage in specified behavior. For example, "When you practice your breathing one more time, then we can use our colored markers."
Create special game rules	The therapist assigns special rules to nonthreatening, typical board games (e.g., checkers). Most often, the special rule is that the child must produce a small amount of work in exchange for a turn at the game. A therapist might introduce this as follows: "Today we get to play checkers, but this is a special kind of checkers. The rule is that before we can take a turn, we each have to tell about a time when we felt mad."
"Turtle Technique"	Developed by Robin (1976), this technique helps disruptive children regain self-control by teaching them to react to aggressive impulses by imagining that they are turtles (e.g., pulling their head into the shell).

child and parents. Throughout the course of therapy, increasing parental involvement is encouraged. The joint therapy is an extension of this, during which parents are taught to be "cotherapists." Teaching parents valuable "therapist" skills helps to improve their relationship with their child, empowers them to become more independent of the therapist, and enhances generalization of treatment gains. Essentially, there is a transfer of dependence and responsibility from the therapist–child relationship to the longer-term and more primary parent–child relationship.

The first two sessions of this play model precedents and routines for all sessions to follow. During these sessions, procedures are explained to the parent as well as the child. The structure of the sessions follows our general four-part outline. During Check-In, consent and confidentiality are reviewed, parents are educated regarding play therapy, the treatment plan and goals are discussed, and a therapy contract is devised. Child's Work involves explaining and modeling play therapy structure for the child. Child's Play is spent in child-directed activities, and Check-Out includes a review of the session's content and assignment of homework.

The content for Sessions 3–7 is more flexible considering that children are referred for short-term play therapy for a variety of reasons. However, these middle sessions should adhere to the same established structure (i.e., Check-In, Child's Work, Child's Play, and Check-Out) and incorporate the same behavior management (e.g., establishing rules, giving good directions) and process skills (e.g., praise, reflection). In terms of content, the therapist should develop a flexible but detailed treatment plan prior to the beginning of Session 3 and progress toward identified goals. The contents of each session should be well planned and build on one another so that skills learned in earlier sessions form a foundation for more advanced skills to be acquired in later sessions. An additional consideration is that the treatment plan should incorporate homework. Assigning meaningful, weekly homework will enhance progress and facilitate parental involvement. Termination themes are introduced at the end of Session 7, because it immediately precedes a major shift in treatment. Sessions 1–7 concentrate on the therapist working individually with the child and involving the parents in the beginning and end of sessions. However, beginning with Session 8, therapy is focused more on the therapist working with the parents and child together.

Essentially, Session 8 begins the transfer of the child's dependence on the therapist to the parents. Decreasing amounts of time are spent individually with the child as the parents are coached in play therapy skills. Parents are asked to attend Session 8 without their child and are taught play therapy skills. In Sessions 9–11, parents are directly coached in the use of these play therapy skills. Their skills are monitored each week by observing the parent–child interaction for 5 minutes and coding specific behaviors using the Dyadic Parent–Child Interaction Coding System (Eyberg & Robinson, 1983). This careful monitoring provides the therapist with a more objective measure of parents' skills acquisition and therefore a valuable piece of information to aid in treatment decisions. After Sessions 9–11, homework is assigned that requires parents to provide daily "play therapy" sessions at home.

Session 12 includes conducting termination rituals with the parents, such as reviewing the treatment plan, examining pre- to posttreatment changes on assessment measures, and praising parental accomplishments. Termination rituals with the child include a review of the course of treatment and a posttreatment party. Typically, one or two "booster sessions" are scheduled to address a few unresolved issues and gradually reduce dependence on the therapist. Parents also are invited to call if they feel it is necessary and are given appropriate resources and referrals.

Teaching Play Therapy Skills to Parents

Parents attend Session 8 without their child and are taught play therapy skills (for a detailed description of teaching play therapy to parents, see Hembree-Kigin & McNeil, 1995). This session is structured so that 10 minutes are devoted to Check-In, 40 minutes are allotted to instruction, and 10 minutes are spent on Check-Out. During Check-In, the previous week's homework and life events are reviewed. The 40 minutes of instruction time is very active for the parents as well as the therapist. Because most people learn best by being involved in the material and by repetition, the therapist strives to incorporate examples relevant to the family, role plays, humor, opportunities for parents to ask questions, and frequent summaries of information during the instruction period. Check-Out consists of a brief review and homework assignment. The assignment given is for parents to spend 5- to 10-minutes of "special playtime" with their child each day.

Parents are told that they will be taught a set of play therapy skills to use with their child in daily 5 to 10 minute play sessions. To help them understand the purpose of this "special playtime," they are told that they can assist treatment progress by serving as cotherapists. Emphasis is placed on how the parents can help their child accomplish more in a shorter amount of time by actively participating in their child's treatment. Special playtime goals are established and individualized for the family. These goals may include increasing child self-esteem, decreasing anger, improving social skills, developing constructive play skills, strengthening family relationships, and using words to communicate feelings.

In conducting special playtime, we ask parents to avoid using commands, criticisms, and questions. Instead, parents are encouraged to use skills such as praise, reflection, imitation, description, and enthusiasm (i.e., PRIDE skills). Parents are taught that a key component for managing behavior and making special playtime a high quality, positive time is the use of attention. Parents are instructed to provide a lot of positive attention (e.g., labeled praise, descriptions, and enthusiasm) to the child when he or she is engaging in appropriate behaviors and to ignore the child when he or she is engaging in inappropriate behaviors during play therapy. This skill is commonly referred to as selective attention–strategic ignoring, or contingent attention.

Parents also are instructed as to how to handle misbehavior during play therapy. The therapist explains that misbehavior can fall into one of two categories: (1) dangerous/destructive, or (2) annoying/obnoxious. Dangerous/destructive behaviors can cause physical harm to people or property. Some examples include hitting, biting, scratching, throwing toys, and writing on walls. Annoying/obnoxious behaviors are inappropriate but do not result in harm. Examples of these behaviors are bossiness, whining, spitting, teasing, and using foul language. Parents are taught different strategies for handling these two types of misbehavior. They are encouraged to stop special playtime if the child engages in any dangerous/destructive behaviors and provide an additional consequence if they feel it is appropriate. In contrast, parents are instructed to use strategic ignoring if the child engages in any annoying/obnoxious behaviors during special playtime.

It is recommended that parents add structure to the special playtime by establishing a routine similar to that of the clinic. Parents are instructed to try to hold play therapy at the same time every day so that it is predictable. This makes the child less likely to beg or nag for special playtime, and makes the parent more likely to remember it. Parents also are instructed that the best materials for special playtime are construction-oriented toys that encourage creativity and imagination, such as blocks, garage and car sets, tea sets, toy farms, dollhouses, and crayons and paper. Toys to avoid include those that have set rules (e.g., board games), encourage aggressive play (e.g., superhero figures, punching bags), require limit setting (e.g., scissors) or discourage conversations (e.g., audiotapes, books, puppets). To start special playtime, parents select three or four acceptable toys or activities and place them in a space free of distracters. The ideal setting is a quiet area where the parent and child will not be interrupted (e.g., the parents' bedroom, a dining room). After the toys have been selected, the parent tells the child that it is time for special playtime and explains the rules as follows:

> "It is time for our special playtime. You can play with any of the toys in front of us and I'll play along with you, but there are two rules you must follow. First, you have to stay right here with me. And second, you have to play gently with the toys. If you wander around the room or play rough with the toys, I will turn around like this and play by myself. Then, when you come back or play nicely again, I'll turn back around like this and play with you again. Thanks for listening to the rules. We can play with anything you want to play with now." (McNeil et al., 1996, p. 68)

The skills taught to parents are very similar to those used by the therapist; however, there are some important differences. Because parents do not have extensive training or objectivity, they are not instructed or encouraged to use interpretations. They also are not prepared to formulate treatment plans or utilize specialized therapeutic techniques, like those used in Child's Work.

Coaching Play Therapy Skills

The direct coaching component of this approach helps to increase time effectiveness. In more traditional, didactic approaches, parents would be taught a skill and sent home to practice it with their child throughout the week. The parents would return the following week and report failed attempts to implement the skill. The therapist would then help the parents make modifications and send the parents home again to practice. In contrast, a direct coaching approach involves teaching parents skills in session and asking them to practice the skills with their child in session. The therapist observes this interaction and provides immediate, specific feedback to the parent regarding their use of the skills. This feedback or coaching can occur with the therapist outside the room (which requires the use of a one-way mirror, intercom speaker system, and a bug-in-the-ear auditory transmission system) or inside the room. When coaching in the room, children are told to pretend that the therapist is not there. It also is explained to the child that the therapist will not talk or play with the child until the coaching is over. Direct coaching is one of the most expedient ways of acquiring new skills because it involves the use of two powerful learning strategies: rehearsal and immediate feedback.

Coaching is most effective when feedback is provided consistently after each parental verbalization. Essentially, the parent makes a comment, the therapist responds, the parent makes another comment, the therapist responds, and so on. This rhythm helps the parent to learn to pause and listen after each comment so that the therapist and parent avoid "talking over" one another and instead communicate effectively. Coaching each parental verbalization also allows skills to be shaped in a time-efficient manner. The parent receives a large quantity of specific, immediate feedback. It is this continuous and active coaching that leads to quick and meaningful improvements in play therapy skills.

Coaches should emphasize the positives. Parents are very sensitive about their parenting skills and little is learned from criticism. If mistakes are made, the therapist should instruct parents as to what to do instead of telling parents what they are doing wrong. Another way to emphasize the positives is to provide frequent labeled praise to parents when they are using skills correctly or engaging in other therapeutic behaviors such as being warm, genuine, or playful. Similarly, coaches should be selective when correcting mistakes. Providing frequent, corrective suggestions may make the session tense, the parent feel overly criticized, and ultimately hurt rapport. Instead, it is better to ignore some minor mistakes even though it may break the coaching rhythm.

Feedback should be brief and specific. Although the therapist may provide an occasional, lengthy observation to parents, the majority of coaching consists of brief, specific phrases. Examples might include "Good description," "Great labeled praise," "I like how you ignored that inappropriate behavior," and "Go ahead and describe that." It is also helpful to coach qualitative aspects of the parent–child interaction such as eye contact, smiles, physical closeness, expression of feelings, patience, playfulness, and creativity. Finally, it is important to be decisive and quick when coaching, particularly when coaching ignoring. When a child engages in a negative attention-seeking behavior, the therapist only has seconds to coach the parent through the situation.

CASE ILLUSTRATION

To illustrate our 12-session model and, particularly, how we include parents in the treatment process, we present a detailed case example of Brian, a child exhibiting sexualized behavior. In a session-by-session format, we briefly discuss the selection of treatment goals, formulation of session objectives, and incorporation of Child's Work and homework activities to address session objectives. As treatment unfolds, we illustrate the increasing involvement that Brian's foster mother, Mrs. Jennings, had in the management of Brian's sexualized behavior.[1]

Background Information

Brian, an 8-year-old boy, was referred for treatment of sexualized behavior subsequent to chronic sexual abuse. Specific behavioral concerns included touching other children's private parts, masturbating in the presence of others, and being indiscriminately affectionate. To help clarify the severity and scope of Brian's behavior problems, several parent report assessment measures were used. For example, Mrs. Jennings completed the Child Behavior Checklist (Achenbach, 1991), and Brian received clinically elevated ratings on the Sex Problems, Aggressive Behavior, and Anxious/Depressed scales.

Sessions 1 and 2

SESSION OBJECTIVES

1. Obtain parental consent and child assent for treatment.
2. Agree on attendance contract.
3. Introduce the parent and child to basic concepts about play therapy.
4. Establish playroom rules and behavioral expectations.
5. Build rapport.

CHECK-IN

During Check-In, the structure of the play therapy sessions was explained to Brian and his foster mother, Mrs. Jennings. The therapist explained the projected course of treatment with Mrs. Jennings, and she agreed to it. Also, Mrs. Jennings and Brian agreed to attend weekly sessions for a minimum of 12 weeks. Brian seemed apprehensive and did not speak much but willingly followed the therapist to the playroom.

[1]A short version of this case originally appeared in McNeil et al. (1996). It has been adapted for this chapter and reprinted by permission from Childswork/Childsplay of Genesis Direct, Inc.

CHILD'S WORK

After they went back to the playroom, the therapist explained the rules of that room. Then, the therapist said, "I know that some of what I talked about with your foster mom might be confusing, but I have a book that explains a little bit more about what we might do together." When reading *A Child's First Book about Play Therapy* (Nemiroff & Annunziata, 1990), Brian was asked what problems he had that could be worked on in play therapy. Not surprisingly, he did not volunteer his sexualized behavior as a problem. The therapist commented that Brian's mother had already talked about how Brian sometimes had a problem knowing when it is okay to touch his own private parts and other children's private parts. The therapist went on to say that although Brian did not have to talk about that in the first sessions, it would be discussed later in play therapy.

CHILD'S PLAY

During Child's Play, Brian quietly played with some clay. He still seemed reserved and did not maintain eye contact with the therapist. To help build rapport, the therapist played alongside him with the clay and described the creations that Brian was making. By the second session, Brian had warmed up to the therapist and was engaged more in shared play.

CHECK-OUT

Mrs. Jennings joined the therapist and Brian for the Check-Out. During this time, the therapist briefly explained Brian's Child's Work session. The therapist provided Brian's foster mother with an inexpensive paperback copy of the book *A Child's First Book about Play Therapy* (Nemiroff & Annunziata, 1990) as a homework assignment to read with Brian at home.

Session Three

SESSION OBJECTIVES

1. Begin to discuss the notion of private parts.
2. Discuss what parts of the body are considered private.

CHECK-IN

Mrs. Jennings reported completing the previous week's homework assignment. To emphasize the importance of completing homework, the therapist praised Mrs. Jennings and then explained that beginning that day, therapy would be more focused on the presenting problems.

CHILD'S WORK

Child's Work began with the following statement from the therapist: "Brian, do you remember a couple of weeks ago when we looked at the play therapy book? I told you then that sometime we would talk about touching private parts. Today, we are going to begin talking a little bit about that. But first, let's draw some pictures together." Brian was asked to draw one picture of a boy and one picture of a girl. These pictures were used to illustrate the concept of private parts. The therapist explained that private parts are all of the parts of the body that are covered by a boy's swimming trunks and a girl's bikini. These concepts were further reinforced by having Brian use a different crayon to draw a bathing suit on each of the figures.

CHILD'S PLAY

During Child's Play, Brian spontaneously picked up a Barbie doll and showed the therapist the location of the doll's private parts. The therapist responded by praising Brian for having been a good listener and remembering what he had learned.

CHECK-OUT

During Check-out, Mrs. Jennings was encouraged to increase her supervision of Brian to prevent opportunities for sexual acting out with other children.

Session 4

SESSION OBJECTIVES

1. Review the concepts of private parts.
2. Begin discussing good and bad touches.
3. Assign homework to involve Brian's foster mother in encouraging good touches with others.

CHECK-IN

When they first arrived, Mrs. Jennings immediately expressed some concern and frustration that the therapy seemed to be making Brian's sexualized behavior worse. He reportedly had been telling other children about private parts and noting the differences between male and female private areas. She was not sure how she should handle these new discussions that Brian was having with others. The therapist suggested that Mrs. Jennings encourage Brian to discuss these issues with her, and to praise him for recognizing private body parts, but also to teach him about being selective in discussing sexual topics with others.

Also, during Check-In, the therapist showed Mrs. Jennings a book about appropriate sexual behavior and asked how she felt about Brian seeing this book. She gave her consent for the therapist to use this book to begin discussing good and bad touches.

CHILD'S WORK

With his foster mother's consent, the book *It's My Body* (Freeman, 1982) was read to Brian during Child's Work. The therapist also used the pictures that Brian made in Session 3 to review the concept of private parts.

CHILD'S PLAY

Brian chose to play with Legos during Child's Play, and the therapist followed his lead. He appeared to enjoy interacting with the therapist and asked, "When do I get to come back again?"

CHECK-OUT

At Check-Out, the therapist and Brian explained the concepts of good and bad touch to Mrs. Jennings. Brian was praised for demonstrating what he had learned, and Mrs. Jennings was pleased that the sexualized behavior was being targeted directly in therapy. She was given a homework assignment to reinforce further these concepts by reviewing them with Brian and praising him for touching family members and peers appropriately.

Session 5

SESSION OBJECTIVES

1. Continue differentiating good and bad touches.
2. Use puppets to role play the different kinds of touches.

CHECK-IN

The homework assignment was reviewed with Brian and his foster mother during Check-In. Mrs. Jennings reported that Brian actively talked about good and bad touches with other members of the family and that she had worked to praise him for good touches. However, she worried that he sometimes was not sure what counted as a good or bad touch when with someone in his family about whom he cared.

CHILD'S WORK

The Child's Work portion again focused on good and bad touches. The book *It's My Body* (Freeman, 1982) was completed and an exercise was conducted at the chalkboard. The chalkboard was divided into three segments: one for good touches (e.g., gentle handholding), and one for each of the two types of bad touches (i.e., aggression and touching others' private parts). Brian was asked to generate examples of each type of touching. Once the board was full, the therapist asked Brian to erase the bad touch segments. Family puppets were used to role-play the different types of touches and appropriate responses when someone wants to touch a child's private parts. Brian was encouraged to practice with the puppets assuming both the roles of the victim and perpetrator. As a metaphor, Brian was taught that interpersonal space is like "a bubble." He was told:

> "When you get too close to someone you can pop the bubble, and people feel yucky when their bubbles get popped. So that people won't feel yucky, it is important to ask permission before you give hugs or kisses. If they give you permission, they can make their bubbles smaller so they won't pop when you hug each other."

CHILD'S PLAY

During Child's Play, Brian was praised for respecting the therapist's bubble, and the therapist used puppets to model how to ask before invading Brian's bubble (e.g., "Could I have a hug?"). Puppets were used for modeling the hug.

CHECK-OUT

During Check-Out, Brian's foster mother was introduced to the bubble metaphor. Her homework assignment was to prompt and reinforce Brian for respecting the bubbles of others.

TELEPHONE CALL

Prior to Session 6, the therapist telephoned Mrs. Jennings to discuss some sensitive information about dealing with masturbation. The therapist explained that an effective treatment strategy would be to begin restricting masturbation to private settings.

Mrs. Jennings was given an opportunity to share her thoughts and feeling about this approach. When she agreed with this strategy, the therapist obtained specific information about the settings in which self-stimulation would and would not be allowed.

Session 6

SESSION OBJECTIVES

1. Discuss masturbation as a private activity.
2. Role-play with puppets.

CHECK-IN

The therapist discussed homework with Mrs. Jennings and reminded her that they were going to talk about private behaviors during this session. Mrs. Jennings nodded in understanding.

CHILD'S WORK

During the Child's Work portion of Session 6, the puppet role plays were continued. The therapist talked with Brian about the times and settings in which it is acceptable to touch one's own private parts. Brian was told that masturbating is a private activity in the same way that using the restroom is done privately. He was also told that people feel uncomfortable watching someone do a private activity. A dollhouse was used to demonstrate the areas of the house in which masturbation is acceptable. Role plays with dollhouse figures were used to help Brian understand the rules for touching one's private parts.

CHILD'S PLAY

During Child's Play, Brian chose to continue dollhouse play, but no sexual themes were evident. The therapist asked Brian whether it would be all right with him to discuss that day's work with his foster mother (specifically, issues regarding appropriate places to engage in private activities). He provided his consent.

CHECK-OUT

During Check-Out, the therapist and Mrs. Jennings outlined a plan for prompting and redirecting Brian when he engaged in self-stimulation in inappropriate settings. Mrs. Jennings was instructed to remind Brian that touching himself like that was a private activity and that he could do that in one of his private rooms, but not in front of other people. She was encouraged to continue prompting and praising Brian for respecting the interpersonal space of others.

Session 7

SESSION OBJECTIVES

1. Continue discussing where it was appropriate to engage in private touching.
2. Continue to talk about good and bad touches.
3. Introduce the idea of Mrs. Jennings participating in therapy.
4. Introduce termination issues.

CHECK-IN

Homework was reviewed with Brian and Mrs. Jennings, who was concerned because although Brian seemed to be very aware of touching other people appropriately, he continued to masturbate publicly. The therapist reviewed what the foster mother should say to Brian when he engaged in this behavior. She agreed to continue prompting Brian to go to a private room when he touched his private parts during the upcoming week and then to check in again with the therapist. To assist her in remembering the frequency of her prompts, the therapist quickly designed a monitoring sheet for Mrs. Jennings to mark with a tally each time she prompted Brian to go to a private room.

CHILD'S WORK

During Child's Work, Brian and the therapist played a therapeutic game addressing safe and appropriate touching. To prepare Brian for upcoming termination, the therapist read the remainder of *A Child's First Book about Play Therapy* (Nemiroff & Annunziata, 1990). The discussed feelings about loss and saying "goodbye." At this point, it was important to begin helping Brian understand that play therapy would begin to be different soon. The therapist told Brian that his foster mother was going to begin participating in their sessions.

CHILD'S PLAY

In Child's Play, Brian chose to continue playing the therapeutic game. While walking to the Check-Out room, Brian asked the therapist for a hug. The therapist responded, "I'm very proud of you for not breaking my bubble! You remembered to ask before touching me."

CHECK-OUT

During Check-Out, Mrs. Jennings was encouraged to continue redirecting inappropriate self-stimulation, to praise Brian for respecting interpersonal space, and to read the termination section of Brian's copy of *A Child's First Book about Play Therapy* (Nemiroff & Annunziata, 1990).

Session 8

SESSION OBJECTIVES

1. Discuss the play therapy (PRIDE) skills with Brian's foster mother.
2. Role-play the skills.
3. Assign the first home-practice of special playtime skills.

CHECK-IN

Mrs. Jennings had been asked to attend this session alone so that the therapist could teacher her the skills for the child-directed play interaction. When she arrived, the therapist asked about the previous week's homework assignment. Mrs. Jennings first gave the therapist the tally sheet she used to monitor the number of times that she prompted Brian, then said she was surprised to see that instead of having to prompt Brian two or three times each day, she had prompted him only once during the last 2 days. Also, she seemed eager to talk about what a difficult week Brian seemed to have had. Brian had told her that he did not like to have to share his therapy time with her. The therapist assured Mrs. Jennings that she would learn skills to facilitate a fun interaction between herself and Brian, and that Brian would quickly learn that the special time would be different from anything else they had ever done together. Also, the therapist explained that this special playtime also would provide a safe opportunity for Brian to express his feelings.

During the session, the therapist explained the child-directed interaction skills and allowed Mrs. Jennings to ask questions. When conducting play therapy with Brian, Mrs. Jennings was encouraged to utilize the PRIDE skills: to use labeled praise for specific things that Brian was doing well, to reflect Brian's talk, to imitate his play, to describe his activities, and to be enthusiastic. She also was discouraged from giving commands and asking questions, because this took the lead away from Brian. Finally, the therapist told Mrs. Jennings to avoid criticizing Brian during special playtime, particularly subtle criticism in the form of the words "No," "Don't," "Stop," "Quit," and "Not." Following the teaching of the skills, Mrs. Jennings role-played the play therapy with the therapist. To establish an example of how Mrs. Jennings should address Brian's sexualized behavior during play, the therapist began to undress one of the dolls in the kitchen area of the dollhouse. The therapist worked with Mrs. Jennings on how to model appropriate behavior with her doll, so that she could explain that her doll would go to the bedroom to undress because undressing is a private activity.

CHECK-OUT

Brian's foster mother was given a handout on the play therapy (i.e., child-directed interaction) skills. Her homework assignment was to begin practicing these skills in a daily 5- to 10-minute special playtime with Brian. Also, Mrs. Jennings was asked to record her special playtimes with Brian on a homework sheet.

Session 9

SESSION OBJECTIVES

1. Coach Brian's foster mother in child-directed play skills.
2. Begin decreasing the amount of time spent in Child's Play in anticipation of termination.

CHECK-IN

Mrs. Jennings decided to continue monitoring the number of times that she prompted Brian when he touched himself and was excited to see that the number of times had decreased to a total of only seven in the previous week. However, she reported that she had forgotten to complete the special playtime homework sheet, but that she had been practicing all week. The therapist spent time delineating each day of the week and asking Mrs. Jennings to discuss the specifics of the special playtime for that day, explaining that the homework sheet was important for tracking positive or negative changes in Brian's behavior. Overall, Mrs. Jennings reported that Brian seemed to enjoy the time they spent together.

The therapist turned to Brian and explained the new structure for the remaining sessions of play therapy. The therapist said, "Today, Brian, I am going to coach your foster mom while she plays with you. I won't talk to you during this time. But, after your special playtime is over, you and I will have some time to spend together alone. During the playtime, you should just pretend that you can't see me or hear me."

CODING

After coding Mrs. Jennings's play therapy skills during the first 5 minutes of special playtime with Brian, the therapist noted that she was upbeat and positive during the play, but that she mostly watched what Brian did. Her verbalizations toward Brian were often acknowledgments such as "Uh-huh" or "Yeah," but she used few reflections. Mrs. Jennings also used seven unlabeled praises, such as "Good" or "That's nice."

COACHING

The therapist began the coaching portion by pointing out Mrs. Jennings's strengths (i.e., her enthusiasm and positive interaction with Brian) and reminded her that one way to let Brian know that she was very interested in what he was saying was to reflect back what he said to her. Her use of reflections immediately increased, and Brian began explaining in more detail what he was building with the Legos. The therapist praised Mrs. Jennings and pointed out that Brian was more talkative with her when she used more reflections.

CHILD'S WORK/CHILD'S PLAY

Because the majority of this session was spent coaching, Brian's individual time was reduced to approximately 15 minutes. Recognizing that Brian was unhappy about reducing his individual time with the therapist, the therapist asked Brian how he felt about having his foster mother join his play therapy. Brian shrugged. The therapist offered, "I know that it can be disappointing to have less playtime. It's also a little sad to think about our therapy ending in a few weeks. Sometimes it helps to talk about it. Tell me what you're feeling." Brian said, "I'm a little sad, but I do like playing with my foster mom." The therapist praised Brian for talking about feelings, and the remainder of Brian's individual time was spent in Child's Play. Brian chose to continue playing with the Legos.

CHECK-OUT

Mrs. Jennings reported that at first, she felt "funny" about being watched as she played with Brian, but when the therapist started coaching, she began to be less worried. Based on the coding that was done, Mrs. Jennings was encouraged to concentrate on changing her unlabeled praises (e.g., "Thanks") into labeled praises for appropriate behavior (e.g., "Thanks for sharing"). The therapist reiterated that labeled praise could be used to increase specific behaviors, such as appropriate touching.

Session 10

SESSION OBJECTIVES

1. Continue coaching Brian's foster mother in child-directed play skills.
2. Spend less time in Child's Play in anticipation of termination.

CHECK-IN

During Check-In, Mrs. Jennings reported that Brian had gotten into trouble at school twice in the past week, and that she had received a note and a phone call from his teacher. She said that although Brian often struggled with his classwork, he typically did not pose any behavior concerns. Brian had gotten into a fight with a girl on the playground, which resulted in him pushing her down and running away. When Mrs. Jennings asked why he was fighting, Brian refused to answer. Otherwise, Brian continued to engage in appropriate touches with the members of his family and other children at home, and Mrs. Jennings said that she had not seen him touch his private parts at all in the past week.

CODING

During the 5-minute coding period, Mrs. Jennings used many reflections when Brian spoke to her but asked a number of leading questions (e.g., "Are you sure you want to play with the dollhouse instead of the blocks?"). Yet she continued to use many positive skills such as praise and descriptions. Brian's behavior was more disruptive than usual, and he acted out a fight between some of the dolls in the house. Mrs. Jennings continued to be enthusiastic as she played with Brian.

COACHING

The therapist began coaching by saying that Mrs. Jennings was doing a great job maintaining her enthusiasm and positive demeanor, especially when Brian's behavior was more difficult. Just then, Brian became very loud and aggressive, making the dolls hit and kick each other. The therapist coached Mrs. Jennings to ignore his aggression and model appropriate conflict resolution. To guide her to ignore the aggression and model a more appropriate response, the therapist said:

> "OK, that's pretty aggressive. I want you to turn your back and ignore the aggressive play, just like we did when you and I role-played. That's it, turn your back completely. I am watching him, so you don't have to worry about his safety. I know this is hard. Now, I want you to model a better way to deal with conflict. Say, 'My doll is going to use her words instead of hitting.' That's it. Have your doll say, 'I'm mad at you and I do not want to play with you anymore. I'm leaving.' OK, he's still being aggressive. Keep ignoring and playing gently with your dolls . . . , hold it . . . , hold it. I know he's asking you a question right now, but he's still being aggressive with the dolls. He needs to learn that hitting and kicking are not appropriate ways to solve problems. OK,

there. He has one of the dolls and is playing gently with it. Go ahead and turn back to him. Please say, 'Thanks for using good touches with the dolls. When you play gently, then I can keep playing with you.' There you go. Nice job with that ignoring. Now I want you to increase your enthusiasm back to where it was before, and start describing his appropriate play."

The remainder of the coaching session went smoothly, and Brian did not engage in other disruptive behavior. This session provided Mrs. Jennings with a good example of how she could use strategic attention and ignoring to elicit more appropriate behaviors from Brian.

CHILD'S WORK/CHILD'S PLAY

This portion was shortened to 10 minutes this session. After reviewing the upcoming termination with Brian (using a picture of a "staircase" to termination), the therapist asked if Brian wanted to talk about the fight he had at school. Brian said that he pushed the girl because she was trying to break his bubble. The therapist praised Brian for talking about a difficult topic and role-played with Brian different options for what to do when someone tried to get too close to him. Brian told the therapist that he did not want his foster mother to know why he had pushed the girl at school. The therapist agreed to respect his request for confidentiality. Then, the therapist allowed Brian to lead the play for the last few minutes of time that they had.

CHECK-OUT

The therapist told Mrs. Jennings that she was making good progress in her use of the play therapy skills, and that she had done a great job ignoring Brian's acting-out behavior. The therapist then told her that Brian had discussed the fight at school but wanted to keep that information private. Mrs. Jennings was asked to continue using the 5- to 10-minute special playtime with Brian. She also was encouraged to use some of the skills outside of that designated time (e.g., reflecting Brian's talk in the car, praising gentle play when friends visited).

Session 11

SESSION OBJECTIVES

1. Coach the foster mother in child-directed play skills.
2. Have foster mother complete posttreatment measures.
3. Further decrease individual time with Brian.
4. Plan the termination ritual with Brian.

CHECK-IN

During Check-In, Mrs. Jennings reported that the previous week had been good. She had not seen Brian engage in any bad touches or private behaviors, and she used a labeled praise to tell him that she was very proud of him for using his good touches. She was asked to complete the same measures she had completed before treatment.

CODING

During the 5-minute coding period, Mrs. Jennings showed good mastery of the child-directed play skills. She seemed comfortable playing with him, and he appeared to enjoy the time with her. The only problem identified by the therapist was that Mrs. Jennings still did not use labeled praise very frequently.

COACHING

To increase her use of labeled praise, the therapist had Mrs. Jennings engage in an exercise with Brian. The therapist asked her to try to use five labeled praises in the next 2 minutes. The therapist praised Mrs. Jennings for thinking of behaviors to praise. Also, when Mrs. Jennings would use an unlabeled praise such as, "Good job," the therapist offered guidance by saying, "That's a good job of doing what?" These prompts helped Mrs. Jennings learn to turn unlabeled praises into labeled praises.

CHILD'S WORK/CHILD'S PLAY

Again, the therapist reviewed the "staircase" to termination picture with Brian. Brian was excited about eating cupcakes at the termination party that would take place the next week. The remainder of time was spent in Child's Play.

CHECK-OUT

The therapist asked Mrs. Jennings to continue using the child-directed play skills during the 5- to 10-minute special playtime at home. She was reminded that the following week, they could review Brian's progress and discuss any additional concerns.

Session 12

SESSION OBJECTIVES

1. Complete termination steps with Brian and his foster mother.
2. Make referrals for any additional needed services.

CHECK-IN

Twenty minutes were devoted to Check-In for this session. The therapist gave a copy of Brian's treatment plan to Mrs. Jennings and discussed the positives in detail. They also discussed progress toward treatment goals, and the therapist provided an assessment of Brian's continuing treatment needs. Brian demonstrated improvements on the Sex Problems subscale of the Child Behavior Checklist but remained elevated on the Aggression scale. Mrs. Jennings commented that she was worried because Brian's teacher continued to express some concern about his academic work. The therapist gave Mrs. Jennings appropriate referral information regarding a psychoeducational assessment. Issues about whether to pursue additional treatment for the aggression were discussed, and Mrs. Jennings decided to wait a couple of months to see if the aggression might decrease on its own.

The therapist then shifted the focus of the Check-In to Mrs. Jennings's accomplishments. She was praised for (1) attending sessions regularly, (2) following through on homework assignments, (3) monitoring Brian's behavior beyond what was requested, and (4) improving her interaction skills with Brian.

CHILD'S WORK

The therapist spent 10 minutes reviewing the course of treatment with Brian. They talked about all the things that Brian had learned and reviewed the various exercises and activities of therapy. Brian was praised for all the hard work he did in play therapy.

CHILD'S PLAY

The termination party lasted for 20 minutes. The therapist and Brian each had a cupcake, and they wrote goodbye cards to each other. Brian said he was sad because he did not want to break the therapist's bubble, but he did not know how to say goodbye. The therapist told Brian that they could shake hands and also that Brian should let his foster mother know if he wanted to talk to the therapist again in the future. Brian was given a certificate as a reward for all his hard work in therapy.

CHECK-OUT

During Check-Out, Mrs. Jennings was reminded about the importance of continuing to practice her skills during special playtime with Brian. She was told to continue praising Brian for good touches with other people and was encouraged to contact the therapist if concerns surfaced in the future.

SUMMARY AND CONCLUSION

The success of this short-term model of play therapy rests on involving and empowering parents in their child's treatment. Parents support therapy by (1) telling the therapist what is happening in the child's life outside the therapy hour, (2) completing weekly homework assignments that reinforce skills learned in session, and (3) learning to conduct play therapy sessions at home. By becoming involved, parents can help achieve goals more efficiently and productively during treatment, and help ensure that treatment gains are generalized and maintained after treatment ends.

REFERENCES

Achenbach, T. M. (1991). *Integrative guide for the 1991 CBCL/4-18, YSR, and TRF profiles.* Burlington: University of Vermont, Department of Psychiatry.

Boggs, S. R. (1990). *Generalization of treatment to the home setting: Direct observation analysis.* Unpublished manuscript, University of Florida, Gainesville.

Brestan, E., Eyberg, S. M., Boggs, S., & Algina, J. (1997). Parent–Child Interaction Therapy: Parent perceptions of untreated siblings. *Child and Family Behavior Therapy, 19,* 13–28.

Capage, L. C., Foote, R., McNeil, C. B., & Eyberg, S. M. (1998). Parent–Child Interaction Therapy: An effective treatment for young children with conduct problems. *The Behavior Therapist, 21,* 137–138.

Eisenstadt, T. H., Eyberg, S., McNeil, C. B., Newcomb, K., & Funderburk, B. (1993). Parent–Child Interaction Therapy with behavior problem children: Relative effectiveness of two stages and overall treatment outcome. *Journal of Clinical Child Psychology, 22,* 42–51.

Eyberg, S. (1988). Parent–Child Interaction Therapy: Integration of traditional and behavioral concerns. *Child and Family Behavior Therapy, 10,* 33–46.

Eyberg, S. M., & Boggs, S. R. (1998). Parent–Child Interaction Therapy: A psychosocial intervention for the treatment of young conduct disordered children. In C. E. Schaefer & J. M. Briesmeister (Eds.), *Handbook of parent training: Parents as co-therapists for children's behavior problems* (2nd ed., pp. 61–97). New York: Wiley.

Eyberg, S. M., Boggs, S. R., & Algina, J. (1995). Parent–Child Interaction Therapy: A psychosocial model for the treatment of young children with conduct problem behavior and their families. *Psychopharmacology Bulletin, 31,* 83–91.

Eyberg, S. M., & Robinson, E. A. (1982). Parent–Child Interaction Training: Effects on family functioning. *Journal of Clinical Child Psychology, 11,* 130–137.

Eyberg, S. M., & Robinson, E. A. (1983). Dyadic Parent–Child Interaction Coding System: A manual. *Psychological Documents, 13,* MS. No. 2582.

Freeman, T. (1982). *It's my body.* Seattle, WA: Parenting Press.

Hanf, C. (1969). *A two stage program for modifying maternal controlling during mother–child (M-C) interaction.* Paper presented at the meeting of the Western Psychological Association, Vancouver, BC.

Hembree-Kigin, T., & McNeil, C. B. (1995). *Parent–child interaction therapy.* New York: Plenum Press.

McGinnis, E., & Goldstein, A. P. (1990a). *Skillstreaming in early childhood.* Champaign, IL: Research Press.

McGinnis, E., & Goldstein, A. P. (1990b). *Skillstreaming in early childhood: Programs for Ms.* Champaign, IL: Research Press.

McNeil, C. B., Capage, L. C., Bahl, A., & Blanc, H. (1999). Importance of early intervention for disruptive behavior problems: Comparison of treatment and waitlist-control groups. *Early Education and Development, 10*(4), 445–454.

McNeil, C. B., Eyberg, S. M., Eisenstadt, T. H., Newcomb, K., & Funderburk, B. W. (1991). Parent–Child Interaction Therapy with young behavior problem children: Generalization of treatment effects to the school setting. *Journal of Clinical Child Psychology, 20,* 140–151.

McNeil, C. B., Hembree-Kigin, T., & Eyberg, S. M. (1996). *Short-term play therapy for disruptive children.* King of Prussia, PA: Center for Applied Psychology.

McNeil, C. B., Hembree-Kigin, T., & Eyberg, S. M. (1998). *Working with oppositional defiant disorder in children: An audio and video training program.* Secaucus, NJ: Childswork/Childsplay of Genesis Direct Inc.

Nemiroff, M. A., & Annunziata, J. (1990). *A child's first book about play therapy.* Washington, DC: American Psychological Association.

Robin, A. (1976). The turtle technique: An extended case study of self-control in the classroom. *Psychology in the Schools, 13,* 449–453.

Schumann, E., Foote, R., Eyberg, S. M., Boggs, S., & Algina, J. (1998). Parent–Child Interaction Therapy: Interim report of a randomized trail with short-term maintenance. *Journal of Clinical Child Psychology, 27,* 34–45.

Zangwill, W. M. (1984). An evaluation of a parent training program. *Child and Family Behavior Therapy, 5,* 1–16.

10

Family Play Therapy and Child Psychiatry in an Era of Managed Care

Thomas G. Hardaway, II

INTRODUCTION

Family play therapy is commonly assumed to be just another form of either play therapy or family therapy. The skills required in individually oriented and developmentally appropriate play therapy are allied with those skills required in family systems therapy. Thus, it is difficult to discuss this topic under the rubric of either play therapy or family therapy.

An unfortunate polarization exists between those who believe that the appropriate treatment of a child's emotional and behavioral pathology is through family therapy and those who believe that individual therapy is the correct treatment. To suggest that one mode of therapy is the only way to treat children makes as much sense as a school of medicine insisting that penicillin is the ideal treatment for all ailments. The role of the psychiatrist is to evaluate the nature of the complaint and its possible diagnosis and etiology. An eclectic decision should be made regarding the kind of treatment mostly likely to cure or alleviate the problem.

Many situations arise in which family therapy is the most appropriate mode of treatment. Although traditional family therapy has proved useful in changing a family system, it presents a major problem with a significant number of families. Psychiatrists commonly treat families with small children. Because these children are preverbal or have limited verbal skills, a brief evaluative interaction commonly occurs with the child present, but subsequent family therapy proceeds either as couple therapy with the parents or as family therapy minus the small child. In the family therapy described in this chapter, the small child is assumed to be as important as any other family member in the pathology of the family. It is further assumed that to exclude the child from therapy is to omit a critical player. Small children have important messages to share, and play is the medium through which small children (and, in fact, some older individuals) are best able to work and express themselves. However, in traditional family therapy, the small child is bored and silent at best, and totally disruptive at worst.

Older individuals are often unable to express the issues and affect that describe the strengths and deficits in the family functioning. Although this information eventually surfaces in traditional family therapy, it comes much more quickly in family play therapy because the issues and affect arise in a literally dramatic and behavioral form, even from the first play interaction.

Important Elements of Family Play Therapy

1. There is a careful evaluation for psychiatric illness or other medical etiology of presenting symptoms. If evaluation indicates a causal relationship between the index patient's symptoms and family system pathology, family therapy is indicated.
2. Conservative, achievable goals are projected over an initial few sessions.
3. All family members are included regardless of age (to include extended family whenever possible).
4. The work of therapy is to be play, at a level where all individuals can be meaningfully involved. Clarifying and interpretive remarks occur more within metaphor.
5. Transference is addressed directly among family members, rather than toward the therapist.
6. There are limited clarifying remarks during the initial play part of session.
7. More interpretive remarks and family verbal processing occur during second half of session.
8. A variety of activities are utilized—free play, drama, sculpting, psychodrama, videotape review, and art.
9. All members of the family are required to remain for processing of play, even those not capable of verbal interaction.

Transferences Acted Out

Another important element in family play therapy involves the nature of transference issues. In individual or group psychotherapy, therapy revolves around transference, with the therapist approximating or paralleling the relationship with the child's attachment figure. In traditional family therapy, this is more attenuated, but it is present. In family play therapy, the transference issues are acted out behaviorally among the family members themselves, with clarification and interpretation directed at the relationship among the attachment figures and with the child.

Thus, the therapist must not only be facile in family therapy and knowledgeable regarding family systems issues, but he or she also must be competent and comfortable with developmental issues and individual play therapy techniques. The therapist must be able to facilitate appropriate play at the developmental level of the youngest individual, while understanding issues pertinent to other individuals and to the family system as a whole. The therapist allows the family to interact spontaneously in play but guides and processes the play in such a way as to point out behaviors that illustrate family issues. At appropriate times, the therapist may make observations to the family regarding family and individual issues as they occur in the room or when the family is ready to hear them.

Relatively little in the literature describes this process. Haley (1973) and Levant and Haffey (1981) described the process of deciding the combination of family members to be treated, including extended family, that will have the most impact on important treatment issues. Zilbach (1982) outlined multiple reasons to incorporate the young child into family therapy using developmentally appropriate activities. Specific activities such as sculpting, psychodrama, videotape review, and puppet play are outlined by Villeneuve (1979). However, much of the literature describing small-child involvement in therapy emphasized the conjoint therapy in a way that implies keeping the child occupied rather than using play among family members as the actual work of treatment. Ackerman (1970) described the important role a small child plays in conjoint therapy by revealing information about the family that might not otherwise be expressed.

Family Play Therapy in the Era of Managed Care

While family play therapy may be considered by mental health providers to be an effective and powerful tool in helping families and individuals, those who pay the bills, mainly third-party payers, are not so convinced. They focus on three main issues:

1. Do the symptoms/complaints require treatment?
2. If so, how does one gauge outcome and effectiveness of treatment?

3. Why pay for family play therapy when individual therapy and medication are seen as the traditionally effective modes of treatment?

How Do Third-Party Payers Define Necessity?

The therapist, when deciding on methods of treatment for the symptoms/complaints presented by parents on behalf of their child, must understand that symptoms and complaints are not necessarily seen by third-party payers as dysfunction. If a patient with an infection, diabetes, or bone fracture is not treated, the outcome is obviously one that is either life threatening or directly affects the patient's overall health. Thus, initial treatment for these symptoms is seen as necessary to prevent further health deterioration or death, or it may be seen as being able to very quickly reverse an acute symptom.

In mental health, and especially in children's mental health, the symptoms and complaints are not as easily seen as life threatening, health threatening, or directly associated with loss of function. Nor is there evidence in many areas of mental health that treatment episodes will quickly, or in a concrete fashion, reverse the complaint.

Assumptions about the Impact of Symptoms upon Subsequent Child Development

Most mental health providers, especially those who evaluate and treat children and families, have both an intuitive and theoretical understanding of the impact that both the child's behaviors and the environment have upon his or her subsequent development and health.

Unfortunately, this is not well understood by those who fund care, or even by other clinical practitioners who refer patients for mental health evaluation.

What is frequently not understood by managed care organizations is that pathologic behavior and mental health symptoms in children have a very direct bearing upon how they will perform in the future in any functional area. When these symptoms and disruptive behaviors are not addressed appropriately, whether at home by parents or, when necessary, by therapists' interventions, children's ability to establish appropriate personal relationships, to learn cognitive skills, to care for themselves, and to operate at baseline function is damaged.

Thus, it is not a far-fetched parallel to compare the child who is allowed to continue being enuretic, disruptive in the classroom, depressed, or otherwise symptomatic to the child who has high blood sugar and requires treatment for diabetes. In the latter, there is ample evidence that denial of treatment will result in acute hospitalizations for diabetic ketoacidosis, life-threatening metabolic complications, with chronic erosion and destruction of kidney, vascular, and limb function. This results in dramatic deterioration of a person's health, both as a child and as an adult, as well as a dramatic increase in costs from acute crisis treatments. What needs to be articulated to third-party payers is that the former is just as significant and health threatening.

These issues point out the similarity of the child who exhibits the behaviors described earlier, whose ability to function academically and socially, and to continue normal psychological development is disrupted. The subsequent requirements for crisis intervention, emergency room visits, and treatment for depression or conduct disorder are equally as devastating not only to the child and developing adult but also to the others involved in his or her life. In addition, the multiple crisis-oriented treatments, both outpatient and inpatient, are predictably more expensive than the planned intervention initially recommended.

The therapist should not assume that the third-party payer shares the same assumptions regarding the parallels drawn here. However, this does not mean that third-party payers are not interested in providing reimbursement for or access to mental health treatment. Their beneficiaries still exert considerable influence on health benefits advisors regarding coverage of various mental health ailments. It is imperative, however, that the providers of such mental health services organize their own thinking and, furthermore, document this thinking around how symptoms translate into critical functioning.

Though the parallel clinical analogy drawn here is obvious to mental health providers, it must be made obvious and clear to those who fund mental health treatment. This is especially true where treatments such as family therapy or family play therapy are recommended as being the preferred mode of treatment.

Thus, it should be clearly articulated that a presenting symptom or behavioral problem is significantly interfering with the child's development—in areas of physical functioning, academic functioning, self-care functioning, or social functioning. Social dysfunction would include evidence that the child's symptoms are a threat to his or her surrounding family, friends, or social structure.

How Does One Demonstrate Outcome and Treatment Efficacy?

By documenting the impact of the child's symptoms upon the aforementioned functional areas, one does multiple things. First, it becomes clear that without treatment, the child's functioning is threatened and requires intervention to prevent further deterioration and or physical harm. Second, it then provides a way to gauge and to demonstrate clearly that the function is improving with treatment.

Thus, as one considers various modes of treatment, especially those that appear more exotic to the outside observer, such as family play therapy, it is important to include a carefully thought out diagnosis that indicates clear pathology to the bill payer. But equally important, the provider must devise a problem list iterating the specific problem behaviors and their impact upon the child's areas of function and his or her surrounding support system.

The treatment plan, if it is to include family play therapy, should indicate clear goals, the achievement of which should be easily obtainable and measurable. If symptoms of obsession and compulsion interfere with the child's ability to go to school and be educated, make him or her socially dysfunctional, and result in worsening dysphoric mood, irritability, and anxiety, these should be documented in such a way as to show necessity for treatment, vulnerability toward further loss of function, and easily observed improvement as treatment is provided.

Will This Mode of Therapy Result in Restoration of Function?

The third question is: "Is this the appropriate mode of therapy?" Any treatment that includes "play" in its name may likely call into doubt its own authenticity. Of course, we could obviate this by changing its name to something like "family activity therapy" or any number of other labels. However, it is more helpful to include in one's evaluation the reason such treatment is considered preferable to other modes. Thus, the therapist should emphasize the following:

1. A careful and well-documented evaluation indicates that there are no other likely medical or psychiatric causes for the child's pathological behavior besides direct family dysfunction, or at least that the family dysfunction is an overriding cause among several contributing factors.
2. Very specific behaviors among family members have been found to contribute to the child's pathology and are sufficiently clear that bringing them to the attention of the family will result in change. Furthermore, this change will leave a direct impact upon the child's pathology.
3. Short-term treatment (four to eight sessions) will be sufficient time for the family to recognize the contributing issues and to make the necessary changes for the most obvious behaviors.
4. It can be predicted that further benefit may be achieved by working on more subtle behaviors because the family has responded to initial treatment of easily achieved objectives.
5. Various measures of outcome can be implemented to track the improvement in the child's (index patient's) function. This can be assessed, for example, by documenting a decreased number of school absences, a decreased number of school incidents, improvement in

academic performance, fewer harmful incidents in the home, and fewer tearful episodes or crisis episodes resulting in emergency room visits.

Although a therapist almost intuitively knows why pathological behaviors or symptoms are destructive to a child's development or well-being, and why treatment is indicated, this "intuitiveness" prevents him or her from conceptualizing and thus articulating the core problems and treatment goals that are necessary to provide the most effective treatment. In addition, being very "concrete" and organized in formulating one's rationale for defining dysfunction and successful outcome are critical in obtaining reimbursement.

What Is "Short-Term" Family Play Therapy?

The clinical case presented results in changes in the family's function and, as a result, improvement in the child's function. By definition, the treatment was short term, and this was even in a training setting where reimbursement issues were not an immediate concern.

The definitions of "long-term" and "short-term" therapy are obviously relative. Unfortunately, too often, in training programs for therapy, "long term" translates into "open-ended" and "not well defined." What trainees then learn is that long-term therapy is therapy provided until the provider moves or the patient moves, whichever comes first. Examination of the documentation of even the most helpful therapy provided over the long term all too frequently does not provide much insight as to the goals of therapy, the necessity for further treatment, or the expectation from further therapy. It is perhaps understandable that those who fund treatment are reluctant to subsidize this.

Mental health providers frequently bemoan the requirement for short-term therapy (generally defined as anywhere from 1 to 20 sessions) as somehow being restrictive and not allowing full benefit of care to the patient who requires it.

To begin with, short-term goals and assessment of progress in function are integral to family play therapy. It is unlikely that families will even embark on this fairly intense and time-consuming form of therapy without a very discrete understanding of the problems, of what will happen in therapy, and of goals sought. If, despite their feelings of inadequacy, families feel that the goals are palpable and achievable in the near future, and that progress can be measured and demonstrated, they will participate and do so with the motivation required for change.

The effective therapist will then utilize this successful experience to embark on further, perhaps more definitive goals and provide the same effective treatment that previously was felt to be obtainable only through long-term therapy. Each time this occurs, the therapist will be able to document the improvement in function of the index patient and the anticipated progress to be made. He or she will also be more successful in obtaining reimbursement for the service.

Thus, long-term therapy can always be an option for the patient and therapist, as long as it is conceptualized as a series of short-term goals, which, if the therapist is effective, will translate into achievement of more definitive and far-reaching objectives.

STRUCTURED SESSIONS IN FAMILY PLAY THERAPY

The structure of our family play therapy sessions is predictable and routine. The sessions last 1 hour and begin with a half-hour of actual on-the-floor play. It is usually obvious from the beginning that the parents have a great deal of discomfort, rigidity, and lack of knowledge concerning how to play with their children. A small amount of guidance is given initially to decrease the intense anxiety felt by the family members, who are frequently at a total loss as to what to do despite the great variety of activities available. After the initial session, we stop giving even that small amount of guidance, so that family members must devise, on their own, what they will do together. Minimal interpretation is offered during this time, and only occasional clarification or observations are made about a behavior at the moment it occurs, or about a message sent by one family member but not received by another.

The second half of the hour consists of a time for the grown-ups (or, in other family constellations, the more verbal members of the family) to sit and process the play. The nonverbal children are expected to remain in the room, playing by themselves but absorbing what is said. It is made clear to these children that they have had time to play with the others, and that now it is time to talk. This time is critical for the verbal members of the family to process behaviors and patterns noted in the previous play and to share interpretations. Because the children in these cases prevent any meaningful dialogue between their parents at home, they act out initially by being disruptive as their parents process the play. The parents eventually recognize this dynamic and how it has been perpetuated, and they are helped to work as a team both to reassure their nonverbal children and to control their disruptive influence. This process is not meant merely as a class in discipline techniques but, more important, as a means of understanding what the family is doing to encourage the disruptive and frustrating behavior.

CASE ILLUSTRATION

In a family we treated with family play therapy, the index patient was a 5-year-old boy who was brought in because of a recent onset of tantrums and hyperactive and assaultive behaviors, especially toward his mother. He had a decrease in appetite and an increasing number of nightmares, with accompanying sleep disturbance. An initial evaluation included a careful history of both the mother's and the father's behaviors and backgrounds, observation and play therapy with the boy, and observation of the interaction among the family members. Various diagnostic possibilities in the differential were ruled out, and we believed that the child's behaviors ultimately reflected family pathology. After an initial attempt at family therapy, the child was excluded after the first session. The parents later said that they realized they were then in marital therapy, and that their concerns about the child were not being addressed. The parents dropped out of treatment, and only when the child's symptoms continued to worsen did they return; this time, they were referred for family play therapy.

We set very simple goals, with a contract for eight sessions. We hoped that through play interaction with their son, the parents would identify destructive roles and alliances within the family that were perpetuating the child's symptoms as well as their frustrations. If they could achieve this, we thought they might use this information in further interaction at home to facilitate a better relationship with the child and assist him in progressing through a more satisfying course of development. If they decided to continue in therapy after the initial eight sessions, we could establish additional goals to help them. A crucial element of family therapy is to help family members develop conservative and achievable goals that will provide them with the confidence they need to progress, especially since frustration usually stems from a downward spiral of feelings of hopelessness and failure.

The pathology of the family interactions surfaced immediately in our work with this family. The destructive roles and alliances between family members were readily apparent in their first play interaction, with an intensity that required quick modulation by the therapist. As the therapist pointed out disabling dynamics on the spot and made suggestions for behavior substitution, the family members could readily identify the dynamic process and feel the shift as they made changes. Rather than operating on a verbal level, they interacted in a play mode that allowed interpretation on a much more affective level. We assigned homework to allow these experiences to generalize and to see what stumbling blocks they still faced as they attempted to reproduce the affect and behaviors at home.

Most noticeable in the first two sessions was how quickly the family learned from spontaneity in play. As the destructive alliance between the child and one parent against the other parent interfered with play, arguments brought projects to a halt, and the dysfunction was clearly manifest at every moment in some play metaphor. The therapist made observations concerning the rigidity of family of family roles and how this was getting in the way of their completing a Tinkertoy house. When the therapist noted that the rigidity of certain members of the family resulted in a kind of tyranny over the others and that this took the fun out of the play, family members were able to see that some individuals' needs were being ignored. This clarification resulted in less threat for everyone to express individual needs and desires more directly. As it became more apparent that most of these needs could in some way be met by mutual cooperation, the anxiety and rigidity decreased, and the necessity for destructive roles and alliances faded.

Viewing videotapes of the sessions demonstrated a principle in which family members had already begun to work. This required some caution, since the parents could quickly see inappropriate behaviors and were likely to be self-conscious and embarrassed. However, viewing certain behaviors within the context of the positive changes they had already made gave the parents more confidence and enthusiasm for the process. Even the child observed that he had feared that any time his parents talked, there would be arguing and hurt. After observing positive outcomes of somewhat heated discussions on the videotape, the child became less disruptive during subsequent processing portions of the therapy.

SUMMARY AND CONCLUSIONS

The benefits of family play therapy are clear. They include positive aspects of individual child therapy by allowing children to express their fears and concerns through play, while addressing family members' responses to the children's behaviors by involving them in the play. Both the therapist and the parents experience an initial anxiety in embarking on a play experience with a young child. However, in families a very young children, even infants, who are experiencing significant interactional pathology, there is no quicker or more powerful way to highlight the dynamics to family members and to engage their affect and involvement than direct play with the young child. This requires much modulation on the part of the therapist, as the issues and affect arise so much more quickly than in traditional verbal therapy. This method is most effective in instances in which families and family members have been carefully evaluated and there are clear indications that the index patient's symptoms are precipitated by a pathological family system.

REFERENCES

Ackerman, N. (1970). Child participation in family therapy. *Family Process, 9,* 403–410.

Haley, J. (1973). Strategic therapy when a child is presented as a problem. *Journal of the American Academy of Child Psychiatry, 12,* 641–659.

Levant, R. F., & Haffey, N. A. (1981). Integration of child and family therapy. *International Journal of Family Therapy, 3*(2), 5–10.

Villeneuve, C. (1979). The specific participation of the child in family therapy. *Journal of the American Academy of Child Psychiatry, 18,* 44–53.

PART III

GROUP PLAY THERAPY

11

A Creative Play Therapy Approach to the Group Treatment of Young Sexually Abused Children

LORETTA GALLO-LOPEZ

INTRODUCTION

"Young children are resilient and adaptable to change." Such statements are often used to rationalize the belief that young children are not significantly affected by traumatic experiences. Child psychotherapists know the opposite to be true. The impact of trauma on young children can be profound and far-reaching. Sexual abuse is among the most potentially damaging sources of emotional distress in young children. According to the National Incidence Study of Child Abuse and Neglect (Sedlak & Broadhurst, 1996), children as young as 3 years of age are as proportionately vulnerable to sexual victimization as older children and adolescents. Treatment protocols for younger children who have been sexually abused, however, are not as readily available as programs for older children. Though it may be true that young children are "resilient and adaptable to change," in most cases, children traumatized by sexual abuse require therapeutic intervention to allow their resiliency and adaptability to emerge.

This chapter presents a comprehensive, time-limited group treatment program for young survivors of sexual abuse. In this work, I aim to provide the reader with a framework of healing opportunities to meet the complex needs of the young sexually abused child.

Sexual abuse has been found to have both an immediate and long-term impact on most child victims. The following list identifies a wide range of symptoms and behavioral responses (most of which are widely cited in the literature) that may be seen in young sexually abused children:

- Nightmares and sleep disturbances
- Extreme anxiety and excessive fearfulness
- Difficulty trusting others
- Damaged sense of body integrity and body image
- Eating disturbances
- Somatic complaints
- Advanced sexual knowledge for age
- Regressive behavior and the loss of premastered skills
- Mood disorders
- Feelings of shame, guilt, humiliation
- Social isolation
- Anxiety related to separation
- Highly sexualized behaviors
- Lack of interpersonal boundaries
- Intrusive thoughts
- Dissociative responses
- Increased distractibility
- Suicidal ideation
- Self-hurting behaviors, including genital injury
- Behaviors that reflect power imbalance—overly compliant or over aggressive
- Behaviors that reflect adult–child role confusion
- Powerlessness and learned helplessness
- Deficient sense of self-esteem and self-worth

Mental health professionals continue to search for effective treatment approaches that will address the significant behavioral and trauma-related symptoms of this population.

Group treatment has long been considered the treatment of choice for latency and adolescent victims of sexual abuse (Mandell & Damom, 1989; Powell & Faherty, 1990). Younger children, however, have historically been treated in individual therapy based on the belief that a group-treatment modality was not developmentally appropriate (Salter, 1988). The literature is sparse in the area of group treatment of young children.

Steward, Farquhar, Dicharry, Glick, and Martin (1986) describe a group-treatment model for young victims of physical and/or sexual abuse that is open-ended, allowing new group members to begin at any time in the treatment process. The model utilizes a nondirective play therapy approach and identifies treatment length as 8 months to 2 years. This approach appears sound, and the treatment goals outlined focus both on healing the wounds of the past and meeting the child's emotional needs in the present and future. However, a directive approach with sexually abused children has been stressed (Salter, 1988; Rasmussen & Cunningham, 1995) as the way to ensure that the trauma is specifically addressed to decrease the child's risk of further abuse. Friedrich (1991) endorses a treatment approach that is "specific, should be sensitive to the child's needs, and should emphasize the interpersonal" (p. 5). (Cohen & Mannarino, 1993) describe a short-term treatment model for sexually abused preschoolers that is highly structured and utilizes individual therapy to treat both the child and the primary caretaker. The model utilizes behavioral interventions to target specific symptoms in an 8- to 12-week format but does not provide opportunities for the child to explore the trauma in terms of its personal meaning.

The model proposed in this chapter attempts to integrate the most essential elements of treatment into a single model. The target population includes both boys and girls, ranging in age from 3 to 10, separated into groups according to age and developmental ability. Although I have found it effective to mix genders in groups with children through age 5, girls and boys should be treated in separate groups from age 6 onward. The treatment model is presented in a time-limited, 16-week format. It relies on group process as a means of targeting the feelings of isolation and stigmatization experienced by many sexually abused children. Nondirective play therapy, directive play therapy, and other abuse-specific strategies are incorporated to meet the complex needs of this population. Such a model is supported by others, such as Rasmussen and Cunningham (1995), who advocate the integration of nondirective and focused strategies in the treatment of sexually abused children. This enables therapists to address trauma-related issues effectively, while providing the child with the emotionally safe environment necessary for the process of healing to begin.

The treatment model is influenced by three distinct but interrelated treatment approaches. The first is based on the long- and short-term impact of trauma on young children. I have found the model of traumagenic dynamics presented by Finkelhor and Browne (1986) to be helpful in the formulation of treatment goals related to symptoms of traumatic stress. The four dynamics—traumatic sexualization, stigmatization, betrayal, and powerlessness—are believed by Finkelhor and Browne to lead to emotional trauma by "distorting a child's self-concept, world view, and affective capacities" (pp. 180–181). The treatment model presented here directly addresses each of these areas to decrease trauma-related symptoms and behaviors.

The second element of this treatment model is that of developmental theory. This approach is formulated to meet the developmental needs of the young child, providing opportunities for mastery of age-appropriate tasks as well as interventions that allow exploration of regressive themes.

Finally, the model incorporates systems theory, focusing on interpersonal relationships and children's view of themselves within their immediate world.

Although this chapter presents only the treatment protocol for the children's therapy group, it is strongly encouraged that counseling be made available for the nonoffending parent/caretaker as well. The ideal situation would allow the parent to attend concurrent group sessions while the child attends a separate group. The parental component should address child development, child sexual development, abuse dynamics, parenting issues, safety issues, family roles and relationships, and ways of enhancing and strengthening the parent–child relationship. Families in which sexual abuse has occurred experience stress and anxiety related not only to the trauma but also to the aftermath. They have difficulty trusting people they perceive to be in authority and have a need to move beyond the abuse.

Working directly with the child's primary caretaker is essential to the success of the child's treatment. By involving nonoffending parents in their child's therapy, we can help parents to align with the treatment process and the treatment providers. Parents may intentionally or unintentionally sabotage their child's treatment if they feel they are in competition with the therapist, or because of their own feelings of guilt and inadequacy. Emphasis should be placed on the important role the parents play in the child's healing. Empowering parents in this process decreases their feelings of inadequacy and enhances their ability to parent their children effectively. Additionally, most parents respond positively to the time-limited treatment approach. Although parents must be informed that their children may need to continue in treatment beyond the 16-week program, having a sense of the range of treatment length appears to ease parents' stress and anxiety and increase their hopefulness.

Assessing Appropriateness for Group

Prior to placement, each child should be individually assessed to determine their appropriateness for the group. Assessment should include examining the child's developmental history as well as completing a clinical interview. The evaluator should attempt to determine the child's developmental level and needs, giving consideration to the possible regressive impact of the abuse. During this initial interview, the therapist must assess the child's level of trauma and evaluate his or her coping skills. It is essential at this point that the therapist ascertain whether the child has given a clear abuse disclosure. A child who has not disclosed abuse, at least in some detail, is not an appropriate candidate for group treatment. Very often, children are referred for sexual abuse treatment when there are allegations of sexual abuse or when they display symptoms such as sexual preoccupation, age-inappropriate sexual knowledge and/or behaviors, or excessive masturbation. Children who present with such symptoms, but have not disclosed sexual abuse, should be seen in individual therapy in order to treat symptoms and assess for the possibility of sexual abuse. This is also true for children who have provided limited details about their sexual abuse but have not made an adequate disclosure. If such children were seen in a group-treatment setting, they would be highly susceptible to contamination by the disclosures of other children in group. Following individual therapy, children can be reassessed for involvement in a group-treatment modality. It is important to note that a child who completely denies being sexually abused is not appropriate for group treatment, even if the perpetrator has confessed to the sexual abuse.

It is not necessary to exclude from group treatment children diagnosed with attention-deficit/hyperactivity disorder (ADHD) or those who present ADHD-type behaviors. Sexually abused children may experience such extreme levels of anxiety that they display symptoms similar to those of ADHD and are often diagnosed incorrectly. As issues are addressed and resolved in treatment, the anxiety-related behaviors usually decrease. These children can be successful in group given that the treatment provider possesses adequate skills and expertise in both sexual abuse and group treatment with children. It is essential that the therapist monitor the level of stimulation the children experience, appropriately intervene when overstimulation occurs, and provide adequate time for closure exercises.

Children who are highly sexualized and impulsive may not be appropriate candidates for group due to the victimization risk to the other children. I would recommend that these children initially be seen individually, with the goal of enhancing impulse control skills and learning strategies to manage the sexualized behaviors. A child who has previously acted out sexually against other children will need to be involved in group or individual treatment that directly addresses the sexual acting-out behaviors and victimization issues. It is important to keep in mind that many sexually abused children engage in age-inappropriate sexual behaviors such as excessive masturbation, preoccupation with body parts, and mutual genital touching with other children. Children who present with these behaviors should not automatically be ruled out as group participants. The bottom line must always be the safety of the other children. This is also true with extremely aggressive children. Children whose aggressive behaviors put others at risk should be seen individually in order to learn to manage their anxiety and excessive anger, and to develop coping skills. They may then be assessed to be appropriate for group treatment.

It is important for children who engage in self-injurious or self-hurting behaviors to be seen in individual therapy in lieu of, or in addition to, group treatment to closely monitor their level of safety. This is also true for children who have engaged in the destruction of animals or other severely aggressive behaviors, or who experience significant levels of dissociation.

These children will need to be closely monitored for psychopathology and will require intensive individual therapy and psychiatric support.

Children in foster care, though presenting with a distinct set of issues and concerns, need not be excluded from participation in group. Foster children can reap great benefit from involvement in the familial type of activities involved in group treatment. They may, however, need the ongoing support of an individual therapist to provide them a greater opportunity to bond and connect with a significant adult.

SHORT-TERM PLAY THERAPY APPROACH

Setting Up the Group

One of the first considerations in setting up a group is its size. Children benefit most from small groups. A generally accepted rule is that the number of children should not exceed the age of the youngest child. In other words, a group whose youngest member is 3 years old should have no more than three children; a group whose youngest member is 4 should have no more than four members, and so on. Having a second group facilitator does not warrant an increase in the group's size.

Group sessions should be an hour in length, with sessions beginning and ending on time. Predictability is paramount. Group rituals are a means of providing a predictable structure that leads to a naturally developing sense of safety and containment within the therapy environment. Beginning and ending rituals contribute to the establishment of trust and security. Anxiety is reduced when children can anticipate what will happen next.

Beginning rituals should be the focus of the first 10 minutes or so of each session. Rituals may include grabbing a pillow or mat and taking a spot in the group circle. This might be followed by a check-in, a group trust-building game, or a welcome song. An important beginning routine is for group members to take turns explaining why they come to group. This serves to strengthen the connection between group members and decrease the stigma and shame harbored by many child victims.

Structured group activities (discussed later in this chapter) should follow the beginning rituals and comprise approximately 20 minutes of the session. The next 20 minutes should be reserved for nondirective play therapy.

The final 10 minutes of the session are reserved for closure and ending rituals. Ending rituals should help provide a sense of closure by offering a chance to process issues that come up in the session. Group members are then prepared to exit the therapy environment intact. Ending rituals may include a song, a movement activity, or any combination of activities that provide a sense of calm and focus. Most children enjoy coming to sessions and resist leaving when the session is over. Therefore, it may be helpful to provide a separate area of the room for ending rituals, so that children physically move from one area to trigger session changes.

I choose to provide a snack as part of the group's ending rituals. Food is helpful for two reasons. First, it is an effective form of tangible nurturance. Even a simple snack of cookies and juice shows children that their group is a place of care and support. Second, snack time parallels a family meal in ways that often facilitate treatment. Since many of the group activities center on domestic issues, groups often end up relating to each other in more or less familial ways. Just as shared meals help strengthen bonds within functional families, snack time provides the group opportunities to process issues, talk through problems, share feelings, and resolve conflicts together.

If you are unable to effect the program within an hour's time, I would suggest adding 10 more minutes for closure and ending routines. This is usually the most difficult time for children, and it takes a good deal of skill for the therapist effectively to redirect the children to the closure activities. I would not suggest lengthening the group time much beyond this, however, as the session then begins to lose its focus and become more like free play or day care than therapy. Whatever length is chosen, time limitations must be set and should not vary from week to week.

The Group Treatment Model

The group treatment model is presented here as a 16-week program. However, it can easily be extended to 20 weeks if necessary. The program is divided into four, 4-week modules. I have outlined below the primary objectives of each module and have described several activities that effectively help achieve these objectives. I have ordered the various activities in the way that I usually sequence them for my groups. Keep in mind, however, that meeting modular objectives is more important than following a specific order, and you may want to add and/or delete activities in accordance with your own style.

In each session, the structured activities are followed by a period of nondirective play therapy. Themes established through the structured activities are usually further explored in the nondirective play therapy that follows. This naturally flowing progression leads to much more purposeful play in nondirective play therapy. Of course, therapist intervention, feedback, and interpretation are essential to facilitating this process.

Within each module, specific themes are identified. The themes of safety and empowerment, however, are arguably the most essential in the treatment of sexually abused children of this age range. Accordingly, these themes are woven into each of the structured activities and are continually reinforced via therapist interventions in the nondirective play therapy portion of each session.

Safety and empowerment must be fostered by the manner in which the therapist interacts with the children. Suzanne Long (1986), stresses the importance of the therapist consistently communicating a sense of "respect, acceptance and faith" in the children being treated (p. 222). This is a wonderfully simple means of characterizing the essential elements of the therapeutic relationship. The therapist must communicate "respect" for children, as well as for children's right to their own feelings, thoughts, and ideas. "Acceptance" enables children to feel confident that they will not be rejected. Finally, "faith" conveys the therapist's belief in children's power to grow, change, and seek resolution.

Sessions 1–4

The tasks of the first 4 weeks of treatment are to set boundaries and establish the group structure, routines, and rituals. Other tasks include encouraging children to bond, increasing their comfort and trust level with each other and the therapist, and forming a sense of group identity. As treatment begins, it is important to talk about feelings and to give children the words to express what they feel, while continually reinforcing the view that group is a safe and supportive place for self-expression.

Initially, children need to understand that they each share a similar reason for inclusion in group. This immediately decreases children's feelings of isolation, alienation, and negative stigmatization. Shame is reduced when this commonality is discussed at the start of each session. Children should be consistently reminded that they have permission to talk about their sexual abuse within the group. Statements such as "Everyone in this group was touched in private places by someone, or was made to touch someone else's privates" help to set the tone for the group. I prefer to stay away from the term "bad touch" to avoid confusing children who may have enjoyed the touching or attention. It is important not to reinforce any negative thoughts or feelings children may have about themselves.

Children are not expected, or asked, to disclose during the first few sessions. Disclosure in group should not take place until the children have developed an adequate level of trust in the group and the therapist. Additionally, children need to understand when it is an appropriate time to talk about their abuse. Because they do not have a clear sense of appropriate boundaries around these issues, many young children disclose information about their abuse to anyone they meet, whether they are strangers or other children at school. The therapist can say, "We'll talk more about this when we know each other a little better," allowing children to begin to understand the need for boundaries and limits regarding disclosure of their abuse.

Safety is a primary concern both in and out of the therapy setting. Not only must the therapist work to provide a safe environment for treatment, but he or she must also work with the parent or caretaker to ensure that the child is safe within the home as well.

THEMES AND OBJECTIVES

- Group joining, establishing group structure, introducing ritual.
- Setting boundaries and limits within the group.
- Setting the stage for the corrective relationship between adults and children.
- Begin differentiating, identifying, and expressing feelings.
- Begin to establish a sense of safety and basic trust within the group.
- Continue to assess each child's developmental and attachment needs, level of trauma through the presentation of trauma-related symptoms, ability to distinguish reality from fantasy, and ability to engage in symbolic and representational play.

STRUCTURED ACTIVITIES

Group Poster. At the start of group treatment, it is helpful to find mechanisms that enhance group cohesiveness while appreciating the individual's uniqueness. This activity involves creation of a group poster highlighting commonalities as well as differences among group members. Areas of focus include likes and dislikes, favorite activities, favorite foods, and so on. Children can be asked to draw pictures, cut pictures from magazines, or make lists. The group may want to choose a group name or theme that can also be incorporated into the group poster. Therapists can create a group ritual by setting up the poster at the start of each session and taking it down at the end. Pictures, photographs, and other items can be added to the poster as the sessions progress.

Puppet Interview. The purpose of this activity is to increase comfort and trust by giving children an opportunity to get to know each other better. Each child should be instructed to choose from a variety of puppets set out on the table or floor. Irwin and Malloy (1975) suggest offering both realistic and fantasy puppet choices in therapy. They propose including domestic and wild animals (specifically those with orally aggressive characteristics), as well as witch, skeleton, king and queen, police officer, and doctor puppets. The puppets are then interviewed using a "talk-show" format. The therapist is "talk-show host" and the children are audience members who take turns asking the puppets questions about themselves. The therapist may direct the child to use the chosen puppet to represent him- or herself, or to create a character. The puppet serves as a distancing tool and vehicle for projection. The therapist should decide the level of emotional distance the children may need at the time the activity is employed. Keep in mind that the further from "self" a character is, the greater the level of distance.

Safe Place Drawing. It is important to assess a child's feelings of safety and to determine what interventions may be necessary to help a particular child feel more protected. In this activity, children are asked to draw a picture of a place where they feel safe and then talk about the drawing. For children who were abused in their own home, this may not be a very secure place. By discussing the characteristics of a safe place, children may be able to identify alternative safe environments. One young girl who had been sexually abused by her biological father indicated that the only place she felt safe was at school. She believed the people there would protect her and prevent her from being kidnapped by her father. In the ideal situation, the home is a safe place for each child. To achieve this goal, it is essential to strengthen the relationship between the child and the nonoffending parent or caretaker.

Self-Portrait. A self-portrait can be a telling representation of children's view of themselves. To facilitate this, children can be given paper and markers to draw a picture of themselves. This can be done with or without the use of a mirror. It is important to have children draw their full bodies, not just their faces, as this gives the therapist more information regarding body integrity and self-image. These self-portraits offer valuable information about issues such as strength and vulnerability, groundedness and self-worth. Size and placement of the figure and body parts, colors, clothing, and facial features and expression deepen our understanding of how children view themselves. It may be helpful to repeat this activity toward the end of treatment, comparing children's self-view over time.

Parent–Child Combined Session: Practicing Listening Skills. The goal of this activity is to bring together parent and child to practice listening skills and enhance communication. The activity begins with the entire group of children, parents, and therapist playing the game of telephone. This is the old childhood game in which a phrase is passed around as it is whispered into each person's ear. Finally, the last person says the phrase out loud, and everyone usually laughs at how the phrase has changed from when it first began. Emphasis should be placed on listening to the person who is speaking. After the game of telephone is played a few times, each parent-and-child team can work together in a separate area of the room to make a telephone using two paper cups and a piece of string. The child can then tell a story into the cup (telephone) while the parent listens. After the story has been told, the parent repeats what he or she remembers of the story. Next, the parent tells a story while the child listens and then repeats the story back again. It may be necessary for the therapist to model this activity first, along with a child or parent. Upon completion of the listening exercise, parents and children should be instructed to engage in structured play together in place of the regular nondirective play therapy time. This parent–child play usually involves the use of puzzles, drawing materials, nontherapeutic board games, and so on. I would not recommend that the parent and child engage in projective or pretend play at this point for fear that the parent might overtly or covertly censor the child's play. This may alter the content of the child's nondirective play in future sessions. Through structured play activities, the therapist can observe a great deal about family roles, relationships, and styles of interaction between parent and child that prove helpful for future treatment planning.

Mask Making for Identification and Expression of Feelings. Appropriate expression of feelings is a basic treatment goal. To accomplish this, children need to acquire the language to communicate what they feel. The structured activity for this session should begin with a group discussion focused on identifying various feelings. A mirror can then be used to explore facial expressions related to particular emotions. Children should then be directed to create several masks, representative of different feelings. Simple materials such as paper plates or precut cardboard can be attached to craft sticks and used to create the masks. Some children have difficulty tolerating masks directly on their faces but are willing to work with masks if they can be held by the stick. When the masks are completed, they can be used for role playing during this session if time permits, or they can be saved for use in future sessions.

Sessions 5–8

At this point in treatment, children usually begin to feel comfortable and accustomed to group routines. Trust in the therapist and group members should be adequately established in order to address safely, issues related to sexual abuse in a forthright manner.

THEMES AND OBJECTIVES

- Continue to identify and express feelings accompanied by modulation of affect.
- Understand privacy versus secrecy.
- Work toward abuse disclosure within the group.
- Repair cognitive distortions related to guilt and responsibility issues.
- Identify appropriate and inappropriate touch.

- Learn about our bodies, establishing a sense of body integrity and awareness.
- Family roles and relationships incorporating the child as part of a system.
- Communication within the family.

STRUCTURED ACTIVITIES

Privacy Boxes. Many children who have been sexually abused do not understand the concept of privacy. Most have not been afforded a sense of privacy within their own homes. To reinforce the idea that everyone deserves privacy in certain situations, children are asked to decorate a cardboard box (a shoebox works well), which is used to hold the children's group projects. The boxes can be painted or colored with markers and decorated with glitter, feathers, buttons, fabric, magazine pictures, stickers, and so on. The boxes are kept in a safe place in a closet or other secure area in the office or playroom. The box becomes a private place to store projects created in group. While the children are decorating their boxes, group discussion should revolve around examples of privacy, secrecy, and surprises. Children should be presented with "What if" scenarios and asked to determine whether the scenario describes an issue of privacy, secrecy, or surprise. Children need to understand that a surprise may be an appropriate kind of secret. An example may be one sibling telling another not to tell Mom what they have gotten her for her birthday. The need and right to privacy can continually be reinforced within the group setting. For example, whenever a group member uses the bathroom, the therapist can remind children to close the door. Discussion can ensue about the importance of closed doors while dressing, bathing, and using the toilet at home. Parents should be learning about the same issues in their group to reinforce these concepts at home.

Body Tracing. The goal of this intervention is to guide children toward making a connection between emotions and what they feel in their bodies. The activity begins with children discussing and listing different emotions. It is recommended to limit the number of emotions and choose the simplest and most common: anger, excitement, jealousy, love, happiness, sadness, worry, loneliness, fear, and confidence. Ask children to talk about what they feel physically when they experience an emotion. To begin, anger is an easy one. Aim for responses such as "When I am angry my hands make a fist," or "When I am worried, my stomach hurts." Once children understand this concept, give each child a set of stickers printed with feeling words and/or the corresponding facial expression. The stickers can be made by the therapist or purchased through therapeutic activity catalogues. Using large rolls of paper, cut sheets to accommodate the length of each child's body. Trace children's bodies either by having them lie on their backs on top of the paper or stand against a sheet of paper tacked to the wall. During this process, it is helpful to describe what you are doing ("Now I am tracing your arm") in order to decrease anxiety related to physical touch. Children can then fill in facial features, clothes, and add anything else they may like. Using the feeling stickers along with the body tracings, children are guided to identify their physical response to a given emotion. Stickers are then fixed to the body tracing in the area representative of the physical response. Connecting the emotional and the physical increases recognition of feelings. Children can then employ newly acquired coping strategies and problem-solving skills to manage and appropriately express their emotions.

Paper Doll Body Figures: Appropriate versus Inappropriate Touch. In addition to offering a healing experience, sexual abuse treatment should provide children with strategies for self-protection. It is important that children understand the difference between appropriate and inappropriate touch, as well as their right to refuse unwanted touches. The following activity utilizes a felt board, and male and female figures representing adults and children. The figures can be made of felt or cut from poster board with felt or Velcro glued on the back to adhere to the felt board. The figures are used to identify private parts of the body and help children distinguish appropriate from inappropriate touches. Clothing can be made for the figures in order to help children grasp the concept that private parts are the parts of our bodies that are covered by underwear or bathing suits. Because this activity directly addresses abuse dynamics, children may become overstimulated and distracted. The felt board provides an area of focus with distinct boundaries, similar to those of a sand tray, thereby minimizing stimulation and anxiety.

Telling Each Other What Happened. An effective way to facilitate disclosures of abuse in group is to highlight initial statements made by children and emphasize the bravery it took for them to tell. Children can be asked to draw a picture of the first time they told anyone about their abuse and then to discuss the drawing. Another approach is to have children use puppets to represent themselves and the person (or people) to whom they disclosed. The therapist may need to take on a role in the puppet play if a child initially reported his or her abuse to more than one person. The discussion about initial disclosures should naturally lead to conversation about the abuse itself. It is not necessary for children to give intricate details about their abuse if they do not choose to do so. It is essential, however, that the therapist correct any cognitive distortions about the abuse, especially those related to the children's feelings of guilt and responsibility. The therapist should also take this opportunity to demonstrate acceptance and validation of children's negative and positive feelings regarding the offender.

Parent–Child Combined Session: Sharing Feelings. The goal of this session is to provide the parent/caretaker and child an opportunity to explore feelings and emotions together in order to begin strengthening their relationship. There are a variety of ways to achieve this goal. One activity involves drawing with a focus on feeling words. Each parent–child pair is given two large sheets of drawing paper folded to make four equal sections. They are also given markers, colored pencils or crayons, glue, and an envelope filled with the following feeling words: "angry," "hurt," "proud," "happy," "sad," "worried," "love," and "afraid." The parent and child each place a hand into the envelope and choose four feeling words. They glue one feeling word at the top of each of the four spaces on their paper, and then draw about a time when they experienced that feeling. When they finish drawing, they share their pictures with the other.

Family Role Playing. Drama and role play are powerful techniques for helping a child explore family relationships as well as his or her own role within the family system. In this activity, children are asked to enact a role within a family. The therapist structures the play by giving a simple direction such as "Let's create a story about a family." In certain groups, everyone chooses a child's role. In other groups, no one chooses to be a child. In most groups, there is a sampling of each. It may be necessary, and can be highly effective, for the therapist to enact the roles of missing family member. Once the roles are established, the therapist asks the group to identify a problem within the family. The children are free to use costumes and props in the drama and basically determine the direction of the play through the actions of their characters. The therapist in character should take this opportunity to infuse certain issues into the play that might help make it more purposeful. Such issues include trust and betrayal, separation and loss, abandonment, stigmatization, guilt, secrecy, coercion, and threats. Role play should be followed by closure, allowing children to let go of the role assumed in play. Closure should involve review of what has occurred and a transition to the "here and now." Themes from this session carry over particularly well to the nondirective play that follows.

Family Sand Tray. Family dynamics can be effectively explored as children create scenes in the sand tray depicting their family doing something together. When the scene is complete, the therapist can facilitate discussion by asking simple questions. Like the Kinetic Family Drawing technique (Burns & Kaufman, 1970), this intervention provides insight into the child's personal view of his or her place within the family. It also captures the child's view of family interactions and functions. In order to facilitate sand tray work in a group setting, it is important to have a separate sand tray for each child. If you do not have multiple wooden trays, rectangular plastic storage containers are an acceptable alternative. These containers can be purchased inexpensively at discount-type stores. I have found that if you sandpaper the inside of the container, paint will adhere better to the surface. Paint the inside of the containers with blue latex paint. It is also important to have enough figures and objects to enable each child to create a scene. An alternative to this intervention is to utilize the Kinetic Family Drawing technique, followed by questions and discussion.

Sessions 9–12

At this point, the children are midway through the treatment program and are usually feeling safe enough in group to begin addressing and directly confronting their fears.

THEMES AND OBJECTIVES

- Identifying and confronting fears and nightmares.
- Enhancing coping and problem-solving skills.
- Reinforcing sense of personal power.
- Safety and protection issues.

STRUCTURED ACTIVITIES

The Nightmare Wall. Nightmares and sleep disturbances are problems commonly seen in young sexually abused children. It is essential that children be given an opportunity to address and confront their fears and work toward resolution. In this intervention, children are asked to discuss and draw their most troublesome nightmares. I have found that some younger children may become frustrated attempting to draw things in a particular way. The therapist may want to assist the child in illustrating the nightmare while the child gives specific drawing directions (location, size, shape, color, etc.). When the drawings are complete, the child is asked to tell the story about the nightmare while the therapist transcribes it onto the back of the drawing or on a separate sheet of paper. The pictures are then displayed on the wall under a sign that reads THE NIGHTMARE WALL. I find that displaying the drawings serves to diminish the nightmare's power over the child and decrease the child's fear. For groups facilitated in a multiuse room, children's drawings can be tacked onto a foam core board or a large sheet of paper and stored out of sight between sessions. Following this activity, children should be asked to draw or list things they can do to feel safe when they have nightmares. Such a list might include sleeping with a special stuffed toy or blanket, using a nightlight, getting a hug from a parent/caretaker, and so on. The drawings or lists should also be posted on "The Nightmare Wall."

Conquering the Monster. For younger children, the "monster" is often representative of things they fear, including the perpetrator or the perpetrator's behavior. There are many effective ways to help children confront the "monster" metaphor. In this activity, children construct an image of a monster and then destroy it. The activity involves a large sheet of paper, some water-based paints (washable), and spray bottles filled with water. This is a very messy activity that should not be attempted if things must be kept clean and tidy. On a large sheet of heavy paper approximately 5 feet long and 3 feet wide, children are asked to paint a scary monster. This can be done by dividing the group in half and having each subgroup work on a monster painting. If the group is facilitated by more than one person, you may be able to have each child create his or her own monster. When the monsters are complete, fill clean spray bottles with water and give one to each child. The next part of this activity can be performed outside by attaching the paintings to a tree or wall. If this is not practical, the paintings can be taped to a wall, with the bottom of the paintings just inside the tub of a water play table or other large plastic tub. Put a large sheet of plastic or an old shower curtain on the floor behind the tub. The children then spray the monsters with the water in the spray bottles, watching the monsters disappear as they are conquered. If there is no way you can attempt this activity due to limitations of your therapy space, a good alternative is to use dry erase boards. Children can draw monsters with the dry erase markers and then use the erasers to make the monster disappear. I have worked with some children who like to make the monsters disappear piece by piece, first its hands, then its feet, then its ears, and so on, until the monster is totally gone. The benefit of this intervention is that, if necessary, children can create and conquer the monster over and over again.

The monster metaphor is often observed in nondirective play and is important for young children to explore in treatment. I once worked with a group of 3- and 4-year-olds whose nondirective play involved capturing, tying, boxing, and hiding a large plastic monster figure week after week. In each session, the monster would escape and have to be conquered again. One week, the children taped the box so securely they could not get the box open, and they asked me to open it for them. The following week, the children left the monster in the closet and it never "escaped" again.

Correcting the Nightmare. The focus of this session is to use problem solving to help children create a corrective, positive ending for their nightmares. Children are asked to draw pictures of their nightmares with these new endings. Most children appear to be empowered by this experience. The initial nightmare drawing of a 6-year-old girl involved the very common theme of the monster in the closet. The drawing depicted the monster hiding in the closet while she lay in bed. In her solution drawing, she glued the monster inside the closet and indicated, "I made the monster scared. I growled at the monster and told him to shut-up, and then I glue him in the closet." A 7-year-old child had asked to take his solution drawing home. He taped it to the wall next to his bed as a concrete reminder that he had the power to manage his fears and anxieties. The second drawings are placed over the original nightmare drawings on "The Nightmare Wall." This is a good opportunity to review the list of things children can do to feel safe after they have had a nightmare and to identify things they can do to feel more secure and less fearful while in bed.

Parent–Child Combined Session: Safety Shield. The goal of this session is for the parent and child to have a dialogue concerning the child's fears. In addition, they need to problem-solve to determine ways the child can feel a greater sense of safety and security. From a sheet of poster board, cut the shape of a shield such as those used by medieval knights, approximately 18″ × 24″. Attach pipe cleaners to each side for handles. Draw a line across the shield about a third of the way down from the top. The parent and child should be asked to work together to draw pictures representing the child's fears on the top portion of the shield. The pair should again work together to identify things that help the child feel safe and draw them on the lower portion of the shield. The shield is an obvious symbol of safety and protection. When each parent and child has completed his or her shield, the parent–child pairs can discuss the content with the group.

Pretend Slumber Party. After focusing for several sessions on fears and safety issues, this activity allows children to utilize some of their newly acquired coping skills to confront fears directly in a pretend-play situation. Prior to this session, determine whether each of the children in group can tolerate being in the dark for an extended period of time. Children are asked to bring a pillow and something they like to bring to bed, such as a stuffed toy or blanket. Each child is given a flashlight and the session takes place in the dark. Blankets are spread on the floor, and children snack on popcorn and drinks. During the session, the therapist can focus the play on fears related to the dark (shadows and sounds) and then guide the children toward finding strategies for confronting and resolving those fears. When working with combined gender groups, a pretend camp out can substitute for the slumber party. Sheets or fabric can be rigged to make a tent and snacks can include popcorn or Smores. One of my favorite ways to end this activity, whether pretending to have a slumber party or a camp out, is to take turns making shadow puppets on the wall. Most children love this, and it is both fun and calming. For certain groups, this activity becomes a weekly ending ritual.

Sessions 13–16

During this period, the group is reviewing and reinforcing themes addressed earlier and preparing for termination. The primary focus is on safety and ensuring that children adequately understand issues of self-protection (having the right to say no, who to tell, how to tell, etc.). Activities in this module utilize more cognitive strategies than activities in previous modules. It is also important for children and their families to begin moving beyond the abuse and strengthen and brighten their future orientation.

THEMES AND OBJECTIVES

- Abuse dynamics: threats, bribery, coercion, responsibility.
- Continuing to confront cognitive distortions.
- Self-protection skills.
- Establishing a sense of security and protection within the family system.
- Change/loss: work toward termination.
- Future orientation.

STRUCTURED ACTIVITIES

Stop and Tell Sign. The goal of this activity is to empower children to resist inappropriate touching and to identify adults they trust to tell. Using poster board cut in an octagonal shape and colored red like a stop sign, the children make a sign that reads STOP on one side and TELL on the other. Dowels or craft sticks can be used as handles. After the signs are completed, each child practices yelling "Stop" loudly and then rehearses telling a trusted adult. The following role-play activity may follow in the same session if time allows.

Role Playing "What If" Scenarios. The focus of these role-playing scenes is to continue to confront and correct cognitive distortions, specifically those surrounding issues of responsibility, threats, bribes, coercion, and the imbalance of power that exists between children and their abusers. It is also an effective way to help children to problem solve and identify strategies and options for given situations. It can be helpful at this point to present a video dealing with safety and inappropriate touch. I have used Disney's *Too Smart for Strangers.* Although the first part of the videotape focuses on protection from strangers, the last segment does an adequate job of addressing issues of inappropriate touch by family members or acquaintances. I particularly like the videotape format in which a situation is created and then viewers are asked what the child in the film should do next. As an alternative, I have assigned parents the task of viewing the film independently, then watching and discussing it with their child.

Parent–Child Combined Session: Safe Place in the Sand. It is important to establish the nonoffending parent or primary caretaker as the child's protector. Give both the parent and child skills to enhance the child's sense of comfort and safety. The following activity enables the parent and child to explore creative solutions together. For this activity each parent–child dyad uses a sand tray and works together to create a safe place in the sand. Together, they choose the elements of their sand tray from a wide variety of figures and objects. When the sand trays are completed, photographs can be taken, and the group is brought together to share what they created. This can be a very powerful exercise, and one in which the parent and child pay close attention to details. One 7-year-old girl had her mother help her build a wall between her home and her perpetrator's home. Another child placed herself in her living room on her mother's lap, with a fence and dog protecting her from the outside world.

Power Masks. Learned helplessness and feelings of vulnerability impact children's sense of self-esteem and place them at risk for further abuse. Helping children to identify the source of their personal power reinforces feelings of strength and independence. This session begins with a dialogue about power. Power should be defined in terms of inner strength as well as the courage and ability to enact change and make choices. The therapist should present a variety of magazine pictures of different people. Examples are a baby, boxer, judge, school child, teacher, parent, and so on. Half of the pictures should be children engaged in various normal daily activities that relate directly or indirectly with the aforementioned definition of power. The children should discuss the power of each person. If they are unable to come up with responses, they should be reminded of the definition.

Examples of correct answers would be as follows: "The baby is powerful, because she smiles to get someone's attention or cries to get what she wants," "The child is powerful, because he can keep his room clean or teach a younger sibling how to play a game." Next, ask each child to identify examples of personal power and then create a mask that represents this power. The mask can be made of precut poster board with a craft stick attached at the bottom for holding. The children should be directed to decorate the mask in any chosen way using markers, glitter, ribbon, beads, feathers, or other available materials. When completed, the masks are displayed by the children. After introductions, each child makes a statement, such as "I am powerful because I . . . "

Termination Activities

Preparation for termination focuses and establishes a positive future orientation; addresses issues of separation, abandonment, and loss; and reflects on growth and change. A variety of activities can be used to facilitate termination of treatment. One activity I especially like involves the use of a sand tray. Each child is instructed to use the sand tray to create the world as a grown-up. If necessary, the therapist can pose questions to children about the things they like to do, or about the people they would like to have in their lives when they are grown. Each child describes the sand tray scene to the group. Following this activity, I turn the focus to a celebration of the accomplishments of the group by reviewing privacy boxes, adding special goodbye messages or wishes to the group poster, or passing hugs around the circle. We always have a party. I also like to present transitional objects to the children when they complete group. I prefer to use something that has some significance to the group, such as pocket flashlights, or objects that symbolize change and growth.

Play Therapy Toys and Materials

When choosing items for the playroom, keep in mind the ultimate function of play materials: fostering a relationship between therapist and the child, enhancing thematic and fantasy play, providing vehicles for projection and emotional distancing, and promoting mastery and self-expression. Include only toys and materials that create comfort. For example, if the therapist cannot tolerate children mixing play dough colors, it is better to avoid using Play-Doh than to risk censoring a child's play. The following is a list of toys and materials for specific use in therapy for sexually abused children. The list includes items for structured and nondirective play therapy. The choice of materials will be dependent on the amount and type of space afforded by the treatment facility. The materials that I consider to be absolutely essential are italicized.

- Domestic and wild animal families.
- Transportation toys (cars, trucks, boats, and planes in various sizes, so that they can be configured as families, if necessary).
- *Two doll houses with several sets of family figures* (preferably bendable, with removable clothes). The figures should represent different races and ethnicities, and be capable of various family configurations (grandparents, multiple child dolls, multiple adult dolls, to represent various family and nonfamily members).
- *Washable boy and girl baby dolls* with doll accessories, specifically, blankets, clothes, bottles, washcloths, and towels.
- Tub for bathing baby dolls.

- Housekeeping props, especially cooking and feeding supplies.
- *Toy telephones:* at least two.
- Doctor kit.
- Sunglasses: enough for each child in group.
- *Flashlights:* enough for each child in group.
- Mirror (unbreakable).
- *Monster figures:* It is important to find monster figures that are not familiar to children (no cartoons or movie monsters), so that they are more effective in projective play.
- Handcuffs with key.
- *Blocks:* I prefer large, sturdy, cardboard or foam blocks which are utilized for building walls and establishing boundaries in play.
- *Puppets:* These should represent family members, adults and children, as well as a variety of negative and positive characters. Puppets should be soft and easy for children to manipulate.
- *Costume box:* Include hats, ties, purses, glasses, capes, jewelry, magic wands, and so on. I also have a large collection of pieces of fabric in different colors, textures, and sizes to facilitate projective play and character development. The fabric can also be used to create different environments in play.
- Musical instruments.
- Soft foam balls in various sizes.
- Puzzles.
- Board games: I prefer nontherapeutic games such as Trouble, Sorry, Don't Break the Ice.
- *Art materials:* These should include a variety of different kinds of paper, including large rolled paper, poster board, and colored tissue paper. Basic materials should include markers, colored pencils, crayons, sidewalk chalk, glue, safety scissors, a variety of beads, stones, string, fabric, ribbons, and other supplies such as tape and a spray bottle. Glitter is a wonderful tool for children who tend to be negative about their artwork or are resistant to working with art materials. I have found that most children enjoy using glitter and tend to be more positive about their creations when they involve glitter. Glitter can be messy, however, and glitter glue pens are a very acceptable substitute. Play-Doh and modeling clay should be included in various colors. Paints are a very freeing tool for children but can be very messy to use. Washable tempera paints are readily available, and watercolors can be just as freeing with much less mess. Boxes and cardboard can be used by children to create boundaries and environments (jails, sleeping areas, adults' vs. children's space, "monster land"). Art supplies can be used to create objects that symbolize healing transformation and self-empowerment, such as keys, magic wands, swords, and power masks.
- *Toys that give permission for aggressive play:* I prefer swords to guns, as they provide greater opportunity for projection. Toy guns are more

familiar to children and encourage imitated play behavior as seen on television and in movies, cartoons, and so on. I have also used foam cylinders, normally used as pool toys, which can be cut and used for safe swordplay. Although I do not normally provide realistic guns in play, I do supply water guns and materials that can be transformed into guns or weapons, such as Legos.

• Tub for water play and water play toys.

• *Sand trays:* Various objects and figures should be readily available for use in sand tray work, including people, animals, vehicles, and environmental objects such as trees, bridges, ladders, fences, and furniture. I also like to include materials such as marbles, stones, feathers, twigs, and string, as well as negative and positive images (wizards, ghosts, dragons, royalty, soldiers, witches, and doctors). I also include a bride and groom, monsters, and an assortment of miniature objects such as swords, food, anchors, tools, and related materials. I like to have the sand tray materials available for both sand tray and dollhouse play.

• Tape recorder.

• Instamatic camera.

• Sports bottles filled with water for regressive play: I have found it difficult at times to convince parents of the rationale and appropriateness of using baby bottles in play therapy. This leads to undue stress and anxiety in the children who fear parents may be angry with them for using a baby bottle, even in play. What I choose to do instead is provide sports bottles filled with water. Each child is provided a bottle labeled with his or her name. The bottles remain in the playroom from week to week and are filled with water before each session. Although the sports bottle does not provide a nipple, it is necessary to suck in order to drink. This provides an experience similar to using a baby bottle. In order to infuse the sports bottles with the regressive qualities already inherent in a baby bottle, children are told that they may use their bottles anytime they wish, even when resting on a pillow or pretending to be a baby in play. In this way, children are provided with an opportunity to engage in regressive play behavior without adding stress to the parent–child relationship. Parents should be advised, however, of the need to tolerate regressive behaviors in their children as part of the healing process.

The Playroom

Ideally, group treatment should take place within a playroom setting. This provides a higher level of expressive freedom than an office or multipurpose room that might restrict the use of certain materials or play activities. However, not all facilities are equipped with a separate playroom, and this should not prevent therapists from establishing a group treatment program. Whatever type of space is used, the primary concern should be the safety of the children. The environment should be free of furniture with sharp corners or edges and breakable or dangerous objects. An inexpensive area rug can be rolled up and stored between sessions to help protect underflooring yet increase the level of freedom. Furniture can be moved, and large pillows or sofa cushions can be used to help define the play space. A table can be helpful for artwork, but artwork can be done on the floor just as effectively. Large pieces of cardboard covered with stick-on shelf paper can help define each child's space and are helpful when working with Play-Doh, clay, or paints. In general, the therapy environment should serve to encourage exploration and freedom of expression while providing the essential elements of security and safety.

CASE ILLUSTRATION

Ashly is a 7-year-old female referred by the Department of Children and Family Services for sexual abuse treatment. Ashly had been sexually abused by an adult male cousin of her mother. The abuse occurred on multiple occasions over a 6-month period. The perpetrator, whom Ashly referred to as Uncle Paulie, had been living with Ashly's family and would regularly be left to care for Ashly when her parents were not at home. Ashly's parents were both physically disabled, requiring walkers or wheelchairs for mobility. They had depended a great deal on Uncle Paulie, who helped with household chores as well as transportation. There was little structure in the lives of this family, and they were easily overwhelmed by normal daily-life stresses.

The sexual abuse of Ashley included oral and vaginal penetration, and a medical exam confirmed extensive internal scarring. The abuse was discovered when Ashly's mother entered the home to find Uncle Paulie in the act of molesting Ashly. The police were notified and upon questioning, Ashly disclosed the details of the abuse. Ashly also indicated that Uncle Paulie had threatened to harm her and her parents if she told anyone about the abuse.

At the time she was referred for treatment, Ashly presented with symptoms including the following: severe anxiety; fearfulness; excessive masturbation; physical complaints such as vaginal pain, headaches, and shortness of breath; increased distractibility; sleep disturbances and nightmares. Assessed to be an appropriate candidate for group treatment, she entered a newly forming group with five other girls between the ages of 6 and 8. The group met every Tuesday afternoon for 1 hour and ran for 16 weeks. I cofacilitated the group with a male intern from a counseling master's program at a local university. Although Ashly's father declined an invitation to participate in treatment, Ashly's mother attended a weekly, nonoffending parents group that ran concurrently with her child's group.

Throughout the first group session, Ashly stayed close to me, rarely venturing from my side. She was cautious and tentative in her play and interactions with others. By the second session, Ashly was more willing to participate with the male coleader and the other group members. She appeared quite comfortable in the playroom, conversing and playing freely and spontaneously. During this session, the group engaged in puppet interviews. The children were given the choice of using the puppets to represent themselves or to create a character. Ashly chose a child puppet but named it Carol and insisted that it did not represent herself. When interviewed, "Carol" reported that she had no parents and that she was a child living by herself. When asked what had become of her parents, "Carol" responded, "I just don't have any." Ashly's nondirective play in this session, and the next six sessions that followed, was chaotic and disorganized. She usually preferred intentional mess-making activities (mixing paint, water, and other substances), in lieu of pretend-play or role-play activities. Ashly's play behavior was a true reflection of her daily life and clearly portrayed the lack of safety and security she experienced at home.

During the third group session, the children were asked to draw a picture of a place where they felt safe. Ashly drew a picture of herself in the playroom with the two group leaders and the group members surrounding her. She indicated that the playroom was safe because the group leaders would not let anyone hurt her or take her away. When questioned about where she felt safe at home, Ashly remarked that she did not feel safe anywhere at home. She worried that the door locks were not strong enough, and she did not believe that her parents were capable of physically protecting her from harm. A great deal of Ashly's fear and anxiety appeared to be related to concerns about her parents' physical health and disabilities. At this point, we realized that a primary treatment goal for this child had to involve enhancing her feelings of safety at home. We discussed this with her mother and established a plan to address this issue in the children's group, the parents' group, and the combined parent–child sessions.

The focus on emotions was continued in the following session, with the goal of connecting emotional and physical responses. After completing the body tracings, the children were helped to identify the parts of their body where they felt specific emotions. Ashly indicated that she felt worry in her head, and that it gave her a headache. She described feeling as if she could not breathe when she was especially fearful, and indicated that when she was excited, "My feet can't stand still." This activity appeared to help Ashly to manage her physical responses to stress. Following this session, Ashly's mother and teacher both reported that Ashly appeared to experience a decrease in headaches and breathing difficulties.

The eighth session brought together the parents and children, with a focus on sharing feelings. Instead of randomly choosing emotions from an envelope, Ashly and her mother were given specific emotions to work on, including "worried," "afraid," "happy," and "safe." Ashly drew about feeling afraid when Uncle Paulie threatened her and her parents, and drew herself worrying whenever one of her parents had to go to the doctor or hospital. She was able to tell her mother that she worried that there would be no one to take care of her if her parents got very sick or died. Ashly's mother was able to talk to Ashly about friends and family members who would help to care for Ashly if her parents could not. They established a plan for handling medical emergencies and later discussed these plans with the friends and family members who would be available to help if needed. Ashly's behavior during nondirective play changed significantly following this session. Her play became more organized and interactive. She rarely engaged in intentional mess-making activities unless she was creating something to be used for role playing.

Nightmares were discussed and illustrated in the group's ninth session. Ashly's nightmare involved a vampire who tied her parents up with ropes and covered their mouths with tape. The vampire then grabbed Ashly and carried her away. Ashly indicated that she had this dream often and always woke from it crying. In the following session, we focused on conquering the children's nightmare monsters. Ashly painted her vampire and enthusiastically sprayed it with a water bottle until it vanished from the paper.

During the next session, the group's 10th week together, we focused on creating new endings for the children's nightmares. Ashly decided that the vampire in her dream would melt if she poured water on him. She drew herself pouring a bucket of water on the head of the vampire as it melted into the ground. After this session, Ashly asked her mother to buy her a spray bottle, which she filled with water and kept beside her bed. Ashly's mother reported that following this session, Ashly's nightmares decreased dramatically.

The following session again brought together the parents' and children's groups to create safety shields. Ashly and her mother discussed the things that Ashly feared; they wrote and drew them on the upper portion of the shield. Ashly identified Uncle Paulie, ghosts, monsters, robbers, and the dark. Together, Ashly and her mother determined what might help Ashly to feel safer. Ideas included a list of emergency phone numbers, a flashlight for Ashly to keep in her room, a nightlight in the hallway, and a new lock for the front door. Ashly also indicated that her favorite pillow, blanket, and teddy bear helped her to feel safer in bed. During the pretend slumber party held the following week, Ashly brought her favorite pillow, blanket, and teddy bear, as well as her own brand new flashlight. She was able to tolerate participating in the group activities in the dark and evidenced a decrease in distractibility and inattention.

The fourteenth group session brought together the parents and children to participate in a sand tray activity. Ashly and her mother jointly created a safe place in the sand. During this activity, Ashly was able to see her home as a safe place. In her sand tray, Ashly placed herself between her mother and her father. A circular wall of sand surrounded them. Ashly instructed her mother to use cardboard to create a door with a large lock, which represented the family's front door. Ashly placed a phone next to her mother and a miniature flashlight in her father's lap. This image represented a great step forward for Ashly and her family. Through her sand tray, Ashly communicated her growing trust in her parents' ability to protect her and keep her safe. And as Ashly's trust in her parents increased, her anxiety-related symptoms decreased. Ashly continued to do well and successfully completed group treatment 2 weeks later. Along with his wife and daughter, Ashly's father attended several family therapy sessions, where the skills learned in group were reinforced and other family issues were addressed. Supportive services for the family were already in place, so no further referrals were made.

SUMMARY AND CONCLUSION

In this chapter, a time-limited group-treatment program has been presented for use with sexually abused children ages 3 through 10. The program attempts to combine the essential elements of therapy with sexually abused children into a treatment protocol that appears to be well-suited for this population. It offers a time-limited approach that directly addresses symptoms of trauma, developmental issues, and the impact of sexual abuse on interpersonal relationships. Though much of the program is directive and abuse-specific, it relies on the healing power of child-centered, nondirective play therapy to enhance the potential for growth and change.

REFERENCES

Burns, R. C., & Kaufman, S. H. (1970). *Kinetic family drawings*. New York: Brunner/Mazel.

Cohen, J., & Mannarino, A. (1993). A treatment model for sexually abused preschoolers. *Journal of Interpersonal Violence, 8*(1), 115–131.

Finkelhor, D., & Browne, A. (1986). Initial and long-term effects: A conceptual framework. In D. Finkelhor (Ed.), *A sourcebook on child sexual abuse* (pp. 180–198). Newbury Park, CA: Sage.

Friedrich, W. (1991, Spring). Child victims: Promising techniques and programs in the treatment of child sexual abuse. *The APSAC Advisor*, pp. 5–6.

Irwin, G., & Malloy, E. (1975). Family puppet interview. *Family Process, 14*(2), 179–191.

Long, S. (1986). Guidelines for treating young children. In K. MacFarlane, J. Waterman, S. Conerly, L. Damon, M. Durfee, & S. Long (Eds.), *Sexual abuse of young children* (pp. 220–246). New York: Guilford Press.

Mandell, J. G., & Damon, L. (1989). *Group treatment for sexually abused children.* New York: Guilford Press.

Powell, L., & Faherty, S. L. (1990). Treating sexually abused latency age girls. *The Arts in Psychotherapy, 17,* 35–47.

Rasmussen, L., & Cunningham, C. (1995). Focused play therapy and non-directive play therapy: Can they be integrated? *Journal of Child Sexual Abuse, 4*(1), 1–20.

Salter, A. (1988). *Treating child sex offenders and victims.* Newbury Park, CA: Sage.

Sedlak, A., & Broadhurst, D. (1996). *Third national incidence study of child abuse and neglect.* Washington, DC: National Clearinghouse on Child Abuse and Neglect Information.

Steward, M. S., Farquhar, L. C., Dicharry, D. C., Glick, D. R., & Martin, P. W. (1986). Group therapy: A treatment of choice for young victims of child abuse. *International Journal of Child Psychotherapy, 36,* 261–275.

12

Play Group Therapy
for Social Skills Deficits
in Children

CHARLES E. SCHAEFER
HEIDI E. JACOBSEN
MARJAN GHAHRAMANLOU

INTRODUCTION

During the last three decades, a growing body of research has indicated that the ability to establish and maintain social relationships in childhood has a significant impact in later life. Peer relationships are particularly influential during the middle elementary school years, when a child devotes a large portion of school and playtime to interactions with peers. Unless children achieve a minimal level of social competence, they have a high probability in adolescence and adulthood of emotional, social, and adjustment difficulties, including low self-esteem, antisocial behavior, interpersonal problems, and school/job failure (Cowen, Pederson, Babijian, Izzo, & Trost, 1973; Kohn, 1977; Parker & Asher, 1987; Vandell & Hembree, 1994).

According to Hartup (1992), "The single best childhood predictor of adult adaptation is *not* IQ, *not* school grades, and *not* classroom behavior, but rather the adequacy with which the child gets along with other children" (p. 2). In fact, children who demonstrate prosocial behaviors are often able to have an impact on their own development by the choices they make and the friends they select (Masten & Coatsworth, 1998). "Children who are generally disliked, who are aggressive and disruptive, who are unable to sustain close relationships with other children, and who cannot establish a place for themselves in the peer culture are seriously at risk" (Hartup, 1992, p. 2).

Social Status

Peer acceptance refers to the extent to which a child is liked or accepted by his or her peer group. Friendship, on the other hand, indicates the existence of a reciprocal and mutually beneficial relationship between a child and one or more other, particular children. Peer acceptance or popularity can be operationalized as a categorical variable; children can be classified into specific sociometric groups such as "popular," "average," "isolated," and "rejected."

Rejected children often exhibit aggressive and disruptive behaviors in addition to low levels of positive peer interactions, such as cooperation and friendliness (Dodge, Pettit, McClaskey, & Brown, 1986). Isolated children, on the other hand, do not usually display externalizing behavior patterns but distinguish themselves by infrequent social interaction and high levels of social anxiety (La Greca, 1993).

Social Skills

It has been proposed that the development of appropriate social skills in a child is an important foundation for adequate peer relationships. Various definitions of social skills have been proposed. Social skills refer to positive social behaviors that contribute to the formation and maintenance of satisfying social interactions. With regard to peers, "social skills" may be defined as the ability to interact with peers in a given social context in specific ways. These interactions are acceptable and valued as well as personally or mutually beneficial (Combs & Slaby, 1977, p. 162). Social skills represent a response class (greeting people appropriately) rather than a discrete behavior (eye contact). Other social skills include communicating effectively, coping with peer provocation, resolving conflicts quickly, group entry skills, and good sportsmanship. "Social competence" is the general term used to describe the overall effectiveness of one's social skills and behaviors (McFall, 1982).

Parenting Practices Associated with Peer Acceptance

Recent studies have investigated the connection between parenting behaviors and individual differences in children's peer competence. The findings are summarized as follows:

- *Authoritative discipline.* Harsh, restrictive, authoritarian discipline has been found to be associated with children's aggression, which in turn is associated with peer rejection (Dishion, 1990; Hart, DeWolf, Wozniak, & Burts, 1992; Pettit, Clawson, Dodge, & Bates, 1996; Travillion & Snyder, 1993). Conversely, socially competent behavior with peers is predicted by an authoritative parenting style. The three main components of authoritative parenting (Baumrind, 1978) are (1) parental acceptance or warmth, (2) behavioral supervision and strictness, and (3) granting psychological autonomy.

• *Attachment.* Children who establish secure attachment relationships with their parents during infancy are reported to be more likely to be competent with their peers than infants who were insecurely attached (Easterbrooks & Lamb, 1979; Sroufe, Carlson, & Shulman, 1993).

• *Arrange peer contact.* Young children of parents who provide them with many opportunities to mingle with other children (e.g., play dates, enrollment in organized activities) tend to have a large number of playmates and be better liked by their peers (Harper & Huie, 1985; Ladd & Golter, 1988; Ladd & Hart, 1992; Ladd, Profilet, & Hart, 1992).

• *Modeling.* Parents who model prosocial behaviors at home (effective conflict resolution strategies) tend to have more socially competent children (Rushton, 1976).

• *Coaching.* Children whose parents actively instructed them to manage challenging peer situations (resolving peer disputes, initiating contact with unacquainted peers) were judged by teachers to be more competent in peer interactions (Finnie & Russell, 1988). Other studies have found that parental coaching is associated with peer acceptance and social competence (Laird, Pettit, Mize, & Lindsey, 1994; Russell & Finnie, 1990). A recent study revealed that preschool girls benefit from their mothers' social coaching, whereas boys demonstrate elevated levels of social competence following their fathers' involvement in play and coaching (Pettit, Brown, Mize, & Lindsey, 1998).

• *Verbal interaction.* Frequent verbal interaction between parents and child correlates positively with peer popularity (Franz & Gross, 1996). Parents who provide verbal support and direction while they stimulate their children to think and problem-solve tend to have children who are more socially competent (Draper, Larsen, & Rowles, 1997). When parents are generally agreeable in interactions with their children, their children are less disagreeable during play with their peers (Putallaz, 1987). Preschool boys whose fathers were physically playful while allowing their sons to regulate the pace and tempo of the interaction were found to be popular with their classmates (MacDonald & Parke, 1984).

• *Interactional synchrony.* Parent–child interactions characterized by interactional synchrony have been found to be related to social competence in children (Mize & Pettit, 1997). Interactional synchrony refers to reciprocal, mutually responsive interactions. Parents and children low in interactional synchrony tend to be unresponsive to one another (ignoring each other or responding with a non sequitur or contrary opinion), change the topic frequently, or show affect that is counter to the prevailing mood of the other person (e.g., mother appears excited, child responds glumly).

• *Stress.* Stressful family events, such as divorce, death of a relative, and relocation, tend to trigger negative emotional states in children, which in turn can adversely affect their relationship with peers.

SOCIAL SKILLS TRAINING PROGRAM

The basic assumption of this social skills training program is that social skills deficits lead to peer isolation and rejection, so that an intervention aimed directly at improving social skills in elementary school children will result in greater peer acceptance. Empirical studies have found that children who have social skills are more sociable, cooperative, altruistic, self-confident, less lonely, and have more friends than children who lack social competence (Newcomb & Bagwell, 1995; Walker, Schwarz, Nippold, Irvin, & Noell, 1994). Children who are rejected by peers, on the other hand, exhibit deficiencies in social skills, in that they are more likely to mistime social initiations, misread social situations, and engage in disjointed peer interactions (Dodge et al., 1986).

Social Skills Curriculum

A 10-session social skills curriculum is presented in this chapter. The curriculum focuses on teaching specific social skills that address common social problems of elementary school children and ensures that they are matched to the social–cognitive ability of these children. The 10 target social skills are selected because of their relevancy to social relationships of children this age. Older children often face similar social difficulties and can benefit from instruction, reinforcement, and practice of the social skills presented in this section. Suggested activities can easily be modified by group leaders in order to meet the needs of children within varying developmental, social, and cognitive levels. Goal selection for the present curriculum is based on the potential effect of the skills to increase peer contacts, increase a child's attractiveness to others, and decrease socially unpleasant behaviors.

This chapter also contains a corresponding 10-session curriculum for parents of the children. Parents meet with a leader in their own group while their children meet with a leader in a separate room. The parents' group is trained to support children's skills transfer into everyday use. The parental component of this training is designed to enhance improvement in children's social behavior in the home setting and maintain improvement over time. Parents play an essential role in facilitating generalization and persistence of treatment effects by monitoring their child's peer interactions. This is accompanied by arranging, prompting, and reinforcing social behaviors in the home setting (Guevremont, 1990).

In the parents' group, the leader explains what is known about social development in children and the importance of social skills and social status. The parents' role in helping children improve their peer relations is also elucidated. Parents are strongly encouraged to provide their children with opportunities to interact with various playmates and to practice learned social skills. Arranging play dates for their children and enrolling them in organized social activities are recommended. Parents are taught the skills of each module and the associated vocabulary for describing the skills that their children are learning. Parents observe segments of their children's group sessions by video feedback about halfway through the training program. They learn how to prompt and reward their child's use of each skill at home using social and token reinforcement. Each week, parents receive a written handout that summarizes the skills module of the week and describes ways to reinforce their child's practice of the skills at home.

In addition to the curriculum for the children's and parents' groups, a handout for teachers is also included. As long as the child is comfortable with this arrangement, parents should be encouraged to inform teachers that the child is enrolled in a "social skills training group" and to provide the teacher with the 10-week outline of skills. The parents may request that teachers pay attention to positive interactions between the child and peers, and reinforce appropriate behaviors. They may also include suggested activities if the classroom teacher is willing to implement them.

Screening

Prior to acceptance into the program, the child and his or her parents come for a 1½-hour screening session with one of the group leaders. The leader interviews the child and parents separately to determine the child's suitability for the group.

Guidelines for conducting the child interview are contained in Appendix 12.1. Once the child interview is complete, the parents are interviewed separately to assess the following information about the child:

- Developmental history
- Family history, including psychiatric disorders and current family stressors
- Social history
- School adaptation
- Special interests and talents
- Physical problems
- Current medications

- Restrictions, if any, on snacks
- Goals the parents have for the child's participation in the group.

Prior to ending the screening session, the parents complete the Child Behavior Checklist (Achenbach & Edelbrock, 1991), and the interviewer meets with the child and parents together to explain the purpose and benefits of the social skills group and the responsibility of group members (attend all sessions, follow group rules, complete homework assignment).

In order to create a positive and safe environment that is conducive to learning new social skills, group leaders are urged to review closely the information obtained from their interviews for purposes of admission to the group. Criteria for excluding a child from the group include the following:

- Severely disruptive, aggressive, or oppositional behaviors
- Bizarre behaviors
- Extreme social withdrawal (no eye contact, lack of verbal responsiveness, no social interest)
- Intense separation anxiety (inability to separate from parents)
- Major depression or suicidal tendencies.

If a child is not accepted for the group, the interviewer advises the parents about other options (e.g., individual psychotherapy, groups in other settings).

Group Composition

Each group consists of four to six children of the same gender. The children in each group are no more than 3 years apart (6 to 7 years old in primary grades, 8 to 10 years old in elementary school, 11 to 13 years old, or preadolescent). An effort is made to mix socially inhibited children with children showing aggressive tendencies to balance internalizing and externalizing tendencies.

Group Leaders

Two group leaders, preferably a male and a female, meet with the same group of children over 10 consecutive weeks. Groups usually meet in the late afternoon (4:00 to 6:00 P.M.) in a clinic room (about 250 square feet) containing a large table and chairs, storage cabinet for table games and art supplies, and a one-way mirror and video camera. A third group leader meets with the parents. Leaders are usually graduate students or therapists in a mental health profession (psychology, social work, counseling).

Leaders have several roles to fulfill in addition to being teachers. A major role of the group leader is cheerleader; he or she becomes excited about the group activities and treats a child's response as if it were a headline in a newspaper. By being very enthusiastic, energetic, and excited, leaders help the children become more interested and involved in the group activities. Enthusiasm is contagious in group sessions!

Leaders should also be playful and fun loving (even a bit wacky at times) in order to capture and sustain children's interest and attention. By showing strong positive affect (smiling, cheerfulness), leaders make the gratifying, fun elements of the group activities more obvious. The group play setting can serve as a rather powerful therapeutic environment where children experience positive emotions that promote learning and practicing new social skills. When these learned skills are associated with pleasant experiences, children are more likely to remember what they have learned and display their positive social skills during interactions with peers.

In addition, group leaders need to have, or develop, good "kid-handling" skills. They must clearly be in charge of the group sessions and comfortable enforcing group rules without becoming harsh or autocratic. Prior experience as camp counselors, classroom teachers, coaches, or youth club leaders can help prepare one to be a group therapist.

Group Sessions

The first 10 minutes of each 60-minute session are devoted to a group discussion wherein the leaders review the previous week's homework and describe the target social skill to be practiced in the current session. The leaders explain in simple, concrete terms what the skill is, why it is important, give examples of the skill in action, and answer any questions about it. This instruction time is followed by 40 minutes of structured activities (games, art projects) that give the children an opportunity to practice the new social skill and receive feedback about their performance.

The final 10 minutes of each session is reserved for snack time (juice, crackers). Snack time serves the following purposes:

- Promote a feeling of being nurtured.
- Enhance the children's self-esteem by giving the leaders time to summarize the group members' performance on the target skill.
- Pass out prizes earned during the group process.
- Present homework for the coming week.

Teaching Methods

A basic assumption of this training program is that children learn social behaviors best when group leaders use a very active instructional approach. This approach includes multiple cognitive-behavioral strategies such as direct instruction, role play, supervised practice activity, prompting, corrective feedback, and monitoring and providing opportunities for independent practice in the natural environment.

Other teaching strategies employed are the following:

- *Modeling.* This method is based on the principle of imitative learning. Appropriate social skills are modeled *in vivo* by group leaders, peers, and use of puppets, dolls, or story characters (symbolic modeling). Following a demonstration by a model, children are given an opportunity to practice the skill.
- *Operant conditioning.* Positive and negative reinforcement are used to gradually strengthen appropriate behaviors (cooperation) and weaken inappropriate ones (aggressiveness).
- *Social cognition.* The emphasis in this approach is not on external behavior but on the thoughts and feelings that underlie such behaviors. The social–cognitive approach is concerned with verbal and cognitive mediators such as finding alternative ways to solve social problems, changing irrational beliefs, or considering the consequences to self and others of one's actions.
- *Coaching.* Oden and Asher (1977) were among the first researchers to use a coaching method to teach social skills to isolated children. The coaching process includes three components. First, children are verbally instructed in social skills (definition and importance). Next, they are provided with an opportunity to practice social skills by playing with their peers. Finally, they have a postplay performance review with the coach (group leader). In coaching, behavior change is based on children's knowledge of specific interpersonal behaviors, their ability to convert social knowledge into skillful social behavior in interactive contexts, and the ability to accurately evaluate their skills performance (Ladd & Mize, 1983).

The fun and enjoyment the children derive from playing group games is another important aspect of the teaching program. Such positive emotions make learning and practicing these skills a positive experience. Learning strategies presented in a game-like context have been found to be particularly effective with elementary-school-age children. The game-like atmosphere enhances and maintains the children's interest and motivation to engage in the activities. By associating the skills with pleasant experiences, the children are able to remember more easily what has been learned in the session.

Finally, the therapeutic factors in the group process (universalization, cohesion, altruism, vicarious learning) are present to enhance the power of this intervention (Yalom, 1985). The safe and realistic environment created in a social skills group provides children with an opportunity to experience and share empathy, regulate emotional states, process social cues, and manage conflict. The major advantage of group play therapy over individual play therapy is the provision of a safe social setting for discovering and experimenting with new and more satisfying ways to relate to peers. The best way for children to learn social skills is in a real-life group situation with peers, and not in individual psychotherapy with an adult therapist.

Management Strategies

Perhaps the most challenging aspect of group work with children is to find ways to manage the broad range of inappropriate behaviors (name-calling, play-fighting, shouting, not listening or participating) that may emerge in group sessions. The goals of group discipline are twofold: (1) to ensure the safety of the children and group leaders, and (2) to create an environment conducive to learning new social skills. Group leaders use the following strategies to prevent or reduce behavioral disturbances during group sessions.

RULES

Rules provide children with concrete guidelines regarding appropriate behavior in sessions and send a clear message that they will be safe in the group. Rules should be formulated during the first session, with the help of the children, and displayed in a conspicuous location in the room. The leaders go over the rules several times and explain the reason for them, using the following guidelines for constructing group rules:

1. Rules should be limited to four to six items because children will not remember more than this number. Give specific directives regarding other behaviors as the need arises.
2. Phrase the rules in a positive ("to do") rather than negative ("don't do") manner ("Stay in your seat" rather than "Don't walk around").
3. Rules should refer to specific, observable behaviors ("Hands to yourself" vs. vague generalities such as "Be nice").
4. Positive consequences (praise, rewards) should result from following rules, with negative consequences (private reprimand, brief time out) applied to rule violations.
5. Review the rules at the start of each session by asking one child to pick a rule and explain it to the group members.
6. Make the rules short and to the point so that they can be easily remembered. Examples of group rules are as follows:
   - Wait your turn.
   - Stay in your seat.
   - Talk quietly.
   - Hands to yourself.

- Raise your hand.
- Play by the rules.
- Listen—Pay attention.

SOCIAL REINFORCEMENT

Social reinforcement (smiles, "Thank you," praise, pat on the arm, nearness, attention) should be given for the children's appropriate social behaviors (Madsen, Becker, & Thomas, 1968). Research has shown that social reinforcement is very effective in increasing children's social behaviors. Group leaders, like classroom teachers, are inclined to take good behaviors for granted and to pay attention only when a child acts up or misbehaves. Give praise ("Good job of sharing the crayons") and appreciation ("I like the way you smile and have fun in the group"; "Thank you for raising your hand") when the children follow the rules and show prosocial behaviors. It is very important to notice as many good behaviors as possible during a group session.

When praising children, try to give "labeled" praise. Labeled praise differs from unlabeled praise in that it clearly specifies the behavior that is being commended. A labeled praise for sharing would be "Eric, nice job sharing your marker with Bill," whereas an unlabeled praise would be "Good work, Eric." The last comment fails to inform the child of the particular behavior that pleases the group leader.

Some additional guidelines for using praise statements are as follows:

1. Be sure every group member is singled out for praise and attention.
2. Vary your expressions of praise rather than continually saying "Good."
3. Attempt to become spontaneous in your praise, and smile while giving it.
4. At first you will probably feel that you are praising a great deal and that it sounds a bit phony. This is a typical reaction. Praising will become more natural with the passage of time.
5. Send frequent praise notes home to children's parents when they have done well in session.

REWARD SYSTEM

For appropriate social behavior in group each child can earn a "happy face" drawn on a piece of paper at the end of the session. For noncompliant and disruptive behaviors, children receive "sad faces." One warning is given before a sad face is given. If the group members receive more smiling faces than sad faces at the end of the session, they earn the privilege of playing the Rewards Target Game. For this game, one child throws a Velcro-lined ball at a target with three numbers on it. Whatever number is hit determines the particular reward (small toy) each group member receives.

Studies indicate that positive reinforcement is most powerful when it includes a combination of labeled praises and tangible rewards (Pfiffner, Rosen, & O'Leary, 1985). Also, children often give their best performance when their individual efforts contribute toward a group reward (Slavin, 1983).

NEGATIVE CONSEQUENCES

For minor or infrequent rule infractions (occasionally interrupting others), the group leaders should try the following: ignoring; reprimanding in private; prompting/reminding about the rules; or leading a group problem-solving effort. However, for more serious or frequent rule violations (physical or verbal hostility, frequent sex talk), group leaders can use time-out or suspension for a session.

Time-out, simply stated, means time away from the group and group leaders. One group leader implements the time-out, while the other continues to direct the group activity. The following guidelines make time-out more effective:

1. A chair in the hallway outside the group room often works well, or use a separate room to isolate the child. Sitting in the corner of the group room (partial separation) can work for preschoolers.

2. Short durations of time-out (5–10 minutes) are preferable. Longer durations have not been found to be more effective and are more difficult to enforce. The child must be quiet at the end of time-out before he or she can return to the group. If a child resists or attempts to leave time-out, enforce by physically holding the child with just enough force to contain him or her, or by ending the session for that child.

3. Children should receive one warning before time-out is enforced. The frequency of time-outs tends to decrease when a warning is given. Keep warnings short and unemotional ("If you continue to shout, you'll have to go to time-out").

4. The group leader (rather than the child) should always control when a child is released from time-out.

5. Time-out works only if the environment one is leaving (often termed the "time-in" environment) is more reinforcing than the time-out area. The relative difference is obtained reinforcement between the time-in and time-out environments, and the main reason time-out is effective (Christophersen, 1987).

6. During time-out, the group leader does not touch or talk with the child.

MODELING

Group leaders should exhibit high rates of prosocial behaviors. Children learn more from what you do than what you say.

PROMPTING

Remind children of appropriate behavior by saying the following:

- "Remember your inside voice."
- "Eyes on me."
- "I need your listening ears."
- "Freeze your body."
- "Right now, it's my turn."

IGNORING

Ignoring means quickly turning away from and paying absolutely no attention to the child who shows annoying behaviors such as talking out of turn or getting out of his or her seat. Everyone in the room must ignore the misbehavior if it is to be extinguished.

REPRIMANDING

In reprimanding, express your disapproval of a child's behavior. Use "I" statements to state how the behavior adversely affects you, your feelings about it, and to suggest an alternative behavior that is acceptable to you. Remember to disapprove of the specific behavior, not the child. Reprimand privately and quietly.

RATIO OF POSITIVE TO NEGATIVE RESPONSES

Leaders should positively reinforce desired social behaviors much more frequently than they apply negative consequences for inappropriate behaviors (about a 5:1 ratio).

PROGRAMMING

If a session is dull or boring, the children will likely be disruptive. It is important to make group activities fun, enjoyable, and interesting for both you and the children.

PROXIMITY CONTROL

Children who argue, fight, or act out when together need to be physically separated from each other. For example, a leader might sit between them during the session.

NOTE HOME

Occasionally, you may need to send a note home or call the parents about a child's misbehavior in a session.

Social Skills Outcome Studies

Numerous studies have demonstrated that social skills can be taught to children. La Greca and Santogrossi (1980) evaluated a behaviorally oriented program (8 weeks) for training groups of children in social skills. The eight skills areas selected for training included smiling, greeting, joining, inviting, conversing, sharing and cooperating, complimenting, and grooming. Relative to children in attention–placebo and waiting-list control groups, elementary school children (grades 3–5) who received the training showed significant improvement in the knowledge and practice of social skills.

Rose (1986) found that children who participated in a 10-session social skills group improved in their assertiveness, empathy for others, popularity, and acceptance among their peers. Other studies have revealed not only an increase in peer acceptance (Gottman, Gonso, & Rasmussen, 1975), but a decrease in social withdrawal and aggressiveness when such behaviors were present prior to the start of the social skills training programs (Brake & Gerler, 1994; Forman, 1993).

Average effect sizes for social skills interventions fall in the moderate range across all outcome measures (Beelmann, Pfingsten, & Loesel, 1994; Schneider, 1992). When a parent-training component is added to children's social skills training, gains in children's social skills knowledge and behavior tend to be higher (Pfiffner & McBurnett, 1997). Also noteworthy is the finding that a parent-generalization component may enhance the transfer of social skills training to the school setting (Ducharme & Holborn, 1997; Pfiffner & McBurnett, 1997).

In general, recent literature has indicated that parent–child interactions as well as children's experiences within their social network contribute heavily to the development of social competence in children (Bost, Vaughn, Washington, Cielinski, & Bradbard, 1998). Notwithstanding recent advances, the question remains whether gains made in training sessions are maintained in natural settings and thus have a widespread and lasting impact (La Greca, 1993). Moreover, even in studies that produce significant gains in the treatment group's peer acceptance, about 40% of the individual children do not make gains in peer acceptance. Further investigations are needed to learn more about the mechanisms underlying the efficacy of social skills training, adapting the training to specific populations and individual child/family needs, and evaluating strategies for sustaining gains over long intervals.

CASE ILLUSTRATION: SOCIAL SKILLS MODULES

Teacher Information

Child's Name: _____

The following is information on the Social Skills Training Program in which my child is currently enrolled. The program is designed to enhance and strengthen social skills, including communication, cooperation, and problem solving. In order for the program to be most effective, children need to practice the skills continually and in many settings, especially in school. The following information is designed to let you, the teacher, know what the child is currently learning and practicing so that, if possible, you can encourage his or her skills. Since social skills are important for all children, there are also suggestions for activities that can be done with the entire class, if you so choose. Thank you *very much* for your help in this process.

WEEK 1—SKILL: CONVERSATION

Date: _____

The specific skills to be covered will include maintaining eye contact and attention, waiting your turn in conversation, answering questions, and asking questions of others.

Activity. Children can pair up and practice interviewing each other, either about personal information such as hobbies, and so on, or about a topic relevant to their current schoolwork.

WEEK 2—SKILL: GROUP ENTRY

Date: _____

Children will learn how to join an ongoing activity or conversation. This includes showing interest, waiting for an appropriate pause in activity, asking to participate, and handling rejection appropriately (by walking away and finding another activity).

Activity. Encourage children in class to invite someone to enter their group during an activity. This would include introducing the new child to the group and explaining the activity and any rules.

WEEK 3—SKILL: SMILE AND HAVE FUN!

Date: _____

According to research, children who smile are seen as more likeable by their peers and tend to have more friends. The goal is to increase the child's tendency to have fun and smile.

Activity. Each child will be given an assignment to bring a joke or a funny cartoon to share with the class. The teacher plays "stone face" and tries to maintain a poker face while the children try to make him or her laugh.

WEEK 4—SKILL: ASSERTIVENESS

Date: _____

The goal this week is to teach children to assert and stand up for themselves without acting in an aggressive manner. The children will be taught to use "I" messages that communicate their feelings or how they are being impacted, without blaming another person or fighting.

Activity. Modeling assertive, passive, and aggressive responses for children is very effective. For example, "When students are whispering to each other, I feel that I can't concentrate on what I'm teaching you, and I'll feel bad if I need to reprimand you. Thanks for stopping." Examples of passive (ignoring but getting mad) and aggressive (yelling) responses could be given in comparison.

WEEK 5—SKILL: SOCIAL PROBLEM SOLVING

Date: _____

The goal is to help children understand the conflict (about wanting the same toy, *not* about blaming another person), generate possible solutions to the problem (play together, or take turns with toy, etc.), and choose a solution to implement.

Activity. Group brainstorming solutions to "What if" problems can be about interpersonal problems ("What if you lost something you borrowed from a friend?") *or* could be tailored to an academic subject. The pros and cons of each possible solution should be discussed.

WEEK 6—SKILL: COOPERATION

Date: _____

The goal is to teach children to share and work together toward a common goal, take turns, and contribute their share of the group work.

Activity. Any game or project that requires cooperation in order to reach the goal can be used. The activity should be one that is impossible to complete if all members do not participate. For example, children could form teams in which one partner is blindfolded and the other partner needs to give directions (right, left, etc.) for the blindfolded child to reach a goal.

WEEK 7—SKILL: COMPLIMENTING

Date: _____

The children will be taught how to give and receive positive feedback, including expressing appreciation, giving praise, and encouraging others.

Activity. Modeling compliments and praise for the children is important; a possible activity could be that, for one day, every comment that an individual makes must begin with praise, compliments, and so on.

WEEK 8—SKILL: AWARENESS OF FEELINGS

Date: _____

In order for children to manage their emotions, they need to be able to understand how they feel, label their emotions, and express them to others. The goal is to help children identify the experienced feelings.

Activity. Have "feeling posters" photocopied for each child's desk and, at various points during the day, call a "Feeling moment." Have the children put a penny on the feeling they are currently experiencing. Also, a possible activity could have children (or the teacher) take turns "acting out" a feeling (using only body language and noises, no words), with everyone else tries to guess the feeling.

WEEK 9—SKILL: GOOD SPORTSMANSHIP

Date: _____

To be a good sport, children must be able to handle losing, accept constructive criticism, and tolerate making mistakes during games.

Activity. Students could discuss professional athletes who are good and bad sports. Also, the class could be divided into two teams for a competitive academic game (science or history facts, etc.), with each child practicing how to be good winners and losers, waiting their turn, and encouraging their teammates, and so on.

Session 1 (Children's Group): Conversation

After introductions, group leaders explain the purpose of the group, that is, to learn and practice some new friendly behaviors. When children get better at their friendship skills, they will enjoy themselves more when with their friends and classmates, and be more popular with their peers.

Ask the group to think up and then select a name for this friendship club of theirs. Then, with the children's input, generate a list of four to five group rules that will help make the group sessions an enjoyable and safe experience for everyone. Post the rules conspicuously on a wall.

LEARNING GOALS

• To enhance children's listening skills, including nonverbal behaviors (eye contact, close interpersonal distance (about 3 feet), forward body lean (pleasant facial expression and tone of voice), and verbal behaviors that indicate that one is attending and trying to understand (questions, noncommittal acknowledgments such as "Um hum," paraphrasing, and empathy).

• To increase children's ability to talk and hold up their end of a conversation (answer questions, engage in small talk, and self-disclose—talk about personal interests and experiences).

INSTRUCTIONS

Introduce this session to the children by explaining that they will be learning some new conversation skills that will help them better initiate conversation with each other, as well as with other children and adults. Then, describe specific behaviors that will enhance conversation, such as the following:

• *Eye contact.* Show your interest in the other person by looking at him or her when you are talking(make eye contact) and by saying the person's name when talking to him or her.

• *Asking questions.* When you ask someone a question ("How old are you?", "What's your favorite TV show?", "Ever play this game before?"), you show that you are interested in the other person and want to learn more about him or her. Showing interest makes it more likely that the other person will like you and want to get to know you better.

• *Talking.* Answer questions asked of you with more than a one-word response. Tell about something interesting that happened to you. Wait for the other person to pause before you start talking. Do not do all the talking—others enjoy talking, too.

ACTIVITY

In dyads, children take turns interviewing each other. Group leaders prompt the types of questions they might ask each other: personal inquiries, such as age, where they live; inquiries about family, hobbies, vacation, school, television and movies, and pets. After the interview, each child tells the group what he or she learned about the person interviewed.

ALTERNATE ACTIVITY

After each child selects a puppet from a large collection, the children pretend that their puppets are having a lunchtime conversation while sitting at a table in a school cafeteria. Group leaders coach the children about appropriate lunchtime conversation, about how to draw each other into the conversation, about how to be courteous, and about being pleasant and agreeable in their comments.

ALTERNATE ACTIVITY

While the group is sitting around a table, one child starts a conversation by asking another child a question about one of the following topics: favorite movie; favorite food; place you would like to visit; person you would like to meet; pet you would like to own. The two children have a brief conversation, then ask other group members to join in by saying something on the topic (a child may say "Pass" if called upon).

HOMEWORK

Give each child a sheet with the following homework assignment.

1. Start a conversation with another child this week.

   Name of child _____
   How did you start _____
   What did the other child say? _____

2. Or try to join a group of children engaged in an activity/game. Use the following three steps in seeking to enter the activity of others:

   a. Stand nearby and observe the other children within the group.

    b. Make a few comments about their activity.

    c. Ask if you can join in the activity or game.

Name of children _____

Where _____

How did you try to join in? _____

What did the other children say or do? _____

_____

_____

Session 1 (Parent Group): Conversation

LEARNING GOAL

To inform parents how they can help their children develop better conversational skills.

INSTRUCTIONS

Children need to speak with others and communicate effectively if they are to interact successfully with their peers. Popular children tend to engage in more verbal discourse with their peers than do unpopular children. Training in conversational skills can lead to improvements in peer acceptance. Researchers have found that popular children ask questions and offer personal information more readily than unpopular children. Conversational skills that contribute to friendship formation include the following:

- Listening skills (asking questions, particularly open-ended questions that require more than a one-word response)
- Talking skills (answering another's questions, elaborating on responses, talking about interests or school activities, and sticking to the topic of conversation)
- Nonverbally attending to the other person while conversing (looking at the person, minimizing distracting movements, etc.)

ACTIVITY

Discuss with the parents ways they can instruct, prompt, reinforce, and model conversational skills for their child at home. List all the ideas on the board and ask the parents to select a few ideas to implement at home that week.

ALTERNATE ACTIVITY

To practice their own conversational skills, parent split into groups of three. One parent is designated the "talker" who shares a personal experience; another parent is the "listener" who responds to the "talker" with good verbal and nonverbal listening skills; the third parent is the "observer" who gives feedback at the end of the 5-minute exercise to the "speaker" and "listener" about ways, if any, to improve their conversational skills.

ALTERNATE ACTIVITY

To demonstrate the difference between "good" and "inadequate" social skills, parents could be shown clips from movies that demonstrate good and bad social skills and asked to identify what behaviors constitute appropriate social skills.

HOMEWORK

Explain to the parents their child's homework assignment and the need for them to monitor the homework, show interest in it, and ensure that it is brought in the following week. In addition, parents are to play the Twenty Questions Game with their child. In this game, parents pick a card with the name of an object written on it. The child tries to guess the object by asking no more than 20 questions. Parents may give children suggestions, such as whether the object is alive or not, or if it is big or little. (The goal of this activity is to give the child practice asking questions—a good conversational skill.)

Session 2 (Children's Group): Group Entry

Review the previous week's homework.

LEARNING GOAL

To improve children's ability to join an ongoing activity or conversation with their peers.

INSTRUCTIONS

Studies show that children with high social competence often attempt to enter an ongoing game by following a three- or four-step procedure. First they stand nearby and watch their peers interacting. Then, they make a positive comment about the game or the group playing ("Good shot!"; "That looks like fun!"). They may then engage in a similar activity on their own (bounce a basketball). Finally, they ask the group members if they might join in the activity.

Similarly, to join an ongoing conversation between two or more of their peers, the following is a good strategy for children to follow:

1. They look at their peers with an interested, pleasant expression on their faces and try to make eye contact.
2. They wait for a pause.
3. They say something on the topic.
4. If this initiative is ignored, they walk away with a good attitude and find someone else with whom to talk.

ACTIVITY

With puppets, have the children practice how one puppet should try to enter the ongoing play activity of two or three other puppets. Group leaders should prompt, model, and reinforce effective entry strategies.

ALTERNATE ACTIVITY: NEGATIVE MODELING

Ask the group to role-play ineffective strategies for joining a play activity of their peers, such as the following:
1. Claiming superiority over the group members ("I can do that better then you").
2. Criticizing group members.
3. Barging right in, without asking permission to play.
4. Protracted hovering about, without any attempt to enter.

ALTERNATE ACTIVITY

To teach children how to invite a peer to join an activity in which they are involved, discuss the following strategy:

1. Ask the other child if he or she would like to join in the group activity.
2. If necessary, introduce the member to others in your group.
3. Explain the activity and any rules to the new child.

Next, children role-play with the group a scenario in which they invite a peer to join in a conversation they are having with two other friends.

HOMEWORK

Have children practice joining a conversation at home or in school three times that week. Remember:

1. Use a pleasant face and voice.
2. Look at others.
3. Wait for a pause.
4. Say something on the topic.

Explain how you joined a conversation.

First time: _____

Second time: _____

Third time: _____

_____

Session 2 (Parent Group): Peer Group Entry

LEARNING GOAL

To coach parents to help their children enter ongoing activities with others.

INSTRUCTIONS

Children's entry behavior refers to how they approach and attempt to enter the ongoing activity of others, particularly their peers. The study of children's entry behavior has received more research attention then any other social skill.

Because successful entry into the peer play group is a prerequisite for further social interaction, it is clearly an important task for children to master.

One of the most effective strategies for joining a peer group activity is to follow a three- or four-step behavioral sequence:

1. *Spectator behavior.* The child quietly stands close by and watches the group activity. This initial spectator behavior allows the child to learn behaviors acceptable to the group and the group's frame of reference, so that he or she can engage in an entry behavior most likely to lead to success in joining the group.
2. *Positive comments.* The child makes a positive statement about the group or the activity.
3. *Mimicking.* The child engages in an activity similar to the group's behavior to show that he or she is interested in the activity and has the needed skills.
4. *Direct request.* The child asks the group if he or she can join in their activity.

Remember that even when children master effective entry skills, they must learn that their peers will probably not accept them immediately into the group. Often, a child must convince others of his or her merits as a play-mate. To inoculate children against the stress of having their initiations ig-nored or rejected, parents might role-play with children that the way to handle this situation is to calmly walk away and seek another activity or playmate.

ACTIVITY

Ask the parents to discuss techniques they used as children to join an ongo-ing peer activity and how they handled peer rejection.

HOMEWORK

Review with the child the steps to join an ongoing conversation with family members, without interrupting the discussion. Encourage the child to use this skill at home this week.

Session 3 (Children's Group): Smile and Have Fun!

Review the previous week's homework.

LEARNING GOAL

To increase children's tendency to smile and have fun with others. (Children who frequently smile and have fun tend to be rated as more like-able by their peers and have more friends than children lacking these be-haviors; Newcomb & Bagwell, 1995).

INSTRUCTIONS

Tell the children that the focus of today's session is to increase their ten-dency to smile and have fun.

Explain the benefits of these behaviors as (1) enjoying time with each other, (2) experiencing mutual friendships, and (3) feeling happier.

ACTIVITIES

1. *Act silly.* Each child takes turns acting like their favorite zoo animal. Other group members try to guess the name of the animal.

2. *Stone face.* A designated child tries to maintain a poker face while the other group members make silly faces and noises to try and make him or her smile. The child who refrains from laughing the longest is de-clared the winner.

3. *Tongue-twisters.* The group plays *Spit It Out*: a fast-paced,

fast-talking, tongue-twisting game. This game contains cards with 96 tongue-twisters for the children to say as often as they can, within a brief amount of time. Examples of twisters are "Three tree twigs" and "Especially suspicious spaghetti." This game is available from The Game Works, Inc., Goletta, CA 93117.

HOMEWORK

1. Select a joke from a children's joke book, and tell it to a family member and classmate. Bring the joke to the next session and share it with the group.
2. Bring in a cartoon to share with the group.
3. Wear a funny hat to group next week.

SOCIAL SKILLS HOMEWORK

Name: _____

This is my joke for the week: _____

_____

_____

_____

Session 3 (Parent Group): Smile and Have Fun!

LEARNING GOAL

To help parents understand that children's lighthearted and humorous behavior tends to increase their social acceptance.

INSTRUCTIONS

One aspect of a child's social interactions that appears to contribute to peer acceptance involves the child's enjoyment of social interactions. Children who are liked by their peers are perceived as more cheerful, as well as laughing and giggling more than disliked children. Therefore, encouraging children to smile and laugh more often during peer interactions may facilitate their social relationships.

HOMEWORK

On two or three separate days this week, parents are to spend 20 minutes playing alone with their child in a way that will bring giggles and smiles to the child's face (have a pillow fight, play piggyback, tell "Knock-Knock" jokes, etc.).

Session 4 (Children's Group): Assertiveness

Review the previous week's homework.

LEARNING GOAL

To teach children how to stand up for themselves without being aggressive or passive.

INSTRUCTION

Assertiveness can be defined as the thoughts, feelings, and behaviors that help a child obtain personal goals or defend his or her rights in a socially acceptable manner.

Children are taught to use "I statements" to assert themselves in conflict situations. The basic components of an "I message" are the following:

1. Briefly describing the behavior of concern.
2. Stating the reason why this is a problem.
3. Requesting an alternate behavior that is acceptable.
4. Showing understanding of another person's good intentions or extenuating circumstances.
5. Sharing negative feelings.

ACTIVITY

First, the leaders should model using "I messages" to handle common conflicts they encounter in daily living. Examples of an "I statement" are as follows: "When put-downs are used, I am disappointed because you're hurting each other. We can't enjoy ourselves in group when we worry about bad names being called." "Tapping your pencil is distracting to me. Thanks for stopping." Model all three common conflict resolution styles: aggressive (verbal and physical), assertive, and passive–avoidant.

Next, ask the group members to role-play being assertive in response to common conflicts with their peers, siblings, or parents:

- A friend will not play by the rules of a game.
- A friend never wants to play anything you want to play.
- A classmate cuts in front of you in line.
- A sibling takes your possession without permission.
- A parent forgets to wake you up on time in the morning.

ALTERNATE ACTIVITY

The group plays a board game designed to teach assertiveness. Example of board games are Assert with Love and The Assertion Game. Therapeutic board games are available from Childswork/Childsplay (800-962-1141).

HOMEWORK

Each child is to practice being assertive three times during the next week and to record the circumstances of each assertion.

SOCIAL SKILLS HOMEWORK

Name: _____

Situation   What I did to be assertive

_____   _____

_____   _____

_____   _____

Session 4 (Parent Group): Assertiveness

LEARNING GOAL

To teach parents how to model assertiveness for their children and to coach them in developing assertiveness skills.

INSTRUCTIONS

Explain that the best way to teach assertiveness to children is by parental example. If a child tracks mud all over the kitchen floor, parents tend to respond in one of three ways:

Aggressive: "How could you be so dumb! You made a mess of my floor. You never think about what you're doing."

Assertive: "I'm really upset. I worked so hard to clean this floor and now you've dirtied it again."

Passive/Avoidant: Parent mutters to self but says nothing directly to the child.

Describe the components of an assertive "I message" (the problem behavior; its concrete effect on you; your feelings about it) and point out how an "I message" differs from a blaming "You message" that attacks a child's personality and is likely to make the child defensive.

ACTIVITY

Parents role-play giving aggressive, assertive, and avoidant responses to problem behaviors of children (child makes a peanut butter sandwich and leaves the kitchen table a mess). For a physical altercation between siblings, an "I statement" would be as follows: "When fights occur, I'm concerned about your safety, and in this house we solve our differences peacefully without fights."

HOMEWORK

In addition to monitoring their child's homework, parents practice giving "I messages" to other family members at home.

Session 5 (Children's Group): Social Problem Solving

Review the previous week's homework.

LEARNING GOALS

To assist children in solving social conflicts by learning the five steps of effective problem solving:

- Step 1: Identify the problem.
- Step 2: Generate alternate solutions.
- Step 3: Choose the best solution.
- Step 4: Implement the solution.
- Step 5: Review solution effectiveness and revise as needed.

INSTRUCTIONS

Explain to the children what a social conflict is, and that they will learn how to solve conflicts in a more effective way. Teach them the five steps to problem solving:

Step 1. A social problem exists when there is a conflict between the needs/desires of two or more persons. If two children are fighting over possession of the same toy, the basic problem is not the fighting but the fact that two children want the same toy at the same time. To determine the source of the conflict (why they are upset), each child needs to take responsibility for his or her own actions and use assertiveness and active listening skills. Children need to learn to attack the basic problem (the conflict), not the other person (by blaming or name-calling).

Step 2. In Step 2, the focus shifts from the problem to solutions. The goal is to brainstorm possible solutions. Each child thinks of a variety of solutions to the problem by following the basic rules of brainstorming:

- No criticism of children's ideas during brainstorming.
- Quantity is wanted (at least five possible solutions).
- Piggybacking is encouraged (modifying another's idea so as to improve it).
- Wild, creative ideas are welcome.

In addition to recording their ideas, the leader suggests some possible solutions when the children are having difficulty producing them.

Step 3. Discuss the pros and cons of each solution (the consequences of each solution) so as to decide on a solution everyone agrees upon. Seek a "win–win" solution whereby each child has at least part of his or her desires met (a compromise).

Step 4. Decide who does what, when, and where in order to implement the agreed-upon solution.

Step 5. At a preestablished interval (a week or a month), all parties to the dispute meet to discuss how well the solution is working and revise it as necessary. If the solution is inappropriate, try another.

ACTIVITY: BRAINSTORMING "WHAT IF" SITUATIONS

Group leaders describe a series of common social-conflict situations in childhood:

- A peer provokes you by cheating on board games.
- Someone takes something without permission.
- You lost something you borrowed from a friend.
- You want something that is not yours.

The group brainstorms as many possible solutions to each problem situation as possible. Explain that a large number of ideas increases the chance that a successful solution will be found. List the ideas on an easel or blackboard and add a few ideas that the group does not mention. To loosen up children's thinking and make the activity more fun, suggest a "way out," completely ridiculous idea.

HOMEWORK

Describe how you applied the problem-solving method to a conflict you had at school or home this week.

SOCIAL SKILLS HOMEWORK

Name: _____

Describe the conflict _____

_____

Describe your solution _____

_____

_____

_____

Session 5 (Parent Group): Social Problem Solving

LEARNING GOAL

To review the 5-step problem-solving process.

INSTRUCTIONS

Explain that when parents articulate the problem, and face and discuss solutions with their children, the children become more aware of the significance of the problem-solving process. When effective problem-solving behaviors are modeled by parents, children emulate these behaviors.

Problem solving is a skill that can be learned and must be practiced. Outline the five steps in effective problem solving:

1. Recognize you have a problem.
2. Brainstorm a wide range of possible solutions.
3. Consider the pros and cons, and choose a good solution.
4. Plan how to carry out the solution and then implement it.
5. Review the success of the solution and modify as necessary.

Often, the most difficult of these steps is identifying the problem. If a child complains, "Alice is hitting me," the basic problem to be solved is not the hitting but, rather, *the reason* why Alice is hitting (perhaps because someone took her toy away). Therefore, the investigation of solutions must relate to the cause of the problem instead of its effect.

The process of problem solving (making choices and learning from them) is facilitated by parents who observe, listen, and ask open-ended questions that further the process. Some useful questions are as follows: "What's the problem?", "What will happen if . . . ?", "What other ways can you think of . . . ?", and "How would you feel if someone did that to you?" Remember that when parents invite "give and take" in a conflict with their child through the use of listening, reasoning, empathy, and compromise, their child tends to employ similar conflict resolution strategies with his or her peers (Crockenberg & Lourie, 1996).

Researchers have found that it is the ability to resolve conflicts quickly and amicably, not the ability to avoid conflict altogether, that distinguishes close peers relationships from other peer relationship in childhood (Carlson-Jones, 1985).

ACTIVITY

Ask a parent to role-play (using the 5-step problem-solving process) a common parent–child conflict at home.

HOMEWORK

Apply the problem-solving process with children at home this week.

Session 6 (Children's Group): Cooperation

Review the previous week's homework.

LEARNING GOAL

To teach children to share, to work together toward a common goal, to take turns, and to do their share of the group work.

INSTRUCTIONS

Explain to the group what "cooperation" means. In a cooperative situation, the combined behavior of two or more individuals is needed to reach a goal. The goal can be attained by an individual only if all the individuals involved can also attain the goal. In a competitive situation, goal attainment by one or a number of individuals precludes attainment by the remaining individuals. Many people believe that our culture suffers from a "cooperation deficiency" and, instead of cooperation, focuses on individual achievement and competition.

ACTIVITY: "CREATE A MONSTER"

Each child in the group draws part of a monster (or creature from outer space). One child draws the head, one the upper body, another the lower body, another the tail, and so on. The drawings are then taped together to form the monster and the group names the creature. Then, the group participates in an "Alternating Line Storytelling" activity involving the creature. You start the story by saying, "Once upon a time, a long, long time ago, there lived a monster named _____." Then, each child, in turn, contributes the next line to the mutual story. Each child should contribute at least two lines until the last child in the sequence gives the last line and says "The end."

ALTERNATE ACTIVITY

This 15- to 20-minute activity centers around the commercial children's game, Perfection (Milton Bradley). The game consists of a 60-second timer, a set of 25 irregularly shaped plastic pieces, and a spring-loaded platform containing a matrix of holes corresponding to the shapes of each of the plastic pieces. Players must race against time to fit as many pieces as possible into their corresponding slots in the matrix. A player may stop the clock (and the game) at any point by pushing a switch. However, if the players fail to stop the clock before time expires, the platform is sprung and all the pieces are dislodged, negating the entire effort. Two children work cooperatively with a single set of pieces, and each partner receives points commensurate with the overall success of the dyad, regardless of individual contributions (both children share equally in whatever level of success the dyad achieves). Each dyad accumulates points over three trials.

ALTERNATE ACTIVITY: "BLINDFOLD DRAWING"

Each child takes turns drawing something while blindfolded. His or her unblindfolded partner helps by giving materials, ideas, directions, and encouragement.

ALTERNATE ACTIVITIES

1. Build a tower, card house, space ship, or other structure as a group.
2. Play Pictionary in pairs (age 8 years and up).
3. Play a cooperative board or card game, such as the Teamwork board game, which fosters cooperation among members of a group. Teamwork is available from Childswork/Childsplay (800-962-1141).
4. Three children work as a team to make something out of clay, or to create a poster using markers and glitter.
5. "Mutual Storytelling": Ask three children to create a story using three random words that you give them.

HOMEWORK

Offer to help someone at home three different times this week.

SOCIAL SKILLS HOMEWORK

Name: _____

Situation 1   Help offered

_____

_____

Situation 2   Help offered

_____

_____

Situation 3   Help offered

_____

_____

Session 6 (Parent Group): Cooperation

LEARNING GOAL

To explain the skills involved in cooperation, the importance of children's cooperation with peers, and to help parents foster their child's ability to co-operate with others.

INSTRUCTIONS

Cooperation is defined as each doing his share, plus aiding or giving assistance to the others, and working together without conflict. This behavior is especially relevant for maintenance tasks around the house. Children will occasionally disagree as to whose job it is to empty the trash or put away the dishes. They will try to avoid the task, wait until others do it, or come to parents to settle the disagreement. These behaviors take time and effort, and can be avoided if children learn to help out around the house at an early age. Young children (3 to 4 years old) can help clean and set the table, put toys away, and help make their bed. Discuss specific chores that each child in the group can do at home.

Some children have difficulty cooperating with their peers because they are too bossy and used to having everything their own way. If a parent observes the child being too bossy with a playmate, he or she should talk with the child in private at a later time. The parent might say, "I don't think Sarah likes it when you insist she follow your rules every time you play together." After citing some specific example of bossy or self-centered behaviors, the parent asks the child, "How would you feel if someone spoke to you that way?" Then, the parents asks the child to think up another way to say what he or she wants without sounding quite so bossy.

Also, explain the need for parents to pay attention to and praise cooperative behaviors by their children. Have the group discuss examples of different cooperative behaviors around the house.

HOMEWORK

Complete a jigsaw puzzle by working together with your child.

Session 7 (Children's Group): Complimenting

Review the previous week's homework.

LEARNING GOAL

To teach children the importance and "how to's" of giving positive feedback ("warm fuzzies") to others as opposed to negative comments ("cold prickles").

INSTRUCTIONS

Warm fuzzies make other people feel good and include such behaviors as the following:

- *Appreciation*: Telling another person what you like about their behavior or appearance. Some examples are "I like that red sweater you are wearing"; "Mom, I like it when you bake cookies"; and "I had a good time playing with you."
- *Praise*: Telling someone that you think they did something well, such as "You really know how to make people laugh," or "You have a great jump shot!"
- *Polite comments*: "Thank you," "Please," "I'm sorry."
- *Agreeableness*: Finding something about another's remarks with which you agree.
- *Encouragement*: Offering encouragement ("You can do it").
- *Affection*: Hugs, pats on the back, saying "I love you."

ACTIVITY

Each child gives a partner a compliment that the other rejects. For example, "That shirt looks really good on you." "I hate this shirt—I had nothing else to wear today." The children then give each other a compliment which they both accept with a "Thank you" and a smile. They then discuss how it feels to have compliment accepted versus rejected.

ALTERNATE ACTIVITIES

1. Each child draws a picture, and the others then say something that they like about it.
2. Play a board game and stop at intervals so members of the group can give positive feedback to each other.
3. In dyads, one child states an opinion about something (favorite baseball team, type of animal he or she likes best, favorite television show), and the other child finds something about the first child's comments with which to agree.
4. At the end of the session, two children are designated by the leaders as "special," and the rest of the group gives compliments to them and/or ask questions to get to know them better.

HOMEWORK

Tell each member of your family what you like about him or her or his or her behavior. Do this three times for each member of your family.

SOCIAL SKILLS HOMEWORK

Name: _____

Name of family member	Appreciation (3×)
_____	_____
_____	_____
_____	_____

Session 7 (Parent Group): Complimenting

LEARNING GOAL

To explain the importance of giving positive feedback to children.

INSTRUCTION

Describe the concept and importance of being a positive person and how this increases one's attractiveness to others. Ask the parents to consider how often they give "warm fuzzies" versus "cold prickles" to their children. Ideally, parents should give five positive comments for every negative one. Discuss the main types of positive feedback (praise, appreciation), rewards (token and concrete), as well as negative feedback (criticism, put-downs, sarcasm, commands, threats, etc.)

There are three main reasons to give children positive feedback:

1. *It bolsters the children's self-esteem.* Children, like adults, like to be noticed. This kind of recognition increases their good feelings about themselves.
2. *It builds a close, warm relationship* between the parent and child.
3. *It is a method of positive discipline.* It gets children to do more of what parents want.

There are three things parents should notice in children: behaviors, ideas, and personal characteristics. For example, a parent can notice and express approval when a child helps clean off the kitchen table, or notice that the child thinks recycling is a great way to care for the environment.

What parents notice can be "big" or "little." They should try to look for *lots* of little things to notice. Often, these little things grow into bigger things. For example, recognizing children for cleaning their plates can lead to their cleaning a couple of serving dishes as well.

Giving positive feedback should not be an isolated occurrence. Rather, parents should be *continually* looking for chances to *"catch 'em being good"* whenever they are with their children. Eventually, this will become a style of relating to their children (looking for positive behaviors, ideas, and characteristics).

HOMEWORK

Parents should list the positive qualities they noticed in their child this week, and what the child did to make the parent notice them. Some qualities that parents have noticed are generosity, pride, caring, helpfulness, cleverness, creativity, and standing up for beliefs.

PARENT HOMEWORK

Characteristic	Activity	Positive feedback

Session 8 (Children's Group): Awareness of Feelings

Review the previous week's homework.

LEARNING GOAL

To help children identify the wide variety of feelings that one can experience, to assist them in identifying situations that lead to different feelings, and to discuss what happens when feelings are kept inside for a long time.

INSTRUCTIONS

Children who have difficulty managing their emotions tend to have few friends. Emotional regulation refers to the ability to modulate one's emotions in response to situational demands. Difficulty regulating emotions is evident in hot-tempered, deliberately annoying, irritable, easily frustrated, hostile, moody, and fearful behaviors.

The first step in emotional regulation is the awareness of one's emotional states and the ability to label and express them to others.

ACTIVITY

Ask each child to choose one feeling from a "Feeling Poster" (a wide variety of posters are currently on the market) and tell the group about a time he or she felt that way and why.

Then give each child a 3" × 5" card with a feeling word written on it (embarrassed, angry). Without showing the card to anyone, each child should act out the feeling (using body language and noises, no words). The other group members try to identify the feeling.

Finally, using a Post-it note with his or her name written on it, each child puts the note on the feeling (on the "Feelings Poster") he or she is experiencing at the moment. They then explain to the group why they have this feeling.

ALTERNATE ACTIVITY

Read to the group the book *I Have Feelings* (T. Berger, 1994, Human Sciences Press, New York). This is a brief, appealing book that illustrates different positive and negative feelings and the situations that precipitate them for children.

ALTERNATE ACTIVITY

Seat the children at a table and bring out a medium-size red rubber ball.

Tell the children that they will have a chance to tell others what makes them feel mad, sad, glad, scared, or whatever feeling you pick for this particular session.

You start by rolling the ball gently to a child. The child catches the ball and tells the group what makes him or her have that feeling ("I feel scared when a dog barks at me").

ALTERNATE ACTIVITY: "GOOD FEELINGS–BAD FEELINGS GAME"

Two children are seated in the center of a circle and the rest of the group members ask them, "What happened this week that felt good?" When the two children are finished describing good feelings, the group asks, "What happened this week that felt bad?" (The purpose of this game is to help children identify their feelings and link them to events in their lives).

ALTERNATE ACTIVITY

Cut out pictures from magazines and newspapers of people (all ages) experiencing strong positive and negative emotions. Ask the children first to identify the emotion being expressed in the picture and then to try to guess why the person is feeling this way.

HOMEWORK

Write down every time this week that you feel scared. Describe what happened just before you got scared and what you did about it.

SOCIAL SKILLS HOMEWORK

Name: _____

Write down every time you get scared:

Date   What happened   What I did

_____

_____

_____

Session 8 (Parent Group): Awareness of Feelings/ Emotional Intelligence

LEARNING GOAL

To increase parents' awareness of their role in developing their child's "emotional intelligence" (EQ).

INSTRUCTIONS

EQ refers to the ability to recognize feeling states in oneself and others, and to control the expression of one's emotions. This ability plays a major role in determining one's success and happiness in all aspects of life. The components of EQ are as follows:

1. *Awareness of feeling states* in self and others. This means tuning in to the body sensations of different feelings in oneself, and empathically putting oneself in another's shoes to imagine what they are feeling at the moment.
2. *Emotional understanding*, the ability to (a) connect feelings to antecedent events (the triggers that produce an emotional reaction, such as feeling sad after losing a ball game); and (b) anticipate how one's emotional reactions will affect future behaviors toward self and others.
3. *Emotional control*, the ability to moderate and control the intensity of one's emotional reactions (feelings and behaviors) by use of such self-control coping strategies as the following:
   - *Catharsis* (emotional release of psychological and physical tension by pounding a pillow, crying, tearing up a newspaper, etc.).
   - *Relaxation* (deep breathing, tense and relax muscle groups).
   - *Imagery* (picturing a calm, comforting place).
   - *Positive self-talk* (calming self-statements).
   - *Physical activity* (going for a walk, shooting hoops, etc.).

EMOTIONS COACHING

Researchers have discovered that parents fall into one of two categories: (1) They give their children guidance about emotions ("emotions coaches"), they reflect and validate their children's emotions, and they are empathic to their children's emotional reactions; or (2) they do not give any substantial guidance in this area.

Research has also indicated that children whose parents coach them on emotions are better off in academics, social competence, emotional well-being, and physical health.

There are five main components of "emotions coaching":

1. Be aware of the child's emotions. Tune in to both the verbal and nonverbal ways children express their emotions.
2. Recognize that negative emotions (anger, fearfulness, anxiety, jealousy) are opportunities for teaching. Help the child express and control their feelings before they escalate and explode. Do not ignore, trivialize, criticize, or punish the expression of negative emotions.

3. Help children verbally label their emotions ("You seem a little bored today"; "You're feeling proud because you worked hard and got a lot done today"). Labeling feelings gives children a sense of being able to cope with them. Studies show that the act of labeling emotions can have a calming effect on the nervous system and help children recover more quickly from upsets.

4. Listen empathically and validate the child's feelings. For instance, if the child is upset about being teased at school, you might say, "I can understand why that would make you feel sad. That's how I feel when people are mean to me." Do not invalidate the feeling with comments such as "That's really nothing to be upset about. Don't let it bother you."

In regard to ambivalent feelings, at about age 7, children can recognize conflicting emotions, so parents can help them understand that it is OK to feel two ways at once ("I imagine you're excited about sleeping over at Marie's house and a little scared too?")

5. Set limits on emotional expression while helping the child problem-solve to find more constructive ways of handling emotionally charged situations ("You brother is not for hitting! What else can you do instead when you are angry at him?")

ACTIVITY: EMOTIONAL AWARENESS

The ability to describe personal emotional experiences (recalling and describing emotional situations) is central to controlling emotional reactions. Knowledge here can lead to better control. For example, self-awareness of sadness can lead to changes in one's thoughts or situations.

Ask the following questions to start a group discussion of emotional awareness.

- "Tell about a time when you felt happy, sad, angry, excited, or loved."
- "How do you know when your child is feeling happy, sad, angry, scared, or jealous?" (body language, empathy)
- "How do you help children tune in to their emotional states?"

Session 9 (Children's Group): Good Sportsmanship

Review the previous week's homework.

Before the end of this week's session, inform the children that there will be a party at the last social skills session the following week, with the parents and children together. Ask them what they think they need for a good party. Write down all suggestions for food, drink, and games in categories on the board for all to see. Then, ask the children to help you narrow the list down to a manageable size. Tell them what you (group leaders) are willing to bring and ask them to volunteer and sign up for the remaining items. Items that do not receive a signature are eliminated.

LEARNING GOAL

To help children understand the concept of good sportsmanship.

INSTRUCTIONS

A good sport is someone who accepts victory or defeat graciously and does not cheat at games. To become a good sport, one must handle the stresses of competitive play, such as losing a game, making mistakes and bad choices when playing, waiting one's turn, and accepting constructive criticism so as to improve one's competence at play.

Some effective ways to handle frustration and stress without losing one's temper or becoming upset are as follows:

1. *Relaxation responses:*
   - Take deep breaths, hold to count of three, release slowly. Repeat two or three times.
   - Count to ten before responding.

2. *Self-talk.* Ask the group to generate and practice saying some comforting self-statements, such as the following:
   - "Stay cool."
   - "I can handle this."
   - "It's OK to lose."
   - "This is helpful advice."

3. *Identifying irrational beliefs.* Help the group examine common irrational beliefs, including the following:
   - "I have to be perfect at everything."
   - "Things *must* go my way!"
   - "It's *awful* to lose or fail!"

4. *Suggest more rational thoughts such as the following:*
   - "It doesn't matter if I win or lose, as long as I try my best."
   - "If I make a mistake, people won't think I'm a failure."
   - "Having a good time with friends is more important than winning a game."

ACTIVITIES

1. Play a competitive game, such as Chinese checkers, and encourage the children to compliment the game winner.
2. Play a game involving waiting turns, such as Trouble or Jenga, and compliment group members who quietly and patiently wait their turn.
3. Have a group discussion of professional athletes who have demonstrated poor sportsmanship during a game.

HOMEWORK

Describe a time this week when you were a "good sport" when playing a game.

SOCIAL SKILLS HOMEWORK

Name: _____

Situation: _____

I was a good sport because I _____

Session 9 (Parent Group): Good Sportsmanship

Before the end of this session, inform the parents that there will be a party for the last social skills session, with parents and children meeting together. Explain that the children will be signing up to bring "goodies" to the party, and ask for the parents' cooperation in bringing the treats their children have agreed to provide.

LEARNING GOAL

To help parents understand the importance of developing good sportsmanship in their children.

INSTRUCTION

Children like to play with other children who are good sports and are able to do things such as keeping a good attitude even when losing a game, after making a poor move while playing, or during other frustrating events.

Children who can cope well with stress and frustration tend to be better sports. Children can cope with frustration without becoming unduly upset in three ways:

1. Relaxation responses
2. Positive self-talk
3. Changing irrational beliefs

[See "Session 9 (Children's Group)" for a description of these coping skills.]

Ask the parents to discuss ways they teach children to be good sports when playing games with them (modeling, prompting, coaching, reinforcing good sportsmanship, and ending the game if they continue to act like poor sports after one warning by the parent).

Session 10 (Children and Parents Together): Wrap-Up

Review the previous week's homework.

To review children's progress in social skills development and to encourage further work in this area.

At the start of the final session, the group leaders ask the children to complete a self-evaluation form (Appendix 12.2) entitled "How Am I Doing with Being a Better Friend *Outside* the Group?" A group leader discusses with each child the completed self-evaluation, commends progress both within the session and outside, and helps the child identify skills that need further improvement. A group leader also meets with each child's parents during the final session to give feedback about the child's progress and to offer recommendations about further growth in social skills.

During the party, a certificate ("Good Player Award") is presented to each child in recognition of hard work in learning new ways of getting along with and playing well with others.

CONCLUSION

The primary objectives of this short-term social skills program are to enhance children's social knowledge, help children translate their concepts into skillful interpersonal behaviors, and foster skill maintenance and generalization of the children's social competence.

Using an active and direct teaching approach, group leaders coach children in social skills within a group format of fun and games. Generalization of the social skills is promoted by the use of homework assignments and by training the children's parents to be social skill coaches in the home environment.

REFERENCES

Achenbach, T., & Edelbrock, C. (1991). *Manual for the Child Behavior Checklist and revised Child Behavior Profile.* Burlington, VT: University of Vermont, Department of Psychiatry.

Baumrind, D. (1978). Parental disciplinary patterns and social competency in children. *Youth and Society, 9,* 239–276.

Beelmans, A., Pfingsten, U., & Loesel, F. (1994). Effects of training social competence in children: A meta-analysis of recent evaluation studies. *Journal of Clinical Child Psychology, 23,* 260–271.

Bost, K., Vaughn, B., Washington, W., Newell, W., Cielinski, K., & Bradbard, M. (1998). Social competence, social support, and attachment: Demarcation of construct domains, measurement, and paths of influence for preschool children attending Head Start. *Child Development, 69*(1), 192–218.

Brake, K. J., & Gerler, E. R. (1994). Discovery: A program for fourth and fifth grades identified as discipline problems. *Elementary School Guidance and Counseling, 28,* 170–181.

Carlson-Jones, D. C. (1985). Persuasive appeals and responses to appeals among friends and acquaintances. *Child Development, 56,* 757–763.

Christophersen, E. R. (1987). *Little people: A common-sense guide to child rearing* (3rd ed.). Kansas City, MO: Westport.

Combs, S. L., & Slaby, D. A. (1977). Social skills training with children. In B. B. Lahey & A. E. Kazdin (Eds.), *Advances in Clinical Child Psychology* (Vol. 1, pp. 161–203). New York: Plenum Press.

Cowen, E. L., Pederson, A., Babijian, H., Izzo, L. D., & Trost, M. (1973). Long-term follow-up of early detected vulnerable children. *Journal of Consulting and Clinical Psychology, 41,* 438–446.

Crockenberg, S., & Lourie, A. (1996). Parents' conflict strategies with children and children's conflict strategies with peers. *Merrill–Palmer Quarterly, 42,* 495–518.

Dishion, T. J. (1990). The family ecology of boys' peer relations in middle childhood. *Child Development, 61,* 874–892.

Dodge, K. A., Pettit, G. S., McClaskey, C. L., & Brown, M. (1986). Social competence in children. *Monographs of the Society for Research in Child Development, 51*(2, Serial No. 213, pp. 1–85).

Draper, T., Larsen, J., & Rowles, R. (1997). Developmentally appropriate parent training for families with young children. *Early Childhood Research Quarterly, 12,* 487–504.

Ducharme, D., & Holborn, S. (1997). Programming generalization of social skills in preschool children with hearing impairments. *Journal of Applied Behavior Analysis, 30,* 639–651.

Easterbrooks, M. A., & Lamb, M. E. (1979). The relationship between quality of infant–mother attachment and infant competence in initial encounters with peers. *Child Development, 50,* 380–387.

Finnie, V., & Russell, A. (1988). Preschool children's social status and their mothers' behavior and knowledge in the supervisory role. *Developmental Psychology, 24,* 789–801.

Forman, S. G. (1993). *Coping skills interventions for children and adolescents.* San Francisco: Jossey-Bass.

Franz, D. Z., & Gross, A. M. (1996). Parental correlates of socially neglected, rejected, and average children. *Behavior Modification, 20,* 170–182.

Gottman, J., Gonso, J., & Rasmussen, B. (1975). Friendships in children. *Child Development, 46,* 709–718.

Guevremont, D. (1990). Social skills and peer relationship training. In R. A. Barkley, *Attention-deficit hyperactivity disorder: A handbook for diagnosis and treatment* (pp. 540–572). New York: Guilford Press.

Harper, L. V., & Huie, K. S. (1985). The effects of prior group experience, age, and familiarity on the quality and organization of preschoolers social relationships. *Child Development, 56,* 704–717.

Hart, C. H., DeWolf, M., Wozniak, P., & Burts, D. C. (1992). Maternal and paternal disciplinary styles: Relations with preschoolers playground behavioral orientations and peer status. *Child Development, 63,* 879–892.

Hartup, W. W. (1992). *Having friends, making friends, and keeping friends: Relationships as educational contexts.* Urbana, IL: Eric Clearinghouse on Elementary and Early Childhood Education. ED 345-854.

Kohn, M. (1977). *Social competence, symptoms, and underachievement in childhood: A longitudinal perspective.* Washington, DC: Winston.

Ladd, G. W., & Golter, B. S. (1988). Parents management of preschoolers peer relations: Is it related to children's social competence? *Developmental Psychology, 24,* 109–117.

Ladd, G. W., & Hart, C. H. (1992). Creating informal play opportunities: Are parents' and preschoolers interactions related to children's competence with peers? *Developmental Psychology, 28,* 1179–1187.

Ladd, G. W., & Mize, J. (1983). A cognitive–social learning model of social skill training. *Psychological Review, 90,* 127–157.

Ladd, G. W., Profilet, S. M., & Hart, C. H. (1992). Parents' management of children's peer relations: Facilitating and supervising children's activities in the peer culture. In R. D. Parke & G. W. Ladd (Eds.), *Family–peer relationships: Modes of linkage* (pp. 215–253). Hillsdale, NJ: Erlbaum.

La Greca, A. M. (1993). Social skills training with children: Where do we go from here? *Journal of Clinical Child Psychology, 22,* 288–298.

La Greca, A. M., & Santogrossi, D. (1980). Social skills training with elementary school students: A behavioral group approach. *Journal of Consulting and Clinical Psychology, 48,* 220–227.

Laird, R. D., Pettit, G. S., Mize, J., & Lindsey, E. (1994). Mother–child conversations about peers: Contributions to competence. *Family Relations, 43,* 425–432.

MacDonald, K. B., & Parke, R. D. (1984). Bridging the gap: Parent–child play interaction and interactive competence. *Child Development, 55,* 1265–1277.

Madsen, C. H., Becker, W. C., & Thomas, D. R. (1968). Rules, praise and ignoring: Elements of elementary classroom control. *Journal of Applied Behavior Analysis, 1,* 139–150.

Masten, A. S., & Coatsworth, J. D. (1998). The development of competence in favorable and unfavorable environments. *American Psychologist, 53*(2), 205–220.

McFall, R. (1982). A review and reformulation of the concept of social skills. *Behavioral Assessment, 4,* 1–33.

Mize, J., & Pettit, G. S. (1997). Mother's social coaching, mother–child relationship style, and children's peer competence: Is the medium the message? *Child Development, 68,* 312–332.

Newcomb, A. F., & Bagwell, C. (1995). Children's friendship relations: A meta-analytic review. *Psychological Bulletin, 117,* 306–347.

Oden, S. L., & Asher, S. R. (1977). Coaching low-accepted children in social skills: A follow-up sociometric assessment. *Child Development, 48,* 496–506.

Parker, J. G., & Asher, S. R. (1987). Peer relations and later personal adjustment: Are low-accepted children at risk? *Psychological Bulletin, 102,* 357–389.

Pettit, G. S., Brown, E. G., Mize, J., & Lindsey, E. (1998). Mothers' and fathers' socializing behaviors in three contexts: Links with children's peer competence. *Merrill–Palmer Quarterly, 44*(2), 173–193.

Pettit, G. S., Clawson, M. A., Dodge, K. A., & Bates, J. E. (1996). Stability and change in peer-rejected status: The role of child behavior, parenting, and family ecology. *Merrill–Palmer Quarterly, 42,* 267–294.

Pfiffner, L. J., & McBurnett, K. (1997). Social skills training with parent generalization: Treatment effects for children with attention deficit disorders. *Journal of Consulting and Clinical Psychology, 65,* 749–757.

Pfiffner, L. J., Rosen, L. A., & O'Leary, S. G. (1985). The efficacy of an all-positive approach to classroom management. *Journal of Applied Behavior and Analysis, 18,* 257–261.

Putallaz, M. (1987). Maternal behavior and children's sociometric status. *Child Development, 58,* 324–340.

Rose, S. R. (1986). Enhancing the social relationship skills of children: A comparative study of group approaches. *School Social Work Journal, 10,* 76–85.

Rushton, J. P. (1976). Socialization and the altruistic behavior of children. *Psychological Bulletin, 83,* 898–913.

Russell, A., & Finnie, V. (1990). Preschool children's social status and maternal instructions to assist group entry. *Developmental Psychology, 26,* 603–611.

Schneider, B. H. (1992). Didactic methods for enhancing children's peer relations: A quantitative review. *Clinical Psychology Review, 12,* 363–382.

Slavin, R. E. (1983). When does cooperative learning increase student achievement? *Psychological Bulletin, 94,* 429–445.

Sroufe, L. A., Carlson, E., & Shulman, S. (1993). The development of individuals in relationships: From infancy through adolescence. In D. C. Funder, R. Parke, C. Tomlinson, & K. Widaman (Eds.), *Studying lives through time: Approaches to personality and development* (pp. 315–342). Washington DC: American Psychological Association.

Travillion, K., & Snyder, J. (1993). The role of maternal discipline and involvement in peer rejection and neglect. *Journal of Applied Developmental Psychology, 14*, 37–57.

Vandell, D., & Hembree, S. (1994). Peer social status and friendship: Independent contributors to children's social and academic adjustment. *Merrill–Palmer Quarterly, 40*, 461–481.

Walker, H. M., Schwarz, I., Nippold, M., Irvin, L., & Noell, J. (1994). Social skills in schoolage children and youth. *Topics in Language Disorders, 14*, 70–82.

Yalom, I. D. (1985). *The theory and practice of group psychotherapy.* New York: Basic Books.

APPENDIX 12.1.
SOCIAL SKILLS ASSESSMENT: CHILD INTERVIEW

The general purpose of the interview is to assess the child's ability to interact in three areas: family, school, and friends. The following is a list of suggested questions to aid in gathering relevant information.

Home Life

Whom do you live with?
How many brothers/sisters do you have? How old are they?
Tell me about them.
How do you get along with Mom and Dad? Brothers/sisters?
Do you like being at home with everyone?
Do they ever do anything you don't like?
Who are you closest to at home?
Who's the boss at home?
What happens when you do something the boss doesn't like?
Is there anything going on at home that you worry about?

Social

How many friends do you have?
How do you get along together? Do you ever get into fights?
Do you ever have your friends over to visit or get together with them outside of school?
What kind of things do you do together?
What do you like best/dislike about your friends?
Would you rather play with friends, or on your own with toys?

School

How do you like school? What grade are you in?
How are you doing in school now?
How do you get along with your teachers and classmates?
What subjects do you like most or least?

General

What is the best/worst thing that ever happened to you?
Do you think you're mostly sad/happy/mad?
What kinds of things make you happy?
What's your happiest memory?
Do you ever get really mad?   (*continued*)

APPENDIX 12.1. (*continued*)

What kinds of things make you angry?
What do you do when you're feeling mad?
What about feeling sad?
What usually happens that makes you feel sad?
What do you do when you feel that way?
What do you like best/least about yourself?
Do you have a special boyfriend/girlfriend? Tell me about him/her.

Motivation for Group

Are you interested in attending our social skills group? If yes, why?
What do you want to get out of attending the group?

After the interview, briefly play a table game (Connect Four, checkers) to observe the child's ability to take turns, sustain attention to a task, handle frustration, and inhibit impulses.

APPENDIX 12.2. SELF-EVALUATION FORM

How Am I Doing with Being
a Better Friend *Outside* the Group?

Instructions: For each skill named, rate how well you feel you are doing now that you have completed the group.

Skill	A lot better	A little better	Not at all better
Conversation			
Group entry			
Smiling and having fun			
Assertiveness			
Social problem solving			
Cooperation			
Complimenting			
Awareness of feelings			
Good sportsmanship			

13

A Play-Based Teen Parenting Program to Facilitate Parent–Child Attachment

SUE A. AMMEN

INTRODUCTION

Adolescent parenthood is a challenging task even if the teen is emotionally mature and has sufficient economic and social support. The vast majority of adolescents have neither the developmental maturity nor the environmental support needed to negotiate the responsibilities of parenthood in ways that do not place their babies at substantial emotional, behavioral, and physical risk. Reviews of the recent literature on adolescent parenting indicate that, as a group, adolescent parents are at greater risk than adult parents to engage in abusive parenting interactions or to be neglectful of their infants' emotional needs (Bavolek, 1990; East & Felice, 1996; Flanagan, McGrath, Meyer, & Garcia Coll, 1995; Passino et al., 1993; Saker & Neuhoff, 1982). They tend to be less sensitive about recognizing their baby's cues, and even when they do recognize them, they often do not respond appropriately because of their limited understanding of child development. They are less verbal with their babies, and their play interactions are less child sensitive. McAnarney, Lawrence, Riccuiti, Plooey, and Szilagyi (1986) described adolescent interaction styles as more like prodding and poking than the reciprocal interactive behaviors seen between a sensitive parent and infant.

The stressors associated with pregnancy and parenting before completing their own development often leave adolescent parents poorly prepared to deal effectively with their children's developmental needs.

> As a result of their asynchronous developmental transition, adolescent mothers [and fathers] are exposed to increased stress which may be detrimental to their well-being and that of their children. Teenage mothers [and fathers] must cope not only with the stressors of adolescence, but also stressors associated with pregnancy and parenthood. These transactions occur at a time when their personal resources for coping with stress are still developing. (Passino et al., 1993, pp. 97–98)

In order to develop a sense of competence in the maternal (or paternal) role, a parent must be able to perceive the child's viewpoint or experience, so that a mutually satisfying relationship can develop between them (Mercer, 1986). This is a significant problem for adolescent parents, because they are normally at a developmental stage in which their thought processes and social awarenesses are egocentric and peer oriented. The teen mother may be able to recognize and meet the infant's needs as long as the infant's needs match her needs to be an all-giving caregiver whose role in life now has a definition. This cognitive and emotional shift becomes more challenging, though, when the child begins to talk and walk and assert his or her needs to move toward greater autonomy and self-definition. This is threatening to the teen mother's self-identity, as well as requiring more complex parenting skills. It is during this period that the teen mother may be at greater risk to have a second baby.

Some adolescent parents are able to negotiate the transition to parenthood successfully. Careful review of the research literature reveals that when adequate social support and socioeconomic resources are available, there are fewer differences between the parental behaviors of teenage mothers and adult mothers (East & Felice, 1996). However, most adolescent parents experience isolation from their peer support group and have limited socioeconomic resources because they have not yet completed their education. This often requires the teen parent to seek emotional and economic assistance from his or her family, which is in conflict with the normal adolescent developmental task of moving toward more independent functioning.

> When pregnancy occurs during adolescence, the typical drive of moving from a more dependent relationship to a more autonomous position is disrupted. An adolescent feels more ambivalent about leaving her [or his] environmental supports and the security of her [his] family, which only adds to the conflict and anxiety of the situation. (Saker & Neuhoff, 1982, p. 108)

If the teen parent and infant are living with the extended family, there may be additional conflicts about who is the baby's emotional mother and who decides how this baby should be parented.

Adolescent parents need support and guidance to learn how to engage in healthy parent–child interactions and to respond in nonpunitive, developmentally appropriate ways in managing their children's behavior. Osofsky, Hann, and Peebles (1993) identify adolescent parenthood as a period of both risks and opportunities, and point out several critical areas that are important in designing interventions for adolescent parents. These include building a trusting relationship with the teen parent, specifically teaching the teen parent how to tune in to the baby's feelings and cues, helping the teen parent recognize and accept the child as an individual, and facilitating the teen's development of his or her own identity. Many interventions that target the early parent–child relationship have utilized home visiting programs over several months (Barclay & Houts, 1995). This chapter is about a short-term, play-based group intervention program that targets the special needs of low-income adolescent parents from diverse cultures.

The Attachment Teen Parenting Program (ATPP) is a 10-week parenting program for teen parents and their babies, ages 1 month to 2 years. The program targets the teen parents' parenting skills and developmental knowledge of their infant children, emphasizes appropriate parent–child interaction from the perspective of attachment theory, and addresses the parents' inner working model of attachment and emerging identity as fathers or mothers within their unique familial and cultural contexts. It differs from many parenting programs in three key ways. First, the content is structured around attachment constructs rather than specific parenting skills. Second, parents and babies are included in the classes, thereby allowing for direct teaching of behaviors and concepts, coaching and modeling by facilitators and the other teen parents, and opportunities to provide immediate feedback. Third, the curriculum is largely experiential and playful.

The theoretical foundation for the ATPP includes a solid understanding of parent–child attachment, adolescent development, infant development, the sociocultural context of parent–child attachment, and the multifaceted problems faced by adolescent parents. The curriculum is organized around the attachment promoting play therapy principles found in Theraplay (Jernberg, 1979; Koller & Booth, 1997). Before moving to a description of the ATPP, attachment, infant development, adolescent development, and sociocultural context are discussed in more detail. This provides both the theoretical foundation for the curriculum that follows and provides references to the key resources used to train others in the curriculum.

Parent–Child Attachment

The quality of parent–child attachment is increasingly recognized as a critical variable in an individual's future social and emotional adjustment (Ainsworth, 1989; Atkinson & Zucker, 1997; Bowlby, 1988; Bretherton,

1992; Colin, 1996; Hartup, 1989; Karen, 1994). Children who experience disruptions or distortions in their attachment relationships tend to have difficulty relating to others, regulating their emotional states and their behavior, and communicating their feelings, which may result in self-destructive or socially destructive behaviors.

The quality of the attachment relationship includes both the experience of the relationship based on actual interactions and participants' "internal working model" of themselves and the relationship (Ammen & York, 1994; Lyons-Ruth & Zeanah, 1993). The interactions between the parent and child lead the child to experience an internal sense of security, which is called a "secure base" (Ainsworth, Blehar, Waters, & Wall, 1978). When the child is very young, this sense of security is directly tied to the physical presence of one or more caregivers with whom the child feels attached. Bowlby (1982) identified two parental variables as strongly related to the development of a secure attachment. The first is responsiveness to the child's signals of his or her feelings and needs, that is, empathic attunement. The second is mutually enjoyable interactions between a parent and child.

As the child matures, this sense of security becomes internalized, and the child is able to move away from the parent to explore his or her world as long as he or she feels safe. The more secure the child feels, the more he or she is able to use the parent as a source of comfort and enjoyment, and as a base from which to explore the world. Furthermore, this sense of security creates in the child a sense of him- or herself as valued, capable, and loved. This experience of security in his or her relationship with a parent also contributes to the child's ability to establish healthy social relationships with others. Thus, the quality of the parent–child relationship, that is, the experience of attachment security, contributes to the child's sense of self, sense of the world, and sense of relationships with others. In other words, quality of attachment is related to development of self-identity, autonomous functioning, and interpersonal intimacy.

As the child begins to develop language, this parent–child relationship typically develops into what Bowlby (1982) called a "goal-corrected partnership." The child begins to acquire insight into the parent's motives and feelings, and the parent and child enter into a partnership dance that involves a two-way communication of feelings, needs, and goals. This is a challenging developmental shift that requires, in one mother's words, "the parenting shift from being the all-nurturing, comforting, loving, mother-presence . . . to setting limits, from giving of myself unstintingly to modeling that mothers also have needs that need to be considered and honored" ("Between the Lines," 1993, p. 2). Oppositional behavior is a normal developmental process during this time. Hughes (1997) describes the importance of "attachment sequences" in responding to this developmental stage.

In healthy parent–child relationships there are countless sequences during the child's second year of life in which the child briefly leaves the felt sense of being securely and joyfully attached with his [or her] parent to some behavioral choice that elicits parental disapproval and instigates the experience of personal shame. In healthy families each such sequence quickly leads back to reunion with the parent that affirms that such shameful experiences have no impact on the ongoing security of the attachment. Because of these experiences, the child manages to actively develop his [or her] sense of autonomy, including a healthy sense of shame, while continuing to be secure in a crucially important attachment. (p. 204)

The critical components of the attachment sequence are parental response to the behavior and underlying feelings with empathy and matter-of-fact consequences, followed by reestablishment of a positive and affirming atmosphere toward the child. The more the parent takes the child's viewpoint into account when dealing with him or her, the faster the rate of development of the child's capacity to grasp the viewpoint of the parent (Light, 1979). Through this process, the child learns to identify and communicate feelings, to modulate or regulate those feelings, to communicate needs and desires, and to recognize others' needs and feelings.

The parent's ability to respond to the child's needs appropriately depends in large part on the internal working model that parent has developed of him- or herself as a parent. Three factors contribute to this internal model: (1) the parent's own experiences as a child in relationship with his or her parents; (2) the parent's current experience as a parent with his or her own child or children, and (3) the parent's understanding of those relationships, both past and present. In other words, if a parent had negative or disruptive parent–child experiences when growing up and has not resolved or come to an understanding of those experiences, he or she is likely to negatively affect the current parent–child relationship (Crowell & Feldman, 1988; Main, Kaplan, & Cassidy, 1985). Most adolescent parents have not yet completed the transition from child to adult in their own relationships with their parents. An adolescent parent under age 18 is in the eyes of the law still considered to be a minor child unless he or she has been emancipated. This requires a consideration of the teen parent's attachment relationship with his or her parents not only as an internal model of past experiences but also as situated in his or her immediate experience.

Infant Development

The focus of this section is not to review infant development in general, as there are many well-written books available that address this topic. Rather, some resources are briefly mentioned that have been found to be particularly useful in the development of this parenting program. Brazelton's

(1992) book *Touchpoints* covers emotional and behavioral development from pregnancy through 3 years of age. He identifies "touchpoints" as

> predictable times that occur just before a surge of rapid growth in any line of development—motor, cognitive, or emotional—when, for a short time, the child's behavior falls apart. Parents can no longer rely on past accomplishments. The child often regresses in several areas and becomes difficult to understand. Parents lose their own balance and become alarmed. . . . When seen as normal and predictable, these periods of regressive behavior are opportunities to understand the child more deeply and to support his or her growth, rather than to become locked into a struggle. (pp. xvii–xviii)

Stern's (1990a) book *Diary of a Baby* provides a powerful description of the infant's experience from the infant's perspective. This book is based on his extensive scholarly works on the development of the infant's sense of self through interactions with the interpersonal world (Stern, 1985, 1995). The following is an excerpt describing the experience of hunger for a 6-week-old baby named Joey.

> *A Hunger Storm: 7:20 a.m.* "A storm threatens. Uneasiness spreads from the center and turns into pain. The world is disintegrating." It is 4 hours since Joey's last feeding, and he is probably hungry. Suddenly his lower lip protrudes. He starts to fret. Soon the fretting gives way to jerky crying, then moves into a full cry. . . . Joey's full cry helps deal with the hunger in two ways: It is a beautifully designed signal . . . to alert his parents to his distress and to demand a response from them. At the same time, it may help him modulate the intensity of the hunger sensation. Hunger, thus, creates in Joey ways to reach the outside world, and to cope with the one on the inside. (Stern, 1990b, pp. 54–55)

First Feelings by Greenspan and Thorndike Greenspan (1985) describes how infants and young children develop their abilities to engage in emotional communication over the first 4 years of life, as well as what parents can do to support this emotional development. They identify six emotional milestones (pp. 4–6):

1. During the first 3 months of life, babies must learn to feel regulated and calm, and to use all of their senses to take an interest in the world. The first milestone is the ability to organize these sensations, to feel tranquil in spite of them, and to reach out actively for them.
2. The second milestone is taking a highly specialized interest in the human world. The human world is experienced as the most enticing, pleasurable, and exciting of all experiences.
3. The third milestone emerges when the baby "says," "Love alone is not enough—I now want a dialogue." As early as 3 months of age,

a baby can enter into a dialogue with his or her parent through reciprocal interactions. A smile is in response to a smile and produces a smile or sound in response.

4. Around 9–12 months, babies learn to connect small units of feeling and social behavior into more complex patterns of behavior that include wishes, intentions, and feelings.

5. The fifth milestone begins around age 18 months, when babies can now create an image of their mother or father in their minds even when the parent is not there. This allows the infant the ability to create ideas and represent his or her world internally. Emotions and ideas are better integrated, allowing for increasingly better control of impulses.

6. The sixth milestone begins around 30 months of age and leads to a full integration of emotions, desires, and cognitive understanding, such that a child can begin to plan, anticipate, problem-solve, set his or her own limits, and experience empathic understanding of another person's experience.

These milestones provide a detailed understanding of the processes involved in the development of the goal-corrected partnership dance between baby and parents.

The Process of Parenting (Brooks, 1991) provides not only in-depth chapters on infancy and toddlerhood, but also a general integration of parenting that brings together both the nurturing and the structuring dimensions as they are embedded in the parent–child relationship. Brooks identifies the two basic tasks of parenting as creating close emotional relationships and establishing effective limits. She also addresses the developmental processes by which parents also grow and change in their own understandings as they learn to parent their children.

Adolescent Development

> Adolescence is a period in life in which critical psychological changes occur. It is a time when character, a person's customary way of being in the world, crystallizes, and identity, the stable sense of who a person is, forms. It is the time that a fundamental psychological issue—achieving an independent identity, rooted in family but reaching out to the world beyond—is confronted and resolved. (Levy-Warren, 1996, p. xii)

In order to understand the ways in which becoming a parent affects an adolescent and being an adolescent affects being a parent, one needs to understand adolescent development. In general, the tasks of adolescence are the development of autonomy, competence, sexual identity, and the capacity for mature intimacy and mutuality in relationships. Major cognitive and biological changes drive these significant interpersonal and intrapsychic shifts. Adolescents develop the capacity for abstract thinking, which allows them to not only think about what is, but also what might be. For some adolescents, this is a frightening experience, as they do not see much potential or identity for themselves in the future. Sometimes, becoming a teen parent reduces, at least for a time, the need to address that anxiety. Levy-Warren (1996) describes adolescence as three separate subphases, each with its own ways of viewing the world, interpersonal focus, and dominant issues and tasks.

Early adolescence is about "decentering." The adolescent's body begins to mature physically, which produces changes in how other's react to him or her. The changing reactions of others force the adolescent to shift his or her perceptions of self and others. Cognitively, the early adolescent begins to see self and others in a more reality-based way, which leads to a derealization of both self and others, especially parents. With this comes the recognition that parents can no longer provide their perception of reality for them—adolescents must find their own identity. In order to accomplish this, the early adolescent focuses on defining how he or she is different from his or her family. If the family is responsive and attuned to the adolescent's process, it can be a secure base from which the adolescent explores this new emotional, cognitive, and social world. The adolescent looks back at childhood and compares prior images to the present: what is the same? What is different? Who am I? During this period of imbalance and struggle, he or she turns to peers for validation, though the process is superficial and without real depth, as the peers are in a similar struggle. So they wear the same clothes and wear their hair the same way and talk the same lingo as they find in this unity a tenuous sense of security.

In middle adolescence, the teen lives in the present, with little interest in childhood or adulthood. This "narcissistic" focus on the self and his or her own needs is needed to make sense of "who I am and what I feel and believe." Friendships are more differentiated, with different friendships helping middle adolescents explore different aspects of themselves. Peers are the primary source of support, identity, and feelings of worth and competence, which may create a sense of isolation from even a supportive family. Middle adolescents tend to be moody, cognitively creative, and emotionally passionate.

Late adolescence is a time of consolidation and looking toward what the future holds. Adolescents are able to see family, friends, and self in balanced and complex ways. They are less preoccupied with themselves, as they have a clearer sense of who they are. They see themselves as competent and able to engage in truly reciprocal relationships. They are able to reconnect with the family as they become aware of what they value from their parents and want in the relationship. They are able to see themselves as similar to their parents without losing themselves. Most individuals do not enter late adolescence until age 19 or later and may enter their mid-twenties before they are able to move into the developmental stage of early adulthood.

An important aspect of adolescent development is developing a sense of belonging in the larger sociocultural world and a sense of connection to cultural and familial traditions. A child obtains a sense of ethnocultural identity from the family directly and from the external world as it is interpreted by the family. In adolescence, the capacity for abstract thought and the desire to find one's place in the larger world trigger a need to develop a self-derived sense of ethnocultural identity rather than one that is simply given through familial custom or authority. Part of the late adolescent consolidation includes integration of this ethnocultural identity (Levy-Warren, 1996).

Adolescent parenthood is experienced differently depending on the stage of adolescent development, the ethnocultural and familial identification of the adolescent, and the larger sociocultural world in which that adolescent lives. Flanagan et al. (1995) studied adolescent development and transitions to motherhood using both qualitative and quantitative methods. They found that maternal role attainment was significantly related to developmental influences. The more immature the mother, the more difficulty she had in interpreting her infant's behavior and alleged motivations. Clinical interventions with teen parents should be designed with an appreciation of these developmental differences in teen parents.

Cultural Context of Parent–Child Attachment

Although attachment is a universal concept, there are fundamental cultural and ethnic differences in its manifestation. Cross-cultural studies provide countless examples of how the sociocultural structure affects, and is affected by, the behavior of the individual. This is particularly true when considering parents and children. Al-Fayez (1998) proposed that the infant's secure base attachment relationship is relatively universal in its expression, while cultural influences become more pronounced as the young child develops language and enters into the goal-corrected partnership with his or her parents and family. Research by Harwood (1992) comparing Anglo American and Puerto Rican mothers supports this idea. Both groups perceived the securely attached child as engaging in healthier and more preferred behaviors than the insecurely attached child, but they had different reasons for the preference of the securely attached child. The Anglo American mothers emphasized the qualities associated with the mainstream American ideal of individualism, such as autonomy, self-control, and activity. The Puerto Rican mothers emphasized qualities of relatedness, such as affection, dignity, respectfulness, responsiveness to the mother and others, and proximity seeking. Al-Fayez's (1998) research on parent–child attachment in Kuwaiti culture also found considerable overlap between the view of the securely attached child in the United

States and Kuwait, but the emphasis was again different. In this case, the U.S. perspective placed more emphasis on the child's monitoring and proximity seeking of the mother in comparison to the Kuwaiti perspective, which emphasized independence and sociability of the child. These differences were seen as related in large part to the more prevalent role of the extended family in Kuwait, providing an attachment network for the child so that the need for the child to maintain proximity to the mother is decreased. Similar differences are likely in minority families or teen families where there is greater involvement of the extended family in the direct caregiving functions with the child.

Zayas and Solari (1994) noted that parents' interactions with their children follow a certain system of priorities, that is, ensuring the child's physical well-being, survival, and self-maintenance as the child grows, while fostering behavioral skills that maximize cultural values. Most parents maintain a constant rationale and approach to socialization that is influenced by ethnic, racial, and cultural beliefs and values. In the United States, minority-group parents have culturally influenced developmental goals for their children, causing their reactions, perceptions, and behaviors to differ from majority-group parents. For example, many Hispanic families socialize children to behave in ways important to the family's culture, whether or not it is in accordance with the norms of the dominant culture. African American families have been found to have a bicultural perspective on parenting. That is to say, they prepare their children to live in the dominant culture that does not recognize their different cultural beliefs while also valuing and developing their African American cultural identity (Cross, 1987; Zayas & Solari, 1994). In general, nondominant culture or minority parents can be seen as having

> distinct beliefs, attitudes, values and parenting behaviors that overlap with, but are also unique from, the dominant culture in the United States. These unique features refer to basic conceptualizations such as the definition and roles of the family; parental beliefs about the determinants of development . . .; as well as what aspects of a child's development are most important (i.e., discipline vs. intelligence) and what the definition of competence is in each of these areas. . . . Most ethnic and minority parents consider what they believe and do (as divergent as it may be from dominant culture parenting norms) to be in the best interest of their children and/or their family system. (Garcia Coll, Meyer, & Brillon, 1995, p. 190)

Parenting practices, family structure, and dynamics are also affected profoundly by socioeconomic status (SES). Parents from different socioeconomic strata tend to have different ideas about parenting and about the ways in which parents perform their parenting functions (Hoff-Ginsberg & Tardif, 1995). Some of these differences are due to external environmental factors, such as the need for greater extended family involvement to provide adequate child care in low-SES families. Therefore, in addition to the primary caregiver, a child becomes attached to several significant adult relatives who are also significant sources of socialization. High-SES parents tend to see their role as fostering development through encouraging initiative and independent thought, while lower-SES parents tend to see their role as ensuring that development follows a particular culturally or socially defined path. Educational and cultural variables also contribute to these differences. Each family also has its unique way of parenting, regardless of cultural, educational, and economic status. Therefore, parenting programs designed to enhance attachment between ethnically diverse, low-income teen parents and their children must be sensitive to the influences of the cultural and familial belief systems and the very real impact of limited economic resources.

Theraplay Principles

Theraplay is an attachment-promoting play therapy approach that is modeled on the healthy interactions between parents and their children (Jernberg, 1979). The principles underlying the Theraplay method are found in the basics of the mother–infant relationship during the first 18 months of the infant's life.

0–4 Months

During the first four months, the mother's sensitivity enables her to respond to her baby's needs. The baby contributes his or her share to the process by crying, smiling, babbling, and sucking. The baby learns that the world can respond to his or her needs.

4–8 Months

The interaction becomes much more a two-way street. The mother and baby begin the give and take of interactive play. The baby learns that she or he can make a difference, can influence the mother to respond to needs. The baby's view of self as a competent, attractive being is developing. The mother's view of herself as a competent, loving parent is increasing.

9–18 Months

Although it starts earlier, clear evidence of discriminated attachment appears during this period. The baby cries in the presence of strangers and clings to the primary caretaker. In the mother's presence the baby feels safe to explore the environment, returning to her side periodically as to a secure base. . . . The parent's presence acts as a source of safety, comfort, and calmness. (Koller & Booth, 1997, p. 208)

Jernberg (1979, 1993) identified the four essential dimensions of these attachment–enhancing behaviors as *structuring, challenging, intruding/engaging,* and *nurturing,* which form the acronym SCIN in recognition that these behaviors occur in a context that includes nurturing and playful physical interactions involving touch.

Structuring refers to those things that a caregiving adult does to provide a safe, orderly, understandable environment for the child. This includes structuring the environment so that the child is safe and feels safe, as well as structuring and guiding the child's behavior so that the child learns the expectations of his or her world. Examples of structuring activities include baby-proofing the house, clearly stated safety rules, and games or activities that have a beginning, middle, and an end.

Challenging is about stimulating and encouraging the child's development. This includes challenging the child to extend a bit, to master tension-arousing experiences, and to enhance feelings of competence. In order to do this in a way that promotes development, the parent needs to be aware of the child's developmental level so that the tasks and expectations are within developmental reach of the child.

Intruding/engaging is about drawing the child into interaction when appropriate, while also allowing the child autonomy appropriate to his or her developmental level. This is about the reciprocal dance of enjoyment that develops between parents and infants. Activities such as peekaboo, blowing on the tummy, and playing "I'm gonna getcha," can be used to draw the baby into enjoyable interactions with his or her caregiver. For the purposes of the ATPP, the language for the intruding/engaging dimension was changed to *enjoying*, though the intent is essentially the same.

Nurturing refers to the soothing, calming, caregiving activities such as feeding, rocking, cuddling, and holding (Koller & Booth, 1997). These four dimensions of the parent–infant relationship were used to organize the curriculum for the teen parents.

SHORT-TERM PLAY THERAPY APPROACH

The ATPP developed as the result of a collaborative project between a graduate program in clinical psychology and an adolescent services program for pregnant teens. The play-based approach described in this chapter is a 10-week parenting program called My Baby & Me for teen parents and their babies, ages 1 month to 2 years, that specifically targets the development of the secure base attachment between infant and parent. The curriculum for the ATPP is still evolving.[1] The program is in the process of developing par-

---

[1]As these other modules evolve, the curriculum for the My Baby & Me classes will also change by shifting some of the content into these other classes. A web page created for the ATTP will be connected to this author's faculty page on the California School of Professional Psychology, Fresno Campus web site (www.cspp.edu), where interested parties can access changes in the program as it evolves.

enting modules that target attachment during the pregnancy, the parenting relationship with a toddler/preschooler, and the internal working models (self-identifications) of the teen parents. Additional program components will also address the specific needs of teen fathers, the partnership relationships between teen parents, and extended family relationships, especially with the teen parent's mother.

The My Baby & Me classes emphasize the following areas, using the structuring, challenging, enjoying, and nurturing (SCEN) dimensions from Theraplay:

1. Appropriate responses that create in the child a sense of security and worth (structuring).
2. Attunement to the child's needs, feelings, and developmental abilities (challenging).
3. Development of an enjoyable, mutually satisfying relationship between the teen parent and child (enjoying).
4. Physically nurturing interactions through learning infant massage techniques (nurturing).

In addition to SCEN, the following areas are also addressed, though with less emphasis:

1. The teen parent's internal models of self, the infant, and the relationship between them.
2. The teen parent's relationships with partners and extended family.
3. The teen parent's identification with and recognition of cultural/familial values and rituals.
4. The teen parent's transformation in self-identity from adolescent–child to parent with a child.

The term "parent" is purposely used in this discussion rather than "mother" even though the primary attachment and caregiving relationship in most cases of teen parenthood is with the mother. The My Baby & Me class is designed to focus on the dyadic relationship between parent and child. Ideally, if the teen father wants to work on his primary relationship with the child, he will bring the child alone, without the mother. In the past, it was found that inclusion of mother and father as a couple reduced the focus on the dyadic relationship between parent and child, as the fathers tended to hold back and watch the mothers engage in the activities. This seemed to interfere with peer-group bonding, as the vast majority of the teen mothers did not have a partner to participate with them. Another My Baby & Me group now includes two teen fathers, along with the mothers of their children. This time, the facilitators are trying to increase the fathers' direct involvement in the activities to see if they can create positive peer-group bonding even with the couples in the group.

Where possible, existing relationships with supportive adults are used to bring the teen parents into the classes. In the ATPP classes, the case managers who had a working relationship with the teen parents contacted them about the classes, transported them and their babies to and from classes, and participated as coleaders in the classes. The first week is the only week that the teen parents come without their babies, as they are completing the pretest assessments. The rationale for not having their babies is attachment based, as it is difficult for the teen parents to focus on paper-and-pencil tasks and the needs of their babies at the same time, and the infants are likely to be uncomfortable in a new place with new people. In reality, many of them bring their babies because they do not have anyone available to watch the baby for them. (In reality, the real world often modifies the curriculum designs, but modeling flexibility and attunement to the changing needs of the participants is also part of the process.)

The curriculum is focused on the development of a secure attachment relationship between teen parent and infant, starting with the creation of a safe environment, followed by the creation of a mutually enjoyable secure-base relationship between teen parent and child. The ATPP tries to present these ideas in the classes without using the abstract conceptual language of attachment theory. In the following paragraphs, the attachment focus is described both in conceptual language and in the language used with the teen parents, followed by specific discussion of the SCEN curriculum and detailed description of some of the play activities. A more complete curriculum guide is available from the author.

Creating a Protective Environment in the Group

James (1994) defines the development of a "protective environment" as the first step in creating the safe emotional space where a therapeutic alliance can develop. A safe emotional space is created for the teen parents and their babies in two ways:

1. *There are three group rules: Confidentiality, respect, and baby's needs.* "Confidentiality" addresses confidentiality within the group, as well as the limits of that confidentiality related to the child-abuse reporting laws. "Respect" means being part of the group by coming each week and accepting what others share even though their own experiences and feelings may be different. "Baby's needs" means that the teen parent needs to respond to the baby's needs whenever the baby needs attention, even when in the middle of a group discussion or activity. Baby's needs come first, but the teen parent can ask for help from the group leaders or other group members as needed. The central concept in the My Baby & Me class is that they,

as the parents, become the most important people in their babies' lives. These rules are reviewed and discussed at the beginning of every group.

2. *The group has a consistent structure that is predictable and understandable.* This structure includes a beginning ritual, activities organized around SCEN, snacks to nurture the parents and babies, and a closing ritual. The beginning ritual includes a review of rules, weather report, ice breaker, and SCEN overview. The weather report asks each parent to share one or two "weather" words describing his or her present emotional state (e.g., "calm," "stormy"). This provides both the leaders and the other group members with a quick gauge of members' affective states and needs. The ice breaker is a specific activity designed to promote group sharing and cohesion. Early ice-breaker activities are more structured and less personally revealing (e.g., the M&M activity where the teen parents take a few M&M's, then share something about their babies or themselves for each M&M. These can be very concrete things, such as how old they are or their favorite ice cream. Later on, after the group members have developed greater cohesion and a sense of safety with each other, the ice-breaker activities are more personally revealing and challenging, such as saying one good thing and one hard thing about having members of their extended family directly involved in their lives as teens and teen parents. For the SCEN overview, the following definitions of SCEN are presented, followed by a statement about what the structuring activity (or challenging, etc.) is for that week.

> *Structuring* is doing things to make your baby feel safe in his or her world. This week . . .
> *Challenging* is how to challenge or help your baby to learn. To do this we need to understand how your baby learns at different ages. This is called "development." This week, we are looking at how your baby . . .
> *Enjoying* is about having fun together. Today, we are going to do an activity called . . .
> *Nurturing* is taking care of your baby—holding her, touching him, feeding her, comforting him. This week, we are going to practice "loving touch" on [part of baby's body].

Following the beginning ritual, the group participates in structuring and enjoying activities, then breaks for a snack, followed by challenging and nurturing activities. The closing ritual includes journal reflection time for the teen parents and story or music time for the children who are old enough, followed by a brief sharing of what they liked or did not like about the group that day.

A small "giveaway gift" is given to the teen parent at each class. These concrete gifts nurture the economically deprived teen parents, as well as contribute to their abilities to provide an attachment-promoting environment. Examples of giveaway gifts to parents include a simple children's book to read to their baby, music tape to sing and dance with baby, a big ball, large children's crayons, safety plugs for electrical outlets, and a baby memory book, specifically designed to capture structuring, challenging, enjoying, and nurturing moments and memories. Polaroid pictures are taken at each class, and the teen parents put these in the memory books and write about them as part of the reflective journaling process.

Creating Mutually Enjoyable Secure Base Relationships

The infant develops trust and a sense of security in the relationship with his or her parent through reciprocal attachment sequences between baby and parent during the first year of life. Levy (Cline, 1992; Levy & Orlans, 1998) calls this process the first-year attachment cycle, which goes from (1) the infant experiencing a need or discomfort to (2) the infant expressing arousal or displeasure, to (3) the parent recognizing what the infant is expressing and responding appropriately in such a way that (4) the infant experiences a sense of relief and relaxation. Thus, the attachment sequence moves from infant need to expression of that need, to gratification of that need by caregiver, to experience of relief and comfort by the infant and experience of competence and closeness for the parent. Over time, these repeated interactions make the baby feel safe on the inside and in the presence of the parent.

In the My Baby & Me class, the teen parents are given specific information about how to (1) recognize these attachment sequences, (2) listen to their babies' moods and messages, and (3) calm their babies using music, eye contact, touch, movement, and soothing words. In addition to directly providing information, secure base attachment behaviors are promoted through specific play activities and the ongoing modeling and feedback that occurs over the course of the 10-week program. There are many times throughout each class when babies express needs. Depending on the teen parent's attunement and skill level, he or she is provided with direct guidance, modeling, and/or positive affirmation for appropriate and successful responding to the infant's needs.

SCEN Curriculum

SCEN provides the organization of the information and activities for each week. However, these four dimensions are not mutually exclusive. The structuring and challenging dimensions are more about what the parent does, while the enjoying and nurturing dimensions are more about specific interactions between the parent and baby. Both structuring and challenging involve the presentation of specific information about safety, communication, discipline, development, and so on. In order to keep the group participants engaged, the curriculum alternates a more didactic dimension with a more interactive, playful dimension. In general, structuring and enjoying are addressed in the first part of the class, followed by nurturing and challenging after the snack break, but the specific sequences also depend on the flow of the curriculum for that day. For example, the developmental information about what babies can *do* at different ages (challenging) is combined with the enjoying activity of playing with a big rubber ball and how that might be done, depending on the age of the baby. The nurturing dimension addresses the actual skills involved in infant massage, while part of structuring addresses how to "structure" nurturing routines at home, such as bedtime, bathtime, and diapering routines that are enjoyable and nurturing.

EXAMPLES OF STRUCTURING ACTIVITIES

1. *Creating a safe physical environment for the babies.* Safety issues are covered by having the teen parents fill out a checklist on baby proofing. Both developmental and familial context issues are addressed. As babies get older, the baby-proofing needs change. Also, many of the teen parents live with extended family members who place restrictions on their ability to baby-proof the home, instead requiring the teen parent to "set limits" with the baby. These challenges are problem-solved by the members of the group.

2. *Boy–girl differences.* Gender-role values and cultural influences are addressed in the group by bringing several gender-specific toys for the babies and having the teen parents talk about how they were raised in terms of gender-specific behaviors, toys, and clothes, and how they want to raise their own children. Cultural and extended-family influences are addressed as they emerge in the discussion.

3. *Discipline.* "Discipline" is defined as helping the baby learn to get along in the world. Two resources are used to address discipline. One is a book on discipline specifically written for teen parents: *Discipline from Birth to Three*, by Jeanne Warren Lindsay and Sally McCullough (1991). The other is a parenting video from Family Development Resources (1996) called *I'm Only Doing This for Your Own Good: Teaching Parents Nurturing Parenting Techniques for Challenging Times with Infants, Toddlers, and Preschoolers.*

EXAMPLES OF CHALLENGING ACTIVITIES

1. *Developmental chart.* A developmental chart describes infant development across five domains: doing, saying, thinking, feeling, and relating to other people. The teen parents identify where their babies are on the chart in general; then, each of the different domains is addressed more spe-

cifically during later classes. Didactic information is presented briefly; then, that information is applied to the different babies of various ages while they engage in the other activities.

2. *Developmental thinking.* Developmental understanding pervades all of the activities and interactions in that appropriate responding requires an understanding of what the infant needs and can understand at that particular age. Therefore, as the parents and babies participate in the classes, they are given ongoing developmental feedback about how their babies experience the world and how they can adapt their activities and responses to the ages of their babies.

EXAMPLES OF ENJOYING PLAY ACTIVITIES

1. *Playing with baby.* Each week focuses on different ways of playing with the infants, starting with face games, because eye contact and face-to-face interactions are primary in promoting attachment interactions. Other enjoying activities include singing songs with the babies and interactive music games. The activities are modified on an individual basis depending on the age of the infant. For example, the Hokey Pokey is an energizing, exciting, and enjoyable dance game in which the participants stand in a circle (parents and babies, and leaders with stuffed animals or toy dolls) and put different parts of the body into and out of the circle as defined by the words of the song. The teen parent learns to modify the activity as needed, so that the small baby is held close to the parent's body while he or she moves in and out of the circle, and the toddler is helped to put his or her own arm, leg, and so on, into the circle as part of the game. The *Nurturing Book for Babies & Children* by Bavolek (1989) is a useful resource that describes several play activities with infants, toddlers, and preschoolers.

2. *Color Your Baby.* This activity is a modification of O'Connor's (1983) Color Your Life activity that targets the teen parent's internal experience and is enjoyable for both babies and parents. During the ice-breaker activity, the teen parents develop a color-feelings chart that pairs the eight colors found in a box of large crayons with eight feelings. These feelings should represent different feelings that they have had about being a parent. During the enjoying activity, each teen parents traces his or her baby onto a large piece of paper. They then color in the baby image using proportionally those colors that represent their own (not the baby's) feelings about being a parent. Group discussion then focuses on how many of them have similar feelings, and how some of the feelings are different, while communicating acceptance of all the feelings as valid aspects of their parenting experiences. This activity is emotionally demanding and is designed for the sixth week of the class, after the group members have had enough time to develop a sense of security and cohesion with each other.

EXAMPLES OF NURTURING PLAY ACTIVITIES

1. *Snack time* provides an opportunity for group leaders to nurture teen parents directly by providing healthy foods, and the teen parents use this as a time to change diapers and feed their babies. Group leaders encourage the teen parents to be playful and nurturing when changing and feeding their babies.

2. *Infant massage.* Leboyer (1976), in his powerful book, *Loving Hands*, describes infant massage as a silent dialogue of love between a mother and her baby. Time during each class is devoted to teaching the teen parents the art of massaging their infants. The term "loving touch" is used instead of "massage," because some of the teen parents associated the term "massage" with sexual touch. Loving touch involves not only physically massaging the infant, which is nurturing and calming, but also listening to what the baby wants and likes, and respecting the baby's feelings and boundaries (McClure, 1989). If the baby is playing and does not want to stop, or is sleeping during this time in the class, the teen parent is given a doll or stuffed animal on which to practice the strokes. The parents are given the small *Nurturing Touch Handbook* by Babeshoff and Dellinger-Bavolek (1993) and encouraged to use loving touch on a daily basis at home. Success and problems in using loving touch at home are discussed each week.

CASE ILLUSTRATIONS

"My Baby Is Too Small to Touch"[2]

One teen mother in particular had a very small baby who was 6 months old but looked a lot younger. The baby also expressed little emotion and had a low activity level. He had been born prematurely and had been kept in the hospital in neonatal intensive care for 2 months. His teen mother treated him as if he were very fragile, and she was afraid to touch him too much. She brought him to the class in a carseat and during the early classes, she left him in it throughout the class. She was very tentative and mechanical in her interactions with him.

It was decided that this teen mother needed some direct modeling, so the therapist became a shadow for this teen mother and her son. Every week, without directly commenting on the mother's lack of interaction with her son, the therapist role-modeled more physical contact and attunement to the baby's needs. The therapist watched the baby's body language and vocal cues

---

[2]This case material was contributed by California School of Professional Psychology doctoral student Andrea Sweeney, who cofacilitated two sections of the My Baby & Me classes.

indicating that he wanted or needed something and animatedly voiced this so that the mother could hear it. The therapist made silly faces at the baby while he was in his carseat and tickled him gently. He was slow to respond, as if he was not used to much attention. He then squirmed in his seat as if he wanted to get out and the therapist said, "Oh, he wants to get out of his seat and join the rest of us!" The therapist pulled him out and onto her lap, making sure the mother was watching the whole scenario and that she was comfortable with the therapist holding him. The very next week, the mother brought him into the class and pulled him out of the carseat herself! She continued to do this for the remainder of the parenting classes.

The therapist played with and cuddled the baby often and identified how his behaviors showed that he enjoyed it. His mother watched her very closely and began to play with him and hold him a little more. He soaked up any attention he received from his mother with obvious enjoyment, and the therapist commented on this. His mother was reluctant to become very involved in the loving touch activity, so the therapist tried to involve her by first role-modeling the procedure without completely taking over, and then praising any steps of loving touch in which the mother engaged. At first, she would put the lotion on her hands and rub the baby a little, but she did not seem engaged with him. As the classes progressed, she took a more active role with him. Amazingly, this baby began to thrive physically and emotionally over the next few weeks. He appeared to gain weight and to be more animated in his facial and bodily expressions. Then, one day, the mother bent down and kissed her baby's nose at the end of loving touch and softly said, "Loving touch is over!" In her eyes, he was no longer "too small to touch," and they were now engaged in a positive attachment dance.

"My Baby Is Too Busy to Touch"[3]

From the beginning of the first session, one teen mother of a very active 2-year-old son caught the attention and concern of the group leaders. When it came time to play with the babies, she made no move toward her active toddler. If others brought him over to her, she interacted briefly, until he moved away again. She made no effort to participate in the loving touch portion of the class. The next class, the therapist actively encouraged and helped her to take off her little boy's shoes and socks and massage his feet and legs. This usually very active boy not only quieted down, he fell asleep. This was very reinforcing for his mother, who experienced his active energy as overwhelming.

Over the weeks, this mother maintained her stance of indifference and nonengagement. She required continued encouragement, prompting, or modeling in order to become engaged in the activities. However, when

[3]This case material was contributed by California School of Professional Psychology doctoral student Carol Sharp, who cofacilitated two sections of the My Baby & Me classes.

questioned about specifics, she revealed that she was doing loving touch with her son at home and that this had become an important ritual for the two of them.

During the closing exercise of the last session, she told the class that nothing had changed as a result of taking the class, but her classmates did not accept this. They told her about the changes they had seen in her as a mother with her son, and they told her about the things she had said that had helped them. Though she did not verbally acknowledge their comments, her smile and body language indicated that she heard them. When the opportunity arose for this teen mother to be involved in a similar class in the future, she volunteered to do so.

"My Baby Doesn't Like to Be Touched"[4]

When the parenting class started, there was obviously a problem between one teen mother and her 2-year-old son. She would come into the class walking at least 10 steps ahead of him, with him dragging behind, trying to catch up. During snack time, she would not help feed him and then became upset when he made a mess of the food. But when she would try to hold him, he would get upset and try to get away. Their attachment dance was out of sync.

For the first two weeks of class she refused to participate in the loving touch, saying that her son did not like to be touched. During the next week, the therapist decided to try to get her to try loving touch on his hands only. The results were amazing. Not only did her son sit still but he also relaxed and enjoyed her physical contact with him. It was a major victory for both of them. She continued to do loving touch on his hands for the rest of the parenting sessions, though she remained resistant to trying any of the other strokes. The mother also reported that she was using the loving touch on his hands at home to help him calm down. She began to help feed him and became more nurturing and loving toward him during the other activities in the classes. By the last week of class, mother and son walked in together, side by side.

PRELIMINARY RESULTS
OF PROGRAM EVALUATION

The program evaluation assessed the teen parents' attachment relationships with their infants, ability to engage in empathic communication, experience of stress and support, and attachment relationships with their own family of origin. Approximately 80 teen mothers and two fathers and their babies have participated in the My Baby & Me classes to date, though only about half of them completed both pretest and posttest data. The first six classes

[4]This case material was contributed by California School of Professional Psychology doctoral student Robyn Salter, who cofacilitated two sections of the My Baby & Me classes.

were 8 weeks long, with a pretest and posttest meeting, and many of the teen parents did not attend the posttest meeting, as they had already experienced closure with the group. So the curriculum was modified to a 10-week program to incorporate the program evaluation into the first and last weeks.

Preliminary results suggest a significant growth in teen parents' empathy, a more positive experience of the parent–child relationship, and increased communication with their peers. However, the results also indicated increased alienation in the teen parents' relationships with their own mothers, which may represent some tension around the teen parents becoming more autonomous and responsible for their parenting role. The curriculum currently is being examined for ways in which it might be modified to prevent this development of alienation even while supporting the teen parents' moves toward greater autonomy. Further research is needed to understand these results better, though the initial observations are quite encouraging.

CONCLUSION

The ATPP is a play-based short-term intervention for teen parents and their babies. The My Baby & Me parenting module described in this chapter is for teen parents and their babies, ages 1 month to 2 years. It specifically targets the development of secure base attachment relationship between parents and babies by utilizing the attachment-promoting play therapy principles found in Theraplay (Jernberg, 1979, 1993), as well as peer-group-process and self-reflection techniques to promote the healthy development of the teen parents' internal working models of themselves as parents and as adolescents moving toward adulthood. Both preliminary research results and observations of the teen parents and their babies as they participate in the classes indicate that the program is facilitating the growth of attachment.

ACKNOWLEDGMENTS

The development of the Attachment Teen Parenting Program was greatly facilitated by two grants from the Family Preservation/Family Support Board of Kings County, California. This project would not have happened without the tremendous support of Susan Elizabeth, Director of Adolescent Services in Kings County, whose passion for finding services for her teen clients and insightful understanding of the importance of attachment opened the door to making a vision become reality. Many doctoral students at the California School of Professional Psychology contributed their ideas and time to design and implement this project, as did many of the Adolescent

Services case managers. In particular, Elizabeth Limberg and Karyn Ewart were instrumental in designing the curriculum, and Susan Bryan and Martha Mossman were invaluable in coordinating all the details to actually make the parenting classes happen. Thank you all.

REFERENCES

Ainsworth, M. D. S. (1989). Attachments beyond infancy. *American Psychologist,* 44(4), 709–716.

Ainsworth, M. D., Blehar, M. C., Waters, E., & Wall, S. (1978). *Patterns of attachment.* Hillsdale, NJ: Erlbaum.

Al-Fayez, G. (1998). *Cross-cultural aspects of attachment behaviors: Use of attachment Q-set in Kuwait.* Unpublished doctoral dissertation, California School of Professional Psychology, Fresno.

Ammen, S., & York, L. (1994). *The many measures of attachment.* Unpublished manuscript, California School of Professional Psychology, Fresno.

Atkinson, L., & Zucker, K. J. (Eds.). (1997). *Attachment and psychopathology.* New York: Guilford Press.

Babeshoff, K., & Dellinger-Bavolek, J. (1993). *Nurturing touch handbook.* Park City, UT: Family Development Resources.

Barclay, D. R., & Houts, A. C. (1995). Parenting skills: A review and developmental analysis of training content. In W. T. O'Donohue & L. Krasner (Eds.), *Handbook of psychological skills training* (pp. 195–228). Boston: Allyn & Bacon.

Bavolek, J. D. (1989). *Nurturing book for babies and children.* Park City, UT: Family Development Resources.

Bavolek, S. J. (1990). *Research and validation report: Adult–Adolescent Parenting Inventory.* Park City, UT: Family Development Resources.

Between the lines. (1993, Fall). *The Doula,* pp. 2.

Bowlby, J. (1982). *Attachment* (2nd ed.). New York: Basic Books.

Bowlby, J. (1988). *A secure base: Clinical applications of attachment theory.* London: Routledge.

Brazelton, T. B. (1992). *Touchpoints.* New York: Addison-Wesley.

Bretherton, I. (1992). The origins of attachment theory: John Bowlby and Mary Ainsworth. *Developmental Psychology, 28,* 759–775.

Brooks, J. B. (1991). *The process of parenting* (3rd ed.). Mountain View, CA: Mayfield.

Cline, F. W. (1992). *Understanding and treating the severely disturbed child.* Evergreen, CO: Evergreen Consultants in Human Behavior, EC Publications.

Colin, V. L. (1996). *Human attachment.* New York: McGraw-Hill.

Cross, W. E., Jr. (1987). A two-factor theory of black identity: Implications for the study of identity development in minority children. In J. S. Phinney & M. J. Rotherman (Eds.), *Children's ethnic socialization: Pluralism and development* (pp. 117–133). Newbury Park, CA: Sage.

Crowell, J. A., & Feldman, S. S. (1988). Mothers' internal models of relationships and children's behavioral and developmental status: A study of mother–child interaction. *Child Development, 59,* 1273–1285.

East, P. L., & Felice, M. E. (1996). *Adolescent pregnancy and parenting: Findings from a racially diverse sample.* Mahwah, NJ: Erlbaum.

Family Development Resources. (1996). *I'm only doing this for your own good: Teaching parents nurturing parenting techniques for challenging times with infants, toddlers, and preschoolers* [Videotape]. (Available from Family Development Resources, Inc., 3160 Pinebrook Road, Park City, UT 84098, 1-800-688-5822).

Flanagan, P. J., McGrath, M. M., Meyer, E. C., & Garcia Coll, C. T. (1995). Adolescent development and transitions to motherhood. *Pediatrics, 96*(2), 273–277.

Garcia Coll, C. T., Meyer, E. C., & Brillon, L. (1995). Ethnic and minority parenting. In M. H. Bornstein (Ed.), *Handbook of parenting: Vol. 2. Biology and ecology of parenting* (pp. 189–209). Mahwah, NJ: Erlbaum.

Greenspan, S., & Thorndike Greenspan, N. (1985). *First feelings: Milestones in the emotional development of your baby and child.* New York: Viking.

Hartup, W. W. (1989). Social relationships and their developmental significance. *American Psychologist, 44*(2), 120–126.

Harwood, R. (1992). The influence of culturally derived values on Anglo and Puerto Rican mothers perception's of attachment behavior. *Child Development, 63*, 822–839.

Hoff-Ginsberg, E., & Tardif, T. (1995). Socioeconomic status and parenting. In M. H. Bornstein (Ed.), *Handbook of parenting: Vol. 2. Biology and ecology of parenting* (pp. 161–188). Mahwah, NJ: Erlbaum.

Hughes, D. (1997). *Facilitating developmental attachment.* Northvale, NJ: Aronson.

James, B. (1994). *Handbook for the treatment of attachment–trauma problems in children.* New York: Lexington.

Jernberg, A. (1979). *Theraplay.* San Francisco: Jossey-Bass.

Jernberg, A. (1993). Attachment formation. In C. E. Schaefer (Ed.), *The therapeutic powers of play* (pp. 241–265). Northvale, NJ: Aronson.

Karen, R. (1994). *Becoming attached: Unfolding the mystery of the infant–mother bond and its impact on later life.* New York: Warner.

Koller, T. J., & Booth, P. (1997). Fostering attachment through family Theraplay. In K. O'Connor & L. Mages Braverman (Eds.), *Play therapy theory an practice: A comparative presentation* (pp. 204–233). New York: Wiley.

Leboyer, F. (1976). *Loving hands.* New York: Knopf.

Levy, T. M., & Orlans, M. (1998). *Attachment, trauma, and healing.* Washington, DC: Child Welfare League of America.

Levy-Warren, M. H. (1996). *The adolescent journey.* Northvale, NJ: Jason Aronson.

Light, P. (1979). *Development of a child's sensitivity to people.* London: Cambridge University Press.

Lindsay, J. W., & McCullough, S. (1991). *Discipline from birth to three.* Buena Park, CA: Morning Glory Press.

Lyons-Ruth, K., & Zeanah, C. H., Jr. (1993). The family context of infant mental health: I. Affective development in the primary caregiving relationship. In C. H. Zeanah (Ed.), *Handbook of infant mental health* (pp. 14–37). New York: Guilford Press.

Main, M., Kaplan, N., & Cassidy, J. (1985). Security in infancy, childhood and adulthood: A move to the level of representation. In I. Bretherton & E. Waters (Eds.), Growing points of attachment theory and research. *Monographs of the Society for Research in child Development, 50*(1–2, Serial No. 209), 66–104.

Mcanarney, E. R., Lawrence, R. A., Riccuiti, H. N., Plooey, J., & Szilagyi, M. (1986). Interactions of adolescent mothers and their 1 year old children. *Pediatrics, 78,* 785–790.

McClure, V. S. (1989). *Infant massage: A handbook for loving parents.* New York: Bantam Books.

Mercer, R. T. (1986). Predictors of maternal role attainment at one year post birth. *Western Journal of Nursing Research, 8,* 9–32.

O'Connor, K. J. (1983). The Color-Your-Life technique. In C. E. Schaefer & K. J. O'Connor (Eds.), *Handbook of play therapy* (pp. 251–258). New York: Wiley.

Osofsky, J. D., Hann, D. M., & Peebles, C. (1993). Adolescent parenthood: Risks and opportunities for mothers and infants. In C. H. Zeanah (Ed.), *Handbook of infant mental health* (pp. 106–119). New York: Guilford Press.

Passino, A. W., Whitman, T. L., Borkowski, J. G., Schellenbach, C. J., Maxwell, S. E., Keogh, D., & Rellinger, E. (1993). Personal adjustment during pregnancy and adolescent parenting. *Adolescence, 28*(109), 97–122.

Saker, I. M., & Neuhoff, S. D. (1982). *Medical and psychosocial risk factors in the pregnant adolescent: Pregnancy in adolescence: Needs, problems and management.* New York: Van Nostrand Reinhold.

Stern, D. N. (1985). *The interpersonal world of the infant: A view from psychoanalysis and developmental psychology.* New York: Basic Books.

Stern, D. N. (1990a). *Diary of a baby.* New York: Basic Books.

Stern, D. N. (1990b, August 20). *Diary of a baby* (excerpts). *U.S. News and World Report, 109*(8), 54–59.

Stern, D. N. (1995). *The motherhood constellation: A unified view of parent–infant psychotherapy.* New York: Basic Books.

Zayas, L., & Solari, F. (1994). Early childhood socialization in Hispanic families: Context, culture, and practice implications. *Professional Psychology: Research and Practice, 25*(3) 200–206

Index